Peer Prejudice
and Discrimination

PROGRAM on INTERGROUP RELATIONS
University of Illinois
Counseling Center
610 E. John St., 206 SSB
Champaign, IL 61820

Developmental Psychology Series

Series Editor, *Wendell Jeffrey*

Peer Prejudice and Discrimination

Evolutionary, Cultural, and Developmental Dynamics

Harold D. Fishbein

University of Cincinnati

WestviewPress

A Division of HarperCollins*Publishers*

To my American and Indian students

Developmental Psychology Series

Copyright © 1996 by Westview Press, Inc., A Division of HarperCollins Publishers, Inc.

Published in 1996 in the United States of America by Westview Press, Inc., 5500 Central Avenue, Boulder, Colorado 80301-2877, and in the United Kingdom by Westview Press, 12 Hid's Copse Road, Cumnor Hill, Oxford OX2 9JJ

A CIP catalog record for this book is available from the Library of Congress
ISBN 0-8133-3052-1 (hardcover).—0-8133-3053-X (pbk.)

The paper used in this publication meets the requirements of the American National Standard for Permanence of Paper for Printed Library Materials Z39.48-1984.

10   9   8   7   6   5   4   3   2   1

CONTENTS

PREFACE

This book indirectly received its start in 1989 when James Lynch asked me to write a chapter on the development of prejudice for a book he was editing dealing with cultural diversity and the schools. I wrote the chapter, and although long in comparison with the other authors', it was too short to do justice to the topic. Shortly after, a sales representative from Wm. C. Brown came into my office and asked whether I had any writing projects. I described the chapter and asked whether Brown would be interested in a book-length treatment. Very quickly I received a "yes" from Michael Lange, the then psychology editor.

Writing this book required more than a little help from my friends. There was so much I didn't know. Ellen Messer-Davidow of the University of Minnesota and Joanne Meyerowitz and Dee Graham of the University of Cincinnati (all the other folks mentioned are from UC) directed me to readings relevant to feminism and American women's history. Dee did some editing in addition. Vibert White lent me books and spent a lot of time talking with me about African-American history. He read and commented on a draft of that portion of chapter 2. Jerry Etienne and Richard Kretschmer, respectively, did the same for the portions dealing with mentally retarded and deaf persons.

Dave Lundgren, Neal Ritchey, and Kathy Burlew spent time with me talking about the social psychology of prejudice. Carl Heuther, in a tradition started in about 1972 while I was writing my first book, spent a lot of time talking with me about evolution and genetics. When I complained to him one day that I couldn't find a clincher for the evolutionary argument I was making, he said that Darwin had the same problem. Somehow that was reassuring. Ed Klein, who has edited a fair amount of my writing, also carefully did so for chapter 7. Dan Berch read a number of different pieces of the book and talked with me about theoretical and organizational matters. Dan has always been very affirming of my longish writing projects. Tony Grasha suggested a change in the book title and helped me to create the present one. Finally, Cathy Johnson, then an M.A. student, did most of the library research and all of the first drafts of the various sections of chapter 6. We spent a year writing it together. Needless to say, her involvement was invaluable.

John Harvey, the social psychology editor, read the entire manuscript (and twice, chapters 1, 2, and 3) and has been enormously helpful and supportive. I've used some of these chapters with my American (Cincinnati) and Indian (Bombay) students. Initially they were a bit skeptical about the genetic/evolutionary approach, but after living with it for a while, they invariably said that it made a great deal of sense to them. Some even wondered how you could do without it. That warms my heart.

Finally, for the second time, my secretary, Lorna Volk, read hundreds of pages of my small handwriting and typed it into highly legible text. I could not have done the project without her. I thank her once again.

I hope you enjoy the text and learn some of the things that I learned while writing it.

Harold D. Fishbein
Cincinnati, Ohio, 1995

Introduction: The Nature of Prejudice

An Encounter

The summer after I graduated from college in 1959 I took a temporary job as a swimming pool attendant at a Chicago Recreation Commission park on the Southwest Side of Chicago. The park was located in a rough working-class neighborhood whose population had shifted during the preceding 10 years from being of extensively Slavic origin to being of mixed Slavic and Latin American. The transition, I was told, had been very tense and many fights had occurred between teenagers of the two ethnic groupings. The Slavs were still in the majority, and many of their adolescents and young adults were strongly anti-Negro. (In 1959, both African-Americans and Euro-Americans referred to the former as "colored" or "Negroes," not "Blacks" or "African-Americans." In fact, referring to a Negro as a Black was considered a potentially prejudiced statement.) The pool was open to the public, free of charge, with no official age, race, ethnic, or sex restrictions.

The lifeguards were male, recent high school graduates of Slavic origin, and residents of the neighborhood. I was the only outsider who worked at the pool, in that I was Jewish and lived in a North Side neighborhood. I had some concerns about my own safety, especially when I worked late and took the evening bus home. I felt fortunate that I was never verbally or physically attacked.

One day at the pool, I was talking with two of the lifeguards when one of the Slavic male teenagers approached the guards with a serious problem. There was a young "colored girl" in the children's pool area. What should they do? The lifeguards told me that colored children weren't "allowed" in the pool and that the last one who had come in, a teenage male several years before, had been thrown out, over the fence. In fact, I never saw an African-American in the park itself during the entire summer. The dilemma the guards faced was that the child, though very dark-skinned with strongly African features, was young and a girl. Should they throw her out now, wait until the end of the hour when everybody had to leave the pool for ten minutes, or do nothing? Just then another male Slavic teenager approached and said there was no problem; the girl was Cuban and spoke Spanish. Everybody breathed a sigh of relief. The girl was not colored; she was Cuban.

The girl was not colored; she was Cuban. What an extraordinary experience. The girl was not a Cuban *and* colored, despite the fact that she had very pronounced black, African features. She was a Cuban, which meant she was a Latin and thus okay. The neighborhood consisted of Slavs and Latins. The battle over that piece of integration had been settled, though I was not aware of any particular friendships between the two groups. They had a working relationship that the majority Slavs were unwilling to challenge. Both groups could peacefully reside in the neighborhood, use the park and pool, and even compete with each other in softball games. But, colored people had better stay clear of the park and the neighborhood. And they did, in 1959.

All of us probably have stories to tell about prejudice and discrimination among children and adolescents. Many of us "ethnics" have been on the receiving end of prejudice. Certainly our parents or grandparents, if they were immigrants to the United States, experienced prejudice either here or in their countries of origin. We are told in our high school history books that the English pilgrims came to the New World to escape religious persecution in their homeland. They were welcomed by Native Americans—the "Indians." Ironically, the descendants of those victims of prejudice and the descendants of other immigrants developed a virulent prejudice and discrimination that nearly destroyed the Indians. That story is not clearly told in the history books used to teach our children.

Definitions of Prejudice and Attitudes

Arguably the best and most influential book written on prejudice since the Second World War is Gordon Allport's *The Nature of Prejudice* (1954). The scope of his book is awesome and the intelligence and sensitivity conveyed are inspiring. Allport starts his book with some anecdotes about "ethnic" prejudice and notes two essential ingredients of it: (1) hostility and rejection and (2) the basis of the hostility being the target individual's membership in a group. These two ingredients are clearly seen in the Cuban colored girl story.

Allport discusses the difference between "ordinary prejudgments," which all of us periodically engage in, and prejudice, a special type of prejudgment. He concludes, "Prejudgments become prejudices only if they are not reversible when exposed to new knowledge" (p. 9). He argues that we emotionally resist evidence that contradicts our prejudices, unlike that which occurs with ordinary prejudgments. Thus, we have a third key ingredient of prejudice: resistance to new knowledge. The swimming pool story indirectly supports this ingredient—the girl couldn't be colored; she was a Cuban. Colored children had to be hostilely rejected, but Cubans were okay.

Allport summarizes his discussion about the characteristics of prejudice with the following definition:

> Prejudice is an antipathy based upon a faulty and inflexible generalization. It may be felt or expressed. It may be directed toward a group as a whole, or toward an individual because he is a member of that group. (p. 9)

A more recent book on prejudice, Howard Ehrlich's *The Social Psychology of Prejudice* (1973), provides an excellent discussion of the concept of prejudice. Ehrlich provides 16 definitions of prejudice excerpted from the works of highly regarded sociologists and social psychologists, published between 1950 and 1966. Nearly all the definitions have the following understanding in common: prejudice is an unfavorable attitude directed towards others because of their membership in a particular group.

Ehrlich concurs with this consensus and defines prejudice simply as "an attitude toward any group of people" (p. 8). Attitudes may be positive or negative. We view prejudice as a negative attitude. But what's an attitude? He defines attitude as follows: "An attitude is an interrelated set of propositions about an object or class of objects which are organized around cognitive, behavioral and affective dimensions" (p. 4).

There are four principal cognitive dimensions of propositions (or fundamental beliefs). The first is *salience,* which is the degree to which the belief is assumed to accurately characterize all the members of a group. Thus, "All Jews are miserly" is more salient than "Most Jews are miserly." The second is *intensity,* which is the degree to which beliefs are accepted and agreed with, or rejected and disagreed with. Thus, "I sort of agree with that belief" is less intense than "I strongly agree with that belief." The third is *evaluative direction,* which is the extent to which the belief about a person or group is good/favorable/desirable or bad/unfavorable/undesirable. Thus, "All Arabs are mildly deceitful" is less negative than "All Arabs are very deceitful." The fourth is *centrality,* which is the extent to which a belief is important to an individual's attitude about others. Central beliefs capture the core or essential aspects of attitudes, whereas more peripheral beliefs can be readily changed without having much effect on an attitude.

The behavioral dimension of attitudes refers to the extent to which one's beliefs are linked with intentions to behave in particular ways. Some beliefs only indirectly relate to behavior; for example, an American employer might say, "Japanese mothers are very nurturing of their children." Others more directly relate to behavior; for example, the same employer might say, "Japanese workers are energetic and diligent." Ehrlich indicates that the above four cognitive dimensions of beliefs can be applied to behaviors.

The affective dimension of attitudes is basically the way a person feels about or emotionally reacts to the object of her attitudes. One pole of these feelings is love/liking/attraction, and the other is hate/dislike/repulsion. People may be strongly attracted to others they evaluate as bad, and conversely may be repulsed by those they evaluate as good. With prejudices, negative beliefs are usually accompanied by negative feelings.

I've spent this much time dealing with Ehrlich's work not because I accept his definition of prejudice, but rather because he shows us how complex the concept of "attitude" is. Prejudice does involve attitudes, and in order to be discussed, these attitudes must be measured. Yet, in virtually none of the studies dealing with children's attitudes is there even a faint approximation to Ehrlich's analysis.

Before I give my definition of prejudice, it would be useful to present two others, those by Milner (1983) and by Aboud (1988), both of whom have written books dealing with children's racial prejudices. Milner's definition is this:

> Prejudiced attitudes . . . are irrational, unjust, or intolerant dispositions towards other groups, and they are often accompanied by stereotyping. This is the attribution of the supposed characteristics of the whole group to all its individual members. Stereotypes exaggerate the uniformity within a group and similarly exaggerate the differences between this group and others. (p. 5)

Like other writers in this arena, Milner maintains that from a psychological viewpoint there are no essential differences between racial prejudices and other forms of prejudice. He notes that the occurrence of physical differences between groups may facilitate stereotyping and prejudice, but those differences are certainly not necessary. Milner's definition is similar to Allport's, especially if we equate "irrational, unjust, or intolerant" with "faulty and inflexible." Additionally, Milner's "stereotyping" is equivalent to Allport's "generalization" about groups.

Finally, Aboud (1988) defines racial prejudice as "an organized predisposition to respond in an unfavorable manner toward people from an ethnic group because of their ethnic affiliation" (p. 4). This understanding fits closely with the core characteristics of prejudice found in Ehrlich's group of 16 definitions. What distinguishes it from Allport's and Milner's definitions is that it lacks the idea of "faulty and inflexible." Thus, a well-founded unfavorable generalization about a group, according to Aboud's definition, would be a prejudice.

Based on the previous discussion, I've adopted a definition of prejudice that closely follows the ideas of Allport and Milner:

> *Prejudice* is an unreasonable negative attitude towards others because of their membership in a particular group.

The quality that makes an attitude "unreasonable" is that it is not readily modified when exposed to new and conflicting information. Prejudice is not an all-or-nothing phenomenon. Rather, like other attitudes, it is graded, as Ehrlich has pointed out. The extent to which children will be prejudiced at any point in time depends on their genetic endowment, their specific experiences of the target group, their own personalities, the prejudiced attitudes expressed to them by family and friends, and the cultural portrayal of the target group by television, books, and schools. Prejudice, of necessity, will change over time, because children gain new information, and their cognitive, social, and emotional understandings and capacities change with maturation and experience.

The measurement of prejudice, as previously defined, has rarely been successfully accomplished with children and adolescents. The major stumbling block has been assessing the "unreasonable" aspect of the negative attitudes. There appear to be no relevant studies that have directly attempted this assessment. The research efforts seem to assume, as an example, that negative attitudes directed towards Blacks or Whites are unreasonable. From an adult viewpoint they may be, but from a child's viewpoint, the negative attitudes may be reasonable. In a simple case, a child is told by its parents that drinking milk is good, crossing streets without looking both ways is bad, police officers can be trusted, strangers in cars are dangerous, and Whites will try to hurt you. Is it reasonable to have positive attitudes towards police and negative attitudes towards strangers in cars, and yet unreasonable to have negative attitudes towards White children?

In another simple example, if a child has had a number of unpleasant encounters with hearing-impaired children, are the child's negative attitudes towards hearing-impaired peers reasonable or unreasonable? Categorization is inevitable, normal, and necessary for adaptive functioning (Allport, 1954). It could be concluded that in the second example, the child's negative attitudes towards those who are hearing impaired are reasonable, in that they are based on a consistent generalization. Is the child prejudiced? Allport would argue, and I concur, that if the attitudes are inflexible and don't change with new and conflicting information, then the child is considered prejudiced (because the attitudes are not reasonable). To state that negative attitudes towards a particular group are reasonable is *not* to say that they are desirable. Frequently, responsible members of a community will try to get children and others to change their negative attitudes. If they are successful, this probably is an indication that these attitudes were *not* prejudiced.

Finally, there is an important area of human beliefs that may appear to lead to prejudice, but technically does not: religion. There are many contemporary and historical examples in which "nonbelievers" have been treated with extreme cruelty by members of fundamentalist religious groups (e.g., Jews and Protestants during the Spanish Inquisition). To the atheist and the agnostic, the beliefs held by fundamentalists are unreasonable; however, within the latters' belief system, they are being reasonable. In our definition of prejudice, an unreasonable attitude is one whose cognitive component can be disproved by contradictory information. If such disproof is not possible, then despite the horror of acts carried out against others by religious fundamentalists, it cannot be asserted that *prejudice* underlies these behaviors. Religious faith and belief are rarely susceptible to proof or disproof. If nonbelievers are thought of as being agents of the devil, and thus treated with suspicion and distrust, there is no obvious way that that belief can be contradicted. Thus, beyond chapter 1 in this book, religion-based attitudes will not be dealt with.

Definition of Discrimination

Prejudices are particular kinds of attitudes that, according to Ehrlich (1973), have three major dimensions: cognitive, affective, and behavioral. The behavioral dimension reflects a *disposition* to act negatively towards others, and not the behavior acts themselves. It is tempting to define discrimination in relation to prejudice. However, it frequently happens that people who are not prejudiced towards a particular target group may act negatively towards members of that group because of their group affiliation. For example, some nonprejudiced real estate agents may not show houses in certain neighborhoods to members of particular ethnic groups, such as Jews, African-Americans, or Hispanics, because the agents have been instructed by their employers or the houseowners not to do so. Or, some female employment managers may not hire women for particular jobs, such as those in construction, because of cultural norms indicating that women don't have the physical capacity to do the work.

Thus, acting negatively (discriminating) towards individuals because of their group membership may or may not be based on prejudice. Accordingly, we adopt the following definition of discrimination. It is similar to definitions offered by Allport (1954) and Marger (1991).

> *Discrimination* involves harmful actions towards others because of their membership in a particular group.

The discrimination can be mild, such as ignoring someone or calling someone a derogatory name behind her back, or it can be extreme, for instance, the mutual killing by ethnic groups between 1992 and 1994 in what was formerly Yugoslavia or the slaughter of Jews by the Nazis in the 1940s. With children, discrimination is usually manifested by avoidance, rudeness, name calling, and, on occasion, fighting.

Although discrimination isn't always based on prejudice, it frequently is, especially if the perpetrator is acting on his own as opposed to acting on behalf of some institution or authority. Children, for example, may be coerced into discriminatory acts by their parents or neighbors. But when children are freely interacting without adult control, it is likely that discrimination and prejudice go hand in hand.

Which comes first, prejudice or discrimination? Frederickson and Knobel (1980) answer in the following way:

> Discrimination may appear to be simply acting out of prior prejudice, but there is evidence to suggest that prejudice becomes fully developed and formally sanctioned only *after* the process of differential treatment is well under way. Attitude and action tend to feed on each other, creating a vicious circle that works to enhance the power and prestige of one group at the expense of the other. (p. 31)

Relationship Between Prejudice and Behavior

In the early 1930s, R. T. La Piere, a White American, traveled widely in the United States with a Chinese couple. The three of them stopped for food at 184 restaurants and for lodging at 66 hotels and motels. Only once did the manager refuse to provide service for them. After completing the trip, La Piere wrote to the proprietors of each establishment, enclosing a questionnaire that included an item asking whether they would take "members of the Chinese race as guests." One hundred twenty-eight returned the questionnaires and more than 92 percent of them stated that they *would not* accept Chinese people as guests (La Piere, 1934).

On the basis of their questionnaire responses, it appears that over 92 percent of these establishment owners were prejudiced against Chinese. Yet, in face-to-face interactions, fewer than 1 percent behaved in a prejudiced manner. How can we understand this dramatic discrepancy?

Milner (1983) and Wicker (1969) have discussed this issue in the broader context of the relation between attitudes and behavior. In general there is a relatively weak correlation between the two. Milner and Wicker identify two groups of factors that play a part in mediating behavior: personal factors and situational factors. Salient among the personal ones are other attitudes held by people and competing motives. Thus, the proprietors in La Piere's study may have disliked Chinese people but may also have held strong attitudes towards treating strangers with courtesy. Further, they may have wanted to reject the Chinese couple but were motivated also to make money. Among situational factors, two of the salient ones are the presence of other people and social norms for proper behavior. The Chinese couple wasn't alone, but rather with a White male friend. Additionally, restaurants and hotels are supposed to care for guests, not turn them away.

Stephan (1985) has summarized much of the empirical research dealing with the relationship between prejudice and behavior. There are several clusters of findings for which accurate generalizations can be made.

In one group of studies involving no direct contact between people, e.g., voting behavior and signing petitions, there was a fairly strong relationship between prejudice and discrimination. For example, White Americans who are prejudiced against Blacks sign documents opposing housing integration. In studies involving direct contact between prejudiced people and the targets of prejudice, the findings were more complex. One of the largest sets of these studies involved "helping" behaviors, e.g., Blacks versus Whites making emergency calls to seek assistance. In these studies, Whites who received these calls and who expressed little prejudice often discriminated the most against Blacks. Stephan suggests that two opposing attitudes are in play: "sympathy for the underdog and feelings of aversion." In responses to a questionnaire, sympathy wins out; but when the individual is asked to take action, aversion predominates.

In a third group of interaction studies, where the measures of prejudice were quite specific and the behavior measured was specific, there was a moderate correlation between prejudice and degree of discrimination. Stephan interprets all the findings in light of how individuals evaluate the relative costs and benefits of expressing particular opinions and acting in particular ways in particular social contexts. So, the link between prejudice and behavior will be strong in situations where individuals believe they will benefit from being consistent in their beliefs and actions, but the link will be weak where the benefits favor inconsistency.

Stereotypes

We saw in the discussion of Milner's (1983) work that stereotypes are closely related to prejudices. The current use and meaning of the term *stereotypes* originated during the 1920s with American journalist Walter Lippmann (Bethlehem, 1985). Nearly all contemporary psychologists define the term in a way similar to his. For Roger Brown (1986), it is "a shared conception of the character of a group" (p. 586). Milner defines the term as "overgeneralizations," usually undesirable, about the characteristics of a group that function to exaggerate the differences between groups. For Ehrlich (1973), a stereotype is "a set of beliefs and disbeliefs about any group of people" (p. 20). Finally, Hamilton and Trolier (1986) define a stereotype as "a cognitive structure that contains the perceiver's knowledge, beliefs, and expectancies about some human group" (p. 133). It is clear from the psychological literature that the development of stereotypes, as categories of beliefs about groups of people, is inevitable, normal, and necessary for adaptive functioning.

Stereotypes may be positive or negative. Negative stereotypes, e.g., "All Asians are secretive," may differ from prejudices in three ways. (1) They may not be "unreasonable" as that term has been defined.

(2) They may not have an affective component; e.g., the conviction that Asians are secretive may be thought about with indifference. (3) They may not dispose one to behave in any particular way. However, because of the ways that stereotypes and prejudices are measured, it is often difficult to determine which one is being assessed. Strongly held negative stereotypes certainly have the look and feel of prejudices. Given the facts that, at a minimum, stereotypes and prejudices share the belief component of attitudes, and that a substantial amount of research has been carried out with stereotypes, we can profit by examining this research. In the following discussion it is highly likely that the conclusions drawn are applicable to prejudices.

Roger Brown (1986) raises two interesting issues about stereotypes that are pertinent to the purposes of this book. The first deals with consequences of the way stereotypes have usually been measured. The second deals with the relation between stereotypes and how we deal behaviorally with individual members of the stereotyped group. The latter discussion gives an explanation of the "Some of my best friends are . . ." phenomenon.

In 1933 two social scientists, Katz and Brady, asked Princeton University undergraduates to select from a large list of traits those that were "typical" for each of 10 ethnic groups. This technique was the way Katz and Brady measured stereotypes. The procedure was repeated in 1951 and 1967 by different researchers for the then current Princeton undergraduates. Table 1.1 contains part of the summary by Karlins, Coffman, and Walters (1967) of the data for four ethnic groups for the three testing periods. As you can see, for most of the groups there is some but not complete continuity from generation to generation. Americans became viewed as less progressive and more pleasure loving from 1933 to 1967; Germans, over the same period, became viewed as more aggressive and nationalistic and less intelligent and stolid. The Jews came to be seen as less mercenary and grasping, and more materialistic and ambitious—more American. Negroes lost the stereotype of being "ignorant" in 1967, but not those of being lazy and musical.

Nearly everyone knows that all these stereotypes are incorrect in the sense that they do not characterize all or even most of the members of the various ethnic groups. As a consequence, we tend to discount them, at least when they are held by others. Part of the problem stems from the way the data were collected: students were asked to identify traits *typical* of each group. No one knows how "typical" was understood, but there is good reason to believe that the students were forced to make absolute judgments about groups rather than relative ones. For example, what does it mean that Negroes are musical? Relative to what or whom?

1933	1951	1967
	Americans	
Industrious	Materialistic	Materialistic
Intelligent	Intelligent	Ambitious
Materialistic	Industrious	Pleasure loving
Ambitious	Pleasure loving	Industrious
Progressive	Individualistic	Intelligent
	Germans	
Scientifically minded	Scientifically minded	Industrious
Industrious	Industrious	Scientifically minded
Stolid	Extremely nationalistic	Efficient
Intelligent	Intelligent	Extremely nationalistic
Methodical	Aggressive	Aggressive
	Jews	
Shrewd	Shrewd	Ambitious
Mercenary	Intelligent	Materialistic
Industrious	Industrious	Intelligent
Grasping	Mercenary	Industrious
Intelligent	Ambitious	Shrewd
	Negroes	
Superstitious	Superstitious	Musical
Lazy	Musical	Happy-go-lucky
Happy-go-lucky	Lazy	Lazy
Ignorant	Ignorant	Pleasure loving
Musical	Pleasure loving	Ostentatious

Source: Karlins, M., Coffman, T. L., & Walter, G. (1969). On the fading of social
stereotypes: Studies in three generations of college students. *Journal of Personality and
Social Psychology, 13,* 1–16. Copyright 1969 by the American Psychological Association.
Reprinted by permission.

Subsequent research by McCauley and Stitt (1978) and others corrected this problem and presented us with a more palatable view of
stereotypes. The essential idea is that a trait is seen to characterize an
ethnic group if it is more typical of that group than it is of people in
general. Subjects were asked the following kinds of questions: (1) What

percentage of Germans are extremely nationalistic? What percentage of people in the world generally are extremely nationalistic? (2) What percentage of Germans are superstitious? What percentage of people in the world generally are superstitious? McCauly and Stitt, for the first question, found that the average percentage of positive responses regarding people in general was 35.4; regarding Germans, it was 56.3. For the second question, the percentages were 42.1 regarding people in general, and 30.4 regarding Germans. By computing the ratio for each pair of percentages, the researcher can determine how much more or less typical each stereotype is for Germans (or for any other ethnic group). Thus, Germans are viewed as much more nationalistic than others (the ratio is much greater than 1.0), but appreciably less superstitious (the ratio is much lower than 1.0).

Are these stereotypes valid? Are Germans really more nationalistic and less superstitious? There is no way to determine the answers. How do you find out how many people in general are superstitious? Stereotypes function to help us bring conceptual order to our experiences, and periodically to make decisions on the basis of them. We assume that the ones we hold are, more or less, valid.

Do we always act on the basis of our stereotypes? Most of us have heard people deride a particular ethnic group, and then soften their stance by saying, "Some of my best friends are." Some of their best friends may really be members of that group. Brown (1986) helps us understand this phenomenon by casting it in the framework of decision-making theory. He points out an important distinction between general *base rate* knowledge about a group of which a person is a member, e.g., lawyers, engineers, women, or Jews, and *individuating information* (specific information) about a particular member of that group. Stereotypes are what are believed to be base rates about groups—for example, "Germans are more nationalistic than people in general." Suppose you wanted to hire a person for international work and it was very important to you that the employee not be nationalistic. All things being equal, if you believed the German stereotype, you would not hire a German for that job. But you might interview several people, one of whom is a German who does not appear to be in the least nationalistic. What do you do?

There is a rule in decision theory, Bayes' Rule, that states that the optimal decision we can make will take into account both base rates and individuating information. Intuitively this makes sense. The individuating information is usually based on a small, potentially inadequate sample of behavior for one particular person, whereas the base rates tell us something based on many people across many situations.

It turns out, judging from a wide variety of laboratory studies dealing with such stereotypes as the relative assertiveness of men, the political conservatism of engineers, and the relative emotional instability of "night" people, that most human beings do not use Bayes' Rule. Surprisingly, people do not use the stereotypes either. When subjects in experiments have relevant individuating information, they ignore the stereotypes and make their decisions on the individuating information. Thus, the employer in the example might very well hire the German applicant.

The social psychology literature has many examples of prejudices overriding individuating information, and of the converse. Nevertheless, the laboratory research makes clear that persons are not necessarily hypocrites or liars when they tell you that "some of their best friends are."

As we have noted, stereotypes are some of the ways we categorize people in order to help bring order to our concepts about them, and to reduce the enormous amount of social information we're exposed to in our daily lives. Hamilton and Trolier (1986) ask what the psychological consequences of categorizing others are. They answer this question in terms of two situations. In the first, when we perceive people as being members of a group as opposed to merely being a collection of unaffiliated individuals, two effects occur. (1) Individuals are perceived as more similar to each other when they are thought to be members of the same group than when they are thought to be unaffiliated; and individuals are perceived as being more dissimilar from each other when they are thought to be members of different groups than when they are thought to be unaffiliated. In addition, (2) when individual members of a group agree with each other, we perceive them as doing so because of the presence of other group members; and when they disagree with each other, we perceive them as doing so because of personal beliefs or convictions. In contrast, when the same people are thought to be unaffiliated, their agreements or disagreements with each other are generally perceived as being based on personal beliefs.

In the second situation, the person herself is a member of one group (the ingroup) and is making comparisons between her group and members of another group (the outgroup). Five interesting effects occur. (1) People believe they are more similar to ingroup members in a host of unrelated ways than they are to outgroup members. (2) Yet, ingroup members believe that there is more personal diversity in the ingroup than in the outgroup; e.g., "They're all alike in that group (the outgroup)." (3) On the other hand, almost in contradiction to the above, when a person rates members of an ingroup and those of an outgroup on various psychological characteristics, outgroup members receive more extreme ratings; e.g., "They're tremendous artists, whereas we're pretty good." (4) Individuals are more likely to remember positive information about ingroup than about outgroup members, and to remember negative information about outgroup than about ingroup members. (5) Individuals are more likely to perceive favorable causes for identical behavior in ingroup members than in outgroup members; e.g., "We do it because we're good-hearted. They do it because they want to look good."

It should be clear from Hamilton and Trolier's research that categorizing people does more than bring order and reduce information flow regarding our experiences. Categorizing also biases the way we perceive, remember, and understand others, thus reinforcing the categories themselves. As a consequence, when new and potentially contradictory information is presented, individuals often unconsciously distort it so that it will be experienced as consistent with their categories. For example, Bigler and Lieben (1993) presented to 4- to 9-year-old Euro-American children stories dealing with traits and social relations that were either consistent with or inconsistent with cultural stereotypes about African-Americans. Children generally had poorer memory for the culturally inconsistent stories than for the consistent ones. Moreover, those who held strong racial stereotypes had the poorest recall overall.

We develop beliefs about others because of their group membership. And as has been seen, it makes a big difference whether they are ingroup or outgroup members. In the next two sections we'll explore some consequences of more extreme beliefs about outgroup members.

Stigmas

During the Second World War, the Jews in Nazi-occupied countries were required to wear six-pointed stars (the Star of David) on their outer garments. This identified them as Jews, who, although they were considered by the Nazis to be less than human, were indistinguishable from non-Jews in nearly all other ways (male circumcision was another way, but was not readily observable). The Jews were stigmatized by the Nazis, and the Star of David was the outward sign of this. Unlike stereotypes, stigmas have an unambiguous relationship to prejudice. Moreover, unlike groups experiencing other forms of prejudice, in which the connection between attitudes and behavior is not strong, stigmatized groups are nearly always discriminated against, sometimes fatally.

Irving Goffman, one of the most imaginative social scientists of our time, wrote a book on this topic entitled, *Stigma, Notes on the Management of Spoiled Identity* (1963). Goffman tells us that the

Greeks originated the term, whose meaning referred "to bodily signs designed to expose something unusual and bad about the moral status of the signifier" (p. 1). The current meaning of the term is derived from its Greek origins, but refers to the "disgrace" itself—some characteristic or attribute of an individual that spoils, discredits, or disqualifies him—and not so much to the physical sign itself. Stigmas help define the social identity of individuals and should be seen in a social context. Thus, a stigma to one group, e.g., a criminal record to middle-class people, may not be a stigma to another group, e.g., a criminal record to members of the Mafia. In fact, for the latter group it may be a positive characteristic.

Stigmas are based upon objective characteristics of people—e.g., being Jewish, African-American, physically deformed, deaf, mentally retarded, homosexual, a former mental patient—but these characteristics usually have no inherent stigmatizing effect. The stigmatized characteristic becomes identified as such by one or more groups in a culture and comes to stand for, or signify, the person herself—e.g., "She's an African-American"; "She's deaf." To be stigmatized is to be dehumanized or depersonalized, which leads to being treated in often discriminatory, predictable ways. The person with the stigma becomes an object, a special devalued one.

Goffman describes three broad types of stigma: (1) physical deformities or incapacities; (2) "blemishes of individual character," such as imprisonment, mental disorder, or radical political behavior; and (3) "tribal" ones of race, nation, and religion. The latter are "inherited," either genetically or through one's family of origin. Goffman views these as having more or less equivalent effects on adults, but I think they may have very different developmental paths for children. As an example, there may be characteristics, such as physical deformities or behavioral abnormalities, that are readily stigmatized by children. Stigmas for more purely culturally defined characteristics, such as religious or sexual preference, may be acquired more slowly or with greater difficulty because they are not readily observable. There may be developmental differences in acquiring stigmas for which the person is blameworthy, e.g., criminality, as contrasted with those for which she is blameless, e.g., race or ethnicity.

The causes for stigmatizing others are probably no different from those underlying prejudice in general. As has been noted before, forming social categories is a natural consequence of processing social information. Certainly stigmas "aid" in that process. Katz (1979) indicates that there is a fair amount of evidence to support a scapegoating cause.

That is, individuals or groups are periodically frustrated or provoked in their attempts to attain certain goals and blame others for their failures—e.g., "The Blacks are getting all the good jobs now." Scapegoating is essentially displaced aggression. Katz (1979) suggests another related cause, which deals with attempts to assuage guilt or moral discomfort based on our knowledge of the existence of stigmatized groups. We see that it's wrong to mistreat homosexuals, or Blacks, or whomever. In order to justify that mistreatment *and* our failures to get others to change that mistreatment, we come to believe that the stigmatized group really deserves it: they *are* morally inferior. This is essentially a dissonance explanation. Still one more possible explanation is that the existence of stigmatized groups makes us feel better about ourselves. We may see ourselves as morally superior, or alternatively, as fortunate that we're "not one of them." Psychologically and socially, status is a powerful motivator of behavior.

One of the consequences of stigmatizing others is that it produces "ambivalent" feelings in us towards members of the stigmatized group (Katz, 1981). The concept of ambivalence has its roots in early twentieth-century psychoanalytic and sociological theory. It refers to dual or opposing feelings we occasionally have towards others, e.g., love and hate, attraction and repulsion. In the realm of stigmas, the opposing feelings are hostility or aversion versus acceptance or sympathy. When these dual feelings are aroused during interactions with stigmatized others, we try to resolve the incompatibility or conflict through a variety of behavioral strategies. One of the important consequences of ambivalence is that our positive or negative feelings get exaggerated or amplified, depending on the situation. Thus moderate concern can be transformed into deep compassion, and moderate dislike into marked rejection.

Katz (1981) develops and tests these ideas through research involving two stigmatized groups in the United States: Blacks and those who have physical disabilities. The dominant feeling many Whites have towards Blacks is rejection, and that held by able-bodied towards disabled persons is sympathy. But rejection towards Blacks is often accompanied by feelings of positive concern about racial discrimination; and sympathy towards disabled persons is often accompanied by avoidance or patronization.

In a typical racial experiment, Katz brings into a laboratory setting White adult subjects, who are met by a Black or White confederate of the experimenter (this partnership is unknown to the subjects) and a White experimenter. Some activity is carried out in which the subjects are asked to do something, e.g., help or insult the confederate. Then the subjects are asked to fill out an impression rating scale about the confederate. Similar procedures are used with nondisabled adults as subjects and confederates who are either able-bodied in appearance or using wheelchairs. The basic measure in all these cases is the subjects' responses to the two types of confederates.

Based on the theory that ambivalence causes exaggerated responses to stigmatized persons, Katz predicted that both positive and negative reactions would be more marked to Black than to White confederates and to disabled than to nondisabled confederates. These predictions were supported in nearly all experiments. For example, in one study White subjects were asked by the researcher to make highly critical statements to the Black or White confederate about the latter's personality. Subsequently, the subjects were asked by the confederate to help him with a tedious task. The Black confederate received much more help than the White ones, which indicates greater sympathy for the Black than for the White persons.

We can see that the ramifications of prejudice and discrimination are complex, but occasionally predictable in surprising ways. Stigmatizing others is perhaps the most debasing form of prejudice and thus the most psychologically destructive for its targets. The physical consequences of stigmatization can also be enormous, as seen in the nearly total annihilation of European Jews by the Nazis during the Second World War.

Official stigmatization of certain groups within a culture does not usually lead to their physical destruction. In fact, it leads to their continuity over time, because of the important functions the stigmatized groups serve for the larger society. We can learn a great deal about the study of prejudice by examining such situations.

Untouchability and the Consequences of Being Stigmatized

This section is based on Herbert Passin's (1955) article dealing with outcasts in India and Japan and on books by DeVos and Wagatsuma (1966) on the Japanese and Isaacs (1965) on the Asian Indians. Although the existence of "untouchable" castes in India is well known in Western culture, comparable groups have existed in Japan for over 1,000 years. There are marked similarities in the origins of these groups in the two cultures, as well as in the social and psychological consequences of being untouchable. Unlike social classes, which imply the long-term possibility of upward or downward movement, castes are more or less permanent inherited characteristics of people.

In both countries untouchability was a legally sanctioned status for substantial portions of the population. In India these groups comprised about 15 percent of the society; in Japan, about 2 percent. People of untouchable castes literally could not be touched by members of other groups without the latter running the risk of being contaminated or defiled themselves. Untouchables lived in segregated villages or neighborhoods and were generally isolated from others. In both cultures untouchables were often viewed as not quite human. In Japan the name for the major untouchable group, "Eta," refers to four-legged animals. Legally they were often restricted in the clothes they could wear, the way they could decorate their houses, and the way they could behave publicly. They couldn't share public facilities with the higher castes. Their legal rights were greatly reduced, and they could not attend school. Also, until present times they could not own land, which in agrarian societies was a powerful hindrance to overcoming poverty.

The category of untouchability was first officially banned in Japan in 1871, and in India in 1949. But, with parallels to the effects of the abolition of slavery in the United States, the Japanese and Indian ex-untouchables remain stigmatized in their societies, socially and physically separated from their fellow citizens.

Passin suggests, and Isaacs and DeVos and Wagatsuma concur, that there were three essential elements required for the evolution of untouchability. The first was that the society have a rigid and hereditary caste system. In both societies, historically there were three or four hierarchically arranged caste groups; below them were the untouchables. The second was the view that status differences between people are inherent in the nature of the universe; and, moreover, that these differences are based on an underlying inherited moral state. For the Indian culture the concept of transmitting one's moral state across generations is based on religious beliefs. For the Japanese, transmission of a "good" or a "base" moral state is not directly based on religious principles.

The third element was the existence of a religious belief that associates the concepts of pollution and ritual impurity with certain substances, usually dirt, blood, and dead animals and people. Excrement falls in the polluted category in India but not in Japan. The key point here is that people with certain occupations, e.g., street cleaners, butchers, and undertakers, regularly and necessarily come into contact with polluted substances, and thus become polluted themselves. The "fact" of this pollution indicates that they have a base moral state that they have received from their ancestors and that they will transmit to their offspring. Thus, even if untouchables are no longer in contact with polluted substances, they are still polluted, and "contagious" to others. Indeed, in both Japan and India the majority of ex-untouchables do *not* engage in jobs that put them in contact with these substances.

Despite the unproven beliefs many Indians and Japanese have that the untouchables come from different racial stock than members of the higher castes, there are essentially no physical differences between the groups. In Japan the untouchables (officially called "Buraku") look exactly like their neighbors. While there are behavioral differences, these are related to education and social class differences. In India there are a number of regional differences in physical appearance. Generally, lighter skin is more highly valued than dark skin. Although the untouchables (now officially referred to as "Scheduled Castes") may often be darker than members of the higher castes, there is substantial overlap in skin color. Thus, a very dark-skinned or a very light-skinned Indian may be from the highest caste—as well as from the lowest castes. In both countries, there are generally no language or religious differences between the untouchables and those of the higher castes.

The original creation of untouchable castes, and their unofficial maintenance today, is largely based on economic, social, and psychological reasons. Economically, the non-outcaste groups are assured that many of the least desirable work activities will be carried out, likely for relatively low wages. In no cultures do high-status, high-paying jobs go to the lowest social classes. For the untouchables, however, employment in these "undesirable" jobs is guaranteed because they have a monopoly on them. Further, these occupations are essential to the maintenance of the society, so the likelihood of unemployment is often less for them than for individuals in the higher caste groups.

Socially, the ex-untouchable groups are given a great deal of autonomy in governing their own segregated communities. They are well known to each other and mutually supportive. This geographic segregation gives the higher caste groups some assurance that they will not come into contact with ex-untouchables. Psychologically, there are benefits to the non-outcastes that we've previously noted in our discussion of stigmas. The status of the ex-untouchables is enormously degrading. Apparently nearly all ex-untouchables carry the emotional scars of this degradation throughout their lives.

In Japan and India, the official elimination of untouchable status came about through changes in the government. In Japan the Tokugawa rulers were replaced by the Meiji, and in India, the British were replaced by the Indians themselves. The elimination of slavery in the South in the United States occurred after the start of the Civil War, not before it. In all three cases, a humane philosophy overcame entrenched cultural practices at a time of political revolution. Thus, powerful conservative forces had to be overcome to produce these humane changes.

Both Isaacs and DeVos and Wagatsuma have written in depth about the psychological consequences of being born into an ex-untouchable caste. They've pointed out some obvious parallels to being born African-American. In both Japan and India the ex-untouchable children usually perform more poorly in school and have a higher dropout rate than do children of other groups. In segregated schools it's often difficult to find higher-caste teachers to instruct them, and in integrated schools, the higher-caste children often discriminate against them. Ex-untouchable children, adolescents, and adults are somewhat apprehensive about leaving their communities for fear of being ostracized. As a consequence of persistent hostility or the threat of it from the larger culture, many, perhaps most, ex-untouchables come to view themselves as contaminated. Because of this persistent discrimination, their expectations about future success in the larger culture are minimal. The safety net is the segregated neighborhood, but at the same time, that is the spider's web.

Education and moving to the cities offer some prospect of escape from untouchability. But escape can be accomplished mainly through "passing": pretending to be a higher-caste individual. The psychological costs are enormous. The individual loses his support system, because he has cut himself off from family and friends, has a constant fear of discovery, and cannot have a normal social life. Moreover, in these two cultures, people are very concerned about "family of origin" and make inquiries about it. You have to lie, but there's a fair chance that the lie will be discovered.

Isaacs and DeVos and Wagatsuma report that some progress has been made against this stigmatization, but it has been slow. No one anticipates that it will be erased before several generations have passed. If the history of prejudice and discrimination towards the Jews and the Blacks is any indicator, "several generations" is an optimistic speculation.

Psychological Consequences of African-American Slavery

As previously noted, several writers have pointed out the parallels between ex-untouchability in Asia and ex-slavery in the United States. This section explores some of the socialization consequences of being raised as a slave and of being descended from African-American slaves. Two consequences will be emphasized here: the positive and the negative consequences, or feeling worthy versus feeling unworthy. The slaves and their descendants have a heritage of being free people from African societies rich in cultural traditions. They were captured by other Africans, and uprooted from their sources of nurturance, protection, and identity. A new, imposed definition of self was given them, a definition that attempted to strip them of dignity. There were contradictions, the most salient, perhaps, being Christianization. As slaves, they were perceived by their masters and society as being human enough, worthy enough to accept the Christian Bible and God. Most developed two personas: the humble, usually obedient, self-effacing presentation of self to White people, and the freedom-loving, self-respectful, mutually supportive presentation of self to Black relatives and friends. A mistake often made by the White population was believing that the persona shown to Whites was the true persona. The slaves' frequent attempted escapes and disobedience were attributed to alleged Black subhuman qualities, as opposed to natural human responses to forced enslavement.

But did the slaves, to some extent, accept the White view of themselves? There is a psychoanalytic concept, "identification with the aggressor," that has been used to understand the apparently contradictory reactions of prisoners to their guards (Bettleheim, 1943). In the Nazi concentration camps, Jews, Poles, and members of other ethnic groups occasionally accepted the opinions of their prison guards about their value. Some viewed the guards as superior beings and themselves as inferior, deserving of their dehumanization.

A more recent theoretical view of comparable phenomena is referred to as the Stockholm Syndrome (Graham & Rawlings, 1991). The syndrome derives its name from observations of value and affectional shifts by hostages leading to bonding with their captors. Four major conditions are prerequisites to developing this syndrome: an individual's survival is threatened by "others," he is unable to escape from those "others,"[1] he is isolated from people who are not similarly threatened, and the "others" periodically show kindness to him. When a person develops the syndrome, he comes to adopt the captors' values as his own and to feel strong affection for them. These four conditions often occurred in slavery conditions, which suggests that many African-Americans at least partially accepted the White people's views of them. That is, many slaves, operating under the psychodynamics of

---

[1]The masculine will be used, but the syndrome applies to both genders.

the Stockholm Syndrome, came to see themselves as less worthy than the Whites who controlled them and threatened their lives, but who periodically showed them kindness.

Graham and Rawlings (1991) have documented the evidence of this syndrome in abused women and abused children. They are in the process of extending their analyses to women in general, in American society. Identification with the aggressor, or the Stockholm Syndrome, likely applies to all oppressed groups in any culture, and not only to hostages, abused people, or slaves. Hence, it makes sense to consider its applicability to many post–Civil War African-Americans, who are still oppressed and still engaged in the struggle for freedom. Thus, the theme of feeling worthy versus feeling unworthy is not restricted to the days of slavery. Rather, there is historical evidence indicating that for African-Americans these contradictory feelings live side by side within the group.

Theories of Prejudice and Discrimination: Individual and Cultural/Historical Influences

Where do prejudice and discrimination come from? Many parents are shocked when their children express prejudiced attitudes that are antagonistic to long-standing family values. Contrariwise, how is it that some children from bigoted families are not in the least prejudiced? Is prejudice in the individual, or is it in the culture?

Gordon Allport (1954) cautions us that the law of multiple causation is at play in all social phenomena, especially those of prejudice and discrimination. That is, there are nearly always several causes underlying the development and expression of prejudice and discrimination. He identified six major "causes" or theories of prejudice, five of which vary along a continuum bounded by individualistic perceptions and beliefs at one end, and by cultural/historical influences at the other. It should be noted that the six causes are oriented towards understanding ethnic prejudice; however, I believe that most, if not all, are applicable to other targets of prejudice. I'll briefly summarize them.

The most transitory and individualistic of the six is called the "Phenomenological Emphasis." In this view, the person's current beliefs, perceptions, and verbal labels chosen regarding any particular group determine how she will react to the situation she is confronted with. There's an immediacy about these reactions, including prejudiced ones, which may be quite different on subsequent occasions.

A more enduring individualistic cause is the "Psychodynamic Emphasis." In this view people develop more or less stable personality characteristics that they bring to all social situations. These characteristics predispose the individual to react in prejudiced ways. Allport notes three types of these characteristics: conflict resolution, frustration reactions, and character structure. Conflict resolution refers to the persistent attempts of some people to gain power or status over others. Frustration reactions, also known as *scapegoating,* are persistent attempts to direct hostile impulses toward minority groups in order to discharge feelings of frustration and deprivation experienced in daily life. Character structure refers primarily to "insecure and anxious personalities who take the authoritarian and exclusionist way of life rather than the relaxed trusting democratic way" (p. 216). In the next section we'll present an extensive discussion of this type.

The third cause is the "Situational Emphasis." In this view, prejudice is seen as arising out of conformity to the current social forces operating in a culture. The focus here is social/psychological, as opposed to purely individualistic or purely cultural/historical.

The fourth cause, "Sociocultural Emphasis," is the principal type of explanation of prejudice offered by sociologists and anthropologists. The total social context is examined with the view of identifying those traditions and conditions that produce conflict among different groups, e.g., job and housing competition and opportunities for upward social mobility. These lead to increased uncertainty about one's values and customs, which in turn leads to prejudice against the groups of people one is in conflict with.

The fifth cause, "Historical Emphasis," recognizes that there is nearly always a long history involved with conflict and discrimination between particular groups in a given culture. This history serves both to justify the prejudices held by dominant groups and to perpetuate them. Many historians believe that economic exploitation is at the heart of the matter. If Blacks, Asians, or Jews are historically seen as morally or "racially" inferior, then negative treatment of them by the economically dominant groups is sanctioned.

The sixth cause, "Emphasis on Earned Reputation," is not on the individualistic and cultural/historical continuum. This cause asserts that there are perceived differences between groups, and that these differences stimulate dislike and hostility. The notion of "earned reputation" acknowledges that at least some of the perceived differences are based on objective reality. Indeed, in our previous discussion of stereotypes we implicitly stated that there is often a reasonable basis for the existence of particular stereotypes.

A more recent analysis of theories of prejudice and discrimination by Marger (1991) both simplifies and extends Allport's conclusions.

Marger identifies three types of theories: psychological, normative, and power-conflict. These are not mutually exclusive, but rather, the causes described often work together. The psychological theories are exactly the same as those of Allport's "Psychodynamic Emphasis," and need not be described again. Normative theories are combinations of Allport's "Situational Emphasis" and his "Historical Emphasis." The essence of these theories is that there are social norms in a given culture that tell us the way we ought to perceive and behave towards members of particular outgroups. These norms are transmitted to our children through the processes of socialization. Sometimes socialization practices are subtle, almost unconscious—e.g., parents' references to the African-American cleaning woman as "the girl"—and other times they are quite blatant. Prejudice and discrimination thus become the normal, acceptable ways to act in society. There is some variation in prejudice among the dominant groups because there are a variety of "reference groups" whose values may be emulated. Different socioeconomic classes, for example, may develop somewhat different ways of expressing prejudice towards the same target group.

Power-conflict theories explain how prejudice and discrimination arise, whereas the previous two categories of theories explain how prejudice and discrimination are sustained and transmitted. The essential idea in power-conflict theories is that dominant groups in a culture are continuously working to maintain the power and privileges they hold. These groups create social, political, and economic institutions to protect their interests and to control any tendencies of subordinate groups to modify the social order. Prejudice and discrimination are protective devices that are aroused when a group in a superior position is threatened by subordinate groups. Marger (1991) suggests that there are usually historical traditions within a culture that support the claims and practices of the dominant groups.

In the next two sections of this chapter, we'll explore aspects of the two endpoints of the individualistic and cultural/historical continuum. In the first of these sections, "The Authoritarian Personality," both a summary and criticisms of some of the principal research findings on this topic will be presented. The material is very important in the history of research on prejudice, and moreover indicates the shortcomings of an individualistic approach. In the second section, "Patriarchy and Female Socialization," a discussion will be presented of how cultural history and socialization practices interact to produce female gender identity. This material is very important in helping us understand how subordinate groups occasionally operate to perpetuate their own subordination.

The Authoritarian Personality

The destruction of the Jewish population in Europe was the culmination of several hundred years of often violent anti-Semitism. The magnitude of the horror was, and is, nearly incomprehensible. That it happened, and that it was directed by the leadership of a highly civilized country, Germany, cannot be denied. But what kind of people could have permitted this to occur? A number of sociologists and psychologists pursued an answer to this question in the United States shortly after the Second World War. Their initial research was published in a 990-page book, *The Authoritarian Personality* (Adorno, Frenkel-Brunswick, Levinson, & Sanford, 1950). Some of the authors continued exploring this area for several more years, and many others joined in. Most of the research and the criticisms of it were completed by the early 1960s. Roger Brown eloquently summarizes this work in the first edition of his book *Social Psychology* (1965). Other more recent studies support his conclusions, e.g., Cherry and Byrne (1976), Forbes (1985).

The basic premise of Adorno et al. (1950) is that certain personality types are more likely to develop strong prejudices than others. The authors concluded that it was possible that particular cultures, e.g., those of Germany and Austria, were more conducive to producing these types of people, but it was also clear that anti-Semitism and anti-Negro prejudices were widespread in the United States. Thus, they sought to describe the prejudiced personality, and not the prejudiced society. Their work is heavily based on psychoanalytic theory, as was much of the personality research carried out in the 1940s and 1950s, and they use this theory to help readers understand the underlying mechanisms of prejudice.

Research on the authoritarian personality used two broad kinds of methods, forced-choice questionnaires and the more clinical techniques of projective questions, interviews, and the Thematic Apperception Test (I'm closely following Brown's [1965] summary now). The subjects for the research were over 2,000 adults from particular organizations: college students, teachers, nurses, union members, veterans, prison inmates, and patients of a psychiatric clinic. Most were White, native-born, middle-class, non-Jewish Americans.

The questionnaires consisted of four scales: the Anti-Semitism scale; the Ethnocentrism scale; the Political and Economic Conservatism scale; and the Potentiality for Fascism scale. The Anti-Semitism scale consisted of statements designed to measure the extent to which the individual held "stereotyped negative opinions describing the Jews as threatening, immoral, and categorically different from non-Jews, and . . . hostile attitudes urging various forms of restriction, exclusion, and suppression as a means of solving the 'Jewish Problem'" (Adorno et al., 1950, p. 71). All the items were written in such a way that agreement with a statement was supportive of an anti-Semitic view. One of the items was this: "The trouble with letting Jews into a nice neighborhood is that they gradually give it a typical Jewish atmosphere."

The Ethnocentrism scale consisted of statements designed to measure the extent to which individuals rigidly accepted aspects of their own culture and rejected what was different. Ethnocentrism is thus a broader form of prejudice than anti-Semitism. The items dealt with various minority groups, foreigners, socially different persons, and the "American Way." As with the Anti-Semitism scale, the items here were worded so that agreement with a statement was supportive of an ethnocentric view. One of the items was this: "Americans may not be perfect, but the American Way has brought us about as close as human beings can get to a perfect society."

The Political and Economic Conservatism scale consisted of statements designed to measure the extent to which individuals held the values of the American conservative right wing. The main components involved keeping things as they were, resisting social change, and valuing ambition, efficiency, and financial success. Unlike the other three scales, the items in the Conservatism scale were *not* all worded in the same direction. One of the items was this: "A child should learn early in life the value of a dollar and the importance of ambition, efficiency, and determination."

The Potentiality for Fascism scale was considered by many to be the scale that measured authoritarianism as a personality trait. It consisted of statements reflecting nine antidemocratic characteristics, all written so that agreement with a statement supported an authoritarian view. The nine characteristics involved conventionalism; authoritarian submission; authoritarian aggression; anti-introspection; superstition and stereotyping; power and "toughness"; destructiveness and cynicism; projectivity; and exaggerated sexual concerns. Two of the briefer statements were these: "Some day it will probably be shown that astrology can explain a lot of things" and "Familiarity breeds contempt."

In general, the split-half reliability of each of the scales was quite satisfactory, indicating that each scale measured a cluster of highly related attitudes. Adorno et al. (1950) constructed these scales believing that anti-Semitism, ethnocentrism, conservatism, and authoritarianism were an interconnected set of beliefs, values, and personality characteristics. Were they? Yes, moderately so. The Anti-Semitism and Ethnocentrism scale scores correlated on average about .80 with each other. Scores on the Conservatism scale correlated on average with Ethnocentrism and Anti-Semitism scores, .57 and .43 respectively. Finally, Fascism scale scores correlated on average with Anti-Semitism, Ethnocentrism, and Conservatism scores, .53, .65, and .54, respectively.

Following data collection for the questionnaires, 80 subjects, half men and half women, were asked to participate in the clinical part of the study. Half of these had scored in the top 25 percent of the Ethnocentrism scale, and half had scored in the bottom 25 percent. The primary goal of the clinical interviews and tests was to develop a deep understanding of the personalities of prejudiced (top 25 percent) and unprejudiced (bottom 25 percent) subjects. This assumes, of course, that the personalities of prejudiced people resemble one another, as do those of unprejudiced people. Prior to the actual clinical sessions, the interviewers knew which groups their subjects were from, and were thoroughly familiar with each subject's questionnaire performance. The two judges who coded the interviews were part of the research team and familiar with the general results from the questionnaire.

Some of the major findings of the clinical data were as follows. Prejudiced subjects tended to have an unrealistic positive view of themselves and their parents, whereas unprejudiced subjects were more objective in their appraisals. When prejudiced subjects did criticize themselves or their parents, they did so in a way that almost denied the validity of the criticism. The negativity was treated as an exception, almost externally forced upon the criticized person, and not a true criticism. The authors argue that the glorification of self and parents alongside the denial of criticism indicates the presence of considerable unresolved ambivalence. The prejudiced person deals with this ambivalence by projecting onto (unconsciously attributing to) minority groups the unacceptable negative characteristics. Why are negative characteristics so difficult to "own up to"? The main reason seems to be the excessive concern prejudiced people have with status and external signs of success. The admission of negative characteristics would lower an individual's perception of his and his parents' status. Finally, prejudiced subjects seemed to have been raised by parents who practiced authoritarian discipline. The aggressive feelings this discipline produced in the subjects could not be directed towards their parents. Instead they were displaced onto minority groups.

Following publication of *The Authoritarian Personality,* a deluge of research and criticism occurred. Brown (1965) sifts through this for us, and I highlight three aspects of his analysis. The first problem with the study involves the construction of three of the four scales such that responses that agreed with the statements always led to high anti-Semitism, ethnocentrism, or potential fascism. It has been documented that many subjects have an "acquiescent response set": a tendency to agree with any kind of assertion. Thus the intercorrelations were spuriously high—so high that the results were meaningless? No. Careful follow-up research showed that acquiescence accounted for only a minor portion of subjects' scores on these scales.

The second problem involves the objectivity of the clinical interviews. The major issue here is that the interviewers were not only knowledgeable about the theory and the hypotheses, but also very familiar with the questionnaire data of each subject. Thus, there were considerable opportunities for biasing the nature of the material the subjects produced. If you know, for example, that a subject is prejudiced, then you can (and might) continue to ask questions until you get the answer consistent with a prejudiced answer. Fortunately, this was not an issue with the other clinical data. These latter data tended to support the conclusions based on the interviews.

The third problem involves the relationships among authoritarianism, education, IQ, and social class (socioeconomic status, or SES). Basically, Fascism scale scores were inversely related to amount of education, IQ, and SES. Some of the questionnaire differences are striking. For example, 80 percent of people with a grammar school education, 60 percent of those with a high school education, and 35 percent of those with a college education agreed with the following statement: "The most important thing to teach children is absolute obedience to their parents." So, is the Fascism scale a measure of personality, or is it a measure related to the cluster of IQ, education, and SES? Fortunately, one doesn't have to choose. The answer is *both*. Poorly educated, low-IQ, low-SES individuals are more likely to develop authoritarian personalities than are others. The fact of this covariation does not undercut the validity of the relations among the four scales. The hopeful aspect of these data is the knowledge that education lessens authoritarianism.

What are we left with? Brown (1965) and others conclude that despite the strong methodological criticisms brought against *The Authoritarian Personality*, there is a personality type, measured by the Fascism scale, that is likely to develop prejudices against outgroup members. More recent research, e.g., Cherry and Byrne (1976), has shown that the situation or context a person is in is a more powerful determinant of whether prejudice will be expressed than are the Fascism scale scores. Other research, e.g., Forbes (1985), has shown that political attitudes, especially nationalist ones, may not be globally related to authoritarianism. Rather, subjects with high Fascism scale scores may be ethnocentric in relation to some but not all outgroups, depending on the nature of the outgroup. Thus, knowledge of an individual's Fascism score is not sufficient to predict her degree of prejudice in any particular situation or against any particular group.

Patriarchy and Female Socialization

Although the first Americans were the American Indians, the most influential Americans in contemporary society were European immigrants and their descendants. Europeans came to this country in increasingly large numbers from the seventeenth century through the early part of the twentieth century, when highly restrictive immigration laws were enacted. These people came from patriarchal societies—societies with an "institutional system of male dominance" (Lerner, 1986)—and brought that mode of social organization with them. Highly supportive of social patriarchy was their Christian religion, with its male dominance and masculine God.

Christianity evolved mainly out of Judaism, but also out of Greek and Roman moral philosophies. Judaism has its roots in the great ancient cultures of the Near East, such as Sumer, Ur, Mesopotamia, Egypt, and Babylonia, all strongly patriarchal cultures. In this religion and these cultures, women attained their status through marriage and motherhood; but it was nearly always a status secondary to that of men and dependent on men.

The Judeo-Christian Fifth and Tenth Commandments are particularly relevant to this discussion. The Fifth says, "Honor your father and your mother, that you may have a long life in the land which the Lord, your God, is giving you." Thus, the masculine God is commanding offspring to honor both their parents. The payoff for this is a long life in the land God gives them. This seeming equality of fathers and mothers is clarified in the Tenth Commandment, which says, "You shall not covet your neighbor's house. You shall not covet your neighbor's wife, nor his male or female slave, nor his ox or ass, nor anything else that belongs to him." Thus, women are counted among the "property" of men, in the same way as are slaves and farm animals. Despite this marked subordination of women to men, as mothers they are the rightful recipients of honor from their children.

The Graeco-Roman influence on the status of women draws mainly on the writings of Aristotle, who predates Christianity by about 350 years. In the Aristotelian position, women are viewed as morally, intellectually, and physically inferior to men. They are incomplete human beings, without fully developed souls. They are irrational, and even with extensive schooling could not attain the intellectual status of men. Their main function is to produce males, who are complete, unified human beings, with fully developed souls. Because of these gender discrepancies, Aristotle maintained that it is a virtue for men to dominate women, and shameful to give women equal treatment (Lange, 1983; Lerner, 1986).

It is clear from reading Lerner (1986) about historical cultures of the Near East, as well as reading contemporary cross-cultural accounts (Freidl, 1975), that the subordinate status of women to men is not restricted to Europe. In general, with the advent of intense agriculture (as opposed to simple horticulture) and warfare, status differences between men and women became exaggerated, relatively independent of historical time or place. The significance of the Judeo/Greek/Roman/Christian influence in the United States is that the justification of the treatment of females by males was based partly on religious grounds. Not only are cultural practices difficult to change, but when those practices are involved with religion, change becomes a sacrilege.

There are at least two important lessons related to the present discussion to be learned from reading history. The first is that whatever the party in power is and whoever constitute its members, there are always some who oppose it. In ancient Greece, there was nearly always a group that sided with the enemy and opened, or was prepared to open, the gates for the attacking army. The second lesson is that many members of subordinate groups take active steps to maintain the status quo. In recent times, many American women fought against passage of the Equal Rights Amendment, arguing in favor of maintaining traditional female roles with such statements as "Women's place is in the home." The significance of these two lessons is that historically, in the United States, there nearly always have been men and women who have contested the traditional roles assigned to women. Indeed, feminism, as a clear voice for gender equality, has existed for at least 150 years (Evans, 1989; Ryan, 1975). On the other hand, we can see that most women did not join the feminist movement and many attacked it, using the same arguments as their husbands, brothers, and fathers.

It is thus likely that at any given point in history, the majority of men and women accepted the then existing gender status quo. Given that men had the dominant and superior positions in nearly all aspects of society, their acceptance of the status quo is understandable. Losing a preferred place has its practical and emotional costs. But why should women have been accepting of their inferior status? Our socialization experiences tell us who we are. The identity is not like a garment that can be shed for a new occasion. We are deeply tied to, committed to, and defined by our identities. Anyone who has been in psychotherapy, as giver or receiver, knows in very powerful ways the adhesive quality of identity, even while perhaps acknowledging its dysfunctionality. A human being not committed to her identity is left very vulnerable to changing circumstances. And circumstances usually do change.

There are also profound cultural/symbolic reasons for the maintenance of the gender status quo, which Lerner (1986) has convincingly written about. Lerner's argument, on the surface, is about the writing of history. But her account should be viewed as a prime example of both the ways masculine values get transmitted in a culture and the ways historical writings help maintain those values. The central idea is that men have controlled both the writing and interpretation of history. They have chosen both what and whom to write about. Not surprisingly, they have written about the activities of men, asserting of course that these are the most important features of culture. Where women have been noted, they are identified as exceptional. Indeed, they are the exceptions that prove the rule: the superiority and centrality of men and men's interests.

The symbols, the rules of interpretation, the concepts employed for understanding history have all been filtered through and processed by men's understanding of society. Thus, until recently, women's activities and concerns have rarely been mentioned in historical accounts. They are taken for granted as the ground upon which the central (and male) figures act out their major roles. As Lerner (1986) notes, women become invisible. The historical disregard of women even carries over into traditionally masculine realms in which women have been successful. For example, until recent years art histories and music histories didn't even mention women's contributions. If the painting or the score was created by a woman, then, historians implied, it wasn't good enough to discuss.

Weren't there women historians? Why didn't they write about women's achievements? There were some, but two factors militated against their presenting a different point of view. First, men controlled the cultural resources, which included higher education, publishing houses, and the media. Thus, women's productions had to pass through men's cultural filters. Second, women historians were trained by men in male-dominant cultures. Thus, the concepts and rules they were taught were those espoused by their male teachers. It's very difficult to break the intellectual and cultural mold into which you have been poured and in which you have cured. So, women historians have used men's symbolic and interpretative frameworks in understanding society.

Let us move the argument out of the realm of history making and into the realm of children's socialization. Traditionally, mothers and other women have been the primary caretakers in the home. In the schools, especially those for young children, teachers have also been women. In our culture the "rules" for understanding, perceiving, and categorizing are based on men's values, but these rules are taught to children by women. One consequence is that the same behavior carried out by boys and by girls may have different meanings for and be treated differently by mothers and teachers. In the extreme, women are full participants in devaluing themselves in support of male-generated values.

Valerie Walkerdine, a developmental psychologist, has documented some of these activities in nursery school settings in England. Following is a quotation from her 1981 article. The children are a 3-year-old girl, Annie, two 4-year-old boys, Sean and Terry, and the 30-year-old teacher, Miss Baxter.

> The sequence begins when Annie takes a piece of Lego to add on to a construction she is building. Terry tries to take it away from her to use himself, and she resists. He says:
>
> **Terry:** You're a stupid cunt, Annie.
>
> The teacher tells him to stop and Sean tries to mess up another child's construction. The teacher tells him to stop. Then Sean says:
>
> **Sean:** Get out of it Miss Baxter paxter.
> **Terry:** Get out of it knickers Miss Baxter.
> **Sean:** Get out of it Miss Baxter paxter.
> **Terry:** Get out of it Miss Baxter the knickers paxter knickers, bum.
> **Sean:** Knickers, shit, bum.
> **Miss B:** Sean, that's enough, you're being silly.
> **Sean:** Miss Baxter, knickers, show your knickers.
> **Terry:** Miss Baxter, show your bum off.
> (they giggle)
> **Miss B:** I think you're being very silly.
> **Terry:** Shit Miss Baxter, shit Miss Baxter.
> **Sean:** Miss Baxter, show your knickers your bum off.
> **Sean:** Take all your clothes off, your bra off.
> **Terry:** Yeah, and take your bum off, take your wee-wee off, take your clothes, your mouth off.
> **Sean:** Take your teeth out, take your head off, take your hair off, take your bum off. Miss Baxter the paxter knickers taxter.
> **Miss B:** Sean, go and find something else to do please. (p. 15)

This is an amazing script. It is so not just because Sean and Terry, at age 4, are already depreciating females as sex objects, but mainly because Miss Baxter colludes with them in the process. Her good-natured tolerance of their behavior—e.g., "You're being very silly"; "Find something else to do please"—indicates that the behavior is expectable, and to some extent acceptable. Miss Baxter, who is a female authority and represents other female authorities, continues to teach both the boys and the girls in her charge that it's permitted for males to demean females. In her discussion with Walkerdine about this incident, she states that what the boys did was natural and harmless. How did Miss Baxter come to these views? Walkerdine, a former teacher herself, asserts that teachers are trained in a "scientific pedagogy." This is a pedagogy that preaches free and natural expression, but an expression that only naturally takes on the characteristics of the society in which it is embedded. In this case, the messages are that females are sex objects and males, even 4-year-olds, are more powerful than they.

The Present Theoretical View

Prejudice and discrimination, as Allport (1954) assures us, have multiple causes. There appears to be a consensus among social scientists as to their nature. For example, John Duckett (1992) examined the psychological research from a historical perspective and arrived at four categories of causes that are quite similar to those of Allport and Marger (1991). However, I believe there is an important "cause" that these and many other writers have overlooked: the genetic/evolutionary bases. We are not only creatures of culture. Rather, as the Nobel Prize winner Konrad Lorenz argued in 1969, and as I concurred in my 1976 and 1984 books, evolutionary processes have designed us to operate in particular ways in particular environments. The enormously influential sociobiology movement started by Edward Wilson in 1975 makes a similar point.

What is meant by a genetic/evolutionary design? To understand this, we must distinguish between *genotypes,* the set of genes that individuals possess, and *phenotypes,* the physiology, anatomy, and behavior of individuals that develop from the genotypes in specific sequences of environments. Genotypes don't vary over the course of a lifetime, whereas phenotypes do, e.g., over infancy, childhood, adolescence, and adulthood. Moreover, the same genotype can lead to somewhat different phenotypes if the individuals are reared in different environments, e.g., identical twins separated at birth. It is genotypes that are inherited, and it is genotypes and environments that determine how phenotypes will develop. Generally there is a close connection between genotypes and phenotypes; e.g., identical twins reared apart do resemble each other. More blatantly, no matter what the rearing, chimpanzees remain chimpanzees and never are transformed into humans. Particular genotypes are transmitted from generation to generation because the phenotypes they develop in given environments reproduce more than those developed by other genotypes. Thus, there is a certain indirectness about the relation between successful phenotypes and successful genotypes.

Returning to genetic/evolutionary designs, the basic idea at the species level (as opposed to the individual level) is that the characteristic genotype of any species emerged because members of the species possessing that genotype were more adaptive than members not possessing it; i.e., they survived and reproduced more viable offspring than the latter. Eventually, because of this differential reproduction over many generations, nearly all members of the species acquired the successful genotype. This characteristic genotype is maintained in a species as long as it leads to successful phenotypes. And this will occur if the environments in which individuals develop and reproduce continue to be supportive of the characteristic genotype. Sounds circular? It's really not. Both gradual and dramatic shifts in the environment can change the characteristic genotype of a species, even causing its extinction.

To say that evolution designed us "to operate in particular ways in particular environments" does not mean that we act only reflexively or instinctively. We are somewhat plastic or flexible, but not infinitely so. Our development is channeled or "canalized," as the geneticist Waddington (1957) has shown for anatomical characteristics, and the psychologist Piaget (1971) has shown for behavior. These behavioral characteristics or patterns emerge provided that individuals are reared in environments falling in a range normal for their species. They are part of the evolutionary design and can be considered as normal, inevitable, and necessary for adaptive functioning. For humans, some of the more obvious behavioral characteristics are language, bipedal locomotion, and coordinated use of two hands, but these also include rule giving and following, reciprocal helping and harming, and particular family and group social structures (Fishbein, 1976). One major aspect of the human design is in the area of "intergroup relations." This is the topic that encompasses the social psychology of prejudice and discrimination (see, e.g., Stephan, 1985). A central conviction of this book is that evolutionary processes have designed us in such a way that the development of prejudice and discrimination towards outgroup numbers is highly likely, and perhaps inevitable. These ideas will be elaborated in the next chapter.

Our genetic/evolutionary heritage provides the initial push towards prejudice and discrimination. We've learned from Allport (1954) and Marger (1991) that cultural norms and values define or identify some of the targets of prejudice and discrimination. Certain outgroups are more likely to be the recipients of prejudice than others. Prejudice towards them becomes expected and normative. However, culture isn't static or stagnant, but rather evolves, i.e., undergoes historical change. Another central conviction of this book is that in order to identify and understand cultural norms towards particular groups, we must understand their historical evolution. The television portrayal of African-Americans, women, or mentally retarded persons in any given year, for example, may not be reflective of long-standing, relatively permanent attitudes and values. The latter do change over time; and it is important to document that change in order to accurately assess where we are today. In that the focus of this book is on peer prejudice and discrimination involving differences in race, sex, hearing impairment, and mental retardation, cultural histories of four target groups will be presented in the third chapter.

Finally, Allport (1954) and Marger (1991) indicate that cultural and group processes are reflected in the behavior of individuals. To a large extent, individuals' behavior is determined by their socialization experiences. Parts of these socialization experiences are the direct and indirect teaching of cultural norms, including those involving prejudice and discrimination. Our discussion of patriarchy and female socialization in this chapter is an example of this. Given that the focus of this book is on prejudice and discrimination of children towards peers, a deep understanding of these topics requires an understanding of their social development. Regarding opposite-sex prejudice and discrimination, we will examine how families, peers, and teachers socialize sex-typing. Sex-typing involves behavior, attitudes, and values about one's own and the opposite sex. Children learn what appropriate and inappropriate behaviors and aspirations are for themselves and others. These valuations set the ground for interactions with and judgments about same- and opposite-sex peers. Regarding race prejudice and discrimination, we will examine how ethnic identity is socialized and develops. One's ethnic identity includes patterns of behaviors, expectations, and values about members of one's racial/ethnic group as well as about other groups. These valuations have differential effects on Black and White children, which are played out in their prejudice and discrimination. Regarding deaf and mentally retarded children, data comparable to those on sex-typing and ethnic identity are, unfortunately, not available. This is a lacuna that I hope other writers will fill in the near future.

Summary

A variety of definitions of prejudice were discussed. Nearly all have in common the idea that prejudice is a negative attitude towards others because of their membership in a particular group. Following the lead of

Allport and Milner, an additional component seemed necessary to distinguish prejudices from other types of negative attitudes: unreasonableness. Allport refers to this component as "faulty and inflexible" attitudes and Milner as "irrational" attitudes. Prejudiced individuals resist modifying their prejudices in the face of contradictory information.

Discrimination was defined as harmful actions towards others because of their membership in a particular group. Discrimination may or may not be based on prejudice, although when children are freely interacting without adult control it is likely that the two go hand in hand. Recent theorizing suggests that prejudice and discrimination feed on and enhance each other.

The relationship between prejudice and behavior is complex. Research shows that when there is no direct contact between people, as in voting situations, there is a fairly strong relationship between prejudice and behavior. However, when people interact with each other, the relationship is weak. Prejudice is just one factor among many that mediates behavior; e.g., other personal attitudes and motives and situational conditions are also influential.

Stereotypes are closely related to prejudices, and often can't be distinguished from them. Stereotypes are categories of beliefs about groups of people that assist us in sorting out the overwhelming social information we receive. We know that our stereotypes are not completely accurate, yet they are often the most reliable guides for making decisions. When we categorize people into ingroups and outgroups, our perceptions and beliefs about them as individuals and as group members are markedly influenced.

One potential consequence of prejudice is stigmatizing others. Stigmas are characteristics of people—e.g., being a member of a particular ethnic group, having a particular disability, or being a former mental patient—that spoil or discredit them. Some likely reasons for stigmatizing others are scapegoating, justifying our failures to help particular groups, and enhancing our own status. But, as Katz's research shows, we are frequently ambivalent about groups we stigmatize. This ambivalence often leads us to exaggerate our responses—either negative or positive—to them.

Historically, there have been groups of people in India and Japan who have been legally stigmatized: the untouchable castes. Although untouchability has been declared illegal in these countries, it still exists and produces profound negative social and psychological consequences. There are some obvious parallels between the treatment of ex-untouchables and that of African-Americans in the United States.

One of the consequences of being raised as an African-American descended from slaves is the development of feelings of unworthiness.

One of the explanations of this phenomenon is called the Stockholm Syndrome, derived from the observation of value and affectional shifts on the part of hostages that produce bonding with their captors. It is thought that the conditions leading to the Stockholm Syndrome often occurred in slavery conditions, which suggests that many African-Americans at least partially accepted the White people's views of them.

A consensus has emerged among social psychologists concerning the bases of prejudice and discrimination. All believe that there are multiple causes that can be construed as falling somewhere on a continuum, with individualistic or psychological causes at one pole and cultural/historical causes at the other pole. The initial motivating force for the development of prejudice and discrimination is the attempts of dominant groups within a culture to continue holding the power and privileges they have.

Research on the authoritarian personality was among the most influential programs on the topic of prejudice. It occupies the individualistic pole of the causal continuum. The original impetus for the study of authoritarianism was the destruction of most of European Jewry by the Nazis during the Second World War. The research was centered in California and was directed towards identifying a personality type that was likely to show ethnocentrism and anti-Semitism. The original studies had some serious methodological flaws, and the original researchers did not study situational influences on prejudice; but there is consensus that individuals with authoritarian personalities are likely to be more prejudiced than other individuals.

Research on patriarchy and female socialization occupies the cultural/historical pole. This research tracks historically how male dominance and female subordination emerged in the United States. It shows how females themselves, who take on the value system of the culture, perpetuate their own subordination in both their professional activities and their socialization of children.

The one causal factor of prejudice and discrimination that most social scientists ignore is our genetic/evolutionary inheritance. The view is taken that genetic evolution has designed us to operate in particular ways in particular environments. Among these ways are patterns in forming and continuing intergroup relations. Although our genetic makeup predisposes humans to prejudice and discrimination, culture identifies the targets. Cultural norms and values are not static, but rather "evolve" over time. Finally, it is individuals who have prejudiced attitudes and act in a discriminatory fashion. In order to gain a deep understanding of these attitudes and acts, we have to understand children's social development.

Plan of the Book

One important question this book addresses is whether generalizations about the development of peer prejudice and discrimination can be made. In other words, can we talk about *the* development of prejudice and *the* development of discrimination? Or do these processes vary with the target groups under consideration? In order to generalize, it is necessary to compare different groupings. In a very extensive search of the psychological, sociological, and educational literatures of North America, I was able to find only four target groupings for which at least several research articles existed and that covered a relatively wide age span. These involved race, gender, hearing status, and intellectual status, i.e., mentally retarded persons versus nonretarded ones. Thus, the selection of these four groupings was completely fortuitous and not based on any underlying theory. Fortunately, the characteristics that distinguish these groups are sufficiently diverse that some confidence can be placed in any generalizations that may emerge.

The central arguments of the book are as follows. Prejudice and discrimination have an evolutionary basis, rooted in the nature of primate and human subsistence groups. Although the existence of cultures is also evolutionarily based, the particular culture in which individuals grow and mature plays a significant role in determining the values assigned to various groups. Members of certain of these groups become the targets for prejudice and discrimination. As with other cultural values, norms, and beliefs, prejudice and discrimination have to be learned. This is often a long process and depends upon the developmental status of the learner, the nature of the prejudice and discrimination to be learned, and the cultural importance of the learning. Prejudice and discrimination are based on attitudes. These frequently can be modified. What are the best approaches for modifying prejudice?

In chapter 2, "An Evolutionary Model for the Development of Prejudice and Discrimination," I attempt to tie together a diverse literature that presents the argument that our evolutionary heritage makes it inevitable that children and adults will develop prejudice and discrimination towards outgroup members. It will summarize research on inclusive fitness, which leads to ingroup favoritism; on our primate evolutionary heritage, which leads to hostility towards outgroups; on authority-bearing systems, which lead to adopting the beliefs that authority figures hold; on children's group processes, which indicate the conditions under which ingroup favoritism and outgroup hostility will occur; and on the development of group identity. The punch line of the latter is that prejudice and discrimination should emerge at about age 4, when children apparently have a well-developed sense of group or social identity.

In chapter 3, "Brief Cultural Histories of Females, African-Americans, Deaf Persons, and Mentally Retarded Persons," I focus on the United States of America and present a historical account of the bases of racism towards Blacks, sexism towards females, and handicappism (prejudice against hearing-impaired and mentally retarded persons). This account focuses on six periods in American history concerning the treatment of women and African-Americans: 1607–1770, Colonization; 1770–1825, Revolution and Consolidation; 1825–1865, Expansion and Civil War; 1865–1920, Reconstruction, World War, and Suffrage; 1920–1945, Prosperity, Depression, and the Second World War; and 1945–the present, Postwar Growth and Change. Cultural histories of the education of those who are deaf and of mentally retarded people involve fewer and different historical periods, owing to the existence of different social forces operating on these two groups.

Chapter 4 is called "Prejudice and Discrimination Towards Opposite-Sex and Deaf Individuals." The first section of the chapter deals with general methodological issues in the study of prejudice and discrimination. The second section is concerned with the genetic/evolutionary and cultural/historical antecedents of prejudice and discrimination. The third section discusses the socialization of sex-typing, and focuses on parents' socialization, the influence of different family types, and the influence of peers and teachers. In the next section, development of opposite-sex prejudice, both research that can be construed as using indirect measures and research more directly measuring prejudice are discussed. The next section deals with opposite-sex discrimination, using playmate preferences and sociometric measures as indicators of discrimination. The final section deals with discrimination towards hearing-impaired individuals. The argument will be made that behavioral differences between ingroup and outgroup members partly underlie both prejudice and discrimination.

Chapter 5 is called "Prejudice and Discrimination Towards Different-Race and Mentally Retarded Individuals." The first section discusses the historically important research by Kenneth and Mamie Clark dealing with alleged self-devaluation by Black children owing, in part, to school segregation. This discussion led to a broader consideration of the development of ethnic identity, in which the important distinction was made between self-identity and group identity. Black children may devalue their ethnic group and still have high self-esteem. In the next two sections, the development of race prejudice and race discrimination are discussed. The emphasis is restricted to Black-White relations. The next two sections deal with prejudice and discrimination by nonretarded children and adolescents towards their mentally retarded peers. The argument is reinforced that behavioral differences at least partly underlie both prejudice and discrimination. In the last section, the development of prejudice and discrimination across the four principal groupings is compared.

Chapter 6 is called "Modifying Prejudice and Discrimination." Arguments are developed and predictions are made based on genetic/evolutionary and cultural/historical considerations. Contact theory and Lewinian theory are also discussed and related to the above. The three major sections of the chapter are concerned with the impact of school desegregation on racial prejudice and discrimination, the impact of mainstreaming on prejudice and discrimination towards disabled persons, and cooperative learning as a vehicle for reducing prejudice and discrimination. The next three sections are necessarily brief accounts of the effects of simulations, the media, and individuation/self-acceptance in efforts to reduce prejudice. The final section attempts to integrate these findings.

In chapter 7, "Recapitulation," an attempt is made to pull together the major themes and findings. Primarily this chapter will give the central punch lines of the previous chapters, in a sense highlighting the summaries. No new material will be presented, but I will try to integrate what has been previously discussed.

2

An Evolutionary Model for the Development of Prejudice and Discrimination

Introduction

The overarching goal of this chapter is to make the argument that our genetic/evolutionary heritage has predisposed us to develop prejudice towards and discrimination against outgroup members. This goal will be reached through the attainment of seven more limited goals. The first is to present an evolution-based genetic model that accounts for species-wide behavioral constancies. The model draws heavily from the work of Waddington (1957), Gottlieb (1991), and Lumsden and Wilson (1981). The essence of the model is that genes, anatomy, behavior, and social and physical environments operate to direct and correct psychological development. Additionally, genes and culture coevolve such that species-specific characteristics will be sustained across generations.

The second goal is to present some results from behavior genetics research that show that individual differences in social behavior are strongly influenced by genetic inheritance. This research indirectly supports the argument that genes can control species-wide behavior characteristics, including the development of prejudice and discrimination.

The third goal is to present research describing the evolutionary history of, and linkages between, the Old World monkeys, apes, and humans. The focus is on common elements and distinctions concerning social organization and social behavior. The central argument is that humans operate socially with mental structures evolved for hunter-gatherer modes of existence. Prejudice and discrimination have their roots in this tribal organization.

The fourth goal is to present the three genetic/evolutionary factors that form the bases of prejudice and discrimination. These factors are ingroup favoritism based on inclusive fitness; authority-bearing systems based on the emergence of cultural socio-genetic systems; and intergroup hostility, based on intergroup relations of the common ancestors of gorillas, chimpanzees, and human hunter-gatherers.

The fifth goal is to present psychological data bearing on the development in children of a group identity. The principal consideration is the idea that prejudice and discrimination are intergroup phenomena that have as a prerequisite the ability of individuals to identify with an ingroup. At what age does group identity emerge, and how does this identity change with maturation?

The sixth goal is to describe some of the psychological processes involved in intergroup behavior. Ingroup favoritism and outgroup hostility are two prominent processes that are obviously connected with prejudice and discrimination. What factors control their emergence?

The seventh, and final, major goal is founded on the premise that prejudice and discrimination partially stem from genetic/evolutionary processes "inappropriately" applied to groups within a culture. We will attempt to identify those processes that lead to successful social interactions within a tribal culture, but to unsuccessful ones in an industrial or post-industrial society.

Canalization

The core assumption of this chapter is that genes determine some aspects of human social behavior. Our genes make *all* of our social behavior possible. But because of our evolutionary design, nearly all humans have inherited a genetic structure that makes certain species-specific kinds of social behavior inevitable. Further, the occurrence of some of these behaviors makes the development of prejudice and discrimination nearly inevitable.

On the basis of the current state of genetic knowledge, it is highly unlikely that the social behaviors themselves are coded in the genes. Rather, particular processes are genetically coded that normally ensure that the evolved social behaviors (phenotypic characteristics) will develop. For example, English and Spanish are not coded in the genes, but language-inducing processes are. If a child is reared in an English-speaking community, she'll learn English. If she's reared in an American Sign Language (ASL) community, she'll learn ASL. Either outcome can occur because the language-inducing processes have developed and are in place.

As noted in chapter 1, a likely genetic process controlling the species-specific developmental aspect of evolutionary design is "canalization" (Waddington, 1957). Gottlieb (1991) has synthesized recent theoretical and empirical research on this topic, which he refers to as "experiential canalization of behavior." In this view, behavioral development involves a hierarchical system of four mutually interacting components. These components are genetic activity, neural activity, behavior, and environment. Genetic activity influences neural development, but the activity of the nervous system also influences genetic activity, by determining which genes will be turned on or shut off. There is a similar bidirectional effect linking behavior and neural activity, and indeed, all other combinations of the four components. Thus, it's not merely genes that ensure that any infant or child attains a species-specific characteristic, e.g., language, but rather, all four components working together. The developmental target is coded in the genes, in the sense that for normal rearing environments, the genes produce nervous systems that activate behavioral processes, which in turn determine that the species-specific behavioral characteristic will be acquired. The genes, the nervous system, the behavior, and the environment all work together to canalize the developing behavior. Thus, as a child starts to speak English in normal English-speaking environments, his English speech is reinforced by others in the environment, who continue to speak English to him. And his nervous system continues to develop the necessary connections to sustain and enhance his spoken English.

When the genes and the various environments, e.g., intracellular, and extracellular conditions, family social interactions, atmospheric pollution levels, are in a normal range for the species, then the developmental targets will be attained. Infants will nurse, crawl, walk, and talk according to the *epigenetic* timetable coded in the genes. (Epigenesis is the emergence of anatomical structures and behavioral and physiological functions produced by the interactions among genes, the developing individual, and the environment.) Moreover, canalization processes are self-correcting in addition to being self-directing. Epigenesis works to put back on the evolutionarily designed developmental track any deviations from the species-specific targets. For example, infants will learn to walk at about 1 year of age even if they've had very little opportunity to crawl, as is the case with Hopi infants. As another example, hearing infants reared by deaf, ASL-using parents learn to speak normally.

Genes, Mind, and Culture

The title of this section is the title of the 1981 book by Lumsden and Wilson. All humans are reared in and live in cultures. These cultures resemble one another in many ways, and yet there are important differences between them, e.g., language, religious practices. Infants and children are required to learn the cultural practices they're reared in, and canalization processes ensure that they will learn some of them. The process of socializing children into their culture is called "enculturation." Enculturation makes us uniquely American, or English, or Mexican. From a genetic/evolutionary view, how might this enculturation come about? Lumsden and Wilson provide a very convincing model as an answer to this question.

We should distinguish three kinds of culturally learned behavior. The first includes species-specific patterns that are seen in all cultures, e.g., nursing by infants, walking, the coordinated use of two hands. The second includes variants of species-specific patterns that distinguish cultures from each other, e.g., language, religious practices, rules for sharing, tool manufacture, whether the bride or the bridegroom leaves the family of origin. Both the first and the second kinds are thus universal patterns of human behavior. The third includes relatively unique practices that are culture-specific, e.g., piano playing, bungee jumping. All three kinds of learning are possible because humans evolved as cultural animals. In a sense, culture is encoded in our genes.

Figure 2.1 is Lumsden and Wilson's (1981) pictorial representation of how genes and culture coevolved—how systematic changes in human genetic structure led to systematic changes in the nature of human culture and vice versa. In the model, the four principal levels of biological organization are shown: molecular, cellular, organismic, and populational. The first three of these levels constitute the details of epigenesis, as defined above. Note that the arrows indicate a particular direction, in contrast to the processes in Gottlieb's discussion. This directionality implies that there is systematic change in each of the levels, as opposed to the maintenance of stable canalized characteristics.

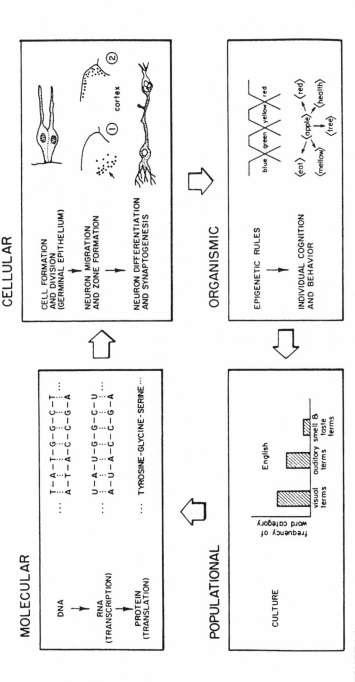

FIGURE 2.1

The full circuit of causation in gene-culture coevolution.

At the molecular level, the genes, which are groups of DNA molecules, produce proteins. These proteins bond together to form all the varied cells in the body. Of particular interest are the brain cells (neurons). The structure and functioning of these neurons produce epigenetic rules for acquiring cultural characteristics and for developing individual cognitions and behavior, e.g., the names of colors, the qualities of apples. The epigenetic rules are canalized, and if the external environment is highly similar for all individuals, then their cognitions and behavior will be similar. The population of individuals who reside and interact in a given region forms a culture and shares a language. The linkage between the organismic and populational levels reflects the translation of genes into culture. The linkage of the populational and molecular levels reflects how evolutionary processes operating on a population of individuals influence gene frequencies.

Let's further examine these latter two linkages. Lumsden and Wilson (1981) identify two broad classes of epigenetic rules: those that transform cultural inputs, e.g., socialization experiences, into "knowledge structures," and those that transform knowledge structures into behavior. Knowledge structures consist primarily of memory and cognitive processes. Behavior is what individuals do in their social and physical environments. The consequences of behavior are different levels of "genetic fitness," i.e., survival and reproduction. If certain types of epigenetic rules lead to behaviors with high genetic fitness within a given population, then those rules will ultimately become the norm for that population. If certain epigenetic rules lead to behaviors with low genetic fitness, then the genes supporting those rules will ultimately disappear. Perhaps the clearest example of this gene/culture coevolution is spoken language. Individuals in a population whose anatomical structures and epigenetic rules led to language behavior had higher genetic fitness than those who lacked these rules. Language is cultural, but language use produced the genetic changes in a population that made language development inevitable.

It's important to distinguish culture-specific from species-specific canalized characteristics. All canalized characteristics started at the culture-specific level. If they spread to other cultures through "intermarriage" and had high genetic fitness in the new cultures, then ultimately those characteristics became canalized in the new cultures. The only reasonable way that a character could become canalized for all members of the species would be that it had high genetic fitness in every culture on earth. Based on the paleoanthropological record, modern humans emerged at least 40,000 years ago, and probably considerably earlier (Fishbein, 1976, 1984). It is thus highly likely that any cultural changes that have occurred in human populations since then either were purely cultural, i.e., not genetic, or were coevolved culture-specific changes.

Recent research by Greenfield and Childs (1991) among the Zinacantecos, a Maya Indian culture, is highly consistent with the Lumsden and Wilson (1981) model. The Zinacantecos have a relatively distinct culture that distinguishes them from neighboring groups—and, of course, from all non-Mayan cultures.

Moreover, they have a distinctive population genetic structure because marriage is largely restricted to other members of their culture. Greenfield and Childs (1991) asked two questions within a cultural/genetic framework. First, do Zinacanteco infants and children show patterns of psychological development characteristic of non-Mayan cultures? Second, do they show culture-specific patterns that have continuity into adulthood? An affirmative answer to the first question provides support for the existence of universal species-specific gene/culture coevolution. An affirmative answer to the second question provides support for culture-specific coevolution.

The data are based on four years of fieldwork carried out in the native language of Tzotzil, and also on 30 years of multidisciplinary studies carried out by other colleagues. Regarding universal species-specific capabilities, the following results were obtained. (1) On mental and motor tests carried out with babies, the sequence of behavioral milestones was the same as that for babies in the United States. (2) In a study of young Zinacanteco children who had no familiarity with "nesting cup" toys, the Zinacanteco children showed the same developmental sequence of strategies for combining the cups as that used by United States children. (3) In several studies using different materials and requiring different cognitive activities, Zinacanteco children between the ages of 4 and 18 showed the same sequences of abilities, at the same ages, as United States children, e.g., the ability to classify different objects in a variety of ways. In some of these tasks, the cognitive abilities tapped for the Zinacantecos were quite novel and, on the surface, inconsistent with cultural learning. Greenfield and Childs (1991) conclude that the above pattern of results supports a universal species-specific developmental sequence.

Regarding culture-specific behavior, Zinacanteco babies show very low levels of physical activity. This "restrained" motor activity is also found among Chinese-American, Navajo, and Japanese babies, but not among Euro-American babies. Children of the four groups who are "restrained" all have different diets and prenatal care from one another, suggesting the existence of a genetic basis for the restraint. Given that these groups also have Asian roots, the assumed genetic basis makes sense. For the Zinacantecos, the behavior of mothers reinforces infants' low activity levels: the babies are swaddled (wrapped) and are nursed at the slightest movement. Euro-American babies rarely receive this kind of treatment. As a consequence of different starting activity levels and different maternal treatment, the activity levels of the two groups of babies become even more divergent during the first week of life. Moreover, relative to Euro-Americans, this pattern of Zinacanteco motor restraint is observed at all developmental levels, including adulthood. It is not the case that Zinacanteco babies are more listless than Euro-Americans. In fact, the opposite may be the case. Research has found them to be more attentive to their surroundings, for longer time periods, than Euro-American babies.

Greenfield and Childs (1991) discuss these results from cultural and genetic/evolutionary points of view. They conclude that in the Zinacanteco culture, motor restraint has an adaptive advantage. Given the apparent long-term stability of their cultural practices, it is likely that this motor restraint is a coevolved behavior characteristic.

Behavior Genetics

Is there evidence to support the concept of canalization, and by implication, the evolution of species-specific phenotypic characteristics? Yes, a limited amount. Fishbein (1976) has summarized some of the genetics research by Alex Fraser and C. H. Waddington that clearly demonstrates the existence of canalized anatomical species-specific characteristics in flies and mice. Gottlieb (1991) provides a strong demonstration of the species-specific behavior response to maternal calling by mallard ducklings. And Ronald Wilson (1978) has shown the existence of canalization of intelligence in human twins. Although the above research is highly competent and imaginative, none of it is directly concerned with canalized human social behavior. However, there is an allied research area, behavior genetics, that does have a bearing on this issue.

Behavior genetics deals with assessing the relative contributions of genes and environment to the explanation of individual differences in behavior. In a sense, behavior genetics is the opposite of canalization, which is concerned with similarities among individuals, i.e., what makes us alike. As Scarr (1992) has pointed out, there is no necessary connection between behavior genetics analyses and canalization analyses. The genes and gene activities that make us alike may operate in a fashion different from that of the genes that make us different. However, behavior genetics analyses demonstrate that genes do, at least partially, control behavior. If it can be shown that genes control individual differences in social behavior, then by analogy the argument is strengthened that genes control similarities in behavior.

Two recent relevant papers are those by Plomin and Daniels (1987) and Eysenck (1992). Plomin and Daniels reviewed their research and that of colleagues concerning the relative contributions of genetic similarity and environmental similarities and differences to variations (individual differences) in personality, psychopathology, and cognitive abilities. Eysenck reviewed his and his colleagues' research concerning individual differences in prejudice. Two of the major methodologies for making these assessments are the adoption design and the twin design.

In the adoption design the experimenter compares either identical twins reared apart, fraternal twins reared apart, non-twin siblings reared apart, or unrelated children reared together (i.e., at least one of whom is adopted). By looking at the correlation in personality, psychopathology, or cognitive abilities in identical twins reared apart, the researcher can make a direct estimate of the genetic contribution to phenotypic variations. For example, a correlation of .50 between identical twins on a personality measure implies that one-half of phenotypic differences between people on that measure are caused by genetic variations. Similar comparisons can be made by examining fraternal twins and other siblings reared apart. Phenotypic variations not explained by genetic variations are assumed to be caused by environmental similarities and differences.

There are two kinds of environmental effects: shared and non-shared influences. The extent to which two genetically unrelated siblings are phenotypically similar reflects shared environmental influences. On the other hand, if pairs of relatives, e.g., siblings, reared together are no more similar than pairs of relatives reared apart, then phenotypic differences between related and unrelated individuals are attributed to non-shared environmental variations.

In the twin design, the phenotypic resemblance of identical twins and same-sex fraternal twins is examined. Each set of twins is reared in the same home at the same time. By comparing the correlations for a particular psychological characteristic for these two types of twins, the genetic and non-shared environmental contributions to that characteristic can be made. If heredity has no effect on that characteristic, for example, then identical and fraternal twins will resemble each other equivalently. The non-shared environmental contribution is assessed by computing the portion of phenotypic variations that distinguish identical twins from each other. Phenotypic variations accounted for by shared environmental influences can be indirectly estimated. This is done by noting the extent of phenotypic variation remaining after the genetic and non-shared environmental influences are subtracted.

What are the results of this research? Plomin and Daniels (1987) report that across a wide variety of studies, the genetic contribution to individual differences in personality, psychopathology, and cognitive abilities ranges from about 30 percent to 60 percent. Regarding environmental influences, nearly all of them consist of non-shared environmental effects. That is, environmental differences *within* families produce individual differences in behavior; but environmental similarities within families have almost no effect on individual differences between related and unrelated individuals. How about prejudice? Eysenck (1992) found a nearly identical pattern as the above for males and females in both England and Australia for six items concerning Blacks and Jews on the Eysenck Social Attitudes Scale. Do Eysenck's results mean that individual differences in prejudice towards Blacks and Jews are coded in the genes? No, but the processes that lead to variations in the development of prejudice probably are. At the present time we don't know what these processes may be.

Hunter-Gatherer Minds in Post-Industrial Bodies

Alice Rossi (1977) has written this:

> The two hundred years in which industrial societies have existed is a short time, indeed, to say nothing of the twenty years in which a few of the most advanced industrial societies have been undergoing the painful transition to a post-industrial stage. Our most recent genes derive from that largest segment of human history during which men and women lived in hunting and gathering societies; in other words, Westernized human beings now living in a technological world are still genetically equipped only with an ancient mammalian heritage that evolved largely through adaptations appropriate to much earlier times. (p. 3)

As noted in a previous section, it is highly likely that the universal species-specific canalizations were in place at least 40,000 years ago, and that evolutionary changes since then have been either purely cultural or genetically culture-specific. We described an example of the latter: motor restraint in the Zinacantecos. There is no evidence of species-specific genetic changes in the past 40,000 years. As a consequence, the assumption being made here is that humans are currently operating with hunter-gatherer epigenetic systems. These systems evolved and supported cultures that were tribal, consisting on average of approximately 500 men, women, and children. The systems were sufficiently flexible to allow the development of agricultural societies, which have been in existence for about 10,000 years. They also permitted the very recent cultural evolution of industrial and post-industrial societies. The fate of the latter is questionable, as can been seen in the mutual destruction many societies are engaged in.

As Rossi (1977) notes, much of our genetic equipment is based on "an ancient mammalian heritage." While that is certainly true, a more profitable approach for the present purpose is to focus on our more recent primate and hunter-gatherer heritages. In this ancestry lie the keys to understanding the genetic/evolutionary bases of the development of prejudice and discrimination.

The Primate Heritage

The primates evolved about 60 million years ago from mammalian ancestors probably resembling contemporary tree shrews (Andrews, 1985). Four major events occurred within that time span: (1) The New World and the Old World (African) primates were separated about 50 million years ago; (2) the Old World monkey-ape split occurred about 40 million years ago; (3) the common Old World ancestors of gorillas, chimpanzees, and humans emerged about 12 to 16 million years ago; and (4) the evolutionary lines leading to distinct gorilla, chimpanzee, and human species appeared about 6 to 10 million years ago. There are two chimpanzee species, *Pan troglodytes,* known as the common chimpanzee, and *Pan paniscus,* known as the pygmy chimpanzee, or bonobo. Of the four species—humans, gorillas, pygmy chimpanzees, and common chimpanzees—the two chimpanzee species have the highest degree of genetic relatedness. Among the primates these four species are apparently more closely related to one another than they are to any other species (Wrangham, 1987).

I've indicated that evolution is an experiment in design. What is the nature of the human design? In that our focus is the evolutionary basis of prejudice and discrimination, we're mainly interested in the social aspects of the design. It has three major components: the heritage we share with the Old World monkeys and apes; that which we share with the chimpanzees and gorillas (which we will discuss in another section); and our hunter-gatherer heritage. As a consequence, our emphasis here will be on those social/behavioral elements that are commonly found among Old World primates and those social/behavioral elements that characterize hunter-gatherer groups. It is noted that the monkey-ape split occurred approximately 40 million years ago, and that the ape-human species have had 6 to 10 million years of independent evolutionary history. All living species are different from the common ancestor. *It is thus assumed that any social/behavioral commonalities that exist between monkeys and apes, or between apes and humans, were part of the design of the common ancestors and continue to be part of the current human design.*

Old World Monkeys and Apes

The primary adaptation of nearly all the Old World primate species, including humans, occurred in order to sustain life as a member of a group (Fishbein, 1976, 1984; Tooby & DeVore, 1987). These species have evolved so that the group provides the framework for (1) subsistence activities, (2) protection, (3) reproduction, and (4) socialization of the young. In these species there is a frequent association of members of all ages and both sexes throughout the lifetime of each individual. In all cases the offspring are typically born singly and are relatively helpless at birth, and they are highly dependent on the adults for a considerable period thereafter. Socialization starts shortly after birth, and occurs primarily through play, observation, imitation, and interactions with group members. The major task of pre-adults is to learn to fit into and contribute to the stability of the social group. In order to accomplish this task they have to develop (1) knowledge of who group members are; (2) a set of social skills important to the group; (3) an enduring set of social relationships with many, if not most, members; and (4) knowledge of the rules of interaction and of the roles appropriate to self and others. These rules and roles are both age- and sex-related. What is tolerated in infants, e.g., tugging on the hair of adults, is often treated harshly in juveniles. Male and female infants and juveniles not only act differently from each other—e.g., males are more active while females stay closer to their mothers—but adults treat them differently.

If the social development of certain maturing members of the group is abnormal, then as adults they will not be able to contribute to the above four vital functions of the social group to which they belong. Natural selection has operated and continues to operate in such a way that individuals that are appropriately developed socially contribute to all four vital functions of the group, and those that are not appropriately developed socially become peripheral members of the group. The latter likely reproduce less than the more central members. This is a negative feedback system involving genes and behaviors. In a stable environment, animals and people with genetic structures such that their social development will be normal develop into normal individuals and reproduce (or get their close relatives to do so), thus passing on their genes in the population gene distribution. Those whose genetic structure is such that they do not readily develop into normal adults have low inclusive fitness, and hence their genes are diminished in the gene distribution (Fishbein, 1976, 1984).

For the present purposes, one of the most significant social aspects of primate groups is the existence of dominance hierarchies. Dominance refers to the ability of one group member to "supplant" another in order to gain access to preferred or scarce resources. Some of these resources are particular foods; locations, e.g., in the shade, near water, in close proximity to certain other group members; and sex with specific individuals. There are three typical ways one member gains dominance over another: (1) defeating the other in a fight, or giving the appearance of being able to do so; (2) forming a coalition with another group member against some or all other group members; or (3) being the son or daughter of a mother that is high in the dominance hierarchy. The latter characteristic typically has importance among the Old World monkeys, and not among the apes. The critical factor here is that in monkey and baboon species, males typically leave their natal groups at adolescence, whereas females remain with their groups throughout their lives. These females form dominance hierarchies, but the males do not (Hinde, 1983).

Primates do not retain their dominance status by constantly fighting with others, or threatening them. Rather, other group members with which they do not have close positive relations simply avoid them, or move away from them when they approach. Two of the consequences of being a highly dominant individual are these: other group members pay attention to the dominant one or try to gain its attention (Chance, 1975); and other group members attempt to "groom" it or get it to groom them (grooming involves one individual searching through another's fur for parasites; Seyfarth, 1983). It has been shown by Strum (1987) and others that one of the consequences of grooming relationships is the development of alliances. These alliances increase a dominant individual's effectiveness in accomplishing goals within the group.

Thus, the picture that has emerged in recent years concerning dominance hierarchies is that the most dominant individuals are not only to be feared, but to be favored. Others want to be allied with them and to be responded to affectionately by them. Although there is no evidence that in nonhuman primate groups highly dominant individuals become role models for younger group members, we will see that this characteristic emerges in human groups.

The Hunter-Gatherer Heritage

As indicated in the preceding section, the evolutionary line leading to the hunter-gatherer design appeared 6 to 10 million years after the emergence of the common ancestor of humans, gorillas, and chimpanzees. The hunter-gatherer subsistence mode and social structure has been a relatively constant human feature for 99 percent of the duration of our existence. What are the major aspects of this design, which differentiates us from the African monkeys and apes? My summary draws on four sources: Fishbein (1976, 1984); Irwin (1987); Tooby and De-Vore (1987); and Wrangham (1987).

At the broadest level, nearly every hunter-gatherer society consists of a set of genetically related subsistence groups that collectively form a tribe. Each subsistence group resides in a certain region and generally has limited contact with other tribal groups throughout the year. Members of the various groups are often closely related, in that sisters and daughters move to other groups for marriage. Their offspring are cousins, nephews, and nieces of members of the natal group. Female departure is the norm; however, in some societies the males usually leave the natal group, and in others either males or females may leave. Unlike the African apes, humans maintain bonds between family members in different groups that continue over time and space. Thus, all members develop strong identification with the tribe as a whole.

Unlike the African primates, subsistence groups are comprised of families. The family is the basic social unit, typically consisting of a married adult male and adult female, their preadolescent male and female offspring, unmarried adolescent and adult sons, and often, parents of the father. Polygyny is tolerated, but infrequent. Marriages are relatively permanent. In primate terms, the couple is pair-bonded, a characteristic rare in the African apes. Depending on the rate of survival, family size may be small or large; this obviously affects the size of the subsistence group. In times of limited availability of food, which is usually seasonal, the group may split into its family components, each moving to an area with enough food to support it.

Unlike the African primates, fathers identify their wives' offspring as their own. Assuming a relatively low frequency of sexual infidelity leading to "illegitimate" offspring, a wife's offspring are in fact the sons and daughters of her husband. In a pattern corresponding to this parental identification, fathers invest a lot of time and energy in helping to raise their children. The extent of this activity is far greater than that among the African apes. In addition to mutual involvement in child rearing and sexual fidelity, husbands and wives have extensive reciprocal and cooperative relationships with each other. Food sharing is an integral part of this collaboration.

Hunter-gatherer groups, as groups, share many goals and activities above and beyond those at the family level of organization. Socialization of children is a group responsibility, as are the division of labor, protection, and food sharing along gender lines. In some societies, hunters are not even permitted to eat their own "kills," but must give them to other group members. They, of course, benefit in turn from the successes of their compatriots. Related to food sharing and group organization, there is extensive male-male cooperation, and relative to the African primates, a marked reduction in aggression and competition. The principal group ethics are sharing and reciprocity. These both produce and require extensive interpersonal interdependencies and social cohesion—much more than that found among the African apes.

Finally, unlike the African primates, the various human tribes, especially those separated by substantial geographic distance, show very marked cultural differences. The term "culture" emphasizes here language, dialect, religious practices, moral rules, belief systems, rituals, dress, art, tools and tool decoration, and any or all activities that characterize a given tribe, e.g., shaking hands as a greeting, or offering particular food or drink to visitors.

Thus, humans and nonhuman primates evolved as members of closely knit subsistence groups. One uniquely human characteristic is that these groups were additionally strongly interconnected through tribal identifications. Members of the same tribe were relatively safe with and could count on nurturance from same-tribe members, even if those members were unknown. Other-tribe strangers, however, were potentially dangerous, especially during the regularly recurring periods of scarce resources. Given that the hunter-gatherer tribal mode of living was in existence for more than 1 million years, it is assumed that genetic/evolutionary processes emerged that led to sustaining tribal autonomy and continuity against neighboring tribes. It is believed that these processes became incorporated into human epigenetic systems and made it nearly inevitable that individuals would be prejudiced towards and discriminate against members of other tribes. When humans recently shifted to nontribal, e.g., industrial, modes of subsistence, our epigenetic systems did not shift. As a consequence, mechanisms that evolved for regulating intertribal contacts became inappropriately applied to within-culture relationships. In other words, humans are predisposed to treat outgroup members of our own cultures as if they were members of different tribes.

I believe that there are at least three genetic/evolutionary factors that have produced this state of affairs. They arose from (1) the inherent nature of Darwinian selection processes acting on relatively closed breeding populations (inclusive fitness); (2) the genetic/evolutionary design of authority-bearing systems in human cultures; and (3) the genetic/evolutionary design of intergroup relations among the common ancestors of human hunter-gatherers. We'll turn now to a discussion of these factors.

Inclusive Fitness

One of the major recent innovations in evolutionary theory is the elaboration of the concept of *inclusive fitness* and its relationship to social behavior (Wilson, 1980). The originator of this concept is William D. Hamilton (1964, 1975), and it has become a cornerstone of the new discipline of "sociobiology." Inclusive fitness refers to the extent to which an individual and her close relatives have surviving offspring. Those with high inclusive fitness transmit a relatively large number of genes to the next generation. Those with low fitness (individuals and their close relatives) transmit relatively few genes to the next generation. One implication of inclusive fitness is that individuals (whether insects or humans) consciously or unconsciously attempt to ensure that their genes are transmitted to the next generation. They can do this in basically two ways: reproduce a great deal, or act in such a way that their close relatives will reproduce a great deal. For example, assuming that my sibling and I have in common one half of our genes, my inclusive fitness would be higher if he had five surviving offspring and I had none than if I had two surviving offspring and he had none. Another implication is that when resources important for survival are limited, individuals will usually show preferences to relatives and act in ways that will decrease the likelihood that nonrelatives will successfully reproduce or survive. They may prevent nonrelatives from mating, withhold food or shelter from them, or kill their offspring. The latter is a strategy that male langur monkeys often perform (Hardy, 1977), but is seen in other primates, including humans.

The most obvious reproductive strategy for getting your genes into the next generation is to mate with your opposite-sex parent or siblings: engage in incest. This level of inbreeding has two negative consequences, one short-term and one long-term. The short-term consequence is called "inbreeding depression." The more closely related two mating partners are, the greater is the likelihood that their offspring will be stillborn, die early, or have mental or physical defects. These conditions all have the effect of decreasing the likelihood that one's genes will survive beyond the next generation (Wilson, 1980). The long-term consequence of high levels of inbreeding is that genetic variability across members of a breeding community is reduced. Thus, when environments change, as they ultimately do, the descendants may not have the genetic resources to adapt to the new environment, and thus die out.

Hence, in attempting to maximize one's genes in succeeding generations, a balance has to be struck between degree of incest and breeding depression. One wants to mate with a relative that is close but not too close, in order to avoid inbreeding depression. There are limited data for humans on inbreeding depression. There is marked depression for immediate-family mating (Wilson, 1980), but in Australian aboriginal tribes, the preferred form of marriage is to first cousins (Tindale, 1974). However, in the United States, first-cousin marriages are uniformly restricted. It can be inferred from the Australian example that inbreeding depression is probably not extensive for first cousins, and is minor for second cousins.

There is another important implication of this line of reasoning. It is that we should prefer that our siblings marry second cousins rather than unrelated persons. Our siblings share on average 50 percent of our genes, our second cousins share about 6 percent of our genes, and unrelated persons share close to 0 percent of our genes. Thus, more of our genes are transmitted to the next generation when one of our siblings marries a second cousin than when that sibling marries an unrelated person. There are some recent historical data consistent with this analysis. Irwin (1987) has analyzed marriage patterns for the Netsilik Eskimos of Canada. They are more likely to marry within the local community than to marry members of a nearby Netsilik community, and relatively unlikely to marry members of other tribes. This pattern of marriages leads to relatively high genetic relatedness in members of the local community.

There are other important genetic, as well as social, consequences of this analysis, which Hamilton (1964, 1975) has described. In short, he shows mathematically that natural selection could operate in such a fashion that, given the opportunity, individuals would behave altruistically towards their relatives. Altruism refers to the performance of some act that benefits another at some expense to one's self, e.g., giving food to a cousin. His analysis demonstrates that altruistic behavior towards one's relatives (and their like behavior in return) increases the Darwinian fitness of both parties. Hence, over many generations the genes of both parties, including those influencing altruism, would become widespread in any breeding population.

In Hamilton's analysis, the Darwinian success of altruistic behavior depends on being able to direct it towards relatives as opposed to nonrelatives. In small inbreeding communities like that of the Netsilik, everyone is a relative, so identifying them is not a problem. From the point of view of prejudice and discrimination, the direct implication of Hamilton's analysis is that we are essentially designed to be ethnocentric: to favor our own group as opposed to others. Some writers have suggested that inclusive fitness also leads to the conclusion that we should be hostile or antagonistic to non-group members (e.g., Irwin, 1987; Reynolds, 1987). The underlying basis of this antagonism is the need to keep valuable resources within the group of relatives to ensure one's genetic continuity.

Authority-Bearing Systems

As emphasized in a previous section, one of the most dramatic shifts human evolution took relative to that of the African primates was in the area of culture. The prominent evolutionary theorist, C. H. Waddington (1960), has referred to this human characteristic as a "cultural socio-genetic system" (which I'll abbreviate as CS-G system). CS-G systems are built on biological hereditary systems, and like the biological systems, are fundamentally involved with transmitting information from one generation to the next. The primary processes used to do this are social teaching and learning. CS-G systems evolve over time, but the mechanisms are different from those of biological evolution, e.g., no genetic changes occur in the former.

CS-G systems involve the transmission of an enormous amount of information. This is made possible by our highly evolved symbolic and communication abilities, and, Waddington argues, by the evolution of "authority-bearing systems." The essence of these systems is that the receivers of information are designed to accept as true or valid the messages transmitted to them by authorities. Human cultures are so complex, for example, that individuals cannot independently test out or evaluate each piece of new information. The mechanism evolution "selected" for overcoming this problem was authority acceptance. Waddington suggests that authority acceptance has its roots in "model-mimic" or "leader-follower" patterns of interaction seen in other animals, but is dramatically extended to encompass conceptual or symbolic materials.

The notion of "authority" is a relative one. Your older sister or brother may take on the role of authority relative to you, but your mother is an authority to them. In general, an authority is a person who has greater legitimate status or power than another person. We saw in the discussion of monkey dominance hierarchies that high-status individuals are attended to more than others, and are sought out for grooming. They hold privileged positions in the social group and others follow their lead and respect their desires. I think that these primate characteristics form the bases for authority acceptance. The principal shift is from the behavioral (nonhuman primates) to the conceptual (humans).

Waddington maintains that much of the information transmitted in a CS-G system is "value-laden" or "ethical" and takes the form of beliefs. Thus, not only do children have to know what items not to eat because they are poisonous and what locations to avoid because snakes or leopards reside there (without personally testing out the validity of this information), but they are required to know and accept beliefs and behaviors concerned with other persons and spiritual entities. There are "right" and "wrong" beliefs and courses of action, and these are often highly culture-specific, e.g., wearing veils, not eating pork, aiding the poor, facing East while praying.

Waddington argues that one essential component of authority acceptance is the psychological internalization of what authorities tell us. We personally take on (take in) the beliefs and values of authorities; this gives these ideas an obligatory character. This is the superego of psychoanalytic theory. In psychoanalytic theory the mechanism underlying internalizing beliefs is the individual's need to identify with authorities in order to avoid punishment by them. We eventually come to extol their values and, in turn, transmit these to others we have authority over. Thus, we not only accept as valid what authorities tell us, but also, in a sense, come to maintain that the ideas are what they *should* be.

Waddington indicates, following psychoanalytic and Piagetian research, that authority acceptance has a developmental path. It appears to peak between the ages of 4 and 7 years, and to decline somewhat as children mature. One reason for the decline is the growing influence of peers on human thoughts and actions. In Piaget's (1932) research, for example, children under age 7 usually say that game rules can't be changed because the rules were handed down by the elders. After age 7 children start to say that they can change the rules if their playmates agree to it. Although authority acceptance might decline after age 7, it remains a potent force throughout the human lifetime. As an example, young men and women go to war, risking their lives (often zealously) because their leaders tell them that doing so is based on a just cause.

There are at least three types of evidence supporting the concept that humans are authority acceptors. The first involves children's ideas about obedience to authority. The literature indicates that there is little change between the ages of 4 and 11 years in children's willingness to obey legitimate authorities, provided that immoral acts are not requested or that the authorities are not intruding upon areas of the children's jurisdiction (Braine, Powerantz, Lorber, & Krantz, 1991; Damon, 1977; Turiel, 1983). This research shows that some of the reasons children give for obedience change with age. Other research (Smetana, 1988) finds that during adolescence, the area of a child's jurisdiction increases, which has the consequence of narrowing the range of others' legitimate authority.

In Braine et al.'s (1991) study, boys and girls between the ages of 6 and 11 years were read stories about children's conflicts with six types of legitimate authority, and two types of unsanctioned authority: a power move by an older sibling and a theft by armed robbers from a store. After each story was read, the subjects were asked how the child in the story felt, what he (or she) should do, why, and how the authority figure would react if the child was not obedient. The major results were as follows (1) Although children indicated different levels of obedience to different types of legitimate authority figures, there were essentially no age differences in extent of compliance. (2) In nearly all cases, children of all ages stated that there would be negative consequences, e.g., punishment, for noncompliance. This suggests that compliance is based largely on avoidance of these bad outcomes. (3) There was a decrease, with increasing age, in the frequency with which the subjects believed that the children in the stories would feel "sad" when placed in conflict. Older subjects were more likely than younger ones to attribute angry feeings to the children. (4) Older subjects gave more varied reasons than younger ones did for complying with legitimate authorities, reflecting greater social knowledge. (5) There were marked differences in the responses of older and younger subjects to the robber story, but not to the older sibling story. These differences were based on the relative values the subjects placed on avoiding physical harm and protecting one's money.

The second line of evidence supporting the idea that humans are authority acceptors involves children's modeling behavior. The assumption made regarding authority acceptance is that children will accept as valid not only what authorities tell them, but also what authorities show them. Thus, children should be more likely to model their own behavior after high-status than after low-status models. A number of studies support this conclusion. In Hetherington's (1965) experiment, groups of 4 1/2-, 7-, and 10-year-old boys and girls and their parents were the subjects. The relative dominance of each parent was assessed by measuring which parent had the most influence in solving hypothetical child care problems. Two measures of children's identification with their mothers and fathers, respectively, and one measure of imitation of each parent were taken. The identification measures involved strength of masculine and feminine sex roles, and similarity of personality characteristics with those of parents. The imitation measure involved judgments of the prettiness of pictures, as modeled by each parent. In general, the results strongly support the importance of parental status in identification and imitation. Both boys and girls were more likely to identify with and imitate the more dominant parent; however, girls were relatively less susceptible to variations in mother-dominance than boys were to variations in father-dominance.

In Grusec's (1971) research, the subjects were 7- and 11-year-old boys and girls who were given opportunities to imitate a same-sex adult with either high or low "power." In the high-power condition, the adult was introduced as a person who was going to select chldren for an interesting trip. Moreover, after the adult and child finished their tasks, the adult was going to interview the child for possible trip selection. In the low-power condition, the same adults were given no special status or relationship with the children. While the children watched, the adults in both conditions played a bowling game and either conspicuously gave some of their winnings to charity (Experiment 1), or used very stringent performance criteria for rewarding themselves (Experiment 2). The adults left the room and the children played the same game. In both experiments, children were found to imitate the high-power models to a greater extent than the low-power ones.

Finally, Brody and Stoneman (1981, 1985) have shown that children are more likely to imitate high-status than low-status children. In these experiments the subjects were either second- or third-grade boys and girls who watched a same-sex "model" child choose his or her favorite foods from pairs of pictures. The model was either younger than (low status), the same age as, or older than (high status) the subjects, who were informed about the model's age. After the models had made their choices, the subjects selected their favorite foods. In both studies, the subjects imitated the choices of the same-age or older children much more frequently than they did those of the younger ones.

The third line of supporting evidence deals with the general question of the relationship between understanding ideas and either believing or disbelieving them (Gilbert, 1991). Gilbert has reviewed and integrated a large number of empirical and theoretical papers concerned with this issue. Interestingly, the framework of his study is philosophical: it contrasts Rene Descarte's view that a person's decision to believe or disbelieve an idea occurs after she has attempted to understand it with Baruch Spinoza's view that believing an idea and understanding it occur at the same time. Spinoza writes that disbelieving an idea requires additional mental processing. Authority acceptance is highly consistent with Spinoza's view, although neither Descarte nor Spinoza qualifies his position regarding the status of the person who transmits the information. Simply put, Spinoza says that we believe what others tell us. Gilbert concludes that Spinoza's view, or one similar to it, is correct. At a minimum, belief of ideas precedes disbelief.

The connection between authority acceptance and the development of prejudice and discrimination is fairly obvious. Children believe what their parents and other authorities—e.g., teachers, political figures, athletes, actors, older siblings—tell them. They also believe what they read in books, magazines, and newspapers, and what they hear and see on television. Much of what they learn conveys consistent messages about various outgroups, e.g., those based on race or gender or mental status. Children not only believe these messages, but incorporate them into their own value systems. As we saw in chapter 1, adults (and presumably children) may hold beliefs that are not readily modified by particular counterexamples. Thus, a Black child may have a White child as a best friend and still believe what his peers, parents, and other family members have instructed him: that Whites are not trustworthy. If this same Black child develops a large number of friendships with Whites, however, these experiences may transform the beliefs he has acquired from his family and friends.

Intergroup Hostility: Heritage from the Common Ancestor of Apes and Humans

Richard Wrangham (1987) has provided an enormously useful integration of research concerned with the social organization of the African apes (both chimpanzee species and gorillas) and hunter-gatherers. These four species share a common ancestor that lived 6 to 10 million years ago. It is assumed that if the common ancestor possessed a given social characteristic, then there is a 6- to 10-million-year genetic/evolutionary continuity of that phenotype.

Wrangham's analysis of the ape species is based on all the long-term (two or more years) major field studies that exist. There are only 10 such studies, two each for the gorilla and pygmy chimpanzee, and six for the common chimpanzee. Thus there may be serious problems with sampling, but this is what we have, and Wrangham's comparative analysis seems to be the most complete available. For the hunter-gatherer data, Wrangham reviewed several sources that deal with their social organization. These include well over 150 ethnographic analyses of different hunter-gatherer societies. Sampling does not seem to be a problem here.

Wrangham (1987) chose 14 categories of social organization that he believes capture the essence of the structure and functioning of the groups formed by the four species. For six of these, he concludes that the common ancestor of all four species had the characteristic being considered, and for two, he concludes that the common ancestor did not have the characteristic. For the remaining six, there is considerable variability across the four species and no conclusions could be made. I'll summarize his results of the eight "conclusive" characteristics.

The first, "social network," refers to whether or not the subsistence group is relatively closed or relatively open to outsiders. The critical observation involves whether non-group members are excluded from the activities of the ingroup. As a point of reference, subsistence group size averages about 25 for hunter-gatherers, 13 for gorillas, 60 for common chimpanzees (Jolly, 1972), and probably about 60 for pygmy chimpanzees (this is inferred from Wrangham's discussion). A distinguishing feature of hunter-gatherers is that they typically are members of a "tribe" averaging about 500 members that consists of many subsistence groups. All three African ape species have closed social networks, and hunter-gatherers are closed with respect to the tribe, and semiclosed with respect to the subsistence group. Wrangham concludes that the common ancestor formed groups with closed social networks.

The second characteristic, "lone males," refers to whether males ever travel alone. Traveling alone is potentially dangerous, in that it may put one in contact with neighboring groups. This occurs with all four species. As a consequence, Wrangham (1987) concludes that this activity occurred for the common ancestor.

The third deals with whether "females breed in their natal group" (the group they were born into). In all four species, females generally leave the natal group, join another nearby subsistence group, and mate therein. This is a very different pattern from that seen in African monkeys and baboons, where the females generally stay in the natal group from birth to death (Hinde, 1983). Wrangham (1987) concludes that in the common ancestor, females rarely bred in their natal group. By contrast, the fourth characteristic in both chimpanzee species and hunter-gatherers is that males generally remain in the natal group. The picture is unclear for gorillas, however.

The fifth through eighth characteristics, perhaps the most important in terms of the development of prejudice and discrimination, deal with "intergroup relationships." These are concerned with how adult members of one social network react to members of other social networks. For the apes, there is one subsistence group in relation to outsiders, and for the hunter-gatherers, there is one tribe in relation to outsiders.

The fifth characteristic, "quality of the interaction," involves the dimension of friendliness versus hostility. For the gorilla, common chimpanzee, and hunter-gatherer species, reactions to outsiders typically are hostile. Violent attacks, occasionally leading to killings, have been observed. In one study of 50 hunter-gatherer societies, tribal warfare typically occurred on average every two years. The major function of hostility towards outsiders is to protect group members from attack or capture. An important secondary function is the protection of scarce resources, e.g., food and water. Few observations have been made of the pygmy chimpanzee, but these indicate interactions with outsiders that are at least tense. Wrangham (1987) concludes that hostile intergroup relations were the norm for our common ancestor.

The sixth characteristic deals with the "identity of the active participants in hostile interactions." Insufficient data are available for the pygmy chimpanzees, but for the other three species, the adult males and occasionally the adolescent males are the usual interactants. In the Old World monkeys, by contrast, adult females often participate in the violence. Wrangham (1987) concludes that "males only" was the pattern for the common ancestor.

The seventh characteristic, "stalk/attack," refers to whether the adult and adolescent males of a group will actively seek out, stalk, and attack outsiders, in addition to reacting hostilely during chance encounters. Again, limited data are available for the pygmy chimpanzees, but stalking and attacking have been observed for the other species. In one study a group of male chimpanzees was observed stalking and killing a female chimpanzee that had formerly been a member of their group (Goodall, Bandora, Bergmann, Busse, Matama, Mpongo, Pierce, & Riss, 1979). Thus, violence is directed not only towards strangers, or towards adult males. Wrangham (1987) concludes that these activities characterized the common ancestor.

The eighth characteristic, "territorial defence," refers to whether these species stake out a particular group territory and attempt to prevent outsiders from entering it. The most common observation is that they occupy a home range that overlaps the ranges of neighboring groups. It is rare for any of them to patrol the perimeter to prevent incursions of outsiders. When outsiders penetrate too deeply into the home range, they will be repelled. Wrangham (1987) concludes that the common ancestor did not engage in territorial defense.

Let me summarize the Wrangham (1987) material. The human evolutionary social heritage from the common ancestor of pygmy and common chimpanzees, gorillas, and human hunter-gatherers is that we were designed as members of relatively closed subsistence groups. The permanent members of these groups are typically the males who defend the group against outsiders. These encounters are usually hostile, and occasionally violent. Males periodically travel alone, and when with other males may stalk and attack non-group members. Females migrate out of their natal group and join other nearby groups. When they do so, they are vulnerable to attack by stalking adult males.

These observations lead to an interesting speculation that the evolutionary basis for prejudice and discrimination differs for males and females. The key data are these: males usually stay with their natal group, whereas females leave at adolescence and join another group; and adolescent and adult males, but not females, defend the group against outsiders, and even stalk and attack them. These behavior patterns show that males are more hostile to non-group members than are females. The observations may mean that males are genetically more predisposed than females to develop commitments to many group members. Adult females form close bonds with their offspring and with only a small number of adult males and/or females. Using evidence consistent with the above, Lever (1978) has shown that boys in Western cultures are more likely than girls both to be members of large groups and to participate in competitive games.

Preadolescent and adolescent females additionally must have a more tenuous identification with the natal group than same-age males, in that they eventually leave it to join another group. Perhaps weaker group identification on the part of females is a necessary condition for their permanent departure. The link between strength of group identification and prejudice and discrimination is that stronger identification may lead to stronger negative reactions to outsiders, and hence, to stronger prejudice.

Although the above prediction about gender differences in prejudice is speculative, the idea of genetically or evolution-based differences in male and female social behavior has been confirmed by David Buss (1994) and his colleagues in a series of cross-cultural studies. The central organizing thesis of this research is that males and females have different degrees of parental investment in their offspring: females are vastly more invested in both time and energy. This differential investment leads to hypothesized differences in men's and women's short-term and long-term mating strategies. Buss lists nine hypotheses that have been consistently confirmed in up to 37 different cultures, e.g., "Short-term mating is more important for men than for women"; "Women will be more selective than men in choosing a short-term mate." The confirmation of these hypotheses in one area of social behavior—mating strategies—certainly doesn't prove hypothesized gender differences in prejudice, but it does make the argument plausible.

Identification of Tribe Members and Multigroup Membership

From the perspective of the development of prejudice and discrimination in contemporary society, two related issues must be addressed: identification of tribe members (or conversely, outsiders); and multigroup memberships. The issue of identification of tribe members relates to two of the three evolutionary factors discussed in this chapter: inclusive fitness and intertribal hostility. It can be assumed that preadolescent hunter-gatherers know relatively few members of the tribe outside their primary subsistence group. How can the young identify strangers who are tribal members (and thus safe) as opposed to outsiders of nearby tribes, who are potentially dangerous? Irwin (1987) suggests that this is accomplished through the evolutionary mechanism known as "badging." Certain groups of birds, for example, identify potential mates through identification of a particular song that only members of their breeding population have learned. Irwin plausibly argues that the young in any tribe readily learn to identify and differentiate most, if not all, of the cultural characteristics that they and fellow tribe-members share. If the stranger speaks the same language with the same dialect, dresses the same, carries the same tools, etc., as do members of the subsistence group, then the stranger is seen not as an outsider, but rather as a fellow tribe member.

The issue of tribal member identification and inclusive fitness has been extensively examined by Van den Berghe (1981) in the context of ethnic prejudice. Van den Berghe discusses three categories of "ethnic markers" that potentially can serve to determine group membership: (1) genetically transmitted "racial" characteristics, such as skin color, stature, and facial features; (2) human-made artifacts that are "worn," such as clothing, body painting, tattooing, and circumcision; and (3) behavioral characteristics, such as speech, manners, and knowledge of particular myths or histories. Many of these are similar to Irwin's (1987) "badges."

The most blatant markers are the genetically transmitted racial differences. As Van den Berghe (1981) points out, from a genetic/evolutionary view, race differences between neighboring tribes were rare occurrences and could not have been the basis for inclusive-fitness choices. Members of nearby tribes are usually racially the same, primarily because they evolved in essentially the same environment and tribal intermarriage (forced or voluntary) occasionally occurred. For example, there is a gradient of hair and eye color in Europe from North to South. Residents of neighboring territories show essentially the same patterns, but the two characteristics in Scandinavians (blond and blue) and in Southern Italians (brown and brown) are very different. Inclusive-fitness choices occurred in relation to the nearby tribes, not between "Scandinavians" and "Italians."

Racial differences only became important as tribal markers during the post-agricultural period, when city-states were founded, armies were formed, and territorial expansion occurred. Black-White hostile encounters are even more recent, perhaps only about 500 years old. Van den Berghe (1981) indicates, however, that with relatively few exceptions, such as South Africa and the United States, where there are strong barriers to interracial marriage, race as a basis for ethnic identity was short-lived. Typically, within several generations, enough intermarriage occurs in a society to obscure racial bases of ethnicity. As a related aside, in historical times the first contacts between members of different races were occasionally friendly, at least in the New World. The Pilgrims in Massachusetts, and the Spaniards in Mexico and Peru, initially were met with curiosity and not hostility by the various indigenous groups. It was only when the Europeans waged war that the native Americans became hostile and fought back. The Pilgrim stories even indicate that the Indians were friendly and saved the lives of those first Euro-Americans. Thus, it appears that racial difference as a basis for prejudice is purely cultural/historical and not genetic/evolutionary.

In his discussion of the "worn" and behavioral ethnic markers, Van den Berghe (1981) argues that the behavioral differences were the most reliable and most difficult to fake. By donning the clothes, hairstyle, and body paint of a neighboring tribe, one could easily look like a member of that tribe. But to affect the mannerisms of the neighboring tribe, especially their language dialect, was often very difficult. Van den Berghe suggests, and I strongly concur, that language differences and similarities were probably the primary ways that tribal membership was assessed. This suggests that there is a genetic/evolutionary basis for strong sensitivities to and responses to speech.

Hunter-gatherers are simultaneously members of a number of groups: a tribe, a subsistence group, an extended family, an immediate family, an age-related group of peers (Eisenstadt, 1956), and a same-sex group ("We are boys"; "We are girls"). Multigroup membership is much more extensive in hunter-gatherers than in the African apes, and probably even greater among urban humans than among hunter-gatherers. The existence of multigroup membership raises two problems. First, how are children able to understand and act on multigroup membership? Second, what happens when conflict occurs between groups of which one is a member? Regarding the first question, it is likely that the tremendous growth in human cognitive abilities, especially symbolic ones, relative to that of the African apes, permits adults, as well as children, to identify simultaneously with several groups. Symbolic labeling is a very powerful social and intellectual tool, especially if it is reinforced by the behavior of other persons.

Regarding the second question, children and adults form a hierarchy of preferred groups, or a rank-ordering of group allegiances. If the groups are in frequent conflict, a person may have to choose to disaffiliate from one or more of the groups, and thus become an outsider to them. In hunter-gatherer societies, which are relatively closed to people outide the tribe, and where there is a strong need for social cohesion, these intergroup conflicts are probably infrequent. But in urban societies they are more common. Tonnesmann (1986) suggests that individuals become more strongly attached to groups where multiple memberships are not possible than to those where membership conflicts may arise. Examples of the former are groups based on race and gender: a person can't simultaneously be a male and a female, or a Black and a White.

Development of Group Identity

The above research and theorizing indicates that three interconnected evolutionary mechanisms are involved in our reactions to ingroup and outgroup members. They are (1) inclusive fitness, which leads to strong ingroup preferences; (2) primate intergroup mechanisms, which lead to hostility towards outgroup members; and (3) authority acceptance, which often leads to ingroup preferences and outgroup hostility. According to this model, individuals who view themselves as members of given groups will react in the described ways above. If a child, for example, does not see herself as a member of a particular dominant group, then she will not react in prejudiced and discriminatory ways towards members of groups that are subordinate to that dominant group. In other words, individuals must develop a group identity before they will develop prejudice and discrimination towards particular outgroups.

At what age do children begin to identify with a group? This question presents issues different from those concerned with the age at which children identify certain characteristics of themselves, such as gender. A child may view herself as being a girl, see herself as being similar to other girls, and yet not identify herself as a member of the girls' group. Being a member of a group entails, at a minimum, the social cohesion of group members—bonding and ingroup favoritism.

There appear to be only three experiments recorded in the English language that directly evaluate the age-related development of group identity for young children. Abramenkova (1983) compares 5- to 6-year-olds with 6- to 7-year-olds; Strayer and Trudel (1984) compare children between the ages of 1 and 6; and Yee and Brown (1992) compare 3 1/2-, 5-, 7-, and 9-year-olds. There are several other studies, however, dealing with the development of children's knowledge of group functioning that bear indirectly on group identity. The assumption is made that if children have knowledge of group processes, then it is likely that they have experienced group identification.

Strayer and Trudel's (1984) research has its origin in the study of primate groups in naturalistic settings. Their subjects were children in 10 day-care groups whose average ages ranged from approximately 1 1/2 to 5 1/2 years. There were two groups at each age level. The researchers focused on dominance and affiliative behavior within the group, because these are central features of primate group social cohesion. Affiliation includes close-in interactions such as touching, holding, and kissing, as well as more distant interactions; dominance includes attacks, threats, competition, submission, and retreat. The central premise of the research, for our purposes, is that if children interact with each other in stable and systematic ways—ways that support social cohesion—then they are operating as members of a social group. This implies that they experience a group identity. If these dominance and affiliative interactions are unstable or unsystematic, the children probably have not attained a group identity.

Strayer and Trudel (1984) measured several types of behavioral interactions that relate to this issue: frequency of conflict, stability of dominance relations, number of dyadic encounters in which dominance is depicted, the relation between dominance status and the amount of affiliation directed towards the child, and the relation between dominance status and number of unreciprocated affiliation behaviors received. The results are straightforward: children under age 3 do not operate as if they were members of groups, for either dominance or affiliation. Groups comprised of 3-, 4-, or 5-year-olds behave similarly regarding dominance relations, but there are more conflicts and more struggles over dominance within groups of 3-year-olds than within the older groups. This means that the dominance hierarchy does not function as effectively for 3-year-olds as it does for 4- and 5-year-olds. Regarding affiliation, there is a shift from the 3-year-olds to the 5-year-olds as affiliation becomes more frequently directed toward the high-status members. In stable human and nonhuman primate groups, high-status members receive more attention and/or affiliation than low-status members. These patterns of results indicate that group identity starts to emerge at age 3 and is well developed by age 5. In general, the group interactions of the 4- and 5-year-olds were more similar to each other than to those of the younger children.

Abramenkova's (1983) study, carried out in the Soviet Union, assessed whether 5- to 7-year-old children would work as hard on a task when only the group leader was punished for poor group performance as they would when each individual was punished. The assumption made is that if individuals identify themselves as members of a group, they will act in a "humane" way toward other members of the group: i.e., they will work as hard to protect their group leader as to protect themselves. Moreover, this humane attitude should be more likely to occur when the members have to interact cooperatively with each other than when they work alone, parallel to each other.

The children were placed into groups of four, based on age and gender, and tested on either a brief interactive task or a brief parallel task. For each task, two conditions were compared: that in which only the experimenter-appointed leader could be punished versus that in which all members could be punished. The measure of a humane attitude was speed and accuracy of performance. The results indicate that a humane attitude was much more likely to occur on the interactive than on the parallel task; groups of 6- to 7-year-olds showed more of this attitude, and showed it more stably, than groups of 5- to 6-year-olds; and the humane attitude was present to some extent even in the younger groups. These findings indicate that by 5 years of age children readily develop identification with a group that is externally formed and lasts for only a brief time period. It would not be surprising to find evidence of a humane attitude in younger children, especially for long-standing groups in nonlaboratory settings.

In Yee and Brown's (1992) experiment, children of ages 3 1/2, 5, 7, and 9 years were first tested on their ability to play the egg-and-spoon game. In this game, players are asked to carry as many eggs balanced on spoons as possible, in a fixed period of time. The timing was rigged such that each child succeeded in carrying exactly 3 eggs. The children were then assigned as members to either a "green" team or a "blue" team. The three other members of the green team each carried more than 3 eggs, while the three members of the blue team each carried only 1 or 2 eggs. The children were shown their teammates' scores and hence could readily note that the green team was fast and the blue team was slow. The children were then asked to make self- and team evaluations, and to indicate whether they would like to switch teams. Children had not met their "teammates," nor did they play the game again. The authors assumed that if children identified with their assigned team, they would tend to evaluate it more highly than they would the other team. However, it was predicted that children assigned to the slow team would indicate a desire to switch teams.

The results are rather complex, in that boys and girls differed somewhat on the various measures. In general, children at all age levels and on both fast and slow teams liked their team better than the opposing one. This was especially pronounced for the 5-year-olds. Children generally were accurate in assessing the performance capabilities of the two teams, although the 5-year-olds on the slow team overevaluated their team's performance capabilities. Finally, most children on the fast team did not want to switch teams, and with the exception of the 5-year-olds, most children on the slow team did want to switch. The authors conclude that children as young as 3 1/2 years can identify themselves as members of ingroups and manifest some intergroup processes. A notable change occurs at about 5 years of age: which children show particular attachment to their groups.

The remaining studies bear only indirectly on the development of a group identity. Sluckin and Smith (1977) were interested in the way 3- and 4-year-olds in two preschool play groups formed a dominance hierarchy. Pairwise dominance was measured by observing the ability of one child to win in aggressive encounters with another. Children's perception of dominance was measured by asking each child to evaluate the "toughness" of each member in his or her play group by ranking photographs of all the playmates.

In both groups a clear dominance hierarchy was found, in the sense that all dominance relations were transitive. That is, if A was dominant over B, and B over C, A was found to be dominant over C. The toughness rankings were carried out twice in the same day, as a check on reliability. Only 8 of the 20 children were reliable, i.e., consistently rank-ordered their peers in the two evaluations. Seven of these 8 children were over 4 years old. Only 1 of the 10 3-year-olds was consistent in his rankings. Especially important was the validity of the rankings, i.e., the statistical relationship between toughness rankings (the two reliability rankings were averaged) and the observed dominance hierarchy. If children can accurately perceive this important dimension of group functioning, it may be inferred that they both perceive their playmates as a group, and identify with that group. The data analyses showed that the children who were reliable in their rankings (predominantly 4-year-olds) also had valid rankings, and that the children unreliable in their rankings (predominantly 3-year-olds) did not have valid rankings. These findings, consistent with the Strayer and Trudel (1984) findings, indicate that group identity emerges between 3 and 4 years of age.

The study by Watson and Fischer (1980) deals with the development of an understanding of social roles in children between 1 1/2 and 7 1/2 years of age. In their research, children were presented with a sequence of eight different levels describing social understanding in preschool play settings. Of particular importance is the distinction made between the *behavioral role* and the *social role* understanding levels. The former concept means that a child can perform several actions in play that fit a particular social role, e.g., doctor, nurse. The latter concept means that a child can do the same, but additionally understands the complementary nature of social roles, e.g., that doctors and nurses interact with each other in particular ways. A child who demonstrates knowledge of a behavioral role may not understand that the role coordinates with other roles. It can be argued that in order for groups to function properly, social roles and not merely behavioral roles must be understood. If a child understands social roles, it may be inferred that he has knowledge of group functioning. It is further assumed that he probably has experienced membership in a group.

The basic technique used by Watson and Fischer (1980) to study these issues was a modeling and imitation procedure. The experimenter would act out a brief story using dolls and then ask the child to act out her own similar story using the same dolls. The portrayed story reflected each of the eight levels in social understanding. If a child could successfully imitate the experimenters' story at a particular level, then it was assumed that the child had social understanding at that level. The results were reliable and straightforward: the maximum level attained by 3- and 3 1/2-year-olds was that of behavioral roles; for 4- and 4 1/2-year-olds, it was social roles. Thus, the findings of Watson and Fischer are consistent with those of Sluckin and Smith (1977) and Strayer and Trudel (1984): 4 years appears to be the age at which a group identity emerges.

The last research to be discussed was carried out by Piaget in the areas of symbolic play (1962) and games with rules (1932). Piaget divides the development of symbolic play into two periods: that from 1 1/2 to 4 years, and that from 4 to 7 years. The first period involves the simple and often haphazard, but novel, use of language and nonverbal symbols with objects. For example, a child places a doll in a pan, covers it with a postcard, and says "Baby, blanket, cold." The pan is symbolic of a bed, and the postcard, of a blanket. In the second period, in contrast to the first, the symbolic combinations are more orderly; the characters and objects used are more realistic, and collective symbolism appears. That is, children can now play together using the same symbols, all taking on roles that complement one another, such as those of mother and father. Thus, in this latter period there is evidence consistent with the findings of Watson and Fischer that the use of complementary roles emerges at about age 4 years.

In the practice of rules of games, Piaget (1932) again distinguishes between the behavior characteristics of 1 1/2- to 4-year-olds and those of 4- to 7-year-olds. For the purposes of this discussion, the importance of games with rules is that they provide symbolic guides for group interaction. The ability to play a game with other children implies that each player sees the rules binding in relation to their collective behavior. Because the rules are somewhat abstract, young children could be expected to have difficulty with them. And they do. But Piaget points out substantial differences between children younger and children older than 4 years in their use of rules. Younger children evidence no understanding of a game governed by rules. Older children play together, claim they are playing by the rules, and even state some of the rules, but they don't play as if the rules were binding, or even shared. It is not until children are about 7 years old that rules regulate their play interactions.

In all the above research, 4 years continues to appear as the age at which understanding of group functioning clearly occurs. These findings support the conclusions based on the Strayer and Trudel (1984) experiment that a sense of group identity emerges by that age. Since understanding of group processes grows appreciably over the next three years, it might be expected that the nature of group identity also changes considerably between the ages of 4 and 7.

Two predictions thus are made based on the above conclusions: the appearance of prejudice and/or discrimination against specific target groups will first reliably appear in 4-year-olds; and the nature of this prejudice/discrimination will change in systematic ways between the ages of 4 and 7.

Intergroup Behavior

In the previous section we found that between the ages of 3 and 4 years, children are capable of developing a group identity. Based upon evolutionary considerations, we concluded that group identity is a prerequisite for the manifestation of certain intergroup processes, i.e., preferential treatment of ingroup members and hostility towards outgroup members. We further argued that intergroup processes are one of the three building blocks of prejudice and discrimination.

What do we know about the development of intergroup behavior in children? And how does this knowledge fit with what we would predict from primate intergroup relations? Surprisingly little research has been carried out in this area. Fortunately, the work that has been done is considered seminal in the field of social psychology. The Sherifs' experiments (Sherif & Sherif, 1953; Sherif, Harvey, White, Hood,

& Sherif, 1961) are among the most imaginative and important in the field of group development and intergroup relations. As far as the subjects knew, they were participants not in experiments, but rather in real-life experiences shared with other preadolescent or adolescent boys. In the first experiment (Sherif & Sherif, 1953), a number of middle-class boys were invited to attend an overnight camp. In the first phase, which lasted less than a week, the children participated in the usual camp activities, ate together, and were given great freedom in choosing their friends. The counselors/experimenters paid special attention to friendship patterns and social networks.

In the second phase, which also lasted less than a week, close friends were placed into two separate groups. The groups were kept isolated from each other as much as possible, eating, sleeping, and carrying out activities in separate locations. One group named itself the Bulldogs; the other, the Blue Devils. Each of the groups developed a set of norms that distinguished it from the other group. For example, the Bulldogs refused to use the color blue, which they associated with the Blue Devils. Most of the boys talked in an "us versus them" fashion and deprecated the other group. Boys who attempted to socialize with members of the other group were called "traitors" by their own group. Within each group, status hierarchies emerged. This system served to further enhance group identification and cohesiveness, and to produce at least mild antagonism towards the other group.

In the third phase, the two groups were brought into competition with each other in order to win points for the group as a whole and prizes for its individual members. The boys competed in sports, tournaments, and camp chores. During this phase, intergroup antagonism escalated to such a degree that the Sherifs made strong attempts to create intergroup harmony. They accomplished this by assigning the groups cooperative tasks necessary for the betterment of the camp as a whole.

In the second experiment (Sherif et al., 1961), two groups of boys were brought into the camp separately, unaware of one another's presence during the first phase. As in the earlier experiment, status hierarchies emerged, which included the development of group norms, cooperation, group identity, and group loyalty. In the second phase, the groups were brought together for a number of athletic competitions. As in the first study, strong negative attitudes and behaviors developed toward the other group. Even neutral contacts turned into conflict, such as a garbage-throwing war following a meal together. At the same time, ingroup feelings were strengthened, often leading to overestimating of the group's competitive abilities. As in the first experiment, the third phase involved having the two groups work together cooperatively, which had the effect of improving intergroup relations.

In summary, the results of these experiments are completely consistent with the findings of the studies on primate intergroup relations. In the process of group formation, preadolescent and adolescent boys developed strong bonds with other group members. A status hierarchy emerged, they developed and adhered to group norms, and they then reacted negatively to outgroup members, some of whom previously had been friends. Competition between groups served to exaggerate these effects. The Sherifs' research indicates that for preadolescents and adolescents antagonism towards outgroup members is an integral part of group formation and group functioning.

The above results raise two important questions about group formation and intergroup relations. First, the Sherifs built into their camp situation a large number of social components designed to create a strong sense of group identity. Are all these components necessary? To phrase it differently, what are the minimum requirements for establishing a group identity (as assessed by ingroup preferences)? Second, the campers showed both strong ingroup preferences *and* outgroup hostility. Do the two classes of behavior always occur together? If not, what does it take to produce both?

The research by Henri Tajfel and his colleagues (see, e.g., Tajfel, 1981; Tajfel & Turner, 1986), known as "minimal" group experiments, were designed to answer the first of these questions. Their results indicate that for adolescents, ingroup preferences are produced even when group identification is based on trivial characteristics and the members of the "groups" have never met, nor will ever meet. In one of the experiments, the adolescents were individually shown slides of paintings by Klee and by Kandinsky (the subjects were not art students) and asked for their preferences. They were then told that they were being placed in the group whose members preferred the same painter they did. In another experiment, the adolescents were shown pictures of dots and asked to state the number of dots. The subjects were then told that they were being placed into a group whose members had either underestimated or overestimated the number of dots in the same manner they had. The adolescents were then individually tested on a number of tasks in which they had to determine monetary rewards for one other member of their "group," as well as for one member in the other "group."

In all the experiments, (at least 30 have been performed), a consistent preference was shown to more highly reward ingroup as opposed to outgroup members. Moreover, in order to discriminate against the outgroup, the adolescents frequently made choices that were less than optimal for their own group. That is, in assigning rewards, they maximized the difference between what the ingroup and the outgroup members received, rather than trying to give the largest reward possible to the ingroup member.

The readiness with which we identify ourselves with a group is astonishing, as evidenced by the experiment of Locksley, Ortiz, and Hepburn (1980). They created two "groups" on an explicitly random basis, the members of which were unknown to one another and would never meet. The researchers still found strong ingroup preferences. Thus, the answer to the first question—what the minimal requirements are for establishing a group identity—is merely assigning people to a group. The results of Yee and Brown (1992) are consistent with this conclusion.

It should be noted that in the minimal group experiments, there was no evidence of hostility towards outgroup members. Discriminating against outgroup members by showing favoritism towards ingroup members often occurs outside as well as inside the laboratory. Indeed, we may even like and show preferences on other occasions to outgroup members we have just discriminated against. This leads us to our second question: Under what conditions will outgroup discrimination involve hostility? The results from the Sherif experiments suggest that competition may be a key factor. Recall that stereotyping and hostility escalated when the two groups were placed in head-to-head competition. Subsequent research has shown, however, that one critical factor is the legitimacy or fairness of the competition (Tajfel & Turner, 1986). If the losers feel that they have lost fairly, they may even elevate their positive feelings towards the winners.

Roger Brown (1986) also suggests that intergroup hostility is related to fairness and places the issue in the context of equity theory. If two groups, for example, feel that the actual or potential distribution of rewards or resources between them is fair, then they will not feel hostility during or after competition. But if a group feels that the distribution is unfair, then that group will express hostility. The two key components of equity are the actual or potential *rewards* gained in relation to the actual or potential *costs* involved in attaining the rewards. Rewards are any outcomes that groups find desirable, e.g., winning prizes, enhancements in respect or status, new privileges. Costs involve two components: (1) any undesirable outcomes, e.g., hard work, pain, threats; and (2) the "assets" or entitlements groups bring with them, e.g., age, status, years of experience, gender. Hence, the giving of an advantage to older, more experienced teenagers while it is withheld from younger, less experienced ones may be seen by both groups as justified, because the older group has more assets. When rewards are scarce, e.g., "winner takes all," then the pressure to closely evaluate equity increases. Consequently, the likelihood of perceiving unfairness also increases. The issue is not the real state of affairs, but rather, the perceived state.

When groups engage in competition, e.g., the Bulldogs and the Blue Devils, they compare themselves with each other in light of the conditions they're placed in. If they have negative stereotypes about each other, if there is a "winner takes all" competition, if there is some ambiguity about the rules, each may feel that the competition is unfair, and initially experience anger. Members of the winning group, of course, will likely change their views, and the losers may feel even more wronged.

When the equity analysis is extended into the realm of prejudice and discrimination, some powerful insights emerge. For example, many members of the untouchable castes feel that the distribution of rewards, i.e., their treatment, is fair, because an asset they have (their caste) justifies the treatment they receive. Parallel arguments can be made for the treatment of Blacks, women, and mentally retarded or physically disabled persons in Western cultures. When the untouchables or Blacks or women or disabled people challenge the way their assets have been evaluated, they then perceive the treatment received as being prejudiced and discriminatory. In other words, prejudice and discrimination are experienced if the treatment is perceived as unfair or unjustified. What often happens is that the higher-status group feels entitled to the distribution of rewards they receive—e.g., better jobs, better pay, more and better housing opportunities—whereas the lower-status group feels cheated, i.e., they reject the old views of their assets. The former group believes that they are being fair, and hence, acting in an unprejudiced manner, whereas the latter group feels the opposite. Obviously, this is a potentially explosive state of affairs, which all too often becomes transformed into a violent actuality.

Hunter-Gatherer Minds Revisited

The preceding material in this chapter leads to the conclusion that several of the processes underlying prejudice and discrimination are genetic/evolutionary, based on tribal and intertribal interactions. These processes are triggered through "normal" interactions, and are inappropriately applied to groups within a culture. Why might this have occurred? Stated another way, why are ingroups and outgroups within a culture prejudiced against each other? There are a number of possible, and not mutually exclusive, explanations.

First, members of a hunter-gatherer tribe have a strong identification with and commitment to other members of the tribe. These cultural commitments and identifications are generally lacking in industrial and post-industrial societies except in times of war, or when one is being mistreated in a foreign land by the locals. In other words, the pull of nationalism is very weak relative to the pull of tribal identity. Second, members of hunter-gatherer tribes are very homogeneous in appearance and behavior, which promotes group identification. In industrial and post-industrial societies, there is usually considerable heterogeneity in appearance and behavior, primarily because of immigration and the incorporation of tribes residing great distances from each other. Hence, badging mechanisms leading to a societal identity are very weak.

Third, the different groups (family and/or task-related) within a hunter-gatherer tribe are highly compatible with one another. If they don't pull together, they'll surely be pulled apart. In industrial and post-industrial societies, groups we identify with are often incompatible with one another, in that they pursue incompatible goals. Fourth, hunter-gatherer tribal members are rarely in competition with each other on a day-to-day basis. Competition is antagonistic to the norms of sharing and reciprocity. If one wins everyone wins; e.g., someone kills a zebra and all share it. If one loses, then all are diminished. In industrial and post-industrial societies, competition is the norm, both within and between groups.

Fifth, hunter-gatherer cultures are highly egalitarian across families, and between parents within a family. Status and power differences between adults would likely be destructive to effective group functioning. There are leaders for particular activities, e.g., hunting, religion, but this leadership does not cut across all activities, nor does it give the leaders general power advantages. In industrial and post-industrial societies, there are obvious power and status differences. Those in power strive to maintain it at the expense of those in subordinate positions. Sixth, competition and status differences in industrial and post-industrial societies are mutually reinforcing. They create "haves" and "have-lesses," and by forming alliances, members of these cultures form ingroups and outgroups. The ingroups are dominant and the outgroups, subordinate.

Seventh, in hunter-gatherer tribes, the goals of socialization are to make the children similar to the adults, who have equal status with each other, but higher status than the children. But if some groups of adults have higher status than other groups, as is the case in industrial and post-industrial societies, then the children will be drawn to and influenced by those higher-status groups. This differential attractiveness reinforces group status differences. Eighth, it is possible that in hunter-gatherer tribes, opposite-sex prejudice and discrimination do exist in children. But these are necessarily modified and redirected during adolescence in order to maintain group cohesiveness and an egalitarian form of functioning. In industrial and post-industrial societies, power differences in gender are the norm and are thus reinforced in adolescence. Racial differences don't exist in hunter-gatherer tribes, and infants with obvious serious physical abnormalities are usually put to death. Thus, in hunter-gatherer societies, there are essentially no opportunities for prejudice based on race or physical handicap beyond infancy.

Finally, authority acceptance in hunter-gatherer tribes is based on authority figures who are the elder members of the family and tribe. They maintain the cultural values, and if necessary, redirect them to benefit the tribe. In industrial and post-industrial societies, there are a large number of authority figures outside of the family. When children go to school, the number increases. Generally, authority figures directly or indirectly instruct the young to accept the values that sustain the status and power of the dominant groups. These values thus reinforce the existence of ingroups and outgroups.

Summary

Our genes determine some aspects of human social behavior. One likely genetic process controlling species-specific development of this behavior is canalization. Experiential canalization involves a hierarchical system of four mutually interacting components: genetic activity, neural activity, behavior, and environment. All four components work together to ensure that developmental targets are attained, buffering developing individuals from genetic and environmental abnormalities.

Humans are a cultural species. Our genes make culture inevitable, but genes and culture coevolved. Systematic changes in human genetic structure led to systematic changes in the nature of human culture, and vice versa. At the heart of this coevolution are epigenetic rules that transform experiences into behavior. Genetic fitness can be assigned to different rules. Some sets of rules led to culture-specific canalized behavioral characteristics. Where the culture-specific characteristics had high genetic fitness across all cultures, they ultimately became universally species-specific.

Behavior genetics research attempts to account for the contribution of genetic and environmental variations to individual differences in behavior. In a sense, this research is the opposite of canalization, which is concerned with the genetic bases of similarities across people. The importance of behavior genetics for the present argument is that it clearly demonstrates the role of genes in controlling social behavior and prejudice.

The essential argument in the chapter is that the three sets of genetic/evolutionary processes that lead to prejudice and discrimination evolved in hunter-gatherer tribes. They were appropriate and necessary for that subsistence mode, which characterizes 99 percent of the duration of human existence. These three sets of processes are put into motion in non-hunter-gatherer contexts because they have been incorporated into our epigenetic systems.

The theory of inclusive fitness leads to the prediction that members of a breeding community will show preferences towards their relatives over non-relatives. In primate evolution, the term "close relatives" is nearly synonymous with "members of the subsistence group." That is, in general, a primate has more close relatives in his or her subsistence group than in other groups. Thus, primates are evolutionarily predisposed to show ingroup favoritism. The existence of scarce resources may, in addition, lead to outgroup antagonism.

Owing to the great complexity of tribal cultures, humans developed authority-bearing systems for readily transmitting information to the young. These systems are probably based on the primate group characteristic of dominance hierarchies, but extend into the realm of concepts and values. In authority-bearing systems, humans not only accept as valid what authorities tell us, but also internalize this information. There may be a developmental trend in decreasing authority acceptance that is related to the increasing autonomy associated with adolescence. Obviously, authority acceptance is one major basis for the cultural transmission of prejudice and discrimination.

Primate intergroup relations are usually tense and frequently hostile. The evolutionary bases of this hostility are closely linked with protecting the young and the females from harm by outgroup members, and secondarily with controlling food resources and maintaining group cohesion. Close examination of intergroup relations among the African apes and human hunter-gatherers suggests that males may be predisposed to develop stronger outgroup prejudices than females.

Unlike the African apes, hunter-gatherers have the tribe and not the subsistence group as the ingroup. Tribes differ from one another culturally, and children acquire knowledge of their own culture through "badging" mechanisms. These mechanisms readily allow children to identify ingroup and outgroup members. It is very unlikely from a genetic/evolutionary view that race differences were significant. Unlike other primates, individual hunter-gatherers are members of several groups, which normally operate in a non-conflictual manner.

The development of prejudice and discrimination is tied to the development of a group identity. The psychological literature suggests that a group identity emerges between the ages of 3 and 4 years and increases for at least several years.

The social psychological study of intergroup relations in preadolescents and adolescents indicates that identification with a group, as measured by ingroup preferences, can occur merely by random assignment of individuals to groups that have no function. Intergroup hostility, however, is based on the existence of unfair competition. An equity model seems to capture the essential features of this phenomenon and leads to valuable insights into the nature of prejudice and discrimination.

Finally, several possible explanations were given as to why the genetic/evolutionary processes underlying appropriate tribal and intertribal interactions are inappropriately applied to groups within a culture. All the explanations acknowledge the fact that industrial and post-industrial societies differ in very significant ways from tribal cultures.

3

Brief Cultural Histories of Females, African-Americans, Deaf Persons, and Mentally Retarded Persons

Purposes

The assessment has been made in the preceding chapters that there are four types of causes underlying the development of prejudice and discrimination: genetic/evolutionary, psychological, normative, and power-conflict. Although these sets of causes are interrelated, they are not static. The genetic/evolutionary ones are the most stable, and the psychological, the least stable. The normative and power-conflict causes fall in an intermediate position and may change over relatively short historical periods. Thus, in order to assess normative and power-conflict influences in the development of peer prejudice and discrimination, it is essential to have a historical perspective. A "snapshot" of the contemporary period may give a distorted picture of the relationship between dominant and subordinate groups. For example, in 1948 the United States armed forces were first racially integrated by President Harry Truman. But it is highly unlikely that discriminatory practices by

Whites towards Blacks immediately stopped. To understand this racial integration, one must examine it in the context of pre– and post–Civil War military practices.

In addition to being "needed" to assess the current situation, a historical approach is required to understand the development of social norms. We stated that historical traditions are used to buttress these norms. And we can know the traditions only by studying them, rather than by inferring them from the current situation.

As noted earlier, four categories of peer prejudice and discrimination are dealt with in this book: prejudice and discrimination towards members of the opposite sex, individuals of a different race, and deaf and mentally retarded persons. These categories were selected because of both their importance in United States culture and the existence of appreciable developmental data for them. Because of these considerations, the present chapter focuses on brief cultural histories of four subordinate groups in the United States: females, African-Americans, deaf people, and mentally retarded people.

Not only will these histories identify the social norms and power-conflict practices of the dominant groups in the United States towards these subordinate groups; a comparison of the histories will also allow inferences to be made about the motivations underlying the norms. It is very unlikely, for example, that economic considerations were the major determinants in discrimination against deaf and mentally retarded people, but they may have been concerning treatment of females and Blacks. Thus, comparisons of histories will broaden our perspective on the cultural bases of prejudice and discrimination.

Comparisons among the four cultural histories will reap another benefit. As will be seen, over the time period studied, discrimination and perhaps prejudice has markedly decreased towards each of these target groups. Comparing the four may allow us to make inferences about the factors that underlie these positive changes.

Before we proceed with the histories, there are two cautions that should be noted. The first concerns the age groups and content historians emphasize. When studying females and African-Americans, they generally focus on adults and on a wide range of content areas. When examining deaf or mentally retarded individuals, they emphasize both children and adults and focus primarily on education, secondarily on employment. Thus, comparisons between the four histories will be based on somewhat different data sets. As a consequence, we'll have to be somewhat cautious about the conclusions we draw.

The second caution is that within each history, there is tremendous diversity among members of the target group. For example, historians have studied females from hundreds of major Native American tribes, as well as females of African-American descent, Asian descent, and European descent. Research has been done on recent immigrants and on females whose families have been in the U.S. for generations. Females across these groups were treated differently, and, of course, there were substantial within-group differences. African-American experiences were markedly affected by region of residence (South versus North), whether the home environment was urban or rural, and, of course, whether or not the subjects or their recent ancestors had been slaves. Similarly, there are many levels of impairment among deaf and mentally retarded persons. Historically, the two groups may have received similar treatment, but obviously there was and is great diversity of experience within and between these groups.

A challenge that any study of the issue of diversity faces is the fact that historians don't write about all subgroupings; implicitly or explicitly, they make choices about whom to focus on. And as a psychologist writing about these histories, I must make additional choices. Fortunately, from this writer's point of view, historical trends can be observed in each of these four major groupings that appear to have wide within-grouping applicability. There does seem to be a "forest" we can observe and discuss, even though lots of individual trees will be unseen as we write about that forest.

Brief Cultural History of American Females

The focus in this section, owing to space limitations, will be primarily on Euro-Americans. The women's histories by Evans (1989) and Ryan (1975), various African-American histories, and the general history of the United States by Nash et al. (1990) suggest the existence of six major cultural periods between 1607, the date of English settlement of Jamestown, Virginia, and the present time. Not surprisingly, most of the periods are identified by the wars that marked them. These periods are as follows: 1607–1770, Colonization; 1770–1825, Revolution and Consolidation; 1825–1865, Expansion and Civil War; 1865–1920, Reconstruction, World War, and Suffrage; 1920–1945, Prosperity, Depression, and the Second World War; 1945–the present, Postwar Growth and Change.

To a large extent the changes in female roles and women's rights from 1607 to the present have involved the social rewriting of the biblical Fifth and Tenth Commandments. In a nutshell, women have gained substantial legal, political, economic, military, sexual, and educational rights since the colonists settled in Jamestown. The changes have not been equivalent in all these areas; the paths of improvement have often been circuitous, with setbacks along the way, and functional equality with men as contrasted with relative legal equality has still not been attained in any of these areas. Women are no longer men's "property," but they still hold subordinate social roles.

Although our treatment must be highly abbreviated, it is useful to indicate some of the most significant findings about women's history in each of the above six periods. This discussion relies primarily on the books by Evans (1989) and Ryan (1975). In the first period, Colonization (1607–1770), women's lives could be captured by the image of cycles of pregnancy, birth, and child care. The average number of live births was eight. Women and their daughters worked very hard in the home and in their gardens. Families were generally economically self-reliant, and men and women had nearly equivalent economic roles in the home. But despite this economic equality, women depended on their husbands' status outside the home in almost every other aspect of life. Females were less literate than males; many schools were closed to girls; married women usually could not own land or businesses independently of their husbands (although widows could own land and businesses); women could not vote, sit on juries (though they could sue for divorce), hold public office, or participate in the religious hierarchy.

Although courtship and femininity were downplayed, women's sexual enjoyment was not suppressed. Premarital sex following engagement to be married was frequent and expected. However, a sexual double standard existed: married men sometimes "fornicated" with other women, but married women committed "adultery" with other men. The chances of a woman successfully suing for divorce because of her husband's infidelity were slim (though she would be successful on a charge of wife beating), whereas her husband's suit would be successful on a similar charge.

The socialization of girls appears to have been relatively straightforward during this period. They worked closely with their mothers and were heavily involved in child care, homemaking, and economic activities related to what could be made at home or grown in the garden. Relatively few had an extensive formal education, and many were illiterate. There were scarce opportunities and no role models for a life not intimately tied to marriage and family.

The next period, Revolution and Consolidation (1770–1825), produced a number of short-term and some long-term changes in women's roles. Prior to and during the war, the country was politicized. Women were forced to look beyond both the home and the nearby community and to become actively involved in ongoing issues and events. Their sons, husbands, or fathers went to war against the British, or took pro-British stances. No one could be neutral or uninvolved. Members of the same church were often in opposition. When their husbands went to war, women often had to take charge of the family as well as the family business. Widowhood made these changes permanent. In some cities, nearly 10 percent of the small shops were owned by women.

Substantial social class differences emerged during this period, due in part to urbanization, in part to immigration, and in part to increased trade. Social roles for women varied, thus providing a wider range of models than had been available in the preceding period. Upper-class women did little economic work and had considerable free time for social activities, shopping, and volunteerism in benevolent and religious societies. Middle-class women were still heavily involved in family life, including economic activities, but they also engaged in volunteer work. Women of the lowest social classes had the greatest autonomy in most aspects of life, but struggled the most for economic survival. Many were employed in the textile industries, receiving considerably lower pay than men. Many lived off welfare provided by the local government and by benevolent societies founded by middle- and upper-class women.

Upper- and middle-class girls received a fair amount of formal education, presumably to enable them to become better wives and mothers. And an increased number of women became schoolteachers during this period. Members of lower-class families received little formal education.

The republican spirit of equality produced by the independence movement had two principal long-term effects on women's roles: it led to the formation of many women's voluntary organizations directed toward promoting social well-being, and it led to greater esteem for the role of motherhood in producing virtuous citizens. Motherhood was celebrated in the first child-rearing manual, which appeared during this period. Schooling was thought to serve this function, too. But women were cautioned to control their displays of education and intelligence lest men feel manipulated by them. Birthrates fell during this time, from eight live births per woman to about six, suggesting a more planned approach to parenthood.

Despite these changes, women's formal political, legal, and property rights remained relatively unchanged. And despite some changes in church-related activities, the religious hierarchy was still controlled by men. Socialization of girls became more complicated during this period. There were tremendous social class differences as well as rural versus urban differences, and schooling became very influential. An active social, religious, and economic life outside the home became a likelihood for many.

The next period, Expansion and Civil War (1825–1865), involved a marked polarization of women's roles. This was most clearly seen in the establishment of two "utopian" societies, the Shakers and the

Oneida Community. Both were economically self-contained, with men and women taking on egalitarian roles. They were communal, and profits from external sales were shared. In the Shaker communities there was rigid segregation of the sexes, with sexual abstinence the governing rule. Within the Oneida Community, monogamy was abolished and sexual intercourse with several concurrent partners was encouraged. Many men and women formed "complex" marriages, which could be readily dissolved.

Although women's sexuality was not *the* central issue in this period, it was important. Magazines, literature, and marriage manuals directed towards middle- and upper-class women defined them as guardians of the hearth, as pure, pious, and embodying the best moral values of the nation. They were encouraged to reign in the home as queens, and care for their children and their husbands, who struggled in the workplace and the political arena. Despite appeals to their romantic natures, and the glorification of romantic love leading to marriage, women were seen as appropriately lacking in sexual passion and men as often being too passionate. Women were responsible for "cooling" their husbands. Those women with strong sexual urges were considered abnormal and surgical removal of the clitoris was occasionally recommended. Long periods of sexual abstinence in marriage were the norm, partially accounting for a further drop in the birthrate in this period, from six live births to five.

Women's moral roles were dramatically extended outside the family to the larger society, where they were viewed as the "mothers of civilization." Large numbers of middle- and upper-class women formed moral reform, temperance, antislavery, and religious evangelistic societies. These concerns enhanced their awareness of the marked gender inequities in the society, which, in turn, gave feminism a large boost. White, nonpropertied men gained voting rights in most states in the 1820s, which further highlighted gender differences in voting rights and other legal entitlements. However, within the next decade many states enacted laws guaranteeing women's property rights independent of their husbands'.

In the early part of this period, middle- and upper-class women rarely were employed outside the home. With Western expansion and increased education for girls, there was a dramatic growth in the need for women teachers, whose pay was typically far less than their male counterparts. Increasingly large numbers of working-class women and female immigrants entered the marketplace, where their pay was usually one-half to one-third that of men. As a consequence of near-starvation wages, many women's labor organizations were founded. A number of labor strikes by women occurred during this period, with limited success. The Civil War brought new work opportunities for educated women to fill the jobs men had, and to directly aid the war effort. The two major occupations were office clerk and nursing. The professional hierarchy was cracked by women: in 1849 the first woman received a medical degree in the United States, and in 1852 the first woman was ordained as a minister in a mainstream Christian denomination. Medical schools quickly closed their doors to women, who, as a consequence, opened several women's medical colleges in the 1850s and 1860s.

Socialization of girls became much more complex than it had been in the previous period, owing to the wide variety of social roles open to them. Books and magazines oriented towards girls from the middle and upper classes emphasized their roles as wives and mothers. But many adult females were highly involved in social action and in jobs outside the home. Some were moving into work traditionally held by men, albeit with lower wages. Feminism as a philosophy of equal opportunity and equal treatment of women and men became embodied in formal organizations, thus challenging traditional social roles.

The next period, Reconstruction, World War, and Suffrage (1865–1920), involved an acceleration of and the resolution of some of the issues that had been prominent in the preceding period. Upper- and middle-class women continued to see one of their major roles as that of being "mothers of civilization," the moral carriers of society, and founded nationwide societies to carry out this role. They started the Women's Christian Temperance Union (WCTU) in 1874 and the Young Women's Christian Association (YWCA) shortly afterwards. The WCTU had considerable influence during the remainder of the century and was an important training ground for female political activists. A national alcohol prohibition act was passed by Congress in 1917. The YWCA focused on helping immigrants and working-class women get settled in their new urban environments. Hull House, a large settlement house for immigrant families, was founded by women in 1889. It was very successful and led to the spread of other settlement houses throughout the country.

The numbers of immigrants and working-class women employed in low-paid, unsafe, and unhealthy environments continued to increase. These groups formed labor unions and periodically went on strike for improved wages and working conditions. Some limited changes occurred, though ultimately child and women's labor laws were passed that did improve work life. Correspondingly, middle-class women increasingly entered the existing professions of teaching and nursing, and the newly created one of social work. Some women even became lawyers, and in 1879 women were granted the right to make presentations to the United States Supreme Court.

Women's cultural organizations, known as "women's clubs," started to flourish among middle- and upper-class women. Women's college organizations were formed that kept women's social and intellectual networks alive. At about the same time, towards the end of the nineteenth century, women founded national ethnic associations, including the National Council of Jewish Women and the National Association for Colored Women. Others followed in the early twentieth century.

Shortly after the passage in 1869 of the Fourteenth and Fifteenth Amendments to the United States Constitution granting voting rights to all males, including the recently freed slaves, the women's suffrage movement gained momentum. Ultimately, nearly every women's organization took up its cause. Although constitutional laws concerning women's suffrage had first been proposed in 1868, it was not until 1910 that women could vote in any state elections. By 1914, nine western states had granted women voting rights, and in Montana, the first woman in the country was elected to Congress. The United States' involvement in the First World War in 1917 and 1918, a fight for European freedom, contributed to the passage of the Nineteenth Amendment. It was ratified in 1920, granting all voting-age women the right to vote.

Birthrates declined further in this period, to four live births per woman. Men continued to be concerned about women's sexuality. Some male physicians writing in the nineteenth century said that women should be discouraged from riding bicycles lest they be overaroused sexually by the seats (Haller & Haller, 1974). By the second decade of the twentieth century, however, sexual freedom had increased, and single women came to be known in the press and magazines as "bachelor girls" instead of "spinsters."

One enduring twentieth-century dilemma for women solidified during this period: career versus marriage. Many working-class women had jobs to help support their families. Many middle- and upper-class women entered professions before getting married. Others no longer had to spend a lifetime raising children because of smaller family size, and chose to work outside the home after marriage. In the years 1890 to 1920, approximately 60 percent of professional women were unmarried and remained so. Thus, for most college-educated women interested in a profession, the choice of a career precluded marriage.

The next period, Prosperity, Depression, and the Second World War (1920–1945), involved marked swings in women's roles. The central issues appear to have been women's sexuality, women's autonomy, women's work, political activism, and career versus marriage. The end of the First World War and the passage of the Nineteenth Amendment led to increasing feelings of autonomy and freedom in women. These feelings joined with the preceding "bachelor girl" decade and the growth of the film industry to create an increased emphasis on and openness about women's sexuality. The 1920s was the decade of the flapper: the bubbly, sexy, outgoing, and fun-loving woman. Through new dance crazes, it became more acceptable to have less of the body covered and to engage in new levels of physical intimacy. Consumerism was on the rise, and with it the growth of advertising. Sex, especially sexy women, sold products to men and women. Single women were working in increasing numbers and had money to spend on themselves, instead of having to help support their parents and younger siblings. Books and magazines directed towards female adolescents became prominent. They emphasized the desirability, and perhaps the necessity, of appearing and being sexy in order to get a man. Marriage was still seen as the primary goal of these activities, a marriage involving romantic love, sexual pleasure, and companionship.

Was there something wrong in women's sexuality? Freud and both his male and his female followers found fault with it. Not only did little girls suffer from penis envy, but women achieved orgasm through clitoral instead of the allegedly more mature vaginal stimulation. Thus women's sexual enjoyment, they maintained, was inappropriately immature. Of course, these pronouncements flew in the face of known biological facts, but the facts were thrown out to support the new theory. Other psychoanalytic doctrine, presumably based on biological considerations, led to the conclusion that the most appropriate role for women was that of a relatively passive wife and mother. A new female disease emerged in the 1940s: frigidity.

Women's success with the passage of alcohol prohibition laws and the suffrage amendment had long-term costs in the attainment of female equality. The steam was taken out of collective efforts on behalf of feminism. In 1923 an equal rights amendment was defeated in Congress. Many women fought against it because the amendment threatened some of the privileges women had attained in previous legislation. With the right to vote, women joined the mainstream of American political life. But the mainstream was controlled by men and men's values. Women's organizations during the Depression and the Second World War were concerned with national issues, not feminist ones. Indeed, feminism came to be seen as self-centered and selfish.

Many of the gains in women's employment opportunities in the 1920s were lost in the 1930s because of the Depression. Jobs were usually sex-segregated; i.e., there were "women's jobs" that were lower-paying but often protected by legislation. Many states passed laws restricting married women to certain types of employment. However, the New Deal of President Roosevelt brought new employment opportunities for highly educated women with administrative experience. Roosevelt's Secretary of Labor for 12 years was a woman. She and Eleanor Roosevelt were instrumental in bringing many women into responsible governmental jobs.

For most women, the Depression had produced a loss in autonomy. The Second World War brought it back, along with new work opportunities and a social partnership with men. Women were barred from few traditional masculine occupations, and worked side by side with men. They received equal pay for equal work, which the unions had fought for. But there was a cloud hanging over this flowering of women's rights: the possibility that the changes were only for "the duration." The war's end, which everyone dreamed of, might also bring to an end women's recent gains.

The last period, Postwar Growth and Change (1945– the present), started with extraordinary joy and optimism. The economy was in full swing, delayed marriages were consummated, and the birth of babies boomed. White married couples started moving to the suburbs in large numbers, and the trend of Black families to move from the South into the northern cities continued. Consumerism prevailed, and this was encouraged in the 1950s by the widespread ownership of television sets.

Although many women lost their jobs to returning veterans after the war ended in 1945, the percentage of working women steadily increased from the late 1940s to the present. Most of their jobs were in the service industries and in traditionally female professions: teaching, nursing, library science, social work. Shortly after the war's end some laws restricting married women's employment were enacted, but all these had been rescinded by the middle 1960s. Jobs were still highly segregated by sex through the 1970s, and to some extent still are. Until the passage of the Civil Rights Act in 1964, women were often paid less than men for the same jobs. And of course, women's jobs in general paid far less than those held by men. It was not until the 1980s that federal and state governments started job reclassification programs assigning equal pay to jobs of comparable worth. These programs are still in process, and although women's pay relative to men's has increased over the past twenty years, parity has not yet been achieved.

The apparent expansiveness of the move to the suburbs brought with it the increased isolation of women from the political, economic, and social aspects of the society. The theme "woman's place is in the home" strongly reemerged after 1945, supported by the sociological studies of Talcott Parsons, the child-rearing books of Dr. Spock, and magazines directed to women and adolescent females. Many women became involved in community organizations, but these were typically child-centered, e.g., the PTA and scouts, and hence oriented toward the family, as opposed to the wider world.

The women's movement was dormant until the mid-1960s. The National Organization for Women (NOW) was founded then, and many "women's liberation" groups emerged. The focus of most of those groups was on equal economic and, by implication, educational opportunities. Many antidiscrimination laws were passed, influenced by women's groups, and new professional education opportunities arose in law and medicine. The number of women elected to local and state offices started to increase markedly, but in the 1990s, the percentage of women in public office is still well below that for men.

The invention and widespread use of "the Pill" as a contraceptive method brought with it considerable sexual freedom. Abortion rights were guaranteed in 1973 in the *Roe v. Wade* U.S. Supreme Court decision. Women's organizations also gave considerable support to lesbianism as a viable and valuable lifestyle. These events gave rise to strong antifeminist reactions among many groups of men and women. Conservative United States presidents were elected in the 1980s, both of whom espoused traditional, i.e., "patriarchal," roles for men and women. Strong antiabortion, antilesbian, and anti "promiscuity" campaigns emerged that threatened the personal freedoms women had gained in the postwar period.

At the present time (the middle 1990s), the socialization of females is very complex and often contradictory. The forced choice of career versus marriage is still problematic for most women. Equality of effort and responsibility in managing a home and family life is rarely the norm for parents who both hold full-time jobs: women do much more than their husbands. Additionally, the prospects of enduring marriages have grown progressively slimmer. Many women are choosing not to bear children, and choosing not to marry. In pre-suffrage days some women found their careers to be a primary source of self-worth. They remained unmarried and also were involved in social causes. Today many women are choosing a similar path. A major vehicle for increased power and autonomy in American society is higher education. But, as Valerie Walkerdine (1990) has convincingly argued, and as we saw in chapter 1, our educational systems place roadblocks in front of that vehicle by socializing young girls to be incompetent in pursuing educational goals. Additionally, career and work advancement is usually controlled by men who typically value more highly the contributions and prospects of other men than those of women. Finally, the issue is still being debated by men and women as to whether females have a "different voice" because of the way they are socialized, or because they are genetically predisposed to be different.

Brief Cultural History of African-Americans

It is estimated that over a 350-year period at least 10 million African slaves arrived in the New World, approximately 5 percent of whom were brought to the North American colonies. It is not clear how many died in transit, but probably at least one in six, and perhaps considerably more (Meier & Rudwick, 1976). Survival in the New World largely depended on the topography of the land and on the climate. Mortality was high in the swampy, insect-infested regions of the West Indies, but relatively low in most regions of the North American colonies.

It is useful to view African-Americans as having had four different types of socialization/enculturation experiences: life as nonenslaved ("free") persons in the North; "free" status in the South; enslavement in the North; and slavery in the South (Nash, Jeffrey, et al., 1990). Prior to the Civil War, 85 to 90 percent of the African-Americans living in the colonies (and states) were slaves, and those who were not were either recently freed or descended from slaves. Being "free" in the North was much less restrictive than "freedom" in the South, but it was not equivalent to the status of White free persons. Northern slaves typically worked in the household, were very familiar to their owner and his family, and often had child care responsibilities as part of their work. Unlike Southern plantation slaves, they lived mainly in urban settings and usually had considerable unsupervised time in the town. The field slaves in the South (men and women) worked extremely long hours, usually under quite unsympathetic conditions. Treatment by their masters was frequently brutal, food supplied to them was often inadequate (they could supplement it by their own extra farming efforts), and they were usually closely watched.

According to a number of writers, e.g., Aptheker (1971), Franklin (1984), and Harding (1981), the central theme in the entire span of African-American history (pre– and post–Civil War) is the pursuit of freedom. This pursuit includes, but is not limited to the goals of justice, equality, and self-determination. There is no convincing evidence that even a substantial minority, let alone a majority, of enslaved Black Africans readily accepted their bondage. Rather, there are ample records that document Africans' fierce struggle for freedom, even before they arrived in the American colonies. For example, many committed suicide by drowning rather than be transported abroad. After arriving in the colonies, many attempted to escape, especially in the

South. Many fled to the North and to Canada. Others went to Florida, where they found acceptance by the Seminole Indians. Thomas Jefferson estimated that in just one year in Virginia, 30,000 slaves attempted to escape (Harding, 1981).

In the Colonization period (1607–1770), dramatic changes occurred in the conception of and treatment of the African slaves. During the early part of the period, slavery itself was defined, and this varied by region (North versus South). By the end of this period, the abolition of slavery was being debated in most of the colonies. Initially in both the North and the South, the slaves were treated in essentially the same way as the White indentured servants. Many of them married, had children, and were freed after a relatively long period of service. Their children were born free, as were those of the White indentured servants. This indentured service status changed over the next forty years into a system of heritable slavery: the Africans legally became slaves for life, and their children were born as slaves owned by their mothers' masters (Harding, 1981; Meier & Rudwick, 1976; Nash, Jeffrey, et al., 1990).

Virginia and Maryland led the way in the negative changes in African-American status in the South. These included prohibitions against education, ownership of weapons, travel, ownership of property, participation in African religious practices, and any legal rights. White Christians attempted to convert them to Christianity, and in 1667 the Virginia legislature passed an act which stated that a person's state of bondage was unaffected by baptism; i.e., a Christian slave was still a slave.

Slavery in the Northern colonies started in 1638 in Massachusetts. Slaves in New England had the greatest legal and personal rights, including the right to sue their masters. In general, their treatment was relatively mild, and their numbers were quite small. In New York, Pennsylvania, and New Jersey (the Middle Atlantic states), treatment of slaves was less harsh than it was in the South, although their slave laws were quite comparable. In New York City, where about 40 percent of households owned slaves in the early 1700s (Nash et al., 1990), there were occasional slave rebellions, and these were responded to violently by the White militia. Rebellions by slaves occurred in both the North and the South during the Colonization period, and nearly always resulted in the killing and mutilation of the rebellious slaves.

Owing to the growth of the slave trade and the number of Southern plantations, the number of African slaves in the South grew dramatically during the Colonization period. What kept the Africans spiritually alive, even thriving? The answer can be found in three interconnected themes that emerge in the various histories of this period: (1) hope of freedom; (2) family life; and (3) religion. Regarding freedom, most slaves were aware of others who had successfully escaped. They knew of many Africans in the South who had legally acquired their freedom from earnings or through formal emancipation by their owners. Moreover, new slaves from Africa frequently appeared who reminded them of an alternative life to slavery.

Family life was the norm for all slaves, including marriage and child rearing. It was an "after work hours" life that was encouraged by the slave owners because families provided inducements to be compliant and to not escape. Family life was not respected by the owners, who readily split up families to sell any slaves as needed or desired. But the bringing of new children into the world is inherently hopeful, and in the case of slaves, embodied hopes for freedom.

Religious life was a major feature of all the cultures from which the African slaves descended. In the highly segregated plantations they could maintain their old religious practices. When Christianity was forced on them, this produced a merger of the African traditions with the new religion (Berry & Blassingame, 1982). The figures of Moses and Jesus became central to their world view: Moses to lead them to the promised land (freedom) in this life and Jesus to lead them to the promised land in the next.

In the second period of American history, Revolution and Consolidation (1770–1825), essentially nothing positive changed for the Southern slaves. Their numbers increased dramatically, in part because cotton became a highly viable crop "requiring" more slaves, and in part because the White agricultural population expanded in the Southwest. The African slave trade in the United States was officially abolished in 1808. After that date many slaves were smuggled into the South, but the majority of slave traffic was from slaveholders on the east coast to the cotton plantation owners farther west.

Ironically, one of the first men killed in the "Boston Massacre" of 1770 was Crispus Attucks, a runaway slave from Framington, Massachusetts (Berry & Blassingame, 1982). At the conclusion of the Revolutionary War most of the Northern states started to end slavery, and two of the Southern states, Virginia and North Carolina, passed laws encouraging slave owners to emancipate their slaves. By 1820, all the Northern states except New York and New Jersey had abolished slavery, but none of the Southern states, who depended economically on the slaves, did so. Despite strong White antislavery sentiment in the North, there was still much racism among Whites. The abolitionists generally were not interested in promoting racial integration. Many believed equality was impossible owing to the "scientifically proven" inherent inferiority of the Africans. As a consequence of these attitudes, various "colonization" societies were formed whose goal was to help Blacks return to Africa. Most, but not all, Blacks opposed this view.

The life of the free Blacks improved after the Revolutionary War, especially for those in the North, where slavery was rapidly declining. Many of them moved to towns and cities, where they lived in segregated neighborhoods. They formed "mutual benefit" organizations to help other free Blacks get work, housing, food, and perhaps most important, education. Schools were nearly always segregated in the North and the South, but they received more private White support in the North, including money and teachers. Of equal importance to the mutual benefit societies was the establishment of "African" Baptist and Methodist churches independent of the White religious hierarchy. The Black ministers became both religious and secular leaders of their communities. Many Southern Whites opposed these churches for fear that antislavery ideas would be promoted, and periodically broke up religious meetings (Harding, 1981; Meier & Rudwick, 1976).

This historical period came to a close with the Missouri Compromise of 1820. The nation had been rapidly expanding to the west, and Northern Congressmen wanted to prevent the spread of slavery. Maine and Missouri had both applied for statehood in 1820, and the following compromise was reached: Maine would be admitted as a free state and Missouri as a slave state, but no other states north of latitude 36° 30' would be admitted as slave states (Missouri itself was north of that line). Thus, the great conflicts between Northern and Southern states on the issue of slavery were put "on hold."

During the next period, Expansion and Civil War (1825–1865), the number of categories of African-Americans dropped to three: all Northern states abolished slavery by 1830. The slave population increased from approximately 1 1/2 million in 1820 to 4 million in 1860, and the number of free Blacks increased during the same period from about 1/4 million to 1/2 million. The latter were evenly divided between the North and the South (Nash, Jeffrey et al., 1990).

Three events occurred in the early 1830s that had powerful effects on the treatment of Southern slaves and Black free people: Nat Turner's insurrection (1831); the founding of the first antislavery society (1833); and England's abolition of slavery (1833). Nat Turner was a religious and highly regarded slave in Virginia. During a session of deep prayer, he believed he received a message from God telling him to slay his enemies, the White slaveholders. He organized a group of slaves and free Blacks and killed all the Whites they encountered (55 in all), including the husband, wife, and children of the family that owned him (Harding, 1981).

In 1833, William Lloyd Garrison, a White editor of an abolitionist newspaper, along with several other Northern Whites and Blacks, founded the American Anti-Slavery Society. This group and allied organizations heavily propagandized state and federal legislative bodies to abolish slavery.

Finally, although relations between England and the United States frequently were tense, Americans often looked towards the mother country with admiration. In 1833 England abolished slavery in all its colonies, which included the nearby West Indies (slavery had been abolished in England in 1772).

Owing to these events, and the preexisting White slaveholders' fears about rebellion, the noose tightened considerably around Southern African-American necks. Most states passed laws prohibiting manumission of slaves, thus discouraging their hopes of freedom. Regarding free Blacks, unrestricted movement within the home state was limited and movement between states was prohibited. They could not serve on juries or give testimony against Whites. Many states imposed an evening curfew on group meetings. Some states required the attendance of at least one White person at both religious and nonreligious gatherings. Legal ownership of weapons was hindered and consorting with slaves was strongly discouraged. Free Blacks convicted of crimes received more severe punishment than Whites, and those convicted of vagrancy or who were unable to pay their debts were occasionally sold into slavery.

Though conditions for the African-Americans in the North were less restrictive than corresponding conditions in the South, they were discriminated against by Whites in nearly all areas of life. They were not allowed to join state militias or the army. Even when the Civil War broke out in 1861, they could not volunteer. The navy, short on recruits, did accept them, and Blacks accounted for about one fourth of its size. In 1863, Blacks were allowed to join the army and served with distinction. Virtually none, however, were permitted to become officers.

Free Blacks had few political rights. By the 1840s, they were disenfranchised in the majority of Northern states (not, however, in New York or the New England states). Most of the "Old Northwest States," e.g., Ohio, Indiana, Illinois, passed laws in the 1840s prohibiting African-Americans from immigrating into their territories. However, free Blacks organized suffrage societies and state and national conventions directed towards combatting discrimination and attaining equal rights.

Not only were Northern Blacks discriminated against in the political arena, but they suffered job discrimination, education discrimination, and discrimination in housing, transportation, and public accommodations, e.g., hotels and restaurants. Regarding jobs, for example, many leading White abolitionist business owners refused to hire well-qualified Blacks. Generally, new White immigrants from Europe were given preferential job treatment. Race riots against Blacks occurred in most major cities, predominantly perpetrated by lower-income Whites. Public transportation was typically segregated, and hotels and restaurants that catered to Whites refused to accommodate Blacks. Schools were nearly always segregated, and until the 1850s, many Northern states refused to fund public education for Blacks. The theme of colonizing Blacks elsewhere was still prevalent in this period. Lincoln himself held these views about the time of his election to the Presidency.

On the positive side of the ledger, Northern Blacks were relatively free. They ran their own churches and businesses, formed independent antislavery societies, founded newspapers and journals, created organizations to assist fugitive slaves, and received charters from England for fraternal organizations such as the Masons and the Odd Fellows (Northern Whites refused to extend membership to Blacks). Many leaders emerged during this period through these activities and organizations. Some were ex-slaves, such as Frederick Douglass and Sojourner Truth. They were dynamic, impassioned, and gifted in delivering either the written or the spoken "word." David Walker's *Appeal*, a 76-page pamphlet written in 1829, and Martin Delaney's *Condition*, published in 1852, are two of the most powerful works in the tradition of Black protest (Harding, 1981).

At the beginning of the next period, Reconstruction, World War, and Suffrage (1865–1920), Lincoln was assassinated and replaced by Andrew Johnson from Tennessee. Johnson was much more sympathetic to the Southern White plantation owners than to the ex-slaves, and indirectly supported efforts of the former to reinstate Black servitude in the South. Over Johnson's vetoes, Congress passed both the Civil Rights Act of 1866 and the Reconstruction Acts of 1867. These acts brought a light into the South that lasted for 10 years, and was not to return for another 90 years (Nash, Jeffrey, et al., 1990).

Southern Blacks (95 percent of whom were ex-slaves) were mainly interested in economic independence, education, religious freedom, legal protection (nearly always against the Whites) and the right to vote. Regarding economic independence, African-Americans were primarily farmers. They had been promised by General Sherman the opportunity to buy, at reasonable cost, forty acres of land. Few plantation owners (all had their land legally returned to them) agreed to sell. As a consequence, almost all the rural ex-slaves worked as "sharecroppers" or moved to Southern cities, and continued their economic dependence on Whites. The only post-Reconstruction change in this pattern occurred in the twentieth century, when substantial numbers of Blacks moved to Northern cities. In 1920, however, about 85 percent of all African-Americans still lived in the South (Meier & Rudwick, 1976).

Perhaps the most long-lived positive change was in educational opportunities. Immediately after the war, both volunteer and government-sponsored Northerners (nearly all were White) came south and opened schools for the Blacks. These continued throughout and beyond Reconstruction and were augmented by funds from state legislators for public education. Essentially all Southern schools were racially segregated (as were those in the North), and those for Blacks were usually the most impoverished. Many Black leaders and White Northern supporters felt that education of African-Americans should be under control of other African-Americans. But few of the latter had the educational background to teach. As a consequence, wealthy Northerners between 1865 and 1870 paid for the establishment of a number of Black colleges in the South, including Hampton Institute, Fisk, Atlanta, and Morehouse. These continue to be influential institutions at the present time (Berry & Blassingame, 1982).

After the Civil War religious freedom enormously increased for the ex-slaves. Membership in the Negro Baptist church and the African Methodist Episcopal church more than doubled. No longer were the African-Americans restricted by White overseers. They could now openly select their own ministers and freely organize their own services. The church became an even more central part of their lives than it had been before the war. This centrality exists into the present time, with many Black leaders, including Elijah Muhammad, Martin Luther King, and Jesse Jackson, having been trained in the ministry (Nash, Jeffrey, et al., 1990).

Congressional Reconstruction required that African-Americans participate in the development of new state constitutions for the ex-slave states, as well as giving them the right to vote. In South Carolina and Mississippi Blacks made up the majority of the population. In the subsequent voting, Blacks were elected to public office in all the Southern states. Two Black men were elected as United States senators from Mississippi; fourteen were elected from various states to the House of Representatives. None were elected governor, but many were elected lieutenant governor, secretary of state, or state treasurer. Blacks held a very large number of local offices. However, in the presidential election of 1877, a compromise was reached between Northern and Southern congressmen in which Rutherford B. Hayes was selected as president and Reconstruction formally ended. Gradually, but completely, over the next 20 years Blacks became disenfranchised in the South. The light was extinguished. Jim Crow laws were passed in all these states that made it legal to discriminate against Blacks. State and federal courts upheld these laws (Berry & Blassingame, 1982; Meier & Rudwick, 1976).

The Ku Klux Klan was founded in 1866 with the support of all Southern White social strata. Organized and spontaneous violence against Southern African-Americans rapidly became the norm. Race riots in all Southern cities occurred, often with the overt support of the police or elected officials. There appears to have been an economic basis for this violence—Blacks and Whites frequently competed for the same jobs—but also many Whites felt the ex-slaves had to be reminded of their "correct" place in society. There was nothing that African-Americans could do to prevent the violence, and little they could do to protect themselves. Fear and intimidation became a way of life for many of them (Shapiro, 1988).

Prior to the end of this historical period, two important Black-oriented national organizations were founded. In 1909, under the leadership of W. E. B. Du Bois, the NAACP (National Association for the Advancement of Colored People) was established to enhance the civil and political equality of African-Americans. In 1911, the National Urban League, under the influence of Booker T. Washington, was established to improve employment opportunities for African-Americans. These organizations have continued to be influential in both the Black and the White communities into the present time.

In the next period, Prosperity, Depression, and the Second World War (1920–1945), Black migration to the Northern cities continued. It slowed during the Depression years, which were devastating for everyone, especially Black skilled workers. Migration then accelerated during the Second World War, when the demand for workers in defense industries increased (Berry & Blassingame, 1982; Nash et al., 1990). By the end of the War approximately 25 percent of African-Americans lived in the North.

The 1920s brought with them a flowering of Black artists, musicians, and writers that has been referred to as the "Harlem Renaissance" (Aptheker, 1971; Meier & Rudwick, 1976). Centered in New York City initially was a tremendous outpouring of African-American creativity. What was new about this was the magnitude of White support, in terms of both patronage and media commitment. The music and literature of this period especially have been incorporated into American culture and continue to be influential in the present time.

The Harlem Renaissance could not mask the extensive segregation and discrimination in both North and South against African-Americans. There was no lessening of discrimination in housing, civil liberties, education, treatment in the armed forces, and until midway into the war, employment. Regarding jobs in the 1920s, all the major unions refused to allow Black membership. In the 1930s, the CIO accepted large numbers of African-Americans, partly because of idealism, but also because of pressure from the creation of independent Black unions and competition within the AFL, which excluded Blacks until the 1940s.

During the early part of the war, defense industries discriminated against Blacks. But in response to a threatened protest march in Washington, D.C., led by A. Philip Randolph (a Black editor, writer, and union organizer), and pressure from other Black leaders and Eleanor Roosevelt, President Roosevelt issued Executive Order 8802, requiring equal employment opportunities for African-Americans. President Roosevelt also brought into the government, at subcabinet levels, a small number of African-American men and women. The New Deal created many federal jobs, which Blacks came to hold in increasing numbers. This trend continued and today a high proportion of federal jobs are held by Blacks (Berry & Blassingame, 1982; Meier & Rudwick, 1976; Nash et al., 1990).

There was one positive outcome of segregated housing in Northern cities: increased political influence. This was especially true in Chicago, which had a large segregated population. In 1928, African-Americans there elected to Congress the first Black member to be elected anywhere in the United States since 1901. Chicago is comprised of many voting districts, and local political jobs are controlled by the leaders of those districts. The same pattern exists in nearly all large Northern cities, with similar positive results for their African-American populations (Meier & Rudwick, 1976).

Somewhat related to the growth of Black political influence in the North were the widespread and effective activities of the NAACP. It was heavily involved in a large number of cases dealing with African-American civil and political rights. Its most famous case in the 1920s involved the defense (Clarence Darrow was the attorney) of Dr. Ossian Sweet, a physician in Detroit, who was accused of murdering a member of a mob threatening his home and family. Dr. Sweet's acquittal by an all-White jury sitting before a White judge in a racially inflamed city was a victory for everyone. In the 1930s, the NAACP became increasingly controlled by African-Americans, both in the office and courtroom. This trend continues to the present time (Shapiro, 1988).

Throughout the 1920s and 1930s a number of major African-American leaders urged Blacks to pursue the course of separatism, Black nationalism, and Pan-Africanism. These included Marcus Garvey, originally from Jamaica, who founded the Universal Negro Improvement

Association, W. E. B. Du Bois, who organized five national and international Pan-African conferences between 1919 and 1945, and W. D. Fard, who established the Nation of Islam (the Black Muslims). Although these were very diverse groups, they held in common the belief that equal treatment by Whites in the United States was unlikely to occur. They argued that Blacks would benefit the most by joining forces with one another, both here and abroad, to obtain the rights and privileges that all humans deserved. Some members encouraged colonization in Africa; Du Bois himself emigrated there shortly before his death. Others encouraged unofficial or official separatism here. The issue of integration versus separatism has not disappeared in contemporary African-American dialogue, although few Blacks seriously suggest emigration to Africa (Berry & Blassingame, 1982).

In the last period, Postwar Growth and Change (1945–the present), substantial gains in justice, equality, and self-determination occurred for African-Americans. These gains came about primarily through the continued activities of the NAACP in the courts, commitment to social change on the part of Presidents Truman, Kennedy, and Johnson, and Black activism, frequently supported by White participants. It can be argued that the most central factor, directly or indirectly, in continued positive changes for African-Americans was their ability to elect public officials.

Three of the signal events in the 1940s were the beginning of racial integration in professional sports (Jackie Robinson broke the color line in baseball in 1947), President Truman's barring of race discrimination in federal agencies, and Truman's desegregation of the military by executive order in 1948. The impact of military desegregation was profound; moreover, it was enhanced three years later, when integrated combat units were sent to Korea. The military academies started accepting African-Americans, and the number of senior Black officers started to increase. From the 1960s to the present, the military engaged in two more wars, with Black and White servicemen performing equivalently. Even though the percentage of Black officers was still lower in 1996 than that of Whites, the highest-ranking member of the Joint Chiefs of Staff, Colin Powell, was an African-American (Berry & Blassingame, 1982; Nash et al., 1990).

Three of the most important events of the 1950s were the decision by the Supreme Court in 1954 banning school segregation; the successful bus boycott in Montgomery, Alabama led by Rosa Parks and Martin Luther King, Jr., in 1955 (about one year later the Supreme Court banned bus segregation); and the Congressional Civil Rights Act of 1957, which further guaranteed voting rights. Black activists and White supporters coordinated their efforts to get these laws implemented. Many White Southerners, including elected officials, often violently resisted these changes. Integration of public transportation occurred relatively rapidly. Integration of Southern schools, including colleges and universities, however, came very slowly; e.g., in 1962 only 8 percent of Black children attended integrated schools (Berry & Blassingame, 1982; Meier & Rudwick, 1976; Nash et al., 1990).

Voting rights in the South came slowly. However, the congressional Voting Rights Act of 1965, which suspended literacy and other voter tests, in conjunction with voter registration drives by Black and White activists, dramatically increased the pool of Black voters. As a consequence, the number of elected Black officials in the South rose enormously, e.g., from 72 in 1965 to more than 1600 in 1974. This trend continued through the 1970s and 1980s, when an African-American was elected governor of Virginia. In both the North and the South, African-Americans were elected mayors of our largest cities, and many were sent to the House of Representatives (Meier & Rudwick, 1976).

African-Americans continued to migrate to Northern and Western cities during the 1950s and 1960s. Since 1970, only slightly more than 50 percent of African-Americans have been living in the South. These population movements have had little effect on a persistent civil rights problem: contact with the criminal justice system. Blacks are arrested more frequently than Whites, are sentenced to prison more frequently, and serve longer sentences. There are relatively few African-American policemen, district attorneys, judges, or prison officials. Berry and Blassingame (1982) point out that Black urban riots have often been triggered by Blacks' perceptions of police brutality towards them. The 1992 riot in Los Angeles is consistent with this view.

The decades of the 1950s and 1960s saw the peak of Black activism. Two important themes, for the present purposes, characterize this period: separation versus integration and violent versus nonviolent methods of achieving African-American goals. To some extent both themes became transformed into a single theme involving Black political power, Black pride, and Black nationalism. The assassinations of Malcolm X in 1965 and Martin King in 1968 probably contributed to the decline of a strategy of violence. The election to public office of African-Americans indicated that Black activism could be directed more towards voting and less towards protest. Black nationalism emphasizes the connection that African-Americans have with one another through a positive common heritage. A major goal of Black nationalism is a pluralistic society rather than a melting pot, with differences between groups being valued (Berry & Blassingame, 1982; Meier & Rudwick, 1976).

The subtitle of Vincent Harding's 1981 book *There Is a River* is "The Black Struggle for Freedom in America." The struggle continues today, reflected in the socialization experiences of young African-American boys and girls. They have to be ever vigilant and have to continue to fight for rights that have not yet been attained. But the history of African-Americans, especially that of the post–World War II period, indicates that ultimately they will succeed.

Brief Educational History of American Deaf Children

Unlike the cultural histories of females and Blacks, those concerning deaf people usually start with a family tragedy: hearing parents learn that their child was born deaf, or through illness or accident has become deaf. Their normal child thus becomes transformed into an abnormal one, or in contemporary parlance, a handicapped or disabled one.[1] To a large extent it is the psychological consequences of that tragedy that have determined the socialization and education of the deaf (Benderly, 1980; Lane, 1984; Sachs, 1989).

Nearly all parents everywhere want what is best for their child. That desire typically involves an expectation that the child will lead a life similar to theirs, get married, have children, be economically self-sufficient, and stay involved with the family of origin. Physically and mentally handicapping conditions often interfere with one or more of these desired outcomes. Historically, deafness and its concomitant, the absence of speech, interfered more profoundly than other conditions, including blindness and lameness. Deaf people without speech in a hearing society were perhaps the most isolated of disabled individuals. Because of an absence of spoken language, their social interactions were limited, as was their knowledge of the immediate environment. Without an adequate symbol system, deaf, nonspeaking people are unable to adequately understand many social and physical events surrounding them (Lane, 1984; Moores, 1982).

However, in North America there has long been another group of families including deaf children that did not experience this tragedy: families in which one or both parents were deaf and used sign language. Their children were not perceived as abnormal, nor were they socially or intellectually handicapped. These children readily learned to communicate fully with their parents and easily became part of a deaf community. Their development was usually normal in all ways (except hearing, of course), and they eventually married (about 80 percent marrying

---

[1] A similar tragedy occurs for parents of mentally retarded children.

other deaf people), became economically independent, had children (about 80 percent of whom have had normal hearing), and in some cases even earned Ph.D.s (Gannon, 1981; Padden & Humphries, 1988). Remarkably, there is no evidence whatsoever to indicate that deafness by itself necessarily interferes with any aspect of a child's development (this, of course, is consistent with "experiential canalization").

The community that nonverbal deaf individuals fully participate in need not consist of even a majority of deaf people. But they must be a "signing" community. Nora Ellen Groce (1985) describes a large network of villages on Martha's Vineyard, a Massachusetts island, in which everyone signed, from approximately 1700 to 1952. It turns out that there was a great deal of intermarriage on the island, which frequently exposed a recessive gene for deafness. In some villages as many as one fourth of the people were deaf, and nearly every person on the island had deaf relatives. In these villages everyone signed and thus freely communicated with one another. Often the hearing individuals would communicate among themselves by signing rather than speech. The last deaf member of this community died in 1952. In interviews with hearing people who had grown up with deaf ones, the latter were never remembered as handicapped, and indeed, without prodding, the interview subjects did not even remember them as having been deaf.

The history of American deaf children is generally not as benign as that of the Martha's Vineyard villages. There are some parallels with the history of American females and African-Americans, in that two of the major foci and stumbling blocks for the deaf have been education and employment. The theme of separatism versus pluralism versus integration has played a continuous role in the treatment of the deaf, as it has in that of females and Blacks. Also, all three groups have had to combat prejudices and discrimination concerning their "handicaps," i.e., deafness, femininity, and race. Yet, the handicap of deafness feels different from the other two conditions. There's a quality of "correctability" about it that's quite different from the characteristics of gender and race. Hearing parents of deaf children, especially those from the middle and upper social classes, have always sought ways to make their children as normal as possible, i.e., as much like hearing children as possible, and to make them lead "normal" lives, i.e., lives like theirs. However, in this process of attempted normalization, they often have overprotected and stigmatized their children. Hearing parents frequently isolated their deaf offspring from certain kinds of experiences, e.g., riding bikes in the neighborhood, playing sports with hearing children. Overprotection may be a form of stigmatization, in that it assumes "incompleteness." But stigmatization has often been more overt, displayed in behaviors such as discouraging "signing" as well as disguising hearing aids (Benderly, 1980; Gannon, 1981; Higgins, 1980; Lane, 1984).

What is deafness? The answer is very complex, involving historical period and many other factors, particularly the availability of useful hearing aids, degree of residual hearing, age of onset, and whether one's parents were deaf (Padden & Humphries, 1988; Quigley & Paul, 1986). To go through all the combinations of these variables would not be very productive for the present purposes, so we will consider only a few of them. Degree of hearing loss is one starting point. Can the individual process spoken language readily? Can she process it readily with an excellent hearing aid? Severely and profoundly deaf persons cannot do so, but they do have some residual hearing. "Stone" deafness is rare. Hearing aids for those who are less impaired may be useful in quiet settings for one-to-one conversations. But in noisy settings or with more than two people talking, children (and adults) often turn them off. Portable hearing aids started to become widely available in 1900, so that date is an important historical demarcation.

The crucial question concerning age of onset (prior to about 1950 most deaf children acquired their impairment from illness) was whether the loss occurred before (prelingual) or after (postlingual) the development of spoken language. Most writers point to age 3 as a useful marker for this, but clearly a child deafened at 16 years has very different language skills and knowledge from one deafened at 3 years.[2] Finally, deaf children of signing deaf parents start to acquire a useful language and communication system during their first year of life. Deaf children of nonsigning, hearing parents usually must wait a considerably longer time until they start to acquire any language. This delay can have dramatic intellectual and social consequences.

It is useful to consider four periods in the history of education of the deaf (Lou, 1988): 1817–1860, Manual Approaches; 1860–1900, Growth of Oralism; 1900–1960, Domination of Oralism; and 1960–the present, Total Communication Approaches. The central dispute throughout the entire history has been whether deaf children should be educated by manual methods, i.e. some form of hand signing, or by oral methods, i.e. speaking English. Until the most recent period, this was usually argued as an "either-or" issue. However, those who strongly advocated manual approaches acknowledged that for some postlingually impaired children, speech instruction would be useful. At the heart of the dispute was a set of wishes and beliefs about deaf children and sign language. Those who advocated oral methods wished that the children

[2]Historically, approximately 1 in 2000 American children have been profoundly or severely prelingually deaf (Gannon, 1981; Lane, 1984). However, the total number of hard-of-hearing and deaf children is closer to 1 in 300 (Moores, 1982).

could be normal and be fully integrated into the normal (hearing) society. They believed that sign language, at best, was a primitive and inadequate version of spoken language. They further believed that exclusive reliance on sign language would interfere with children's development and thought processes, make them unemployable for skilled work, socially isolate them from their families, and force them into an inferior deaf community (Lane, 1984). The arguments against sign language, especially between 1860 and 1900, were often virulent and not founded on fact. As will be seen, they were wrong in many ways. The amount of heat generated by many of the oralists without the shedding of light was still another tragedy for the deaf.

Chance plays a major part in the story of the first period. In 1815 Thomas H. Gallaudet was hired by some wealthy New Englanders to go to Europe to learn the methods for teaching deaf children so that a school for them could be set up in Connecticut. He first went to England to learn oral methods from the Braidwood family, which apparently was running successful schools there. For financial reasons the Braidwoods refused to teach him, and by chance Gallaudet was told about the highly successful French manual methods introduced by Abbe de l'Epee in 1755. Gallaudet went to France, was welcomed by l'Epee's successors, and started to learn the French methods and sign language. He persuaded Laurent Clerc, a deaf teacher of the deaf in the French schools, to leave Paris to help him set up his school. They returned in 1816 and in 1817 opened their public school, the first in America.

American Sign Language (ASL) is a direct outgrowth of French Sign Language, with about a 50 percent vocabulary overlap today. ASL is not signed English, but rather has a different grammatical structure. For example, an ASL translation of "I gave a man a book" is "I-give-him man book" (Padden & Humphries, 1988). In order to make English speech and sign language nearly identical, additional signs have to be employed, e.g., to mark tense and number. Initially, in the American school, as in the French schools, these additional signs were used in the classroom, thus paralleling the relation between spoken and written English. A major problem with signed English is that the additional grammatical signs aren't really necessary for understanding, and indeed, may interfere with it. As in the French schools, the students "talked" to each other outside of class in the more natural sign language (ASL). By 1835, signed English was dropped and instruction occurred in ASL (Lane, 1984).

In 1818 the New York School for the Deaf opened, and between then and 1860, more than two dozen others followed throughout the country. All used ASL as the primary mode of instruction, and most of the principals and chief teachers had been students of Laurent Clerc (Lou, 1988). In this period about 60 percent of the teachers were hearing male college graduates who learned their craft on the job. About 40 percent of the teachers were deaf themselves and had been students in one of the schools for the deaf. With few exceptions, these schools were residential, i.e. boarding schools, and students returned home on weekends and/or during vacation periods. The minimum age of enrollment was never lower than 8 years, and the average age of enrollment was about 11 or 12. For the overwhelming majority of children, these schools were their first introduction to the deaf community and their first fully social lives. Given that nearly all of the prelingual deaf were without spoken language, and illiterate, it is difficult to imagine what their pre-residential-school lives were like.

The period from 1860 to 1900 saw the beginning and growth of strictly oral instruction in North America. Although the manualists had a clear field until this time, three factors worked against their continuing exclusive control. First, there were strong, and apparently highly successful, strictly oralist schools in Germany and England, two countries in which many Americans had their cultural roots, and all had their intellectual roots. Second, several prominent American educators and scientists, as early as Horace Mann in 1844, went to England and Germany to learn about oral methods and came back home enthusiastic about them. Third, many teachers of the deaf and most parents of postlingually deaf children believed that speech training would be highly desirable. In 1867 two purely oral schools opened, one in New York and one in Massachusetts. They were not necessarily antimanual, but rather enrolled postlingually deaf children who did not have profound or severe hearing losses. In 1865, the National Deaf-Mute College (in 1894 renamed Gallaudet College) was opened with Gallaudet's son, Edward Miner Gallaudet, as its chief executive. Although instruction was primarily in ASL, Edward argued strongly that oral methods, including "speechreading," should be emphasized for those who could benefit by it (Lane, 1984; Lou, 1988). In 1869, Horace Mann opened the first permanent day school, and purely oral methods were used.

Between 1870 and 1890 Alexander Graham Bell (the inventor) carried out an active campaign promoting purely oral methods and disparaging manual ones. Although his wife was deaf, he developed a set of genetic principles whose goal was to prevent inherited deafness. That he persisted in the latter is amazing given the then available knowledge that deaf parents primarily have hearing offspring and that more than 90 percent of deaf children have hearing parents (Lane, 1984). In 1880, the International Congress on Education of the Deaf met in Milan, Italy. The deck was stacked against manual methods; the participants voted overwhelmingly to suppress these methods and adopt strictly oral methods of teaching. The five Americans attending voted against these resolutions (Lane, 1984). The impact in Europe was almost immediate— teaching in sign was abolished—and of course, the voting had supported those Americans pressing for pure oralism. By 1900, approximately 50 percent of deaf students were taught by oral methods.

Two other significant educational changes occurred during this period. First, the percentage of both hearing male teachers and deaf male and female teachers declined markedly. The reduction in deaf teachers is explained by the growth of oral methods, whereas the increase in women teachers was likely caused by their lower pay scale relative to that of men. By the end of the century, approximately two-thirds of the teachers were hearing, non-college-educated women, and only about 20 percent of all teachers were deaf (down from 40 percent prior to 1860). Second, many of the day schools, all of which used purely oral methods, started accepting young children, some as young as 3 years old. Thus, hearing parents could more readily participate in their children's early education.

The next period, 1900–1960, brought to an end purely manual instruction, and in almost all schools, instruction by ASL was prohibited. By the end of the First World War, Lane (1984) estimates, 95 percent of deaf students were receiving instruction in spoken English. Thus, the central goal of schools for the deaf became the teaching of English skills. Students spent an enormous part of their day in listening, speaking, and speechreading. Where manual methods were used, they served only to augment the understanding of English, e.g., finger-spelling or signed English, not to transmit information or promote thinking skills. Profoundly or severely prelingually deaf individuals received even more of this combined instruction than others, because they had so much more to learn.

Three factors contributed to the nearly complete victory of oralism. First, battery-operated hearing aids became available in 1900, followed by vacuum tube hearing aids in 1921 and transistor hearing aids in 1950. These were dramatic improvements both in amplification and portability over the earlier sound-capturing devices. Hearing aids became analogous to prescription eyeglasses, in that they allowed children to be normalized. Second, a more integrative, scientific approach to understanding deafness and teaching spoken language to the deaf emerged. The leader in this new approach was Dr. Max Goldstein, who founded the Central Institute for the Deaf in 1914. His "acoustic method" was applicable for anyone who had any residual hearing, and not just those who were mildly or moderately hard of hearing (Gannon, 1981; Lou, 1988). The third factor was the accumulation of research comparing the academic achievement of those taught by predominantly manual methods to that of those taught by predominantly oral methods. Quigley and Paul (1986) have summarized much of the significant data collected between 1916 and 1927. In these studies students taught by purely oral methods, especially those in day schools, displayed, on average, reading and English language understanding skills that were about one year higher than the comparable skills of children taught by manual methods. However, these same studies showed that deaf high school graduates were performing at about only a fourth- or fifth-grade level. Further gains in reading and language for the deaf after about age 15 were quite small.

The current period, 1960 to the present, is witness to the dethronement of pure oralism in favor of "total communication" methods. These primarily consist of the simultaneous use of spoken and signed English during instruction as well as the teaching of finger-spelling, speechreading, and manual signing. The two central goals of total communication are to teach English and to teach educational content. Currently only a minority of schools still adhere to pure oralism (Benderly, 1980; Moores, 1982). Several factors contributed to the demise of oralism. First, as noted in the previous paragraph, oralism was an academic failure. The data for the early part of the twentieth century, unfortunately, were replicated in studies carried out 50 years later (Quigley & Paul, 1986). Not only were deaf students far behind in English; they lagged behind hearing students in all content areas. Moreover, only a small percentage of prelingual deaf ever developed understandable speech, and only a minority could "read" speech effectively.

Second, a wealth of research became available during the 1960s that clearly showed that deaf children of deaf parents, i.e., students who knew ASL well, performed much better academically than those of hearing parents, i.e., those who didn't know ASL. Often, the former students performed as well as hearing children. Moores (1982) notes that proportionately, far more deaf children of deaf parents go to college than do deaf children of hearing parents.

Third, a series of studies by William Stokoe, starting in 1960, convincingly showed what most signing deaf had known all along: that ASL was a genuine natural language capable of all the subtlety and profundity of thought manifested by spoken English. This legitimation of ASL helped remove much of the stigma placed upon ASL in both the hearing and the deaf communities.

Fourth, the academic failures of oralism led to an increased emphasis on, and enrollment of children in, preschool education for the deaf. The reasoning was that oralism failed because it wasn't started early enough. Moores (1982) summarizes research indicating that no positive lasting effects on academic achievement have been found for those receiving preschool oral education.

Fifth, a reanalysis of the earlier research favoring oral over manual instruction showed that the children receiving oral instruction had had higher IQs and better entering language skills than those receiving manual instruction. In short, the studies had been biased to favor oralism (Quigley & Paul, 1986).

At the present time, there is no one method of "total communication." The field is in flux, but ongoing research should indicate how best to match type of teaching method with type of deaf child (Schlesinger, 1986).

Two other changes have occurred in the current historical period that are at least partially related to the civil rights movement of the 1960s. First, pluralism as an accepted mode of minority status started becoming applicable to the deaf. In this regard, the National Theater of the Deaf was created in 1966 and began touring the next year. Signing and captioned speech started to occur on television and are now prominent at political conventions. The children's television program *Sesame Street* has a character who uses ASL. Local deaf clubs and deaf athletic competition have become commonplace. There are several deaf national organizations. There is a deaf culture that is different from the hearing culture, and relies on ASL. The members of this culture usually have a history of residential education, as well as other experiences unique to the deaf (Padden & Humphries, 1988). Some deaf people comfortably move in and out of this culture, periodically joining with the hearing, but others do not, because of their incapacities with spoken English.

The second change involves the types of schooling available to the deaf. Federal legislation guaranteeing equal educational access and freedom of choice for "least restrictive" educational environments have caused dramatic shifts in patterns of school enrollment. Opportunities for college education, including technical education, now extend far beyond Gallaudet College in Washington, D. C. There are other programs on both coasts and in the heartland. The "least restrictive" law has required local public school districts to provide adequate "in-house" schooling for deaf children residing in their communities. This has resulted in a dramatic decrease in residential school enrollment and a dramatic increase in integrated classrooms, i.e., mainstreaming. It is not at all clear whether the effects of these latter changes will in the long run be positive or negative for either the social or intellectual achievements of deaf persons.

Looking back over this 175-year history, we can see civil rights gains for the deaf, and a decline in the stigmatization of deafness.

However, it is not yet clear whether there have been appreciable educational gains for profoundly and severely prelingually deaf children of hearing parents. The chief stumbling block appears to be their relative deprivation of a working language relationship with their parents, which may in part be brought about by stigmatization. Many of these parents are unwilling or unable to learn ASL and to continuously use it with their prelingually deaf children. As a consequence, these children often have marked language and conceptual deficits, which hamper progress in formal educational settings. Many have argued that bilingualism should be the goal of deaf education: using ASL and reading/writing English. But until parents commit themselves to learning and using ASL, the bilingual goal will be achieved with difficulty and with possible consequent academic deficits for the children. For children who can readily benefit from the use of hearing aids, or who were deafened well after spoken language was acquired, the picture is more optimistic. Many of them do well academically and have well-adjusted social lives.

Brief Educational History of American Children with Mental Retardation

Although there are some similarities between the educational histories of deaf and of mentally retarded children, the differences are more pronounced. There has rarely been a problem in identifying a young child as normally hearing versus hearing impaired. Certainly there are degrees of impairment, and occasionally deafness and mental retardation have been confused. But in nearly all cases, children who appear to be normal but who cannot speak and cannot understand spoken language are hearing impaired. The degree of impairment has its main effect on the ease of teaching the child to speak and to understand speech. Identification of mental retardation has usually been much more difficult; its definition has varied considerably with the historical period; and the degree of retardation has dramatically affected how children were educated and cared for. Although deafness and sign language have received and still do receive stigmas, these stigmas are mild compared to the frequent compulsory segregation and the history of sterilization of retarded persons.

As noted in the previous section, the incidence of deaf and hard-of-hearing children is about 1 in 300. The incidence of mental retardation—at any degree from mild to profound—is about 3 in 100, a rate nine times greater than that of hearing impairment (Patton, Payne, & Beirne-Smith, 1990). Those who are mildly retarded generally look and act like normally developing children, but progress socially and intellectually at a slower rate, and reach a lower level of final development. This retardation is often not identified until they are 5 or 6 years old. Many marry and have children. Those who are profoundly retarded look different and act very differently from normally developing children, develop at a far slower and different rate, and have much lower social and intellectual attainments. Many in this group never learn to talk or to gain bowel control. Approximately 75 percent of mentally retarded people fall in the mild range, about 20 percent in the moderate range (these individuals have sometimes been described as "trainable"), and about 5 percent in the profound range (Patton et al., 1990; Zigler & Hodapp, 1986).

There are three basic types of causes of mental retardation. The first Zigler and Hodapp (1986) refer to as "familial." This is most often mild retardation genetically transmitted from one or both parents who are themselves mildly retarded. The second type is genetically transmitted by nonretarded parents (97 percent of these parents are not retarded), and usually involves brain damage produced by some genetic anomaly, e.g., Down Syndrome, Fragile X syndrome. The children are usually moderately to severely retarded. The third type is produced by environmental insults during fetal development; at birth, e.g., oxygen deprivation; or in early childhood, e.g., lead poisoning. The children may be severely, moderately, or mildly retarded. Zigler and Hodapp suggest that a fourth possible type, retardation produced by lack of environmental stimulation, is rare. It is important to note that regardless of the causes, the level of retardation reached can be positively or negatively affected by the social, emotional, and intellectual environment the children are reared in.

Based on a reading of the books listed, which in whole or part deal with the history of the education of mentally retarded persons in North America, four major historical periods can usefully be identified (Kanner, 1964; Pasanella & Volkmon, 1981; Patton et al., 1990; President's Committee on Mental Retardation, 1976, 1977; Rotatori, Schwenn, & Fox, 1985; and Wallin, 1955). The first period is 1848–1896, Residential Care; the second is 1896–1950, Special Education and Sterilization; the third is 1950–1975, Advocacy and Expanded Education; and the fourth is 1975–the present, Deinstitutionalization, Mainstreaming, and Inclusion.

A central underlying theme that cuts across all four periods is the question of how much change towards normal development can be produced by educational interventions. Although the European pioneers in this field in the early 1800s initially believed that retarded children could be completely normalized, this gave way by 1850 to the belief that at best only substantial gains could be obtained. At certain points in this history many maintained that no gains were possible, and indeed, that mentally retarded people were dangerous to society. Few people hold the "danger" view any more, but it subtly became transformed into a belief that mental retardation is harmful to society, at least in financial costs, but probably also in social costs. As an example of this attitude, each year tens of thousands of pregnant women pay for amniocentesis, an expensive surgical test to determine whether their fetus has a genetic defect. Nearly all of these women pay for an abortion if the test results show that their child will be mentally retarded.

Although in 1818 some mentally retarded children were temporarily placed in the Hartford School for the Deaf, the first historical period, Residential Care, started in 1848. In that year the state of Massachusetts, at the urging of Samuel Gridley Howe, paid for the residential education of 10 mentally retarded children in a wing of the Perkins Institute for the Blind. Several other public residential institutions were opened in the next 10 years, and by 1898 24 institutions existed in 19 different states. There were also a number of private institutions, but these comprised less than 10 percent of the residential population. In 1876 the medical directors of these public and private schools formed a national association and published a journal. That association exists today as the American Association on Mental Retardation (Patton et al., 1990).

Who were the residents of these early institutions? As previously stated, the definition of mental retardation has changed considerably with historical period. Since intelligence tests did not emerge in the United States until 1910, other means of identification were employed, mainly in the context of medical diagnosis and examination of social functioning. The first students were generally 7 to 14 years old and primarily cretins (children with severe mental deficiency caused by severe thyroid deficiency), those with Down Syndrome (then known as "mongolism"), those with very slow language development, and children with serious behavior-control problems. Excluded from these schools were all children whom the directors believed could not be developmentally improved. These included the "insane," children who were epileptic, paralyzed, or severely brain injured, and children with hydroencephaly (markedly enlarged heads). From the point of view of mild, moderate, profound, and severe retardation, it appears that most of the residents were moderately retarded, with a small proportion in the mild range (some of those who had behavior problems) and a small proportion in the profound and severe range.

Wolfensberger (1976) divides this historical period into three partially overlapping stages. In the first, from 1848 to 1880, the goals of the residential schools were to educate these children so that they would develop (to use Hervey Wilbur's words of 1852) "nearer the common standard of humanity, in all respects, more capable of understanding and obeying human laws; of perceiving and yielding to moral obligations; more capable of self-assistance, of self-support, of self-respect, and of obtaining the greatest degree of comfort and happiness with their small means" (Wolfensberger, 1976, p. 49).

The institutions in this first stage were small, typically containing 10 to 20 children. They were seen as analogous to boarding schools, from which the students would be returned to society to carry out useful roles. The directors of these schools believed that by segregating the retarded children and giving them loving care and education in a family-type context, they could cause the desired outcomes to occur.

By 1870 some data concerning success were in. Probably no more than 20 percent of the residents were able to return to their communities and become self-sufficient. Moreover, the nature of the institutions had changed dramatically. They had become much larger and admitted many children who were unlikely to ever attain self-sufficiency. Long waiting lists developed. These problems worsened over the next 10 years. In this second stage, from 1870 to 1890, the institutions became transformed from "schools" into "asylums," whose main goal was permanent custodial care.

Given this goal, three trends occurred in the development of these institutions (Wolfensberger, 1976). They were built in isolated locations, far from urban centers, presumably to increase the happiness of the inmates. Second, they were substantially enlarged, presumably for the benefit of the residents, e.g., they could be protected more easily, they would have more of their "own kind" to associate with. Third, they were run in increasingly economical ways. The increased size helped to accomplish this, but also costly educational programs were eliminated. In many cases the institutions ran farms, and occasionally the most able residents were kept on the farms to work (with no wages) rather than being returned to the community.

In Wolfensberger's third stage, 1880 to 1900, mentally retarded individuals were progressively seen as a social menace that should be controlled. Not only were the institutions a financial drain, but many started to believe that retarded individuals had criminal instincts, were sexually promiscuous, were prone to alcoholism, and in general, lowered the moral standards of the community. Many directors of institutions and politicians argued that those who were retarded should not be allowed to marry, should be sexually segregated within institutions, and should even be sterilized. At least three events occurred that supported these attitudes. A famous study of the Jukes family was published in 1877 that "showed" the close links over many generations between criminality, immorality, and mental retardation (a well-known comparable study on the Kallikaks was published in 1912). Second, many young mentally retarded criminals were, in fact, being sent to these institutions for custodial care. Third, a strong eugenics movement emerged in the 1870s, based on Darwin's theory. Recall that Alexander Graham Bell was then advocating eugenic control of the deaf. Thus, in this first historical period, "hope" became transformed into "fear."

The next historical period, 1896 to 1950, started with the establishment of the first special class for mentally retarded students in a day school in Providence, Rhode Island (Kanner, 1964). The idea of special classes (as opposed to residential care) spread rapidly in the next 10 years to many major cities. With few exceptions, during this entire period these special classes were for children who were mildly retarded. The first training school for teachers of special classes opened in 1905.

As noted above, placement in residential asylums had been based on medical diagnosis and social behavior. These criteria excluded the vast majority of mentally retarded children, who behaved acceptably and were normal in appearance. So, what happened when special classes were established for these latter children? Basically, compulsory education created a new category of children with social problems: children who learned very slowly and couldn't keep up with their more intelligent peers. They were not much of a problem initially, because in 1880 only 6 percent of all children over the age of 13 were enrolled in school. Moreover, the younger children (90 percent of whom were enrolled) attended class about half as many days as do children today (Fishbein, 1984). As school terms lengthened and more adolescents went to high school (about 30 percent in 1920), those among them who were mildly retarded became a greater social problem.

The number of special education classes grew rapidly until about 1920, from which time they remained stable, until about 1950. Although most educators saw the potential benefits of special education for mildly mentally retarded children, state legislatures were reluctant to increase funding for them. Indeed, legislation was frequently passed to exclude many moderately, severely, and profoundly retarded from school altogether. Thus, the overwhelming majority of these children had essentially no educational opportunities.

The second major event during this period was the adaptation in 1911 of the Binet-Simon intelligence tests for North Americans. Binet and Simon were two French scientists who were asked by the French government to devise a test to determine the most appropriate type of schooling for retarded children. Their scale, which measured mental age, first appeared in 1905 in France. In the United States, as in other countries, educators for the first time had an objective means for assessing the educability of its children. The term "mildly retarded" eventually emerged from this test and described children whose intelligence quotient, or IQ (mental age divided by chronological age), was between 2 and 3 standard deviations below average, i.e., between 55 and 70. School systems and state legislatures started to make educational and funding decisions for retarded children based on their IQ scores. Social adaptation level still was used to assess degree of retardation, but it took a distant second place to IQ.

The third major event during this period was the widespread enactment of eugenics laws. Indiana passed the first sterilization law for the mentally retarded in 1907. By 1926, 23 states had them, and by 1930, 30 states had passed laws permitting involuntary sterilization of retarded individuals. In 1927 the United States Supreme Court in an 8-1 vote declared these laws constitutional. The great jurist Oliver Wendell Holmes wrote the majority opinion, in which he declared, "Three generations of imbeciles are enough," referring to the genetic transmission of mental retardation. It is estimated that as many as 40,000 "mentally retarded" individuals were sterilized, the last probably in Virginia in 1972. It appears from the diatribes in favor of involuntary sterilization that a high percentage of those labeled as "retarded" were criminals, prostitutes, never-married mothers, and paupers who were residents of the asylums. They were sterilized to prevent further reproduction of "morally inferior" citizens.

After about 1935 involuntary sterilization slowed down considerably. Many of the early ardent advocates changed their minds. Some did so for humanitarian reasons, but most did so because sterilization didn't seem to work. Only a small percentage of those eligible were actually being sterilized, and recent scientific evidence had indicated that the links between criminality and mental retardation were weak. Thus concluded quite an extraordinary historical period in the treatment of the mentally retarded, one that indicated the inhumaneness and destructive power of prejudice and ignorance.

The third period (1959–1975), Advocacy and Expanded Education, started with the founding of the National Association for Retarded Children, a group mainly comprised of parents of mentally retarded children. By 1959 it had about 50,000 members, including a large number of professional workers involved with research and teaching in mental retardation. This group has strongly and persistently advocated for more research on, more and better educational opportunities for, and more humane treatment of the mentally retarded.

Two other organizations made up predominantly of professionals also had a strong impact on changing attitudes and practices towards the retarded: the American Association on Mental Deficiency (AAMD) and the Council for Exceptional Children (CEC). The AAMD membership grew from 664 in 1940 to approximately 12,000 in 1975. The organization took very active positions on setting standards for facilities and delivery of services, litigation on behalf of the retarded, development of social policy, and support of research. The CEC is concerned with all exceptional children. Its membership grew from 3,500 in 1938 to 67,000 in 1975. In 1963 it created a division on mental retardation. Its goals are similar to those of the AAMD, but it places more emphasis on promoting research concerning education of retarded individuals and on developing legislation to benefit retarded persons.

A fourth major nongovernmental organization that strongly advocated for the mentally retarded was the Joseph P. Kennedy, Jr. Foundation, founded in 1946. The foundation was named for the older brother of the then future president of the United States. It became a powerful influence in the field after John F. Kennedy assumed the presidency in 1961. Important legislation creating research centers and the National Institute of Child and Human Development was affected by efforts of this foundation. The foundation either gave substantial monies, or helped raise money, for research, education, and clinical treatment. It was also instrumental in creating the Special Olympics and other physical fitness programs for retarded persons. Through its contributions to the President's Panel on Mental Retardation of 1962, it helped determine the future course of government action on behalf of retarded individuals.

Thus, in a trend starting in 1950 and greatly enhanced by the election of a strongly supportive U.S. president in 1961, mental retardation came out of the closet and started to occupy a more central stage in the educational arena. The most dramatic changes occurred in special education programs, predominantly for the mildly retarded. In 1950 fewer than 100,000 children were enrolled in such programs. This number rose to about 250,000 in 1962, 750,000 in 1970, and 1,250,000 in 1975. Public advocacy provided the push, but federal and state legislatures provided the money, and teacher's colleges and school systems provided the personnel. During this same historical period, moderately retarded students (with IQs from about 30 to 55) received expanded educational opportunities. In some states, separate schools for the handicapped were created. These accommodated small numbers of moderately retarded children who could not be taught in the public schools. For the profoundly and severely mentally retarded, little change in residential treatment occurred. There was a growing sentiment, however, in favor of either enhancing educational programs in these institutions or bringing the children home to be educated in their own communities.

In the last historical period (1975–the present), the signal event was the passage in 1975 of Public Law 94-142, the Education for All Handicapped Children Act. There were at least four major provisions of this law affecting education of mentally retarded children: (1) that free appropriate public education be provided for every handicapped child; (2) that this education occur in a "least restrictive environment," which meant that to the extent possible and appropriate, handicapped children be educated in regular classes with nonhandicapped children; (3) that an individualized education program be written for each handicapped child in conjunction with that child's parents; and (4) that due process legal procedures on behalf of the handicapped child be followed if parents and educators cannot agree on the appropriate education for that child. This law also mandated that states provide educational services for handicapped individuals between the ages of 3 and 21 years. During the next few years after 1975, other legislation was enacted that both clarified and expanded this law.

The consequent changes in residential treatment and educational practices were marked. First, what started as a trickle of deinstitutionalization in the 1970s became a flood. The number and size of asylums for the retarded have dramatically been reduced. Currently only the most profoundly retarded and multiply handicapped persons are in institutional care. All the rest are being cared for in the home and educated in the community. Second, moderately retarded children are being educated in public schools, spending some of the time in the same classrooms as normally developing children, in the educational practice of "inclusion" (or "mainstreaming"). Third, many mildly retarded children are being fully included in classrooms with nondisabled students; if trends continue, most will be in the future. This means that the number of retarded children in special education classes has declined since 1975.

Mainstreaming of mildly retarded children has been supported by considerable research showing that segregated retarded students (i.e., those in special classes) perform no better academically than retarded students who are taught in integrated classrooms, but receive tutoring services (Pasanella & Volkmor, 1981). Moreover, recent research has shown that social acceptance by their normally developing peers is greater for integrated than for segregated retarded children, and that self-esteem is higher for integrated than for segregated retarded children (Strain & Kerr, 1981).

From this 145-year history, it is clear that educational opportunities for mentally retarded persons have undergone marked positive changes. The starting point was the recognition that retardation takes many forms, which require different educational experiences. Progress was set back by the unfortunate belief that immorality and retardation were closely linked. Parental advocacy moved things forward again, and progress gained tremendous momentum through the efforts of a charismatic president who had a mentally retarded sister. At the present time, children with mental retardation are increasingly being educationally integrated with their normally developing peers. Normalization processes for mentally retarded individuals are now in high gear, and these promise to ultimately produce a reduction in prejudice and stigmatization.

Comparisons Among the Histories

In the following discussion, I'll first focus on the common features concerned with the maintenance of prejudice and discrimination towards the target groups. Then I'll point out some of the salient differences among them regarding this maintenance. Finally I'll address the issue of changes in prejudice and discrimination.

From the earliest historical period, all four groups occupied a subordinate status in society, and continue in that position today. One can imagine alternative scenarios: groups starting in a dominant position and becoming subordinate, e.g., conquerors who are overthrown; groups starting in a subordinate position and becoming members of the dominant group, e.g., Irish immigrants to the United States in the later nineteenth and early twentieth centuries. The present target groups were initially, and to some extent still are, viewed by the dominant culture, i.e., White males, as being inherently inferior, perhaps as handicapped or incomplete. This presumed inferiority was, and to some extent, still is used as a justification for paternalistic and discriminatory treatment. The dominant groups frequently appealed to, and to some extent still appeal to, "scientific" evidence to support their beliefs, thus giving the appearance of an objective assessment of inferiority. Consistent with an enduring subordinate status, each history contains long-standing themes of prejudice and discrimination, which are modified, transformed, and replayed over time. Very few new "deficits" that feed into prejudice and discrimination have emerged over the course of these histories. An exception to this rule was the transitory linkage between mental retardation and immorality seen in the early part of the twentieth century.

The dominant groups have attempted to control the sexuality, the education, and the job opportunities of all four target groups. Regarding sexuality, regulation and/or prevention periodically have been attempted. Public education has typically been limited and often prohibited. Job opportunities have been controlled through restrictions on educational opportunities, apprenticeships, and hiring practices. At a conscious level, these controls have been exerted because of the presumed inferiority of the target groups. Perhaps at a more unconscious level, the controls have ensured that the status quo would be maintained, that the target groups would stay subordinate.

In the 1960s all target groups and the dominant culture started to deal with the issue of pluralism. Does equality in our culture mean "sameness"? Does "different" imply "inferior," or does "different" imply "different but equal"? Individuals and groups have strengths and weaknesses. As members of the dominant culture have been slowly acknowledging the "equal but different" and "strengths and weaknesses" arguments, this has led to renewed thinking about prejudice and discrimination.

There are notable differences in the histories. Black, deaf, and mentally retarded persons have been consistently stigmatized by the dominant culture. White females have not, though their "limitations" have been pointed out. Contrariwise, unlike the other three groups, women have had their moral strength and leadership acknowledged throughout the entire history. No comparable psychological or moral strengths have been alluded to for the other target groups. Another set of differences relates to whether the target groups had the capacity for normal functioning, i.e., being like White males. Initially, expectations of normalcy were applied to the mentally retarded and the deaf. Following the Civil War, a window opened for African-Americans, but it then closed for about 90 years. After the First World War, such a window opened for women. Currently, expectations based on a broader view of normalcy exclude many of the mentally retarded, but include the other three target groups.

Economic competition is one of the major motivations for White males to attempt to keep Blacks and females in a subordinate position. This motivation seems to be lacking regarding the deaf and mentally retarded, although economic considerations certainly played a role in their treatment. Deaf and mentally retarded children were stigmatized because of their impairments, their deviation from the norm. Unfortunately, efforts by some parents and well-meaning others to make them "normal" have occasionally sustained the stigmatization.

Regarding change, with the possible exception of limited educational progress for some deaf persons, the histories provide evidence that discrimination (and perhaps prejudice) have markedly declined for all the target groups. Opportunities now exist for members of these groups that could only be dreamed of before the Second World War. However, issues of equality and pluralism are not yet sorted out, nor will they be in the near future.

There appear to be three interrelated factors that together led to changes in discrimination, and perhaps prejudice towards all four subordinate groups. These are self-advocacy by members of the subordinate groups (or by their families) for change; advocacy for change by powerful and/or substantial numbers of the dominant group, i.e., White males; and changes in law through either legislation or executive edict.

Self-advocacy was clearly evident among Blacks both prior to and after the Civil War, among women especially after the Revolutionary and Civil Wars, and among families of the deaf and the mentally retarded, for whom family members urged the development of special schools. This form of advocacy brought persistent pressure on the dominant culture to change. It was effective because members of the subordinate groups had developed organizational and leadership skills through the clubs, special interest groups, and churches they belonged to and participated in. There is power in collaboration, as contrasted with individual action, especially if the cause is just.

Powerful members and/or substantial numbers of the dominant group had to take up the causes of the subordinate groups. They were encouraged by the latter in at least two ways: moral persuasion and political influence. From colonial days onwards, there were always members of the dominant groups who felt that prejudice and discrimination were wrong. Through the efforts of the subordinate groups, this sense of "wrongness" became transformed into feelings of obligation to make changes. But many motives for action are always in play, and they have to be weighed before change occurs, e.g., feelings of obligation versus the anticipation of losing status. An added inducement is the threat to political power. When subordinate groups started to influence voters, then the equation for motivation to change was further strengthened.

Finally, changes in the law had to be made in order for widespread decreases in discrimination to occur. These changes were made by powerful members of the dominant culture, aided and influenced by the advocacy of members of subordinate groups. School segregation based on race was declared unconstitutional by nine White men on the United States Supreme Court. The case was argued by a Black lawyer from the NAACP. Passage of women's suffrage, racial integration of the armed forces, and public education for deaf and mentally retarded persons, all came about through changes in the law. And these changes were made by members of dominant groups. Frequently the president of the United States acted alone, as Harry Truman did in racially integrating the armed forces. The federal civil rights laws of the 1960s were an important turning point for all four groups. These groups now had antidiscrimination laws on their side along with high-ranking advocates upholding the laws. Also, they had the courts, which attempted to impartially allow advocates to challenge the ways that the laws were being enforced.

Despite the great progress that has been made, the histories indicate that there is a long way to go to attain the goals of equality and self-determination. But the fact that real progress has occurred gives hope for the future.

Summary

In order to obtain an accurate assessment of the normative and power-conflict causes of prejudice and discrimination, it is necessary to carry out cultural-historical analyses. Two cautions are noted about these analyses for the four target groups: (1) the age groups and content areas considered differ among them; and (2) there is tremendous diversity of experience among members within these target groups.

For American females and African-Americans, six major cultural/historical periods were discussed: 1607–1770, Colonization; 1770–1825, Revolution and Consolidation; 1825–1865, Expansion and Civil War; 1865–1920, Reconstruction, World War, and Suffrage; 1920–1945, Prosperity, Depression, and the Second World War; and 1945–the present, Postwar Growth and Change. Women have made substantial legal, political, economic, military, sexual, and educational gains over this time span. Although they have attained legal equality with men, there is still not functional equality in any of these areas. Some of the greatest gains were made in times of war, when new demands and opportunities occurred for women. Females of different social classes have had very different socialization experiences from the post–Revolutionary War period to the present, which have led to unique opportunities to combat prejudice and discrimination.

During the first cultural/historical period, African-American slaves came to be defined as inheritable bond servants rather than indentured servants. Prior to the Civil War approximately 90 percent of African-Americans were slaves living in the South, 5 percent were "free" in the North, and 5 percent were "free" in the South. But throughout the entire history, freedom for Blacks was never equivalent to that of Whites. For about 10 years after the Civil War, during Reconstruction, an extraordinary window of freedom opened for Southern Blacks. They owned land, attended school, voted, and elected officials to state and federal offices. In the ensuing 90 years, Jim Crow laws were enacted, and gains against discrimination were minimal. The major exception was President Truman's racial integration of the armed forces. From the 1960s to the present, African-Americans have made substantial progress towards the goals of equality, freedom, and self-determination.

Four periods in the history of the education of deaf individuals were discussed: 1817–1860, Manual Approaches; 1860–1900, Growth of Oralism; 1900–1960, Domination of Oralism; and 1960–the present, Total Communication Approaches. Perhaps the central issue of this history has been attempts by adults to make their children "normal," i.e., just like their non-hearing-impaired parents. Deafness has been regarded by the dominant culture as "handicapping" rather than as "disabling"—in other words, deaf people were viewed as incomplete and deficient instead of different. In this context, the educational and communication battles have been over the role of sign language. Initially academic instruction occurred primarily in American Sign Language (ASL). Efforts by Alexander Graham Bell and like-minded oralists eventually led to the prohibition of its use. Subsequent research showed that exclusive reliance on these methods was associated with poor academic progress, and for the profoundly and severely deaf, poor social adjustment with the nonimpaired. Currently, ASL has regained acceptance in educational settings, and instruction occurs in it and in various oral methods.

Four periods in the history of the education of children with mental retardation were discussed: 1848–1896, Residential Care; 1896–1950, Special Education and Sterilization; 1950–1975, Advocacy and Expanded Education; and 1975–the present, Deinstitutionalization, Mainstreaming, and Inclusion. A central underlying theme cutting across all four periods is the question of how much change towards normal behavior can be produced by educational interventions. In the first period, there was widespread belief that with small, family-like residential care and instruction, substantial progress towards normality could be accomplished. During the next period, educational efforts started to shift towards special classes for mildly retarded children and custodial care only for severely and profoundly retarded children. Many retarded adults were involuntarily sterilized because of the presumed link between retardation and criminal activity. During the next two periods parental advocacy and a sympathetic president of the United States paved the way for expanded educational opportunities and more compassionate treatment.

A number of common features emerge concerning the maintenance of prejudice and discrimination towards these groups. Among them are these: the four groups have always held subordinate positions in the culture; all were initially viewed as incomplete or inferior; and the specific themes of prejudice and discrimination for each are long-standing, rather than recently developed. The dominant groups in the culture have attempted, and in many cases continue to attempt, to control the sexuality, education, and job opportunities for these target groups.

There have been notable differences in the histories. For example, the moral strength and leadership of American women has always been acknowledged. Changes in discrimination, and perhaps in prejudice, have been produced by organized self-advocacy, supportive leadership by prominent members of the dominant groups, and changes in the law. Current discussions of pluralism as a goal for a democratic society also further the cause of reducing prejudice and discrimination.

Prejudice
and Discrimination
Towards Opposite-Sex
and Deaf Individuals

Introduction

The juxtaposition of the two sets of studies dealt with in the present chapter is based mainly on convenience rather than on conceptual considerations. Basically, the literatures related to opposite-sex and race prejudice are relatively large, whereas the literatures dealing with deaf and mentally retarded people are relatively small. The pairing of topics in this chapter was arbitrary and atheoretical. A comparison of the four literatures will occur in chapter 5.

There are four goals of this chapter. The first is to understand the methodological issues involved in the study of prejudice and discrimination. As noted in chapter 1, prejudice and negative stereotypes are not equivalent. To what extent can they be distinguished in the published research? In addition, several techniques have been employed in the study of discrimination. What are the unique characteristics of these techniques, and how is generalizability affected? The second goal is to develop predictions for the development of opposite-sex prejudice and discrimination based on genetic/evolutionary and cultural/historical considerations. The third is to describe the socialization of sex-typing, which plays an important role in children's development of opposite-sex prejudice and discrimination. Sex-typing refers to concepts, preferences, behaviors, and personal identity related to maleness and femaleness. These characteristics incorporate the differential cultural values about males and females that in large part form the basis of how peers interact with and evaluate one another. The fourth is to summarize as completely and accurately as possible the two designated literatures. I previously attempted a brief summary (Fishbein, 1992), but many important details were omitted in that effort.

Methodological Considerations

Prejudice

As was noted in chapter 1, prejudice, as defined in that chapter, has rarely been measured. In virtually every study in which the attitudes of children and adolescents were assessed, no attempt was made to determine their "unreasonableness," i.e., the resistance of the negative attitudes to new and conflicting information. Thus, it is not clear whether the "prejudice" research is about prejudice or about negative stereotypes, or some combination of the two. On theoretical grounds, this methodological issue is important. On pragmatic grounds, it may or may not be.

Related to the above consideration is the strong bias in the literature towards the assessment of "beliefs" as contrasted with the "affective" and "behavior dispositional" components of attitudes. Prejudicial beliefs and negative stereotypes closely resemble each other, as noted above. If all three attitudinal components were highly intercorrelated, and relatively stable across age, then the belief bias would not be a serious issue. McGuire (1985) indicates that with adults, the three components are moderately correlated. But no comparable developmental research has been carried out. However, a number of developmental studies have contrasted several similar measures of prejudice (e.g., Brand, Ruiz, & Padilla, 1974; Katz, Sohn, & Zalk, 1975), and have found the intercorrelations among them to be low. Aboud's (1988) recent review concurs in this judgment. The major implication of these findings is that developmental patterns across a variety of studies should be examined, with relatively little weight given to any particular experiment.

A third methodological concern is that the testing context has been shown to influence children's expressed attitudes. For example, Katz et al. (1975) found that race of the examiner (Black versus White), age of the child, and race of the child (Black versus White) had interactional effects on children's assessed prejudice. Hence, even experiments that have used the same testing materials with same-age children, carried out in school settings, may have reached different conclusions because the races of the examiners were different. Analogously, Brand et al. (1974) have shown that different results may occur as a function of geographic region, social class of the children, and/or construction of the test materials, e.g., intensity of skin color differences between "White" dolls or pictures and "Black" dolls or pictures. Thus, caution must be observed in interpreting conflicting results from highly similar experiments.

A fourth methodological concern is that "forced-choice" materials and methods have typically been used in assessing prejudice, e.g., the *Projective Prejudice Test* developed by Katz et al. (1975), and the *PRAM II* developed by Williams and Morland (1976). With these methods children must choose between two stimulus materials, e.g., a drawing of a White child versus that of a Black child, on the basis of some physical or psychological attributes: "Which is the ugly child?"; "Which is the naughty child?" Aboud (1988) identifies three problems with these methods: (1) no index of intensity of prejudice can reliably be inferred from differences in preferences; (2) group frequencies or percentages are often interpreted as if they were mean scores of individuals; and (3) most critically, forced choice confounds preference of one group with rejection of the other. Children may like both White and Black children, but their showing a consistent preference for one race will give the impression that they are prejudiced towards the other.

A fifth methodological concern was raised by Soder (1990) about tests assessing prejudice towards disabled persons; however, this concern readily generalizes to other groups. Specifically, the tests fail to distinguish between reactions to the disability (e.g., deafness) and reactions to disabled persons (e.g., deaf people). Nondisabled individuals don't want to be disabled and don't envy those who are; disabilities as such are devalued. Research shows that disabled people evoke strong feelings of sympathy and altruism among nondisabled people, which indicates that *disabled persons* are not devalued. Analogously, given the history of African-Americans, it is highly unlikely that many Euro-Americans want to trade places with them. As was noted in Katz's

(1981) research, cited in chapter 1, White adults often show stronger sympathy for Blacks than for Whites; these findings are similar to those regarding disabled individuals. Soder suggests, in an analysis consistent with Katz's views, that "ambivalence" may be a more appropriate description of dominant/subordinate attitudes than "prejudice."

A sixth methodological concern, raised by Spencer and Markstrom-Adams (1990), deals with the issue of whether tests of prejudice assess children's attitudes towards various target groups as opposed to their knowledge of social stereotypes. In North America, Whites have higher status than Blacks. If children, Black or White, choose the White doll as smarter, more helpful, less ugly than the Black doll, they may merely be indicating to the examiner that they know the socially correct answer.

The last methodological concern, somewhat related to the above, is that apparent developmental decreases in prejudice may reflect changes in knowledge of social desirability, and not changes in prejudice (Aboud, 1988, Katz et al., 1975). Research findings suggest that prejudice measures that are relatively transparent in purpose indicate greater age-related decreases in prejudice than do less transparent measures. However, all the data are not consistent with these findings, especially those showing that older children are less likely than younger ones to be concerned with social approval on a general measure of social desirability. Thus, as with the other methodological concerns, caution should be used in drawing conclusions about developmental trends.

Discrimination

Discrimination was defined in chapter 1 as "involv[ing] harmful actions towards others because of their membership in a particular group." As far as I can determine, this trait has never been systematically assessed in North American children or adolescents. What have been measured and used as a "proxy" for discrimination are playmate or friendship choices. It has been assumed that if children of one gender, for example, exclude children of another gender from their circle of friends, the exclusion is based on gender differences. The exclusion is considered harmful, and hence discriminatory. Obviously, any particular child, for a variety of nondiscriminatory reasons, may have a circle of friends restricted to the same race, gender, or absence of disability. However, when opportunities exist for a large group for friendship with children who are of a different race or the opposite sex, or who have various disabilities, and these friendships don't occur, then discriminatory processes may reasonably be inferred.

Basically, six different procedures have been used to make these measurements: peer nominations, peer ratings, teacher nominations, teacher ratings, behavior observations, and peer assessments (Hallinan, 1981; McConnell & Odom, 1986; Terry & Coie, 1991). In virtually all the research, the data were collected in school contexts, and children's friendships or playmate preferences from among their classmates were assessed. Thus, we know very little about discrimination outside of school settings. This is a very serious methodological concern, because friendship choices have been shown to be markedly influenced by structural characteristics of the school and classroom. For example, in traditional classrooms, friendship choices are largely based on academic achievement, whereas in open classrooms this is not the case (Hallinan, 1981). In that African-American students, for example, typically perform more poorly than Euro-Americans, traditional classrooms would most likely have fewer cross-racial friendships than open ones. The problem is exaggerated in schools that have ability tracking.

Returning to the six procedures, the three most commonly used are peer nominations, peer ratings (these two are known as "sociometric" procedures), and behavioral observations. There are two types of peer nominations, fixed-choice and free-choice. In fixed-choice methods, children and adolescents are given a list of their classmates, or their photographs, and asked to name their three best friends, the three individuals they like the most, or some other characteristic. Often they're also asked to list the three people they like the least. With free-choice methods, no restriction of numbers is given. There are several problems with these two procedures. First, in fixed-choice methods, some individuals may be erroneously excluded or included, e.g., the respondent only has one best friend, or has five best friends, but is asked to list three names. Second, in free-choice studies, too many choices may be inadvertently encouraged, some of which don't really fit the criteria the researchers had in mind. Third, for both types, it is also possible that esteem or admiration is being evaluated, rather than friendships. Fourth, it is highly likely that children interpret the tasks differently at different ages. Finally, for both types, reliability in nominations is moderate, and improves if negative nominations are used.

In peer ratings, children and adolescents are given a list of their classmates and asked to make the same judgment about each one, usually on a 3- to 5-point scale, e.g., "How much do you like each classmate: a lot, a little, not at all?"; "Is this classmate a good friend, a friend, or not a friend?" Peer ratings are fairly sensitive to differences in the characteristics being rated, e.g., play with, work with. The major problem with this procedure is that most classmates get rated in the middle category. Moreover, young children tend to rate everyone the same, probably reflecting an unclear understanding of the task. Still, generally, peer ratings have a higher reliablity than peer nominations.

Researchers who frequently use sociometric techniques believe that peer nominations and peer ratings assess different types of relationships. The former probably measure friendships or popularity, whereas the latter measure social acceptability. As a consequence, conclusions drawn about discrimination may differ dramatically as a function of the type of sociometric technique employed.

Behavioral observations of interactions are the most direct way of assessing discrimination or friendship. If nondisabled children, for example, are rarely seen positively interacting with mentally retarded children, then it is likely that they have no mentally retarded friends. The two principal problems with behavioral observations are the limited opportunities in school settings for making the observations and the large amount of time needed for making reliable assessments. Once they are past preschool, children and adolescents have nearly all their school time structured. The three exceptions are lunch, recess, and walking to and from school. These provide a limited sample of friendship activities. As a consequence, beyond the preschool level, relatively few studies use observations as the principal method of assessing friendship choices.

Teacher nominations and teacher ratings parallel peer nominations and ratings. They are most often used with preschool- and kindergarten-age children, usually as methods to validate peer reports or behaviors. The two major problems with teachers' data are that they don't know all the children in their classes equally well, and they use somewhat different criteria from those of children themselves for determining friendships. However, experienced teachers can provide very valuable information about their students' peer interactions.

If the five procedures discussed above were all assessing friendship patterns in equivalent ways, then one would expect that the intercorrelations among them would be moderate to high. But in their literature review, McConnell and Odom (1986) found the intercorrelations to vary from low to moderate. This is problematic and indicates that one should be cautious in interpreting the results of any single study.

Finally, we consider "peer assessments." Strictly speaking, this is not a technique for assessing friendship, but is used to assess the behaviors that may underlie friendship choices. In this procedure, children and adolescents are given a list of behavioral characteristics, e.g., smart, athletic, unhappy, a bully, and are asked to identify three classmates who best fit each description. In Terry and Coie's (1991) study, peer assessments of eight characteristics were examined in relation to both peer nominations and peer ratings of popularity. They found that the different popularity categories, e.g., popular, average, rejected, were associated with unique patterns of peer assessments. Additionally, they found that peer nominations were more strongly related to peer assessment than were peer ratings. This last finding is consistent with the conclusion that ratings and nominations measure different aspects of interpersonal relationships.

As with the measurement of prejudice, the above discussion, considered as a whole, should warn the researcher that caution must be exhibited when evaluating studies concerning the development of discrimination. The various measures apparently assess different things. The wise course would be to look for developmental patterns across studies that utilize various assessment procedures.

Antecedents of Opposite-Sex Prejudice and Discrimination

Opposite-sex prejudice and discrimination are the outcome of three factors: the genetic/evolutionary predisposition to form and differentially evaluate ingroups and outgroups; cultural norms that attach higher status and dominance to males than to females; and the socialization of sex-typing.

In this section I'll briefly discuss the implications of the evolutionary and cultural perspectives on the development of opposite-sex prejudice and discrimination. In the next section I'll present an extensive description of the socialization of sex-typing. To a large degree, socialization practices encompass and are built on the above two factors. In the following section I'll discuss the relevant literature on opposite-sex prejudice. It should be noted that little of this literature was produced from the viewpoint of prejudice, but rather focused primarily on stereotyping. Finally, I'll conclude with a discussion of opposite-sex discrimination.

Genetic/Evolutionary Predispositions

As was noted in chapter 2, the genetic/evolutionary bases of prejudice and discrimination evolved in a tribal context for which protection of group members from other tribes and competition for scarce resources with those tribes was the norm. Two of the genetic/evolutionary processes most pertinent to the present discussion are authority-acceptance and the acquisition of badging mechanisms, i.e., behavioral and nonbehavioral characteristics that differentiate groups from one another. In contemporary North American cultures, unlike hunter-gatherer tribal cultures, a large number of different groups exist that are in competition with one another and differ in power and status. Authority figures in North America condone these differentiations, which include groupings by gender. Infant boys and girls are extremely similar physically and behaviorally. However their parents produce gender differences in appearance and encourage behavioral differences. These provide badges for distinguishing the two sexes—e.g., pink for girls, blue for boys; long hair and bows for girls, short, unadorned hair for boys (the behavioral effects will be discussed under sex-typing). Badging differences are maintained throughout childhood and adulthood.

The genetic/evolutionary model predicts ingroup, i.e., same-sex, favoritism, and outgroup, i.e., opposite-sex, hostility. The section of chapter 3 concerning the history of American females confirms these predictions for male attitudes and behavior, but is mute about females. The present chapter will remedy that gap. The discussion in chapter 2 of female immigration to other groups and extensive male involvement in intergroup hostility in human and nonhuman primates led to the speculation that males would develop stronger prejudices than females. This speculation can be evaluated here. The discussion in chapter 2 of the genetics of prejudice concluded that family influences were minimal. This leads to the prediction that family influences on the socialization of sex-typing will be minimal.

Finally, the discussion of the development of group identity in chapter 2 led to the prediction that prejudice and discrimination would emerge between the ages of 3 and 4 years, and undergo a marked change at about 7 years of age. These age-related changes are consistent with the conclusions of Fischer and Bullock (1984) based on a thorough review of the research literature in cognitive development. They identify four large-scale age-related reorganizations of thought, which occur at ages 4, 6 to 7, 10 to 12, and 14 to 16 years. Other research in social cognitive development indicates that a further reorganization occurs at about age 18 or 19 (Colby, Kohlberg, Gibbs, & Lieberman, 1983, for moral development; Damon & Hart, 1988, for development of self-knowledge; Kohlberg & Ullian, 1974, for development of sex-role knowledge; Selman, 1980, for development of interpersonal knowledge; and Turiel, 1983, for development of social conventions). These findings lead to the prediction that additional changes in prejudice and discrimination should also occur at these older age periods, i.e., 10 to 12, 14 to 16, and 18 to 19 years.

Cultural Norms

One of the central arguments made in chapter 1 was that prejudice and discrimination were normative in a culture, owing in part to the differential power and status of ingroups and outgroups. The dominant groups attempt to maintain their superior position through prejudicial and discriminatory acts directed towards subordinate groups. Members of subordinate groups, owing in part to their unfair treatment by dominant groups, respond to the latter in prejudiced ways, and where possible, in a discriminatory manner also. We saw in chapter 3 that American females from colonial days to the present have been discriminated against by the dominant males, whose prejudicial attitudes have undergirded that discrimination. What is not clear from that historical research is the extent to which status differences occurred between young boys and girls (the differences were obvious in adolescence, as reflected in academic and occupation opportunities). It is possible that children recognize male/female status differences among adolescents and adults, but not among themselves (there are a number of permutations on this theme, of course).

There are several likely consequences of the cultural/historical differences between males and females. First, fathers, who have more at stake than mothers in maintaining the dominance status quo will show greater differentiation than mothers in socializing their sons and daughters. That is, fathers should be more likely than mothers to encourage traditional sex-typed behavior in their children. Second, owing to gendered status differences, girls should acquire knowledge of opposite-sex-role stereotypes earlier than boys. Third, boys should show more traditional sex-typing than girls, and this difference should increase with age, owing to their increasing awareness of cultural values. Fourth, owing to self-perceived lower status, females should be more likely to adopt male sex-typed behaviors and values than the converse. This difference should increase with increasing age. Fifth, owing to gendered status differences, self-esteem in males and females should be more highly related to masculine than to feminine characteristics. Sixth, owing to gendered status differences, with increasing age, opposite-sex prejudice should be diminished for females more than for males.

Socialization of Sex-Typing

As we noted in the introduction, to a large extent opposite-sex prejudice and discrimination are built on the differential sex-typed socialization experienced by males and females. With increasing maturity, the "badges" of masculinity and femininity become more pronounced, insuring that grouping on the basis of gender will strongly occur. Sex-typing, however, is multidimensional, as Huston (1983, 1985) has clearly documented. Table 4.1 is her attempt to visually indicate some of this complexity. The table displays a matrix consisting of two factors, sex-typed *constructs* and sex-typed *content*. The constructs involve four different ways, approaches, or constructions of sex-typing. These are gendered concepts or

TABLE 4.1 A Matrix of Sex-Typing Constructs by Sex-Typed Content

Content Area	Construct			
	A. Concepts or Beliefs	B. Identity or Self-Perception	C. Preferences, Attitudes, Values (for Self or for Others)	D. Behavioral Enactment, Adoption
1. **Biological gender**	A1. Gender constancy.	B1. Gender identity as inner sense of maleness or femaleness. Sex role identity as perception of own masculinity or femininity.	C1. Wish to be male or female or gender bias defined as greater value attached to one gender than the other.	D1. Displaying bodily attributes of gender (including clothing, body type, hair, etc.)
2. **Activities and interests:** Toys Play activities Occupations Household roles Tasks Achievement areas	A2. Knowledge of sex stereotypes or sex role concepts **or** attributions about others' success and failure.	B2. Self-perception of interests abilities; **or** sex-typed attributions about own success and failure.	C2. Preference for toys, games, activities, attainment value for achievement areas: attitudes about sex-typed activities by others (e.g., about traditional or nontraditional roles for women.	D2. Engaging in games, toy play, activities, occupations, or achievement tasks that are sex-typed.
3. **Personal-social attributes:** Personality characteristics Social behavior	A3. Concepts about sex stereotypes or sex-appropriate social behavior.	B3. Perception of own personality (e.g., on self-rating questionnaires).	C3. Preference or wish to have personal-social attributes **or** attitudes about others' personality and behavior patterns.	D3. Displaying sex-typed personal-social behavior (e.g., aggression, dependence).

	A. Concepts or Beliefs	B. Identity or Self-Perception	C. Preferences, Attitudes, Values (for Self or for Others)	D. Behavioral Enactment, Adoption
4. **Gender-based social relationships:** Gender of peers, friends, lovers, preferred parent, models, attachment figures	A4. Concepts about sex-typed norms for gender-based social relations.	B4. Self-perception of own patterns or friendship, relationship, or sexual orientation.	C4. Preference for male or female friends, lovers, attachment figures, or wish to be like male or female, or attitudes about others' patterns.	D4. Engaging in social or sexual activity with others on the basis of gender (e.g., same-sex peer choice).
5. **Stylistic and symbolic content:** Gestures Nonverbal behavior Speech and language patterns Styles of play Fantasy Drawing Tempo Loudness Size Pitch	A5. Awareness of sex-typed symbols or styles.	B5. Self-perception of nonverbal, stylistic characteristics.	C5. Preference for stylistic or symbolic objects or personal characteristics or attitudes about others' nonverbal and language patterns.	D5. Manifesting sex-typed verbal and nonverbal behavior, fantasy, drawing patterns.

Source: Huston, A. C. (1983). Sex-typing. In P. H. Mussen (Ed.), *Handbook of child psychology*, Vol. 4. Copyright 1983 by John Wiley & Sons, Inc. Reprinted by permission.

beliefs, which include sex stereotypes; gender identity or self-perception; gender preferences, attitudes, and values towards self or others; and gendered behavior. Huston identifies five content areas to which each of these constructs apply: biological gender; activities and interests; personal-social attributes; gender-based social relationships; and stylistic and symbolic content. For example, personality tests assessing masculinity and/or femininity would deal with one's gender identity (construct) of personal-social attributes (content).

As can be seen, we cannot simply talk about the socialization of sex-typing. The various cells of the matrix may involve different developmental paths and different developmental levels attained. Some of the general attainments may even be contradictory, e.g., a girl prefers playing with dolls to playing with trucks, but thinks it appropriate for women to be doctors. Thus, when we discuss sex-typing, we have to specify the particular measures employed. Huston points out that in general, the research indicates greater male/female overlap in the personality traits and social behavioral areas than in play activities, peer preferences, and occupations.

Socialization of sex-typing starts shortly after birth (Huston, 1983; Katz, 1983). Research has found that parents of day-old boys see their babies as "big" to a greater extent than do parents of day-old girls, despite equivalence of length or weight. Boys are seen as "stronger" and "firmer," girls as "softer" and "finer." In an experimental study with the same 3-month-old infant, adults unfamiliar with the child treated it differently depending upon whether the infant was identified with a boy's or a girl's name. When they believed it was a girl, for example, they used a doll more frequently in play interactions. When they thought it was a boy they talked about "his" absence of hair and strong grip. Analogous findings occurred in research with 6-month-old and 9-month-old infants.

The home physical environment of boys and girls is also markedly different during infancy (Katz, 1983; Pomerleau, Bolduc, Malcint, and Cossette, 1990). The quality and quantity of toys, colors, types of clothing, and motifs of rooms vary considerably by infant's sex. Boys are provided with more sports equipment, tools, and vehicles; girls are given more dolls, fictional characters, and furniture. Thus, parents strongly proclaim to the community at large, to themselves, and to the child, that "he is a boy" or "she is a girl." The stakes are obviously high.

Socialization of sex-typing occurs in films, television, and books, and is performed by teachers, peers, parents, and other adults. Regarding television, where differential gender stereotyping of males and females is very marked, Huston (1983) and Signorielli and Lears (1992) suggest that its influence on socialization of sex-typing of children may be even greater than that of parents. In television, males are much more highly developed behaviorally and psychologically than are females. Usually females do little more than follow the lead of their more central male companions. Men have the most prestigious and interesting jobs, and are nearly always supervisors of women. As we noted in chapter 1, the chief players in history books are men, and Huston points out that this is typical in children's storybooks and textbooks.

Parents' Socialization of Sex-Typing

In this section we address the following three questions. (1) Do parents treat their sons and daughters differently? (2) Are fathers more likely than mothers to differentiate in their treatment of sons and daughters? (3) How do mothers and fathers affect the sex-typed behavior of their children? For all these questions, we focus on traditional White, middle-class families, on which most of the research has been carried out. In the next section, we will examine the impact of family type on socialization.

There are three extensive reviews, by Huston (1983), Lytton and Romney (1991), and Siegal (1987), and a recent experiment by Kerig, Cowan, and Cowan (1993), dealing with the first two questions. The conclusions of all are quite similar. Lytton and Romney carried out a meta-analysis of 172 published and unpublished studies dealing with parents' differential socialization of boys and girls. Their analyses encompassed three age ranges—0 to 5 years, 6 to 12 years, and 13 years to adulthood—and eight major socialization areas, including "encourage sex-typed activities." The other areas were interaction, encourage achievement, warmth, encourage dependency, restrictiveness, discipline, and clarity/reasoning.

With the exception of sex-typing, there was a great deal of variation of effects in all the socialization areas. The meta-analyses showed that overall differences between parents, and differential treatment of boys and girls at any age, were very small and statistically insignificant. In the area of sex-typing, though, at all ages mothers and fathers did significantly treat their sons and daughters differently. For example, both parents encouraged sex-typed toys, activities, and household chores. Generally, parents were similar in their sex-typing; however, fathers were more likely than mothers to both encourage male sex-typed behavior in boys, and discourage male sex-typed behavior in girls. There was also a tendency for fathers to interact more with sons than with daughters, with the converse holding for mothers and daughters.

The research in this area indicates that parents do treat their sons and daughters differently as this treatment relates to socialization of sex-typing. Sons are encouraged by mothers and fathers to be active, assertive, and competent; daughters, to be dependent and compliant. In general, fathers are more likely than mothers to differentially socialize boys and girls. This supports the prediction made in the section in this chapter on cultural norms that fathers, as members of the dominant male group, have more at stake in maintaining cultural values and norms than do mothers, who are members of the subordinate group.

How do fathers and mothers influence the sex-typing of their children? We'll examine two categories of experiments in answering this question. The first category briefly deals with fine-grain analyses of interactions between parents and their 1 1/2- to 2 1/2-year-old children. This is the age range in which children are developing a verbal gender identity and a preference for sex-typed toys. The second category briefly deals with the effects of mothers' employment outside the home on older children's sex-role stereotyping.

Three recent experiments deal with fine-grain analyses. In the first, Eisenberg, Wolchik, Hernandez, and Pasternack (1985) studied 1 1/2- to 2-year-old boys and girls in their homes, separately interacting with their mothers and fathers. The experimenters returned approximately six months later to repeat their observations. In the second, Fagot and Leinbach (1989) observed 1 1/2- to 2-year-old boys and girls interacting at home with both parents present. The researchers returned 9 months later for additional observations. In the third, Caldera, Huston, and O'Brien (1989) observed 1 1/2- to 2- year-old boys and girls interacting separately with their mothers and fathers in a laboratory setting.

Some of the principal results were as follows. Eisenberg et al. (1985) and Fagot and Leinbach (1989) found that parents of boys generally selected masculine-typed toys for them to play with, and parents of girls selected gender-neutral toys for them. Because of their greater availability, boys were more likely to play with masculine than with feminine or neutral toys, and girls more likely to play with neutral than with feminine or masculine toys. Eisenberg et al. observed that parents of different families varied somewhat in how much they differentially reinforced same-sex versus opposite-sex toy play. The extent of this differentiation during the child's third year of life (but not second year) was positively related to the development of gender identity. Fagot and Leinbach found, however, that parents' high affective involvement (positively and negatively) with their child's same-sex and opposite-sex toy play during the second year of life (but not the third year) led to the development of early gender identity.

Caldera et al. (1989) found that fathers were initially most interested in masculine toys when they were with their son, and mothers were initially most interested in feminine toys when they were with their daughter. However, after this initial reaction, parents' nonverbal involvement in play, verbal behavior, and proximity to their child were influenced by the type of toy played with, independent of sex of parent or sex of child. In contrast to the above two studies, 1 1/2- to 2-year-old children were more engaged with same-sex than with opposite-sex toys, controlling for any systematic differences in parents' behaviors. This finding probably reflects both parents' initial reactions to sex-typed toys and the differential experiences with sex-typed toys that boys and girls bring to the laboratory.

Taken together, the above three experiments indicate that two factors largely determine the early development of gender identity in children: parents' differential selection of toys for their sons and daughters; and the extent to which parents are involved with or concerned about their child's sex-typed play. These factors start manifesting their effects as early as 1 1/2 years, and have taken hold by age 2 1/2.

Turning now to the effects of mother's employment outside the home, Fishbein (1984) and Huston (1983) examined much of the relevant literature, and arrived at similar conclusions. However, two more recent experiments, by Baruch and Barnett (1986) and McHale, Bartko, Crouter, and Perry-Jenkins (1990), indicate that the issue is quite complicated, with no clear answer. Fishbein and Huston found for two-parent middle-class families that children between the ages of 5 and 12 years with externally employed mothers held fewer sex-role stereotypes than those whose mothers were primarily housewives. The effects were somewhat larger for girls than for boys. For children in working-class families, some research showed similar effects, but other research showed no effects of maternal employment. Fishbein explained the social class differences in terms of working by choice in satisfying jobs versus working to help support the family in less desirable jobs.

Baruch and Barnett (1986) found that for middle-class families, mother's external employment had no effect on children's sex-role stereotypes. However, mothers who held nontraditional attitudes towards the male role had children with relatively nontraditional sex-typed attitudes. McHale et al. (1990) found that for middle-class children, sons' (but not daughters') evaluation of their own participation in male and female sex-typed household chores was influenced by mother's work status and father's attitudes and behaviors. If mothers worked externally and fathers helped with chores, then sons evaluated their own carrying out of chores positively. If mothers had no external employment and fathers helped little with chores, then sons evaluated their carrying out of chores negatively. Girls were unaffected by any of these factors.

Influence of Family Type on Socialization

We'll now look at three studies that examine the effects of nonconventional family structures and/or orientations on the sex-typing of children. A "conventional" family is one in which children are reared by male and female married parents who hold traditional sex-typed attitudes and generally accept prevailing cultural norms. Mothers may or may not be employed outside the home in conventional families, but they do carry out most of the domestic and feminine-typed household tasks. Obviously, being "conventional" is not an all-or-nothing category; there is some variation among conventional families in the degree to which they hold traditional beliefs.

Weisner and Wilson-Mitchell (1990) report on the sex-typing of 6-year-old boys and girls who were raised either in a conventional family or in one of five categories of nonconventional types of families. The latter varied considerably in terms of their commitment to a stable nuclear family lifestyle; e.g., one of these five lived in communal settings. They also differed somewhat in their practice of sex-egalitarian beliefs and activities, as well as in their opposition to other conventional cultural norms.

The major findings were as follows. On measures of observed free play and children's stated play preferences with toys and with friends, no differences in children's sex-typing were found as a function of type of family they were reared in. Similarly, there were no family-type-related differences in psychologists' ratings of children's gender-appropriate appearance or behavior; nor were there differences as a function of family category in parents' ratings of children's sex-typed personality characteristics. However, family category did influence children's sex-typing of occupational classifications and preferences, as well as sex-typed knowledge of toys and objects. Specifically, children from the nontraditional family categories gave more non-sex-typed responses than those from conventional families. The extent of this difference was related to the degree of family nonconventionality. Finally, all children showed considerable knowledge of sex-typing and sex roles, with girls being less traditional in their responses than boys.

These results indicate that marked differences in family orientation and structure have minimal effects in development of sex-typing by 6-year-old children. The primary influence was on children's beliefs about occupations and objects, which were consistent with the nontraditional gender belief systems of their parents. As the authors of this research indicate, all families are embedded in essentially the same American culture, and the gendered cultural norms pervade most areas of children's lives. The values of an individual family can have only a small impact on modifying cultural meanings and norms.

The above conclusions are strongly supported by the results from Stevenson and Black's (1988) literature review on the effects of paternal absence and children's sex-role development, and Patterson's (1992) literature review on the sex-role development of children reared by lesbian and gay parents. The general conclusions of Stevenson and Black were that on a variety of measures of sex-typing as a function of father absence, the effects on boys were small, and the effects on girls were generally absent. The typical findings for boys were that those living with both parents held slightly greater sex-role stereotypes and chose slightly greater male sex-typed activities and preferences than those raised by only their mothers. However, teachers' and mothers' ratings of aggressive behavior show father-absent boys to score higher than father-present boys. For all these findings, the largest effects were found for boys whose fathers were away on military service, as contrasted with boys whose fathers were absent due to divorce or death. Age, race, and SES effects were generally small, and somewhat questionable on methodological grounds.

Patterson (1992) indicates that owing to tremendous societal and methodological problems, the research on lesbian and gay parents is not extensive and sample sizes are generally small. Among the societal problems, for example, are the legal threats to homosexuals maintaining custody of their children. Thus, most lesbian and gay parents will not openly agree to be studied in the context of their homosexuality.

Most of the research compares boys and girls reared by divorced lesbian mothers with children reared by divorced heterosexual mothers. These mothers were the household heads, although some currently lived with another woman (lesbian mothers) or with a man (heterosexual mothers). The former situation was much more frequent than the latter. Another potentially important difference between the two groups was that children of lesbian mothers were more likely to have contact with their biological fathers than children of divorced heterosexual mothers.

In general, the boys and girls studied were in the primary grades. For these children (ages 5 to 12), researchers, using projective techniques and interviews, found no differences in same-sex gender identity between those raised by lesbian mothers and those raised by heterosexual mothers. Using questionnaires and observations, no group differences were found for children's sex-typed interests, activities, behavior, or peer relationships. Regarding adolescents and adults, the male and female children of lesbians and gays were no more likely to report having homosexual preferences than comparable-age individuals in the population as a whole.

On the surface the Patterson (1992) findings are remarkable: children raised by lesbian and gay parents develop traditional sex-typed beliefs and behaviors. The fact that the findings appear to be remarkable hinges on the linked assumptions that parents who are homosexual will also be nontraditionally sex-typed in other important ways and moreover, they will consciously or unconsciously attempt to transmit those values and behaviors to their children. Both assumptions may be false. Indeed, lesbians and gays may try extra hard to transmit traditional sex-typing to their children in order to protect them from a hostile society.

Taken as a whole, the above three studies indicate that variations in sex-typed family structures, beliefs, values, and behaviors have only a limited effect on the development of children's traditional sex-typing. This is consistent with the prediction, based on genetic analyses of prejudice, that extrafamilial influences would be much stronger than within-family environmental influences. As previously argued, culture is powerful, and it is nearly impossible for families to not expose their children to and involve them in the norms of their culture. Not only the media, but peers, teachers, and other adults transmit and reinforce traditional sex-typed norms.

Influence of Peers and Teachers on Socialization

Several recent experiments have explored the roles of teachers and peers in shaping traditional sex-typed behavior in infants, toddlers, and young children. Two classes of behavior are focused on: the development of assertive/aggressive acts, and choices of sex-typed toy play. Fagot and her colleagues provide important information of the first class (Fagot, Hagan, Leinbach & Kronsberg, 1985; Fagot & Hagan, 1985).

Fagot et al. (1985) studied 13-month-old infants in infant play groups, and the same children 10 months later, when they were in toddler play groups. During infancy no sex differences were observed in frequency of communicative behaviors, e.g., gesturing, talking, or assertive/aggressive behaviors, e.g., hitting, grabbing objects from a peer. However, teachers punished and rewarded boys' assertive/aggressive behaviors more than they did girls', with the converse holding for communicative behaviors. Peers did not differentially respond to boys and girls for either category of behaviors. During toddlerhood, boys and girls showed somewhat different patterns of communicative and aggressive/assertive acts. Teachers responded equivalently to boys and girls for both categories of behavior. But for assertive/aggressive acts, boys received more negative reactions from peers than did girls, and girls were ignored more than boys.

Fagot et al. (1985) interpret these results as follows. Teachers hold stereotypic views about sex-typed behavior predispositions. Boys are assumed to be more aggressive than girls, and girls are assumed to seek attention through lower-intensity communicative acts. During infancy, where there were, in reality, no behavioral differences between boys and girls for these categories, teachers responded as if there were, and essentially shaped sex-typed behavior. During toddlerhood, boys' and girls' sex-typed behaviors conformed to stereotypes, and teachers now responded to children's behaviors, and not to their gender. Peers responded to a combination of gender and behavior; such responses may further shape sex-typed gender differences.

Fagot and Hagan (1985) then focused on assertive/aggressive behavior (hereafter referred to as "aggression") and sought to extend the above results. They studied three age groups of toddlers in multi-age play groups: children were 20 months, 27 months, and 33 months old. The question they addressed was the impact of teachers' and peers' reactions on the continuation of aggressive acts. The first finding was that there were no sex differences in these effects. Second, for the youngest group, reward, punishment, or ignoring had no differential effect on terminating or sustaining the aggressive behavior. For the two oldest groups, however, negative peer and teacher reactions prolonged aggression relative to positive reactions or ignoring the aggression. Given that girls' aggression is more likely to be ignored, and boys' aggression more likely to be responded to negatively, these results indicate that boys', but not girls', aggression is indirectly encouraged by teachers and peers.

What effects do peers and teachers have on more broadly defined sex-typed activities than aggression? Fagot (1985) addressed this issue for 2-year-old children in multi-age nursery school play groups. Male-typed play included rough-and-tumble activity and play with large blocks; female-typed play included play with dolls and dressing up; gender-neutral play included climbing and sliding, play with clay, and doing puzzles. Continuation or termination of play following teacher or peer reactions were used as the measure of the effect of the reaction.

The results are somewhat surprising. When male peers rewarded boys' activities (relative to punishing or ignoring them), irrespective of gender-typing, boys continued the activities longer. Teachers' and female peers' differential reactions had no noticeable effect on the continuation of boys' activities. When teachers and female peers rewarded girls' activities (relative to punishing or ignoring them), irrespective of gender-typing, girls continued the activity longer. Boys' differential reactions had no noticeable effect on girls' activities. Additional analyses indicated that boys, but not girls, periodically received peer sex-typed punishment—e.g., "That's dumb, boys don't play with dolls"—when they engaged in female sex-typed play.

Fagot (1985) interprets these results as follows. Boys' male peers encourage them to stay away from female-typed activities and to play with other boys. Girls' female peers encourage them to play with other girls, but do not discourage them from engaging in male-typed activities. Teachers appear to encourage in boys and girls the kind of classroom calmness that is associated with female-typed and gender-neutral activities.

Lamb and his colleagues (Lamb & Roopnarine, 1979; Lamb, Easterbrooks, & Holden, 1980) examined the effects of peer reactions to sex-typed play in 3- and 4-year-old nursery school children (Lamb & Roopnarine) and in nursery school and kindergarten children (Lamb et al.). Their categories of male and female sex-typed activities, peer reactions of reward and punishment, and effects of the latter on continuation of play activity were all similar to those used by Fagot (1985).

The major results were as follows. In both studies boys and girls generally engaged in sex-appropriate activities. Both male and female peers rewarded boys more than girls for male sex-typed play, and rewarded girls more than boys for female sex-typed play. Punishment for sex-typed play infrequently occurred, but it had the effect of terminating play. Finally, boys further continued rewarded male-typed play more than girls did, and girls further continued rewarded female-typed play more than boys did. Additionally, Lamb et al. (1980) found that boys terminated female-typed play more rapidly than girls did following punishment; and girls terminated male sex-typed play more rapidly than boys did following punishment. There were no age differences in any of these results.

The above findings suggest to the authors that 3- to 5-year-old children have acquired the knowledge of sex-appropriate and sex-inappropriate activities, and the motivation to carry out these activities. Children reward and punish peers for adherence to or deviation from the gender norms. These results further suggest, as compared to the findings of Fagot (1985), that one major development that occurs between the ages of 2 and 3 years is boys' and girls' susceptibility to gender role enforcements (rewards and punishments) by both male and female peers.

Taken together, the data on the socialization of sex-typing indicate that parents, peers, teachers, the media, and all forms of cultural norms transmission operate to ensure that males and females will develop very different gender identities and behaviors from a very early age. That even 2-year-olds contribute to this differentiation is remarkable. Nearly everyone in the culture becomes invested in these identities. The children themselves manifest a variety of "badges" to ensure that the two gender groups will not be confused. The adopting of another badge is readily noted, and peers especially, take corrective measures to get things straight. There may be a genetic component to gender roles, but even if there is not, sex-typing seems to develop like canalized behaviors. Even such apparently nontraditional family types as those with two homosexual parents have little effect on the development of gender. As will be seen in the next two sections, the outcomes are significant for males and females and for the culture as a whole.

Development of Opposite-Sex Prejudice

Indirect Measures

In an earlier section of this chapter, "Cultural Norms," six predictions were made based on the consequences of status and dominance differences between males and females in North American societies. Only one of the predictions directly addressed developmental changes in opposite-sex prejudice. The other five indirectly dealt with prejudice, in that they involved either a female sex-role devaluation or a male sex-role enhancement. The first prediction, confirmed in a later section, on socialization, was that fathers would be more involved than mothers in traditional sex-typing of their children because they had more to gain by maintaining the status quo. The effect of encouraging compliance in girls and assertiveness in boys is likely to lead to prejudice against females in a society where males make and enforce the rules.

The above prediction dealt with parents, whereas the others deal with children. The second prediction was that owing to gendered status differences, girls should acquire knowledge of opposite-sex stereotypes earlier than boys. On the surface, there's nothing prejudiced about this. However, given a theory that links knowledge acquisition to the social value of that knowledge, if girls acquire opposite-sex knowledge before boys do, this implies that male sex-typing is more valuable social knowledge than female sex-typing. Is this not merely a restatement of the cultural norm that males have higher status than females? Of course it is. In this way female and male children essentially acknowledge the higher valuing of male roles over female roles. But it is an *indirect* measure of prejudice. In the remainder of this section we'll examine the research relevant to the four predictions dealing with indirect measures of opposite-sex prejudice in children.

O'Brien (1992) and Levy and Fivush (1993) have reviewed literature relevant to the above prediction concerning the acquisition of knowledge about opposite-sex stereotypes. In the typical experiments, boys and girls are shown pictures of objects or activities associated with male and female children and adults, and are asked to identify which sex the object or activity is usually associated with. Preschool boys and girls ages 2 and older have greater knowledge of same-sex than of other-sex gender-typed knowledge. However, the discrepancy is greater for boys than for girls. Indeed, in some studies, girls showed knowledge of the two sex-typed categories that was equalled only by the same-sex knowledge attained by boys. Thus, the second prediction is confirmed.

The third prediction made was that boys should show more traditional sex-typed preferences than girls, and owing to increasing awareness of cultural values, the difference should increase with age. This prediction differs from the second one above in two ways: it focuses on preferences rather than on knowledge, and it predicts age-related developmental changes. The research literature strongly confirms this prediction (Huston, 1983; Katz, 1983; Katz & Boswell, 1986; O'Brien, 1992; Signorella, Bigler, & Liben, 1993). Interestingly, most researchers refer to the shift to more opposite-sex preferences by girls as evidencing their increased "flexibility" relative to boys.

The experiment by Serbin and Sprafkin (1986) is an excellent example of research in this area. The authors tested boys and girls from five age groups between 3 and 7 years old on various measures of sex-typed knowledge and sex-typed preferences. The authors found essentially no differences between boys and girls in their ability to identify children's and adults' sex-typed objects and activities. Regarding preferences, one of their tests, "affiliation," involved pictures of men and women, with the same-sex adult doing nothing, and the opposite-sex adult doing something interesting. The children were asked which adult they would like to be with. Girls choose females about half the time at each age level (40 percent at age 3). Boys, on the other hand, showed a pronounced increase in choosing males, from 30 percent at age 3 to 75 percent at age 7.

The fourth prediction made was that owing to their self-perceived lower status, females should be more likely to adopt male sex-typed behavior and values than the converse. This prediction is similar to the third one, except that the focus here is both more specific, i.e., on behaviors, and more general, i.e., on values. Although we would expect similar predictions to have similar outcomes, Huston (1983) has taught us that sex-typing is multidimensional and that development of the various sex-typed components are not necessarily correlated with one another.

Huston (1983) and O'Brien (1992) summarize literature that supports this prediction. Baruch and Barnett (1986) and others have found that girls are more likely than boys to perform opposite-sex-typed household chores. Smetana (1986), in studying preschoolers' conceptions of sex-role transgressions, found that both boys and girls judged male sex-role transgressions more severely than female sex-role transgressions. In the area of occupational aspirations, Etaugh and Liss (1992), studying children from kindergarten through eighth grade, found girls, but not boys, increasingly interested in opposite-sex-typed occupations. Finally, in reviewing literature on children's preferences for being like various television characters when they grew up, it was found that boys almost never chose a woman but about one fourth of girls chose a man (Fishbein, 1984).

The fifth prediction made was that owing to gendered status differences, self-esteem in males and females should be more highly related to masculine than to feminine characteristics. There is a corollary prediction that owing to the connection between self-esteem and depression (Harter, 1993), females should be more likely than males to suffer from depression. Although the data are somewhat limited concerning the fifth prediction, two large studies with high school students confirm it (Massad, 1981; Spence & Helmreich, 1978).

In both studies concerned with self-esteem, the Personal Attributes Questionnaire (PAQ) developed by Spence and Helmreich (1978) was used to assess masculine and feminine personality traits. The assumption underlying the development of the PAQ was that masculinity and femininity were independent personality dimensions; i.e., one could score high on either or both of them. In developing the PAQ, they included only those characteristics that were positively valued by both male and female adolescents. Spence and Helmreich found for both males and females that self-esteem was moderately to strongly positively correlated with masculinity scores; i.e., high masculinity was associated with high self-esteem. However, femininity for both sexes was weakly correlated with self-esteem. Massad (1981) found that males with high masculinity scores had higher self-esteem than those with low masculinity scores, and that their femininity scores had no effect on this relationship. Females with high masculinity and high femininity scores had the highest self-esteem, and those with low scores on both had the lowest self-esteem. Thus, masculine characteristics boosted female self-esteem.

Regarding the development of depression, two recent papers have reviewed the literature, reaching identical conclusions (Cantwell, 1990; Petersen, Compas, Brooks-Gunn, Stemmler, Ey, & Grant, 1993). Distinctions should be made between depressed mood, depressive syndrome, and clinical depression. The three categories can be seen as points along the continuum of severity of depression, with clinical depression apparently occurring in 3 to 5 percent of adolescents and close to 0 percent in preadolescent children. In the other two categories adolescents also have a higher occurrence than preadolescents. For each of these three categories the data are very consistent: preadolescent boys and girls, i.e., 8- to 12-year-olds, have approximately equal rates of depression, whereas for adolescents aged 14 and older, females have higher rates than males. The latter pattern persists into adulthood. Petersen et al. suggest that one causal factor for the gender differences is that the biological changes in puberty strengthen one's gender identity. Obviously, from the present point of view, stronger identity with a subordinate group (females) would be more depressing than that with a dominant group (males).

In summary, all four predictions concerning either the enhancement of male sex-typed characteristics or the devaluation of female sex-typed characteristics were supported. This may give the impression that opposite-sex prejudice is unidirectional. However, as will be seen in the next section, which deals with more direct measures of prejudice, males and females both evidence opposite-sex prejudice.

Direct Measures

Opposite-sex prejudice is discussed in two ways. In the first, we look at the negative and positive sex-role stereotypes that boys and girls hold for themselves and for the opposite sex. For example, if boys hold stronger negative female sex-role stereotypes than girls do, and weaker positive female sex-role stereotypes than girls do, it may be inferred that boys have prejudiced attitudes towards girls. Three studies use this approach. In the second way, we examine children's evaluations of counterstereotyped (or opposite-sex) behavior that they and/or male and female peers carry out, e.g., girls playing with trucks or footballs. Negative reactions to counterstereotyped play can be viewed as a devaluation of the opposite sex, and hence, as an indicator of prejudice. Three studies take this approach.

Kuhn, Nash, and Brucken (1978) compared knowledge of sex-role stereotypes for 2 1/2- and 3 1/2-year-old boys and girls involved in a nursery school. The children were shown two paper dolls—one clearly resembling a girl, the other a boy—and asked to identify them. All did so correctly. The children were then read a list of seventy-two statements which dealt with traits, e.g., "I'm strong"; [activities,] e.g, "I like to play ball"; or future roles, e.g., "When I grow up, I'll fly an airplane." These were all items that adults and older children had clearly identified as being sex-role-stereotyped. For each statement, the children were asked to point to the doll that best fit in.

The results showed that children agreed with adult stereotypes about two thirds of the time, a rate that is statistically well above the range of chance. There were no age or sex differences in amount of stereotyping. Significantly, boys and girls sometimes disagreed about the statements that they stereotyped. Boys, but not girls, believed that girls cried, were slow, and complained about hurt feelings and not having a turn at play. Girls, but not boys, believed that girls looked nice, gave kisses, never fought, and said, "I can do it best." Thus boys held more negative attitudes and fewer positive attitudes towards girls than girls held about themselves.

How do beliefs about boys fit into this picture? Girls, but not boys, believed that boys enjoy fighting, are mean, weak, and say, "I did wrong." Boys, but not girls, believed that boys enjoy hard work, are loud, are naughty, and make people cry. Except for the last three items, which may be too ambiguous to categorize accurately, girls held more negative attitudes and fewer positive attitudes towards boys than boys held towards themselves. It can be inferred from these findings that 2 1/2-and 3 1/2-year-olds do hold opposite-sex prejudices.

The study by Albert and Porter (1988) deals with sex-role stereotypes among 4-, 5-, and 6-year-olds enrolled in preschool programs. The children were shown both a male and a female doll and told two stories, one concerning the child's home, and the other the school environment. Intermittently throughout the stories, the child was asked to point to the doll that engaged in the activity or event just described. In all, 32 activities were noted, all judged by adults to be either positive or negative, as well as clearly sex-role-stereotyped. For example, the item "Which one throws toys around when told not to?" is a negative male sex-role stereotype; "Which one goes over to take care of the little child?" is a positive female sex-role stereotype.

Overall, children were found to be more accurate, i.e., to agree with adult ratings, in the sex-role stereotyping of their own than of the opposite sex. Older children were also more accurate in their sex-role stereotypes than were younger children. Girls were more likely than boys to associate all the negative male sex-role stereotypes with the male doll. Moreover, the strength of these judgments was greater for older than for younger girls. For all of the positive male sex-role stereotypes, boys scored higher than, or the same as, girls. In findings similar to those for the negative stereotypes, older girls were less positive than younger ones.

A similar pattern was found for female sex-role stereotypes, with boys and girls holding reversed positions. That is, boys generally viewed girls more negatively and less positively than girls saw themselves. The opposite-sex disparity, however, was not as great as that seen for male sex-role stereotypes.

Zalk and Katz (1978) tested second- and fifth-grade Black and White children on race and gender biases. For the latter, they were shown slides of boys and girls and given either a positive or a negative description of one of them. The participants were then asked to point to either the boy or the girl who best fit the description, e.g., "Which child always answers the teacher's questions wrong?" The descriptions dealt with both academic and nonacademic characteristics, with six involving positive attributes, and seven involving negative ones.

The pattern of results was similar for second- and fifth-graders, although the older children were less biased than the younger ones. Both males and females rated same-sex children more positively than opposite-sex children, consistent with the above results for preschoolers. Females rated males much more negatively than they did females; but unlike the above results for preschoolers, males rated males somewhat more negatively than they did females. One possible explanation for the discrepancy with males is that in these school settings boys are more frequent troublemakers than girls and are criticized by teachers for this. Four of the seven negative descriptions involved school-related activities; hence, children's negative evaluations may partially reflect their school experiences.

Taken together, the results of the above research indicate that opposite-sex prejudice starts to emerge at age 2 1/2, is clearly seen in 4-year-olds, and increases until about age 8 (the second-graders in Zalk & Katz, 1978). Between ages 8 and 10 it declines somewhat, probably because of increases in sex-typed flexibility and an increased ability to balance beliefs and experiences.

The experiment by Bussey and Bandura (1992) dealt with nursery school children's self-evaluation of how they would feel after they had played with same-sex or opposite-sex toys, and with their evaluation of older boys and girls they saw on television playing with opposite-sex toys (special videotapes were produced for this task). The children were taught to indicate their evaluations by pressing light switches that were associated with the following five categories: real great, kinda great, nothing special, kinda awful, real awful. For purposes of data analyses the preschoolers were divided into two groups, with average ages of 3 years and 4 years, respectively.

The major findings were as follows. For self-evaluations, the 3-year-olds tended to evaluate same-sex toy play positively and opposite-sex play negatively, but this was not statistically significant. For the 4-year-olds, this pattern was quite pronounced, and statistically significant. Regarding evaluations of televised older children, there were no age or sex differences, but generally, the participants reacted negatively to opposite-sex toy play, e.g., boys playing with dolls, girls with trucks. These results are consistent with the above studies dealing with preschoolers' negative judgments of opposite-sex characteristics, and positive judgments of same-sex characteristics.

Martin (1989) studied two groups of boys and girls with average ages of approximately 4 1/2 and 8 1/2 years. The participants were shown pictures of same-age boys and girls and read descriptions about their friends and interests. Only one target child was shown at a time. Four of the target children were boys and four were girls. One of each sex was depicted in a gender-neutral way; one of each as having same-sex stereotyped interests; and one of each as having opposite-sex counterstereotyped interests. Finally, one boy was labeled as a "sissy" and one girl as a "tomboy." After each description was read, the participants were asked to make three "liking" ratings, ranging from "not at all" to "a lot": (1) How much do you like the target? (2) How much do other boys like the target? (3) How much do other girls like the target?

In a pattern consistent with those observed in work previously mentioned, overall, boys liked male targets better than female ones, with the converse holding for females. The younger boys and girls disliked the "tomboys" more than all other target children, whereas the older boys and girls disliked "sissies" the most. There were no significant differences in liking or disliking as a function of depicted neutral, stereotyped or counterstereotyped interests. Regarding the judged liking of the target children by other boys or girls (second and third questions), the identical pattern seen for the younger children was found for the older participants. For the younger participants, the only significant finding was their expectation that other boys would like boys better than girls, with the converse holding for girls.

From the perspective of opposite-sex prejudice, the most important results involved the age-related shift from younger children most disliking "tomboys" to older children most disliking "sissies." One possible explanation of these results involves the idea that for both age groups, male characteristics are seen as somewhat more valued than female characteristics. The younger children assume that male characteristics "belong" to males, and thus see tomboys most negatively. This is consistent with Smetana's (1986) results, noted in the previous section. The older children, however, value male characteristics in both sexes, and view sissies most negatively because they have rejected these characteristics.

The paper by Lobel, Bempechat, Gewirtz, Shoken-Topaz, and Bashe (1993) follows these leads from Martin's (1989) research in very imaginative ways. The possible drawback to their research is that it was carried out in Israel with 10- to 12-year-old Israeli children. Although the article was published in a North American journal and Lobel et al. took a number of measures that demonstrate the comparability of these children's responses with those of North Americans, Israel is nevertheless a different culture. In this experiment, the researchers constructed four videotapes, all involving 10- to 12-year-old children. In the first, one boy (the target) and three girls played "Chinese jumprope" together (a girls' game in Israel). In the second, one girl (the target) and three boys played soccer together (a boys' game). In the third, a boy played soccer with three other boys. In the fourth, a girl played Chinese jumprope with three other girls. The participants were shown only one of the videos and then asked (1) to rate the target child on 16 masculine and feminine traits; (2) to rate the popularity of the target with his or her peers; (3) to rate how much they personally liked the target child; and (4) whether or not they would like to engage in a variety of activities with the target child.

Regarding rated masculinity and femininity, the target boy and target girl who played soccer were both rated about the same, and more masculine than feminine. The target boy and target girl who played jumprope were both rated about the same, and more feminine than masculine. Regarding judged peer popularity, the least popular was the boy who played jumprope with girls. The popularity of the other targets was essentially the same. This pattern is consistent with that found by Martin (1989) for the older children; i.e., "sissies" were disliked most. Regarding personal liking, girls playing with girls, i.e., in a traditional sex-typed way, were liked the most by both boys and girls. There were only slight differences among the other three conditions. This is inconsistent with Martin's findings, and may indicate a level of comfort that older children feel with traditional girls. Finally, boys would most prefer to engage in other activities with the girl who played soccer with the boys, and girls would prefer engaging in activities with the boy who played soccer with other boys. This finding is consistent with the view that masculine characteristics are most highly valued by boys and girls. Additionally, it indicates that heterosexual interests are starting to play a role in opposition to opposite-sex prejudice.

Taken together, these three experiments indicate that opposite-sex prejudice emerges at age 3 and is strongly in place at age 4. At these ages the prejudice is bidirectional: boys devalue girls' characteristics and girls devalue boys'. Between the ages of 4 and 8 years, in a pattern consistent with the results reported in chapter 2 concerning group identity, a shift occurs. Both girls and boys reject boys who take on female characteristics. Although the underlying processes may be different, both sexes at about age 8 effectively state that male characteristics are more valued than female ones. Between the ages of 8 and 10 years, the enhancement of male characteristics strengthens, but a new element enters and opposes opposite-sex prejudice: heterosexual interest. Boys want to be involved with masculine girls, and girls want to be involved with masculine boys. The picture is somewhat cloudy during preadolescence, in that boys and girls personally like traditional girls the most.

The results in this section have bearing on the prediction made in the "Cultural Norms" section that owing to gendered status differences, with increasing age opposite-sex prejudice should diminish for females, more than for males. The results from the first three experiments, dealing with negative judgments about opposite-sex stereotypes, are inconsistent with this prediction, but those concerned with evaluations of counterstereotyped behaviors support the prediction. There is no obvious resolution to this disparity.

Development of Opposite-Sex Discrimination

As discussed earlier, opposite-sex discrimination as defined in chapter 1 has apparently never been studied in North American children and adolescents. The basic assumption made here is that freely chosen gender segregation reflects exclusion based on gender differences. This exclusion may be harmful, and hence, discriminatory. In the following studies two principal methods of assessing segregation have been employed: for preschool and kindergarten children, behavioral observations; for older children, peer nominations (a sociometric technique). Only five experiments will be described out of potentially dozens, primarily for illustrative purposes. That is, the age-related pattern of gender segregation is clear. The Shrum and Cheek (1987) and Shrum, Cheek, and Hunter (1988) research were selected because they studied virtually an entire school system from grades 3 through 12. The others were chosen because of the clarity of their methods and results.

LaFreniere, Strayer, and Gauthier (1984) studied 15 long-standing play groups of children 1 1/2, 2 1/4, 3, 4, and 5 1/2 years old. They observed how frequently children directed positive social initiatives to same- and opposite-sex peers. For the 1 1/2-year-olds, no sex preferences were shown; 2 1/4-year-old girls, but not boys, showed same-sex preferences; by age 3, both boys and girls were directing twice as many initiatives to same-sex as to opposite-sex peers. This ratio remained stable for the girls; for the 5 1/2-year-old boys, however, the ratio changed to 3 to 1. Thus, 3-year-olds of both sexes are reliably showing opposite-sex discrimination.

Maccoby and Jacklin (1987) studied the social play of groups of 4 1/2-year-old nursery school children and 6 1/2-year-old kindergarten children. For each child engaging in either parallel or interactive play, it was noted whether the child's partner was of the same or the opposite sex, or whether the child was part of a mixed-sex group. Both age groups participated in mixed-sex groups approximately one third of the time. The 4 1/2-year-olds were about two and a half times more likely to be playing with a same-sex than with an opposite-sex partner, but the

6 1/2-year-olds were eleven times more likely to be doing so. The results for the 4 1/2-year-olds are consistent with those reported by LaFreniere et al. (1985) and those for the 6 1/2-year-olds are consistent with other published data. Thus, a dramatic increase in opposite-sex discrimination occurs between the ages of 4 1/2 and 6 1/2.

The results of the research on both opposite-sex prejudice and opposite-sex discrimination for young children are very consistent. By age 2 1/2, children show attitudinal and behavioral preferences of the same sex over the opposite sex. These remain relatively stable until about age 4 1/2, after which they grow stronger. By age 6 1/2, the phenomenon of opposite-sex discrimination is striking. The dramatic increase in children's sex discrimination after age 4 1/2 is consistent with the argument that group identity emerges between the ages of 3 and 4 and increases between ages 4 and 5.

Hayden-Thomson, Rubin, and Hymel (1987) conducted two experiments using sociometric techniques to assess same-sex and opposite-sex preferences of children in grades K through 3 (Experiment 1) and grades 3 through 6 (Experiment 2). The children in each classroom were given a set of photographs of each of their classmates and asked to place them in one of three boxes. One box was for "children you like a lot," the second was for "children you sort of like," and the third was for "children you don't like." In each experiment children rated same-sex classmates higher than those of the opposite sex. Both boys and girls in Experiment 1 showed an increasing negative bias towards opposite-sex classmates with increasing age, i.e., from kindergarten to grade 3. However, in Experiment 2, there were no particular trends for either boys or girls as a function of age. Most conservatively, one could conclude that opposite-sex discrimination increases from grades K to 3, and remains relatively stable from grades 3 to 6.

Shrum and Cheek (1987) and Shrum et al. (1988) studied virtually all the third- through twelfth-graders in a racially integrated school district in a southern community in the United States. The data were collected in conjunction with an ongoing biomedical research program. The single question analyzed in both studies was, "Who from school are your best friends?" Using sophisticated statistical methods, Shrum and Cheek analyzed the answers in order to understand how age, race, and gender influenced the social networks in the schools. In particular, they sought to discover how three social categories—isolates, liaisons, and groups—changed as a function of age, and how gender and racial heterogeneity of groups changed with age. In simple terms, an isolate is a person who has zero or one reciprocated friendship. A liaison is a person who has reciprocal friendships with several others, but not exclusively with members of a particular group. A group is a set of at least three in- dividuals who have linked friendships.

In general, the proportion of children and adolescents who were isolates decreased slightly from grade 3 to grade 12; the proportion of liaisons strongly increased from grades 3 to 12, with the biggest changes occurring from grades 7 (entrance into junior high school) to 12; and group membership mirrored liaison status, with the largest drop occurring between grades 7 and 12. Thus the entrance into junior high school is a "watershed for the development of peer relations." What about the gender composition of groups? In grades 3 through 6, an av- erage of only 17 percent of groups were mixed in gender. In grades 7 and 8, this rose to 66 percent, and in grades 9 to 12 (senior high school), 100 percent of groups were mixed-gender groups. These re- sults indicate that the relatively rigid gender segregation seen in ele- mentary school starts to markedly change in junior high school, where heterosexual affectional interests come into play.

Shrum et al. (1988) present a fine-grain analysis of friendship choices (as distinct from group membership) indicating that extensive gender integration is far from the norm at any of the ages studied. Two measures of level of opposite-sex friendship were analyzed: segrega- tion and preference. Both assess the extent to which gender friendships occur relative to chance expectations; i.e., if no sex discrimination oc- curred the proportion of male-male, male-female, and female-female friendships would be tied to the proportion of males and females in the school. The two measures are similar in this regard, and hence the age- related pattern of results was quite similar. Both showed that mixed- gender friendships were very infrequent throughout grades 3 to 12. Starting in junior high school, the frequency increased somewhat and continued through grade 12. The patterns were slightly different for males and females. Same-sex preferences were highest for the boys at grades 3 and 6; for the girls, they peaked at grade 7. At a minimum, children and adolescents in all grades reported an average of at least 5 times as many same-sex as opposite-sex friends.

How does one explain the presence of opposite-sex discrimination in 2 1/2-year-olds and its continuation through adolescence? Maccoby (1988, 1990) has presented a thoughtful analysis of this phenomenon, and links gender segregation to preferred play and interaction styles. She suggests that in nursery school, discrimination is not closely tied to sex-typed activities because many of the activities are gender-neutral. Same-sex preferences are also unrelated to children's own degrees of masculinity or femininity as personality traits.

Two factors seem to be involved in same-sex segregation in nurs- ery school. First, boys in this age range are more likely than girls to enjoy rough-and-tumble play and to be oriented more toward competitive and dominance-related activities. Girls seem to find these activities less pleasurable and often even distasteful. Boys tend to be more excitable, and girls calmer and quieter in their experiencing of these activities. Second, by age 3 1/2 girls find that they are not able to influence readily the play activities of boys, but they can do so with girls. Boys can influence both sexes. (Fagot (1985) showed the lack of influence at age 2 to be symmetrical.) There is a difference between the approaches of the two sexes: girls make polite suggestions, while boys make direct physical and vocal demands. Thus boys learn to enjoy being with boys, and girls with girls, in approximately a 2 to 1 ratio. This ratio remains stable for about two and a half to three years, and then dramatically increases when boys develop a male group identity and girls a female group identity.

As boys and girls remain in same-sex groups, they powerfully socialize themselves in sex-typed interaction styles, interests, activities, and social structure. For example, girls are more likely than boys to become members of smaller groups, to congregate in private homes as opposed to public spaces, and to form intimate friendships with one or two girls, as opposed to boys' less intense friendships with many others. Boys continue throughout childhood and adolescence to be more concerned with dominance and competition, whereas girls continue to be more concerned than boys with collaboration and seeking agreement. Thus, the same-sex group interaction patterns seen in preschool are very similar to those that develop in childhood and adolescence.

A recent study by Bukowski, Gauze, Hoza, and Newcomb (1993) of children in grades 3 through 7 confirms some of Maccoby's (1988, 1990) conclusions. Bukowski et al. examined personality and behavioral correlates of children's own same-sex and opposite-sex friendship choices, and their popularity with same-sex and opposite-sex peers. Among the principal findings were these: same-sex preferences were primarily due to liking same-sex peers rather than to disliking opposite-sex peers; boys who preferred to engage in large-motor activities, e.g., playing ball, riding bicycles, had a stronger preference than other boys for same-sex friends; the more a child was rejected by opposite-sex peers, the more likely that child was to prefer same-sex friends; and high levels of aggressiveness were negatively related to friendship choices, but especially so for girls. The latter points to the important role of behavior in mediating same-sex and opposite-sex segregation.

How do the results concerning opposite-sex prejudice and discrimination fit with the prediction based on the development of group identity and cognitive development? Five age-related shifts in knowledge organization were identified, at ages 4, 6 to 7, 10 to 12, 14 to 16, and 18 to 19 years. The research on development of prejudice identified that shifts in either magnitude or direction occur between ages 3 and 4, 4 and 8, and 8 and 11 years. These are consistent with the first three age periods. There are apparently no data available for the two older age periods. The research on discrimination identified shifts between ages 3 and 4, 4 and 6, 6 and 9, 11 and 13, and 14 and 18 years. These are consistent with the first four age periods, with two exceptions: there is a shift between ages 6 and 9; and the 14- to 18-year-old age range partially overlaps two of the above age periods, i.e., 14 to 16 and 18 to 19 years. These findings point to the effects of a strong cognitive factor in the development of both opposite-sex prejudice and discrimination. It would appear to be linked with those cognitive processes involved with the development of social and perhaps self-knowledge.

Development of Discrimination Towards Deaf Individuals

This section reviews practically all the recent research involving hearing-impaired (deaf) and normal-hearing (hearing) children and adolescents in integrated settings.[1] These studies have utilized either behavioral observations or sociometric techniques for comparing the two groups. None of the studies evaluated prejudice on the part of normal-hearing children towards those who are hearing impaired. There is some literature bearing on this issue, but the attitude measures are embedded in scales dealing with prejudice towards the "physically handicapped." In that research little information is given about the experiences the hearing children have had with the deaf children, and as a consequence, is of limited value for the present purposes.

The major problem with this research area is the rarity of integration of more than one deaf child or adolescent into a classroom with hearing students. The main exceptions are the preschool studies and the two experiments involving college students at the Rochester Institute of Technology. Thus, for children between the ages of 6 and 18 years, nearly all the research deals with the reactions of hearing students to the single deaf student in their classroom. A second problem involves the effects of degree of impairment of the deaf children. In most studies there was a great range of hearing disability, from mild to profound deafness. This means

---

[1]In the recent literature on hearing impairment, the word "deaf" is quite acceptable, as is "hearing-impaired." "Hearing" is preferred to "normal," but is equivalent in meaning to "normal-hearing."

that even with hearing aids the range of understanding and using speech was quite varied. Children with only mild hearing impairment can readily understand and use speech with hearing aids. Those with profound losses can generally do neither. Given the centrality of speech to interactions, generalizations may be limited.

Six of the papers using observational methods deal with preschool children aged 3 1/2 to 6 years. One additional paper deals with first- and second-graders (McCauley, Bruininks, & Kennedy, 1976), and one with first- through sixth-graders (Antia, 1982). Age effects are not reported in any of these studies, primarily because of the small number of deaf children involved.

In the Brackett and Henniges (1976) study, all the deaf preschool children used hearing aids and had mild to profound hearing losses. Both deaf and hearing children spent part of each day in a structured language learning class and part in a free-play setting. Each child's behavior was observed in both settings. For purposes of analysis, the deaf children were divided into two groups based on their language abilities. The major finding relative to discrimination was that the hearing children interacted more with deaf children having good language abilities than with those having poor language abilities. The latter children interacted mainly with their teachers and with other hearing-impaired children. The results of research by Arnold and Tremblay (1979) and Levy-Shiff and Hoffman (1985) are consistent with these findings: Preschool hearing and deaf children interact primarily with children of similar hearing status.

Cause-effect relationships are difficult to determine in this research. Do hearing children reject the deaf with poor language abilities, or do the latter only seek out teachers and other deaf children to interact with? Brackett and Henniges (1976) do not provide enough clues for an answer. The Vandell and George (1981) and Vandell, Anderson, Ehrhardt, and Wilson (1982) experiments do help with this question. These studies took place in the same setting: an integrated preschool focused on the hearing impaired. Equal numbers of deaf and hearing children were involved and spent part of each day together. The children were systematically observed in pairs in a separate playroom. In the Vandell and George experiment the focus was on children's interaction initiatives: their frequency, type, and success. The major findings were that pairs of hearing children had the highest levels of interaction, and mixed pairs—i.e., hearing with deaf children—had the lowest levels. Deaf children initiated more interactions with hearing children than the reverse; also, the deaf children were more likely to be ignored or rejected by the hearing children than were the hearing by the deaf. Both groups of children used the same kinds of social initiatives, and the deaf children were more persistent in their attempts to interact. Finally, mixed pairs were more likely to use inappropriate initiatives—e.g., signalling to a peer when the child's back was turned—than were pairs of hearing or pairs of deaf children. These results indicate that normal-hearing children would rather interact with other hearing children than with deaf children, despite the persistence of the latter in initiating interactions.

The Vandell et al. (1982) experiment dealt with attempts to modify the "frequent and persistent refusal of normal children to interact with profoundly deaf peers." The researchers spent 15 to 30 minutes a day for 15 consecutive days with half of the hearing children, training them to be more knowledgeable about and to develop more appropriate communication skills for interacting with hearing-impaired children. The other half of the hearing group received no special training. The results were striking. In virtually every measure concerning interaction success between deaf and hearing children, the trained hearing children performed more *poorly* than those who were untrained. It appears that sensitizing normal-hearing children to the needs of deaf peers makes them less willing to interact with the latter.

The research by Lederberg, Ryan, and Robbins (1986) provides some insight into the above findings. Lederberg et al. paired deaf 5- and 6-year-olds once with each of four different play partners. The pairs were placed alone in a small playroom with age-appropriate toys. One of the partners was a familiar deaf playmate; one, a familiar hearing playmate; one, an unfamiliar but "experienced" hearing playmate who was a friend of another deaf child; and one, an unfamiliar hearing playmate who was "inexperienced" with deaf children. None of the deaf children had developed spoken language.

A variety of measures of social interactions, communication styles, and type of play were coded. Some of the major results were as follows: deaf children interacted most frequently and effectively with other deaf children, and next most effectively and frequently with familiar hearing playmates. Familiar hearing playmates were more likely than unfamiliar ones to modify their communication styles to accommodate their deaf playmates. For example, the familiar playmates were more likely to use visual communication techniques than the two unfamiliar ones. In general, there were few differences between unfamiliar experienced and inexperienced hearing playmates: both had considerable difficulty interacting with their deaf playmates. The above pattern of results indicates that for hearing preschool children, interaction success with a deaf playmate stems from knowing and having experience with the particular playmate, and not from the use of generalized skills acquired in interactions with other deaf children.

McCauley et al. (1976) observed first- and second-graders in the classroom, with one deaf child per class. The deaf children had moderate to profound hearing losses; all wore hearing aids, and all were receiving speech therapy. McCauley et al. do not report the relative frequency with which hearing children interacted with the deaf child. Rather, they report on the types of interactions both groups had—i.e., positive versus negative, verbal versus nonverbal—and the individuals with whom they interacted—i.e., peers versus teachers. The hearing and deaf children were similar in all ways but one: the hearing children interacted more with their peers than with the teacher, whereas the reverse was the case for the deaf children. The authors suggest that deaf children seek out teachers because interactions with them are more rewarding than those with normal-hearing children.

Antia (1982) observed deaf and normal-hearing first- through sixth-graders in integrated classes and the same deaf children in special segregated classrooms. Antia took essentially the same kinds of measures that McCauley et al. (1976) had taken. The major findings were these: hearing and deaf children were rarely isolated within the classroom, and thus had ample opportunity for peer interactions. As in McCauley et al. (1976), the deaf children were more likely to interact with teachers than were the hearing children, and less likely to interact with peers. The hearing children also interacted more frequently with other normal-hearing children than with their deaf peers. In the special classes the deaf children increased their interactions with teachers, but not the frequency of peer interactions.

The above experiments point to the following conclusions. Normal-hearing children from preschool through sixth grade prefer interacting with other normal-hearing peers to interacting with deaf children. The latter children prefer interacting with teachers and with other hearing-impaired peers to doing so with hearing peers. The motivation behind these choices seems to be ease of communication and the rewards of the interaction. In a sense, both groups of children follow the path of least effort.

Recent research investigating communication styles in deaf and hearing children support these conclusions. Jones (1985), who observed 6- to 8-year-old deaf and hearing children from segregated schools, found that in face-to-face interactions deaf children keep about 25 percent more distance from each other than do hearing children. Musselman, Lindsay, and Wilson (1988) found that among deaf 3- to 9-year-old children in segregated settings, those with the greatest hearing losses had the greatest difficulty in peer interactions. Finally, McKirdy and Blank (1982) studied the verbal "dialogues" among deaf and hearing 5-year-old children in segregated settings. All had IQs in the normal range. The dialogues among the deaf were much more restricted than those among the hearing. Levels of complexity, both as initiators of interactions and as responders, were much lower for the deaf than for the hearing.

We now examine research using sociometric methods for evaluating acceptance by hearing children of their deaf peers. The participants in these experiments were between the ages of 7 and 18. Four studies were carried out in school settings, and one, by Hus (1979), in a summer day camp. Hus' paper assessed only five deaf and four normally hearing children. Age effects were not reported or found in any of the research.

Kennedy and Bruininks (1974) studied first- and second-grade deaf children enrolled in integrated classrooms. Their degree of hearing loss ranged from moderate to profound, with the majority falling in the severe/profound categories. All wore hearing aids full-time and had been previously enrolled in preschools with hearing children. Best friends and roster and ratings measures were used to assess sociometric status. The principal results were that the scores for deaf and hearing children on all measures were essentially the same. However, there was a strong trend for the children with profound/severe losses to be more popular than the average normal-hearing child in their classes. Those with moderate losses tended to be less popular than their normally hearing peers. The number of mutual choices for best friends was equivalent for deaf and hearing children. Thus, the higher sociometric scores for those with profound/severe losses cannot readily be attributed to unidirectional, i.e., hearing to deaf, sympathy. One possible explanation for these surprising findings is that the children with profound/severe losses required positive special attention from their teachers and classmates, which had the effect of making them better known and more likable.

Kennedy, Northcott, McCauley, and Williams (1976) followed 11 of the severely to profoundly deaf children from Kennedy and Bruininks (1974) for two years. They administered the same tests as in the above study, and additionally carried out observations of peer and teacher interactions. In the second year of the followup, when nine of the students were in third grade, a very different pattern of results emerged: these students were now either less popular (on one measure) or equally popular (on another measure) as the average normal-hearing child in their class. The number of mutual friendship choices was equivalent in the hearing and deaf groups. Regarding behavioral interactions, the quality of these interactions, i.e., positive, negative, verbal, nonverbal, was equivalent for the two groups; but in a pattern similar to that found in previously reported research, the deaf children interacted more with their teachers and less with their peers than did the hearing children.

The experiment by Elser (1959) helps us understand whether the relative popularity of deaf children is related to age and/or degree of impairment. Elser measured both friendship choices and reputation (status and personality) in 9- to 12-year-olds (grades 3 through 7) with predominantly moderate hearing loss, in fully integrated classes. None of the children had profound losses. For the purposes of data analysis, Elser divided the deaf children into two groups: those with losses of less than 50 db (mild and moderate), and those with greater losses. Virtually none of the children in the former group wore hearing aids full-time. Generally, results were consistent with Kennedy et al. (1976): both groups of deaf children were perceived by their hearing peers as being in the lower third of the class in both friendship choices and positive reputation. There were no differences in personality traits. Results were also somewhat consistent with Kennedy and Bruininks (1974): children who did not wear hearing aids (had a milder impairment) were less accepted than those who did.

Elser suggests that the lower popularity of children without hearing aids may be due to their appearance of having normal hearing ability, which predisposes others to assume they will behave similarly to non-impaired children. That they socially interacted differently, for no apparent reason, may have led normal-hearing children to be somewhat rejecting of them.

The overall reduction in popularity of deaf children relative to the first- and second-graders in Kennedy and Bruininks (1974) is buttressed by the findings of Hus (1979). In her summer camp study, severely/profoundly deaf 8- to 10-year-olds were liked far less than their hearing peers.

We can summarize the results of the above four experiments as follows. Six- and 7-year-old deaf children with severe/profound losses are more popular than their hearing peers, whereas those with moderate losses are less popular. From about age 8 on, deaf children decline in popularity, especially those with less severe impairments. By age 12, the deaf children are now rated as less popular than their hearing peers. These results suggest that older and younger children use different criteria for sociometric friendship choices.

Selman's (1980) analysis of friendships and peer groups helps us understand these phenomena. Six- and 7-year-olds tend to view friendship as one-way assistance rather than reciprocity. The latter is an important aspect of 9- to 12-year-olds' conception of friendship. Six- and 7-year-olds view peer groups as consisting of unilateral relations, not involving common goals. Nine- to 12-year-olds see peer groups as consisting of bilateral relations and common goals. Thus, the assistance that hearing 6- and 7-year-olds give to deaf peers might lead to the development of friendship. But that same assistance by 9- to 12-year-olds would not, since it is not reciprocated or bilateral.

Ladd, Munson, and Miller (1984), in a two-year longitudinal experiment, studied hearing and deaf juniors and seniors in public high school occupational education programs. In these programs, deaf and hearing students frequently work closely together on laboratory projects. The deaf students were mainstreamed into these schools when they were juniors, typically with one or two deaf students per class. The hearing students had been enrolled since at least their sophomore year. The researchers used sociometric scales, qualitative observations, and parent, teacher, and student interviews to assess how successfully the deaf were socially integrated. Unfortunately for the present purposes, no data were presented for the hearing students, and few comparisons were made between deaf and hearing students.

Some of the principal findings were these: deaf students socially interacted more with hearing students during their senior than their junior years; and peer ratings by hearing students of several personality characteristics of the deaf, e.g., social ability, considerateness, yielded no appreciable differences between the hearing and deaf. Interviews with parents of deaf adolescents indicated that few hearing peers from school ever visited their homes. The teachers of these adolescents reported frequent in-school friendships between hearing and deaf students, but were aware of few out-of-school friendships. The overwhelming majority of deaf and hearing students reported having in-school friendships with students of a different hearing status, i.e., hearing and deaf. These results indicate that in-school friendships among older deaf and hearing students readily occur, especially after both groups have had extensive experience with each other.

The last two experiments are concerned with normal-hearing students' reactions to deaf college students who were integrated in both classrooms and residence halls. Emerton and Rothman (1978) gave a questionnaire to hearing freshmen and transfer students at the Rochester Institute of Technology (RIT) concerning attitudes towards the deaf. RIT is also the home of the National Technical Institute for the Deaf (NTID), which in 1990 enrolled approximately 1,200 deaf college students. Students at NTID have the choice of taking some or all of their courses at RIT, with full support services available. The hearing students were given the questionnaire before entering college, and six months later. In general their attitudes were positive; i.e., they rejected about 80 percent of stereotypes about the deaf. However, these attitudes became slightly more negative after six months. The latter scores were unaffected by whether the hearing students lived in integrated (deaf and hearing) or segregated dorms. On the sixth-month questionnaire, the majority of the hearing students saw the deaf relative to the hearing students as immature, having more psychological problems, and passive about taking leadership roles.

The study by Brown and Foster (1991) dealt with the same two populations of students at RIT and NTID. Theirs was a qualitative research project in which the hearing students, who had been at RIT for an average of 2 1/2 years, were interviewed using in-depth open-ended strategies. Half were men, half had lived in integrated residence halls, and all but one had taken at least one course with a deaf student. Some of the principal findings were as follows. The hearing students felt that the deaf were equally capable of performing well in class, and were unconcerned by the special instructional and support services the latter were given. However, the structure of the classroom essentially precluded positive interactions between the two groups. The deaf students always sat close to the front, where they could readily see the teacher and the interpreter. The hearing students sat in other locations, and formed acquaintances through casual conversation with their hearing neighbors. Any out-of-class communications the hearing had were with these acquaintances. However, several hearing students reported much more positive social experiences with deaf partners in laboratory settings.

The hearing students reported a fair amount of difficulty living in the same residence halls as the deaf students. They usually either spoke in negative terms about the deaf or identified a small number of deaf students as "exceptional." Some of the negative behaviors were making too much noise, pushing in line, blocking the hallway. Some of the negative attitudes mentioned were rudeness, cockiness, arrogance, self-centeredness. The "exceptional" deaf students usually had good speech, read lips, behaved similarly to the hearing students, and showed a desire to interact with hearing students. Very few hearing students reported any long-standing friendships with deaf peers. On those explicitly social occasions to which deaf and hearing students were invited, the two groups rarely mixed. Generally, deaf and hearing students joined separate clubs and enjoyed separate social networks.

Brown and Foster (1991) understand these findings as reflecting a conflict between the deaf culture and the somewhat inappropriate expectations of the hearing. For example, deaf persons often get someone's attention by pounding on a table. When conversing, they establish a "sign visibility distance," which, as previously noted, is greater than the usual distance between hearing speakers. Both examples are disruptive to the hearing student: the former behavior is seen as inconsiderate, and the latter as rude, when a deaf person blocks a stairway or hallway. Because deaf students look like hearing ones, attend the same college, and have equivalent intellectual abilities, the hearing expect them to act like hearing students. In other words, hearing evaluate deaf students "with reference to a hearing norm."

It can be concluded from the Ladd et al. (1984) and Brown and Foster (1991) research that friendships between deaf and hearing older adolescents and young adults can occur within certain types of classroom situations. These are most likely found in laboratory settings, where the deaf and hearing work together closely and collaboratively. But the friendships rarely go beyond the classroom. Foster and Brown (1989), based on in-depth interviews with deaf students at RIT, suggest that neither deaf nor hearing students are strongly motivated to develop friendships with each other. Simply put, it takes a great deal of effort and patience to attain comfortable social interactions. Given other available options for developing satisfying relationships, intense involvement with those of a different hearing status is not pursued. Thus, separate social networks emerge where social and emotional needs are more readily met.

Summary

Seven methodological concerns about research on prejudice development were discussed. First, no clear distinction exists in the literature between "prejudice" and "negative stereotypes." Second, different measures of prejudice often lead to different conclusions. Third, the testing context (persons and materials) has been shown to influence children's expressed attitudes. Fourth, forced-choice techniques may confound preference of one group with rejection of the other. Fifth, tests assessing prejudice fail to distinguish between reactions to some characteristic of the target group and reactions to the members themselves. Sixth, tests of prejudice fail to distinguish between children's attitudes towards target groups and their knowledge of social stereotypes. Seventh, apparent developmental decreases in prejudice may reflect changes in knowledge of social desirability, and not changes in prejudice.

Six different procedures have been used to infer level of discrimination: peer nominations, peer ratings, teacher nominations, teacher ratings, behavior observations, and peer assessments. In most cases, data were collected in school settings. Thus, relatively little is known about discrimination outside of these settings. Additionally, various classroom structures have been found to have differential effects on friendship choices. Concerning the different measures, children of varying ages may interpret the tasks differently. Teachers and children may interpret them differently from each other. Moreover, the correlations among the measures are typically low to moderate.

Genetic/evolutionary predispositions and cultural norms were discussed as antecedents of opposite-sex prejudice and discrimination. Several predictions were made based on these factors concerning developmental, gender, parental, and familial effects on prejudice and discrimination.

In the section concerned with the socialization of sex-typing, the complexity and multidimensionality of sex-typing was emphasized. Sex-typing of infants starts virtually at birth and pervades nearly all aspects of children's physical and social environments. Parents socialize their sons and daughters differently. Fathers are more likely to do so than mothers, a practice consistent with the cultural norms of male dominance. The development of gender identity is strongly affected by parents' toy selection and by involvement in their child's sex-typed play. Consistent with earlier predictions is the finding that variations in family type, e.g., conventional versus nonconventional family, single parent versus two parents, single homosexual parent versus single heterosexual parent, have very little effect on either boys' or girls' development of gender identity. Teachers and peers in preschool settings, however, appear to have strong effects on the differential gender identity in boys and girls.

The development of opposite-sex prejudice was assessed by both indirect and direct measures. In the section dealing with indirect measures, four predictions based on the consequences of male and female status and dominance differences were evaluated. The predictions concerned either the enhancement of male sex-typed characteristics or the devaluation of female sex-typed characteristics by children and adolescents. All four were supported by the data.

For the direct measures, two categories of experiments were examined. In the first, we looked at the negative and positive sex-role stereotypes that boys and girls hold for themselves and for the opposite sex. In the second, we assessed children's evaluations of counterstereotyped behavior that they and/or male and female peers carried out. Results of research for the first category indicate that opposite-sex prejudice starts to emerge at age 2 1/2, is clearly seen in 4-year-olds, and increases until about age 8. Between ages 8 and 10 it declines somewhat. Data for older children are unavailable. Results of research for the second category are somewhat inconsistent with the above. Between ages 4 and 8 years, both sexes start to value male more than female characteristics, which tends to produce female prejudice among females. Between 8 and 10 years this enhanced valuing of male characteristics strengthens, but the emergence of heterosexual interests after age 10 complicates the developmental pattern.

The research on opposite-sex discrimination identified developmental shifts between ages 3 and 4, 4 and 6, 6 and 9, 11 and 13, and 14 and 18 years. These are fairly consistent with predictions based on the development of group identity and cognitive development. These results point to the effects of a strong cognitive factor mediating this discrimination. Analyses by Maccoby and others concerning differences between males and females in sex-typed interaction styles, interests, activities, and social structure suggest that these differences underlie opposite-sex discrimination.

Research using observational methods concerning discrimination towards the hearing impaired indicates that normal-hearing children from preschool through sixth grade prefer interacting with other hearing peers than with deaf children. Deaf children prefer interacting with teachers and deaf peers than with hearing children. The motivation behind these choices seems to be ease of communication and the rewards of interaction. Research using sociometric methods indicates that 6- and 7-year-old deaf children with severe/profound losses are more popular than their hearing peers, whereas those with moderate losses are less popular. From about age 8 on, deaf children decline in popularity. By age 12, the deaf are now rated as less popular than their hearing peers. Selman's analysis of developmental changes in understanding friendships and peer groups was used to explain the sociometric phenomena.

Research with older adolescents and young adults in academic environments indicates that friendships between deaf and hearing students can occur within certain types of classroom settings. However, social distance is the norm outside of the classroom, primarily because it requires too much effort for members of the two groups to attain rewarding and comfortable interpersonal interactions.

Prejudice and Discrimination Towards Different-Race and Mentally Retarded Individuals

Introduction

There are five goals of this chapter. The first is to present a brief summary of perhaps the most socially significant research that has been carried out in North America by psychologists: Kenneth and Mamie Clark's work on the development of race prejudice in children. The Clarks' studies played an important role in the judicial decision to prohibit school segregation along racial lines. Their research also helped set the stage for and provided a major impetus to the study of racial prejudice. The second goal is to evaluate several hypotheses related to the genetic/evolutionary and cultural/historical material previously discussed. These hypotheses will parallel those presented in chapter 4 for opposite-sex prejudice. The third goal is to summarize as accurately as possible the literatures dealing with the development of prejudice and discrimination based on race and mental retardation. The literature discussing race will emphasize Black and White racial groups. The fourth goal is to summarize the literature dealing with prejudice and discrimination toward mentally retarded individuals. The fifth goal is to integrate the four prejudice and discrimination literatures discussed in the present and the previous chapter in order to find common themes in this research.

Regarding the second goal above, one speculation and two predictions were made based on the genetic/evolutionary material. First, in our evolutionary heritage adolescent females (but not males) migrated to other groups; females also were less involved in intergroup hostility than males. This suggests that males may be genetically predisposed to form stronger commitments to ingroups, a possibility that leads to the speculation that males would develop stronger degrees of prejudice than females. This speculation was supported for opposite-sex prejudice, and is probably applicable to race prejudice and discrimination. Second, family influences in the development of prejudice will be minimal. This prediction was based on the behavior genetics research and was confirmed for the socialization of sex-typing. It is likely that this prediction will be supported in the literature on race prejudice and discrimination. Third, based on the group identity and cognitive development literature, it was predicted that prejudice and discrimination would emerge between the ages of 3 and 4 years and undergo age-related shifts at 7, 10 to 12, 14 to 16, and 18 to 19 years.

There were six predictions made concerning opposite-sex prejudice and discrimination based on the cultural/historical dominance of males over females. Four of these predictions are applicable to race prejudice and discrimination, given the cultural dominance of Whites over all other racial/ethnic minority groups. First, Blacks and other minority groups should acquire knowledge of White cultural norms prior to Whites' acquisition of knowledge of minority cultural norms. Second, owing to their self-perceived lower status, Blacks and other minorities should be more likely to adopt White cultural behaviors and values than the converse. Third, owing to the high status of Whites relative to that of other racial/ethnic groups, self-esteem in all races should be more highly related to White cultural behaviors and values than to the behaviors and values of their own races. Fourth, owing to the higher status of Whites than that of other racial/ethnic groups, with increasing age, race prejudice and discrimination should diminish on the part of minority groups more than on the part of Whites.

Brown v. Board of Education

The psychologist Kenneth B. Clark prepared a report in 1950 for the Mid-Century White House Conference on Children and Youth, called "The Effects of Prejudice and Discrimination on Personality Development in Children." This report and other social science studies were extensively relied on by the U.S. Supreme Court for its 1954 decision in the case entitled *Brown v. Board of Education.* The justices noted that so-called "separate but equal" public education facilities were inherently unequal when the segregation was based on race. They maintained that such racial segregation denoted the "inferiority" of Negroes, which affected children's motivation to learn. When segregation was sanctioned by law, it tended to "retard the educational and mental development of Negro children." Therefore the segregated Negro children were being "deprived of the equal protection of the laws guaranteed by the Fourteenth Amendment." Such segregation in public education was ruled unconstitutional by the Court.

In 1955, Clark revised his White House paper and published it as the book *Prejudice and Your Child.* In 1963 the book was enlarged to include several appendices related to the Supreme Court decision, leaving intact the 1955 material. What follows is my brief summary of those aspects of the book dealing with the research carried out by Clark and others concerned with the development of a racial self-image.

The starting point for Clark's research, which he began in the late 1930s with his wife, Mamie Clark, was the conviction that Negro and White children (in Clark's words) "learn social, racial, and religious prejudices in the course of observing, and being influenced by, the existence of patterns in the culture in which they live" (1963, p. 17). How do these American cultural patterns affect the racial awareness and racial preferences of Negro children? The Clarks initially studied this question with 3- to 7-year-olds using the "dolls" test. The children were presented with four dolls that were identical, with the exception that two were brown and two were white. The children were asked by the Negro experimenter to identify the "White doll," the "colored doll," and the "Negro doll." More than 75 percent of 4- and 5-year-olds living in both the North and the South correctly identified the "races" of the dolls. This percentage increased with increasing age.

Clark points out that Negro children whose skin color was indistinguishable from that of White people showed a delayed ability to reliably identify the dolls. However, by age 5 or 6, the majority of these children made correct social identifications, i.e., that Negro dolls were brown, and White dolls were white, despite the fact that they themselves had "white" skin color. Clark concluded that racial awareness developed in Negro children as young as age 4. He noted that other researchers found parallel results with White children.

The Clarks additionally asked the Negro children to point to the doll "which is most like you." Overall, approximately two thirds of the children were correct, with the percentage increasing with increasing age: 37

percent of 3-year-olds and 87 percent of 7-year-olds chose the brown dolls. Again, children with light skin color had more difficulty with this task than the darker children. Thus, there are close parallels between the development of racial awareness and that of racial identification.

The Clarks then went on to study racial preferences of Negro children. The researchers asked the following four questions:

1. Give me the doll that you like to play with.
2. Give me the doll that is the nice doll.
3. Give me the doll that looks bad.
4. Give me the doll that is a nice color. (p. 23)

They found that the majority of children of all ages preferred the white doll to the brown one. Other researchers have found comparable white-over-brown doll preferences for White children. Clark concluded that the self-rejection of Negroes as indicated by their preference to be White "reflects their knowledge that society prefers [W]hite people" and their acceptance of this racial attitude.

What are the personal and emotional consequences of racial self-rejection by Negro children? The Clarks carried out another experiment, called the "coloring test." They report both objective and more impressionistic or clinical data from this research. Children were given a sheet of paper with drawings of familiar "things," such as a leaf, an apple, a boy, and a girl, along with a box of crayons. The children were asked to color all the things except the boy and the girl. Only the 5- to 7-year-olds consistently used the correct colors in this task. The researchers then asked these children to color the same-sex drawing "the color that you are" and to color the opposite-sex drawing the color they liked little children to be. All the light-skinned Negro children colored the same-sex drawing with a white or yellow crayon, and 15 percent of the children with medium or dark-brown skin did the same, or used a "bizarre color like red or green." When asked to color the opposite-sex child, 48 percent of all these children chose brown, 37 percent chose white, and 15 percent chose an irrelevant color. These results are generally consistent with the dolls test and indicate racial self-rejection.

Were there differences between results for Negro children from the North and those for Negro children from the South? Yes, dramatic ones. About 80 percent of the Southern children, but only about 36 percent of the Northern children, colored their preferences brown. Moreover, Southern children rarely used bizarre colors, but 20 percent of the Northern children did so. Additionally, only 20 percent of Northern children, but 82 percent of Southern children, spoke to themselves or to the researcher as they worked, indicating guardedness by the Northerners. Finally, none of the Southern children, but some (no percentages are given) of the Northern children, were very distressed by this task, e.g., crying, refusing to finish the task without coaxing.

What do these numbers and observations mean? Clark believes that the Northern Negro children actually had a psychologically healthier reaction to the inner conflict between who they were racially and whom the society valued. Their preference for white over brown, choice of bizarre colors, relative silence during the task, and intermittent emotional upheaval indicates that they did not willingly accept a devalued racial identification. The acceptance of a "brown" racial status by the Southern children indicates an acceptance of an "inferior social status." In the dolls task, for example, some of the Southern Negro children would point to the brown doll and say, "This one. It's a nigger. I'm a nigger" (p. 45).

Clark concludes this section of the book with the following powerful statement regarding the implications of his research:

> As minority-group children learn the inferior status to which they are assigned and observe that they are usually segregated and isolated from the more privileged members of their society, they react with deep feelings of inferiority and with a sense of personal humiliation. Many of them become confused about their own personal worth. Like all other human beings they require a sense of personal dignity and social support for positive self-esteem. Almost nowhere in the larger society, however, do they find their own dignity as human beings respected or protected. Under these conditions, minority-group children develop conflicts with regard to their feelings about themselves and about the value of the group with which they are identified. Understandably they begin to question whether they themselves and their group are worthy of no more respect from the larger society than they receive. These conflicts, confusions and doubts give rise under certain circumstances to self-hatred and rejection of their own group. (pp. 63–64)

Development of Ethnic Identity

From a psychological viewpoint the central argument of the Clarks was that identification by Black children with a minority group having an "inferior status" (Blacks) leads to "deep feelings of inferiority" and "a sense of personal humiliation." Clark based this conclusion on both qualitative observations of racial conflict among Black children and the children's systematic identification with and preference for White dolls over Black ones. However, it is possible that direct measures of self-esteem may not conform to this conclusion. That is, Black children may identify with and prefer White dolls or pictures more than Black ones, and *not* have low self-esteem.

What do the data show? Overall, in studies carried out both before and after the start of the civil rights movement and passage of civil rights legislation in 1964, for both children and adolescents, there is no systematic relationship between measures of self-esteem and measures of racial preference or ethnic identity (Aboud, 1988; Cross, 1987; Phinney, 1990). That is, children and adolescents may have high or low self-esteem and either positively or negatively value their own ethnic group. This is a surprising result, counter to Clark's conclusions, and apparently counter to the prediction that Black self-esteem will be positively related to White cultural values and behaviors. How is it explained?

Let us first start with some definitions. Racial groups and ethnic groups are not equivalent. In the United States they do tend to be covariant; e.g., African-Americans, Chinese-Americans, Mexican-Americans do form racial/ethnic groups. But Jewish-Americans, Greek-Americans, and Italian-Americans are all White and often indistinguishable physically. In Canada, French-Canadians and English-Canadians look alike, but form distinct ethnic groups. Recent research in the United States usually compares different racial/ethnic groups with each other or with Whites as a whole. The ethnic groups chosen are primarily the subordinated minority groups, especially African-Americans, which are equally defined by the terms "race" and "ethnicity."

Nearly all writers in this field offer definitions of ethnic groups. Rotheram and Phinney's (1987) definition captures the essential features of the concept. An "ethnic group" is "any collection of people who call themselves an ethnic group and who see themselves sharing common attributes" (p. 12). Note that race and minority status are not relevant to the definition. "Ethnic awareness" refers to a person's ability to make distinctions between different racial/ethnic groups. "Ethnic identity" goes beyond this. It "refers to one's sense of belonging to an ethnic group" and acquiring its behavior patterns. Thus, being Jewish-American, or African-American, or Japanese-American does not automatically place an individual in an ethnic group, though others may think it does. If the person herself does not have a sense of belonging to, and does not share behavior patterns characteristic of a particular ethnic group, then the person does not identify as a member of that group. However, that person may certainly be "aware" of the existence of different ethnic groups. "Ethnic preference" refers to an individual's valuing or preferring one racial/ethnic group over others. The preferred group is not necessarily the individual's racial/ethnic group.

Ethnic awareness is typically measured by presenting children with dolls or pictures depicting different racial/ethnic groups and asking them to point to the picture/doll of a specific group, e.g., White, Native

American, Black, Chinese. Another technique involves presenting children with three pictures of people, two from the same racial/ethnic group and one from another group. The children are asked to choose the two who are most similar. Ethnic identity is typically measured by showing children dolls or pictures depicting different racial/ethnic groups and asking them to point to the doll/picture that most looks like them. Ethnic preference is typically measured the way the Clarks did, as described in the previous section. Children are shown pictures or dolls representing different ethnic groups and they are asked questions about which doll they'd like to play with, which is the nicest, and so forth. We'll defer discussing research dealing with ethnic preference until the section on the development of prejudice.

Rotheram and Phinney (1987) and Beuf (1977) each hypothesize three stages in the development of children's ethnic identity. The following is a synthesis of their views. In the first stage, which characterizes most groups of 3- and 4-year-olds, children have little awareness of racial/ethnic differences. In the second stage, ages 4 to 6 years, most Black and White children show accurate ethnic awareness, but Native Americans, Chinese-Americans, and Mexican-Americans do not. White children tend to acquire awareness earlier than children of other racial/ethnic groups. Also in this stage, White children demonstrate accurate ethnic identity, but children in the other North American ethnic groups do not. They typically point to the White doll/picture equally or slightly more frequently than to that of their own racial/ethnic group in response to the question "Which doll (picture) looks like you?" In the third stage, between 7 and 10 years of age, all groups of children demonstrate accurate ethnic identity and have developed an understanding of "racial constancy." Prior to this stage, children believe that they can willfully change their race, or that variations in apparel or hair, e.g., wearing Native American clothes or a blond wig, produce changes in one's race. White children achieve racial constancy at earlier ages in this stage than do children of other racial/ethnic groups. These findings are consistent with the prediction that Blacks and other minorities should be more likely to adopt White cultural behaviors and values than the converse.

The phenomenon in the second stage in which children of non-White ethnic groups identify with White dolls/pictures rather than their own ethnic dolls/pictures has been referred to as "misidentification" (Rotheram & Phinney, 1987). This is a crucial part of the phenomena the Clarks discovered, which formed the basis for their conclusions about Black self-devaluation. We have seen above that misidentification is unrelated to self-esteem. What does it mean, then?

Beuf (1977), Cross (1987), and Vaughn (1987) offer similar explanations of this phenomenon. The essential aspects of their models are as follows. The self-concept can be viewed as comprised of two major components, a social identity and a personal identity. One's social identity includes all the various social groupings, including ethnic groups, that a child is aware of and belongs to. To a large extent the social structure of a society, which includes devaluation of certain minority groups, determines the social groupings that children are aware of. In developing their individual social identities, children make comparisons between attributes of those groups they are aware of, and locate themselves as members of some of the groups. Thus, minority children learn they are members of ethnic groups devalued by the majority culture. A child's personal identity includes all the attributes that she notes in making interpersonal comparisons with other individuals she is in contact with. These include beliefs, emotional states, skills, interpersonal competence, and self-esteem. Hence, one can acquire high self-esteem but identify with a devalued minority group.

When minority children in the second stage are asked who they look like, and then point to the White doll/picture, the above writers argue that the children are interpreting the question not as one of personal identity, but rather as one of preferred social identity. These authors maintain that children in the second stage know which the most highly valued group is (Whites). Since they believe that race is a fluid category, it can be changed at will. Hence, their pointing to the White doll/picture reflects that belief and their desire to be part of a highly valued group. In the third stage, children no longer misidentify their ethnicity. That's because they have acquired racial constancy, which is parallel to other attainments in the stage of concrete operations (Piaget, 1971). They now accept their membership in a particular ethnic group because that membership cannot be willed or wished away.

A critical feature of being a member of an ethnic group, especially from the viewpoint of prejudice and discrimination, is that one has acquired patterns of behaviors, beliefs, and feelings that distinguish ingroup from outgroup members. In that groups differ in a large number of ways, the question must be answered, "Which ways are most central?" Rotheram and Phinney (1987), after an extensive survey of anthropological and social psychological literature, have identified four dimensions that capture the essential types of social rules involved with structuring ingroup interpersonal interactions. These can be construed as behavioral badges, which can be used to identify group members. The four dimensions are as follows:

1. An orientation toward group affiliation and interdependence versus an individual orientation emphasizing independence and competition.

2. An active, achievement-oriented style versus a passive accepting style.
3. Authoritarianism and the acceptance of hierarchical relationships versus egalitarianism, and
4. An expressive, overt, personal style of communication versus a
restrained, impersonal, and formal style. (p. 22)

Thus, members of ethnic groups that differ substantially on any of
these dimensions are likely to experience conflict when they interact
with one another. This was clearly seen in Maccoby's (1988, 1990) discussion of gender differences, in which males and females were found
to differ on the first dimension. Presumably, ethnic groups that differ
on two or more dimensions will experience considerable conflict. One
major consequence of this intergroup conflict is a confirmation of
boundaries between ingroups and outgroups.

In addition to these four dimensions, other writers, e.g., Heller
(1987) and Kochman (1987), emphasize differences in language and
communication styles as being fundamental to conflicts between different ethnic groups. Heller maintains that members of an ethnic group
participate in particular social networks, have access to particular social
roles (including various work and play roles) and share resources controlled by the group, e.g., certain churches, neighborhoods, shops.
"Shared language is basic to shared identity, but more than that, identity rests on shared ways of using language that reflect common patterns of thinking and behaving, or shared culture" (p. 181). Heller argues that language shapes identity formation in two essential ways: it
marks the boundary between groups and it carries the meaning of
shared experiences. Perhaps the most dramatic cases illustrating
Heller's views involve the different languages used by the deaf and the
hearing, as described in the previous chapter. Different languages keep
outsiders out, and reinforce the shared experiences of insiders. Language may be the primary badging mechanism used to define ingroup
membership.

Kochman (1987) is in essential agreement with Heller (1987) that
certain features of language are "boundary maintaining markers."
Members of ethnic groups know these features well and use them to af-
firm self and others as ethnic group members. In the African-American
community "Black intonation" and "expressive intensity" are two such
features. Black intonation is a speech pattern of rising and falling pitch
that is distinctive among Blacks. Blacks who don't use this pattern are
often accused of "acting White." Expressive intensity involves a great
deal of animation and vitality in speech, as opposed to subdued, low-
key communicative acts. When Blacks talk in the latter manner they are

also accused of "acting White." Other components of Black talk, especially heard among male adolescents, are "Black boasting" and "Black verbal dueling." Both involve a type of sense of humor and self-presentation that are characteristically identified with African-Americans.

A recent study by Rotheram-Borus and Phinney (1990) illustrates how membership in different ethnic groups influences children's interpretations of the same social experience. In that different interpretations lead to different social expectations, it is but a short step to infer that conflict and the consequent boundary marking is a likely outcome.

In their experiment, the participants were third- and sixth-grade African-American and Mexican-American boys and girls attending the same ethnically integrated schools. The children were shown eight videotapes of brief social encounters involving same-ethnic-group peers, which were designed to tap the four dimensions of cultural variation previously described by the authors (Rotheram & Phinney, 1987). Two of the scenes dealt with the issue of group versus individual orientation, two with attitudes toward authority, two with excessive versus restrained emotionality, and two with active versus passive responses to social situations. After each scene was presented, the children were asked what they would do if they were the principal character in the scene; e.g., a teacher shown scolding a child because she is disappointed in him. "If you were the child, what would you do?" Children's responses to each scene were coded by the experimenters into three or four different categories. These categories are the measures of social expectations.

The principal findings were as follows. There were relatively few differences in social expectations among Mexican-American and African-American third-graders for any of the four discussions of cultural variation. However, the two ethnic groups differed considerably in sixth grade. In a sophisticated statistical test that assesses the similarity of responses to same- and different-ethnic-group children, there were, with few exceptions, well-defined response patterns for all members of each of these two ethnic groups. Generally, Mexican-American sixth-graders were more group-oriented than African-Americans. They also relied more on authorities for solving problems than the latter group did. On the other hand, African-Americans were more emotionally expressive and verbal than Mexican-Americans. Finally, African-Americans used more active coping strategies in response to social situations, whereas Mexican-American sixth-graders were more willing to accept situations as they were. The authors point out that the sixth-grader findings are consistent with other research using adult members of the two ethnic groups.

The above age-related findings are connected to another important aspect of the development of ethnic identity: bicultural socialization (Cross, 1987; Rotheram & Phinney, 1987; Vaughn, 1987). This concept has been implied in much of the preceding discussion, but was conceptualized as minority children identifying with the White majority. The more accurate way to discuss the socialization of ethnic minorities is that they acquire at least two ethnic identifications: those of the majority culture and of own-group minority culture. It is obvious that in order to be minimally competent in society one needs to know some of the majority-group social rules of that society. Moreover, in North American societies, virtually everyone is exposed to majority culture through television, printed media, and the schools. Majority children, on the other hand, have little pressure to acquire knowledge of minority cultures, and often have little exposure to minority groups. Even in integrated settings, social rules are usually determined by the majority culture. This analysis is consistent with the prediction that Blacks and other minority groups should acquire knowledge of White cultural norms prior to Whites' acquiring of knowledge of minority cultural norms.

Two of the consequences of differential socialization of majority and minority children is that the former readily develop a clear social identity at a relatively early age, and the latter develop at least two social identities, which are occasionally in conflict. Thus, there may be confusion in members of the latter group at early ages, which leads to a delayed development of a minority identity. Our previous discussion of the three stages of acquisition of ethnic identity support this view, as do the results of the Rotheram-Borus and Phinney (1990) study. What further complicates the picture for minority children, however, is that their own ethnic group is devalued by the majority culture. As noted earlier, when race constancy emerges, minority children must identify with this devalued group.

Vaughn (1987) suggests that there are three possible outcomes of the latter phenomenon. Children may accept their group's inferior status, they may fight it, or they may emphasize what is uniquely positive in their ethnic group. It's likely that members of minority groups do all three: the first because of lifelong conditioning by the majority culture, and the second and third because ingroup valuing and outgroup devaluing nearly always occur, and individuals usually strive for a positive self-image. Thus, from Vaughn one might expect that for minority children and adolescents, after race constancy is acquired, same-race preferences would progressively increase with increasing age. This is counter to the prediction that as children get older, prejudice and discrimination should diminish for minority groups more than for Whites.

Development of Race Prejudice

As previously noted, owing to a voluminous literature, this section will emphasize Black and White racial groups. Fortunately, two excellent reviews of most of this research have been reported by Aboud (1988) and Williams and Morland (1976). We'll frequently rely on their discussions.

Most of the research carried out since the 1960s with young children has been strongly influenced by the materials and methods developed by Williams and Morland (1976), which they fully describe in their book. Researchers use variants of their two forced-choice tests: the Color Meaning Test (CMT) and the Preschool Racial Attitude Measure II (PRAM). In the CMT, children are shown different-colored photographs of two animals that are identical except for coloring: one is black and the other white. After the experimenter reads a short story about each of these animals, the child is asked to identify the animal described. For example, "Here are two cats. One of them is a bad cat and scratches on the furniture. Which is the bad cat?" Half the stories depict positive qualities, and half negative qualities. If a child consistently chooses one color for the positive qualities, e.g., black, and the other color for the negative qualities, e.g., white, the child is assumed to have, in this example, a pro-black color bias.

In the PRAM, children are shown photographs of two nearly identical drawings of humans—male and/or female, young and/or old—except that the skin color of one is pinkish tan and that of the other is medium brown. The children are read brief stories about one of the people and asked to make a choice. For example, "Here are two little girls. One of them is an ugly little girl. People do not like to look at her. Which is the ugly little girl?" As with the CMT, half the qualities are positive, and half negative. It is assumed by researchers that consistent pro-light-skin ("white") or pro-dark-skin ("black") choices reflect racial bias. With older children a variety of attitude measures have been employed. A frequent measure is the social distance scale. With this scale participants are asked questions like the following: "Would you feel comfortable living next door to a Black family?" Possible responses are listed thus: "Yes, definitely; yes, probably; I don't know; No, probably; No, definitely."

As we indicated in chapter 4, there may be serious methodological difficulties stemming from the use of forced-choice methods to infer the development of race prejudice. Consistently choosing the "white" over the "black" picture certainly indicates a preference for white over black, but it does not necessarily indicate a rejection of black. For example, I may nearly always prefer chocolate to vanilla ice cream, but in the absence of chocolate, I'd readily consume vanilla. In order to overcome the forced-choice problems, Aboud and Mitchell (1977) used a continuous measure of how much 6- and 8-year-old White children like their own and three other racial/ethnic groups: Asian, Hispanic, and Native American. Generally, they like their own group the best, but only slightly more than their next-preferred group. The least-liked group was rated relatively neutrally, as contrasted with being disliked. Thus, pro-White did not mean anti-non-White. Unfortunately, very few studies of race prejudice (but not race discrimination) have used continuous measures.

In our presentation of the three-stage model of ethnic identity, we stated that most children show accurate racial/ethnic awareness between 4 and 6 years of age and that White children show accurate ethnic identity in this age range. Children of other racial/ethnic groups do not consistently choose pictures or dolls of their own ethnic groups until age 7 or older. Not surprisingly, ethnic preference follows this pattern. Three types of procedures have been used to assess these preferences. In the first, children are given depictions of children of two or more racial/ethnic groups, including their own, and asked which children they'd most like to play with. In the second, they're asked to choose the picture or doll they would most rather be (racial/ethnic self-preference). In the third, with White and Black children, the PRAM, CMT, or other attitude measures have been employed.

For ease of understanding, we'll present findings for White and Black children separately. White children clearly show White ethnic preferences at 4 years of age. The strength of these preferences, in most studies, increases until about 7 or 8 years, and then either declines or levels off between ages 8 and 12 (Aboud, 1988; Williams & Morland, 1976). At all ages, however, Whites most prefer Whites. Moore, Hauck, and Denne (1984), using a non-forced-choice social distance scale, found no decline in race prejudice for White adolescents between ages 12 and 16 years; but Williams and Morland, using the evaluative scale of the semantic differential, do report a decline for adolescents between 14 and 18 years. Baker and Fishbein (1993) found a decline in prejudice for males and females between the ages of 8 and 17 years with a non-forced-choice social distance measure comparable to that of Moore et al. With a forced-choice behavior disposition measure, they found no change in that age range for females, but an apparent increase in prejudice for males. For the latter measure, White children and adolescents in grades 3, 6, 7, 9, and 11 were presented with a sheet of photographs of unfamiliar same-age children, four each of White males, White females, Black males and Black females. They were asked to select five photographs of individuals whom they would like to know better. The age curve for females was relatively flat. But for males, the curve was flat for grades, 3, 6, and 7, but far fewer Black adolescents were chosen by the participants in grades 9 and 11. Instead, the White males in these higher grades selected more White females than their younger schoolmates.

Baker and Fishbein (1993) suggest, following the argument of Katz et al. (1975), that social desirability may mediate the age-related decline in prejudice when relatively transparent measures are used. Also, it is not clear whether prejudice towards Blacks increases or same-race interest increases. Thus, the data do not allow us to conclude whether White prejudice towards Blacks increases, decreases, or stays the same during the junior and senior high school years. It is possible, of course, that the different components of prejudice—beliefs, affect, and behavior dispositions—have different developmental courses (Katz & Zalk, 1978), but there are not enough data for conclusions to be drawn.

In the introduction to this chapter, three predictions were made based on genetic/evolutionary considerations: males would be more prejudiced than females; family influences in the development of prejudice would be minimal; and shifts in prejudice would occur at ages 4, 7, 10 to 12, 14 to 16, and 18 to 19 years. Concerning sex differences, Aboud (1988) has reviewed the relevant literature for preadolescent children and has concluded that there are no reliable or consistent sex differences in prejudice. However, three recent studies with adolescents and young college students reach a different conclusion. Moore et al. (1984), studying Black and White 12- through 16-year-olds, found females to be less prejudiced than males on nearly all measures of prejudice. There were no race-by-sex or grade-by-sex statistical interactions. Baker and Fishbein (1993) found females in grades 3, 6, and 7 to be equally or more prejudiced than males on two measures of prejudice, but on both measures males in grades 9 and 11 were more prejudiced than females. Finally, Qualls, Cox, and Schehr (1992) tested undergraduates from a nearly all-White liberal arts college (mean age of 19.6 years) on a questionnaire assessing opposite-sex, homosexual, and racial prejudice. They found that females had less racial prejudice than males. Thus, it may be concluded that for adolescents, but not preadolescents, White males express more racial prejudice than White females. This is partially consistent with the genetic/evolutionary hypothesis. It is not clear why this phenomenon does not hold for younger children. One possibility is that the latter have less of a commitment to group norms and identity than do adolescents.

Regarding the second hypothesis, we noted in chapter 2 that Eysenck (1992) found variations in prejudice between siblings in the same family to be as great as variations between members of different families. Thus there were no overriding family effects on the development of prejudice. Aboud (1988) has reviewed the literature concerning parental ethnocentricism and authoritarianism on children's prejudice and has concluded that White ethnocentric parents occasionally produce ethnocentric children. The data are conflicting. Authoritarianism in parents is typically not associated with the development of prejudice in their children. Unfortunately, few studies have been carried out since the 1960s; hence, the database is quite small on which to base firm conclusions. However, the evidence, as it exists, indicates that family effects are small, consistent with the genetic/evolutionary hypothesis. We'll defer a discussion of the third hypothesis until the end of this section.

We'll now turn to research concerning the development of racial prejudice in Black children. Aboud (1988), Williams and Morland (1976), and the present author have reviewed a large number of studies dealing with this issue. Most of the studies employed the PRAM or some variant of it. The principal findings are as follows. Black 4-year-olds generally equally prefer Blacks and Whites or show a greater preference for White dolls or pictures. Their pro-White bias usually increases between 4 and 6 years of age. Between the ages of 7 and 10 years, in most studies, Black children develop a positive Black preference. Those children who had previously been pro-White become racially neutral in their choices, and those who were neutral become pro-Black. There is some evidence, however, from Semaj's (1980) study that during the age range of 8 to 10 years, pro-Black attitudes decline somewhat. Thus, pro-Black attitudes form a curvilinear relationship with age. An important finding is that in studies where researchers have independently assessed attitudes towards White and Black children, as Black children become more pro-Black, their attitudes towards Whites become neutral, as opposed to negative.

As with White racial attitudes, the data for Black adolescents are not nearly as extensive as those for preadolescents. Moore et al. (1984) report no age-related changes in Black racial attitudes between the ages of 12 and 16 years. Williams and Morland (1976) report that Black attitudes towards Whites became progressively more negative between the ages of 14 and 18 years. Patchen (1982) does not report age effects for his senior high school students (presumably, there were none), but states that only about 11 percent of these students held negative attitudes towards Whites. For some attitude categories, e.g., "willing to help Blacks," "fun to be with," Blacks were much preferred to Whites. But for most categories, e.g., "starts fights," "are mean," "expect special privileges," Black students perceived both racial groups equivalently. Given the small number of studies as well as inconsistent results, no conclusions can be drawn regarding Black adolescent racial attitudes.

Before turning to the genetic/evolutionary hypotheses, we will describe one important study, that by Bagley and Young (1988). The authors gave the PRAM and CMT to preschoolers in Britain, Jamaica, Canada, and Ghana. They found that 4- to 7-year-old Black children of Ghanian parents living in England, Canada, and Ghana generally had positive Black and negative White biases on both tests. This implies that the positive White biases reported above for other Black children is linked to their being raised by Black parents who themselves were raised in White dominant cultures. Thus, it is not inevitable that Black preschoolers in North America will initially develop positive White and negative Black biases.

Returning to the hypothesis of sex differences in prejudice among Black children, the data are inconsistent with younger children and too sparse with adolescents to allow us to make an assessment. Regarding family influences, however, the data are more certain. Branch and Newcombe (1980, 1986) and Spencer (1983) found that for young children, parents' attitudes towards Whites, Blacks, the civil rights movement, and racial awareness could have positive or negative effects on pro-Black attitudes. To some extent this was age-related, changing direction at about age 6 to 7 years. But the effects were not strong in any of the studies. Hence, the hypothesis of limited family influence on the development of prejudice is supported.

Regarding the third hypothesis concerning age-related changes in prejudice, the literature supports only the first two predicted age shifts. No consistent changes are found for any of the other age periods. At age 4, children develop a positive White racial bias. At age 7, marked changes occur for both Black and White children, which are correlated with the development of race constancy. Aboud (1988) indicates that between the ages of 8 and 12 children of both races shift in their ethnic judgments towards individualization and away from group membership. These shifts are correlated with decreased prejudice. However, the decline in prejudice starts at about age 7 to 8 years, and hence does not fit into the 10- to 12-year-old age period.

One relevant prediction was made based on the cultural/historical literature: with increasing age, race prejudice should diminish more for Blacks than for Whites. This is not supported. Both Black and White children showed a decline in race prejudice between 8 and 12 years, and the data are inconsistent during adolescence.

Development of Race Discrimination

Basically, there are three kinds of research dealing with racial discrimination: one based on sociometric ratings, a second on observations of behavioral interactions, and a third on self-reports of behavioral interactions.

The sociometric procedures are of two types (Singleton & Asher, 1977). In the first or "best-friends" type, children and adolescents are given the names of all their classmates and asked to identify their best friends or those they most prefer playing with. In the second—roster and rating—children and adolescents are given the names of all their classmates and asked to rate on a five- or seven-point scale how much they like to play with or to work with each of them. These two procedures often lead to very different conclusions about racial discrimination. In the behavioral research, the children and adolescents are observed in the classroom, school playground, and cafeteria. The researcher notes with whom they are interacting. In the self-report research, the children and adolescents are asked to indicate how frequently they interact with or talk to members of different races and/or opposite sexes. Self-reports are more similar to behavioral observations than to sociometrics, and hence will be grouped with the former. We'll first describe the observational research, restricting our discussion to research carried out in the United States.

The earliest three studies, concerned with preschool children observed during free play, found no systematic relationship between play partner preferences and race (Stevenson & Stevenson, 1960, for 2 1/2-year-olds; Goodman, 1952, for 4-year-olds; and Porter, 1971, for 5-year-olds). However, the sample sizes in these studies were small, and gender preferences were not controlled. Fishbein and Imai (1993) corrected this problem and measured dyadic playmate preferences and behavior patterns of play activities, social involvement, verbalization, and negative acts for all 90 children enrolled in an urban preschool. The behavior patterns were similar for boys and girls and for Black, White, and Asian racial groups. Overall, all groups of children preferred playing dyadically with same-sex classmates. Girls showed a preference (relative to chance expectations) for playing dyadically with same-race, same-sex classmates, and a greater relative avoidance for White boys than for either Black or Asian boys. Boys, on the other hand, showed a relative preference for dyadically playing with White/same-sex classmates, and least relative avoidance for same-race girls. These results obviously are inconsistent with implications from the racial attitudes literature, in that playing with White children would be the preferred choice for both boys and girls. The Fishbein and Imai results for Black and White playmate preferences were replicated in an independent study carried out by Fishbein, Stegelin, and Davis (1993). There were not enough Asian children in their study to carry out the relevant playmate analyses. Fishbein and Imai offer an explanation for these findings, which we will shortly consider.

Finkelstein and Haskins (1983) observed White and Black kindergarten children during both classroom instruction and playground recess periods in both the fall and spring academic quarters of a single school year. The authors examined four categories of interactions—group-play, talk, negative, and command—and assessed whether observed and chance expectations were significantly different. Comparable measures were made for dyadic interactions. During the fall quarter, both racial groups preferred same-race to other-race contacts (sex differences were not analyzed). These same-race preferences were greater on the playground than in the classroom. In the latter situation, teachers have a strong influence in directing interactions. During the spring quarter, same-race classmate preferences increased in strength, suggesting that children's interracial experiences strengthened their segregation tendencies. The authors propose, based on their observations, that race-based differences in behavior predispositions underlie the increased segregation. For example, Black and White children differed in how much they used talk, negative behavior, and commands in their interactions. This explanation is consistent with the argument of Rotheram and Phinney (1987) concerning the effects of different ethnic socialization on behavioral predispositions and interethnic conflict.

The above pattern of results is different from those found by Fishbein and Imai (1993), in that here, both Black and White children preferred same-race playmates. Unfortunately, Finkelstein and Haskins (1983) did not separately examine the four race-by-sex combinations used by Fishbein and Imai. However, in the age range studied, boys overwhelmingly prefer playing with boys, and girls, with girls—probably leading to same-race/same-sex preferences. Regarding the "fit" of these results with the prejudice literature, at ages 6 to 7 Black children are shifting to a positive Black bias. Although no attitude measures were taken, it is likely that the same-race behavioral preferences were consistent with changes in racial attitudes.

Another study to observe classmate preferences on the basis of race was carried out by Singleton and Asher (1977) with third-grade children. The observations were made in classroom settings, as contrasted with the playground. The authors assessed whether there were race or sex differences in the frequency of children being alone, interacting with the teacher, or interacting with peers. There were no significant effects. The authors also assessed whether there were race or sex differences in the percentages of peer interactions that were positive. With the main exception that Black males had relatively fewer positive interactions with Black peers, there were no appreciable race or sex effects on this measure. Also, there were very strong same-sex preferences, in results consistent with those of the above two studies. However, inconsistent with the findings of both other studies, were the present research observations that females preferred interacting with same-race peers, whereas males showed no racial preferences. Unfortunately, the authors did not examine preferences on the basis of the four race-by-sex combinations; but it can be assumed that for the girls, preferred interactions were with same-race and same-sex peers.

In the Schofield and Sagar (1977) study, seventh- and eighth-graders in a newly and voluntarily racially integrated school were observed over the course of a single year. The focus was on seating arrangements in the school cafeteria. Students' choices were analyzed by sex and race; specifically, the authors asked, relative to chance expectations, what the sex and race were of schoolmates sitting next to and directly across from each student. Unfortunately, data analyses did not consider the four race-by-sex combinations. The results were very clear. Seating segregation by sex was stronger than segregation by race for both seventh- and eighth-graders. However, in both grades adolescents significantly preferred sitting next to members of the same race, with females showing a stronger effect than males. In seventh grade, where no academic tracking existed, cross-racial seating choices increased over the academic year. In eighth grade, where academic tracking did exist and led to increased classroom segregation, same-race seating segregation increased over the academic year. Thus, the cross-race experiences that adolescents had within the school affected their interracial contacts.

Schofield and Francis (1982) studied classroom peer interactions in the racially mixed accelerated eighth-grade classes from the same school investigated by Schofield and Sagar (1977). The majority of these students had been enrolled for two years, but some had newly transferred the year of the study. The race and sex of peers interacted with (the four categories used by Fishbein & Imai, 1993); the tone of the interactions (positive, negative, or neutral); and the orientation (task-related or social) of the interactions were coded. The students overwhelmingly interacted with same-sex peers. The females showed a strong preference for interacting with same-race peers, whereas the males showed no such race preferences. There were no race or sex differences in tone, with all but 1 percent of interactions being positive or neutral. There were no sex differences in orientation; however, same-race interactions tended to be social in nature, and cross-race ones tended to be task-oriented. The pattern of results showing same-race preferences by females but not males is consistent with the classroom results of Singleton and Asher (1977).

Before attempting to pull all these findings together, we will present one additional experiment, that by Damico and Sparks (1986).

These authors asked seventh-grade students in two structurally different schools to indicate "how frequently they talked to every other student" in their grade. Their four choices ranged from "a lot" to "never." This question was not restricted to in-class interactions. One of the schools (with no tracking) organized students in teams; classes were heterogeneous in ability, and substantial in-class peer interactions were encouraged through cooperative learning activities. The other school (with tracking) ability-tracked students and used teacher lecture and student recitation instructional methods. Thus, limited in-class peer interactions occurred. The data were organized along the lines of the four race-sex categories previously described. A consistent picture emerges across both types of schools. Students of both races most preferred talking with same-race/same-sex peers. White students next preferred talking with cross-race/same-sex peers, but Black students tended to have their second preference for opposite-sex/same-race peers. All four race/sex groups least preferred interacting with opposite-sex/cross-race peers. Overall, there was less cross-racial interaction in the tracking than in the no-tracking school.

The principal race-related results of these six studies can be summarized as follows. In free-play or other non-classroom settings, from kindergarten through grade 8, males and females prefer interacting with same-race/same-sex peers. In preschool, this is true for females, but males prefer interacting with White males. In classroom settings, in grades K through 8, females prefer interacting with same-race peers, and males show little (in kindergarten) or no race preferences. Thus, there are two issues to be resolved: (1) the shift for Black males in free-play settings from preschool to kindergarten; and (2) the discrepancy between classroom and non-classroom settings.

One plausible interpretation for the first issue follows that proposed by Fishbein and Imai (1993). Briefly, there is substantial experimental evidence that children's playmate choices are influenced by two factors: racial status and physical attractiveness. Status can be roughly approximated by scores on tests of racial bias, such as the PRAM. For preschool-age children, Whites have higher status. For older children, same-race children have higher status. It is assumed that males and females evaluate same-race peers as more atractive than other-race peers. The research literature shows that physical attractiveness is more important for females than for males as a determinant of friendship choice, but is a factor for males also (Krantz, 1987; Smith, 1985; Vaughn & Langlois, 1983). In preschool, physical attractiveness outweighs racial status for Black females, but for Black males the opposite occurs. There is no conflict between the two factors for White children.

In kindergarten, racial status has shifted for Black children in a positive Black direction, and hence they show a same-race bias, and prefer interacting with Black peers.

One plausible explanation for the classroom/non-classroom discrepancy also hypothesizes the operation of two factors: sex differences in friendship bonds and the constraints of classroom settings. Schofield and Sagar (1977) and Schofield and Francis (1982) have argued that males cast a wider social net than females, owing to their interest in large-group activities as well as competition and dominance striving. Females prefer interacting with small groups of close friends. Both males and females prefer same-race friendships, but females are more closely bonded to their friends than are males. In classroom settings the primary social constraint operating is the focus on academic tasks, and secondarily on maintaining friendships. Owing to their stronger bonding to close friends, females merge the primary and secondary social constraints and interact most with same-race females. Males do not do so. In the absence of an academic task constraint, males also prefer interacting with same-race/same-sex peers.

The last material to be discussed here deals with self-observations by high school students of interracial interactions (Patchen, 1982). Patchen's study is remarkable in scope, in that it included interviews and/or questionnaires with over 5,000 students, 1,800 teachers, and administrators from all 12 public high schools in Indianapolis, Indiana. Unfortunately, Patchen did not report his results by grade, but the sheer numbers of participants minimize that concern. Patchen asked students a number of questions about three categories of behaviors concerned with same- versus other-race interactions: interracial avoidance, friendly contacts, and unfriendly interactions. For interracial avoidance, the majority of Black and White students reported avoiding sitting near an other-race student at least once during the current semester. About half reported avoiding talking with other-race students, and substantial minorities reported avoiding standing or walking near other-race students. Strong majorities of White and Black students were uninfluenced by race concerning attending school events, joining activities, or going to parties. There were essentially no race differences for the avoidance category.

Friendly cross-racial contacts were frequent within the school setting, but much less frequent off campus. Interracial dating and visiting the homes of cross-racial peers were very infrequent. About half the students reported never doing things with cross-racial peers outside of school. However, the overwhelming majority reported greeting, having friendly talks with, and walking with cross-racial peers in school. The majority reported doing schoolwork with cross-racial peers. There were essentially no racial differences for this category.

For unfriendly interracial interactions, there were substantial differences between the reports of Black and White students. White students were more likely than Blacks to report being talked to in an unfriendly way, being called bad names, being purposely blocked from passing, and being threatened with bodily harm. There were much smaller disparities in reports of interracial arguments, pushing, and fighting. These approximated the frequency for same-race reports. Thus, White students perceived themselves as being more threatened by Black students than the converse, but hostile physical contact between the two groups was equivalent.

Patchen (1982) does report race-by-sex correlations for these three categories. In general, Black males and Black females responded similarly, with one small exception: females reported fewer unfriendly contacts than males. For White students, there were more consistent sex differences. Females reported less avoidance, fewer unfriendly contacts, and more positive racial attitudes than did males. In all the above cases, the correlations were relatively small.

The Patchen (1992) findings show a fair amount of interracial wariness among these high school adolescents, especially on the part of the White students. However, friendly acts frequently occurred, primarily in the school setting. One important response was this: when students were asked "what kind of experiences you have usually had with other-race people at this high school," the answers were equivalent for both racial groups: 13 percent said "not too friendly or unfriendly," 55 percent said "fairly friendly" and 32 percent said "very friendly." The interracial wariness and friendliness indicate considerable ambivalence in these relationships.

We'll now turn to the sociometric experiments. Jarrett and Quay (1984) used both roster-and-rating and best-friends techniques in assessing kindergarten and first-grade playmate preferences in two long-standing integrated schools. In a finding consistent with those of the above research, sex was a more powerful factor than race with both techniques in determining peer preferences for all groups of children. But the two sociometric techniques led to very different results regarding race preferences. With the roster-and-rating method, both Black and White kindergarten and first-grade children had a stronger positive preference for White than for Black peers (no analyses were carried out on the four sex-by-race categories), and a stronger rejection of Black peers. With the best-friends technique, however, kindergartners showed no racial preferences, but first-graders showed same-race preferences. Jarrett and Quay also performed correlational analyses between the two techniques and found children's scores to be unrelated.

The authors suggest that the higher status of White children may underlie the results with the roster-and-rating techniques.

Singleton and Asher (1977) used a roster-and-rating scale to assess two kinds of preferences among third-grade children: how much they liked to play with each of their classmates, and how much they liked to work with them. The data were analyzed for the four race-by-sex categories described above. The results were very similar for the work and play categories. Children of both races strongly preferred same-sex to opposite-sex peers. They showed a mild tendency to prefer same-race peers. The percentage of variation in preferences accounted for by sex of peer was about 40 percent, but for race of peer it was only 1 percent. This pattern of results for race is different from that of Jarrett and Quay (1984), and different from Singleton and Asher's (1977) own results using observational methods.

Singleton and Asher (1979) asked the same questions of the same children three years later, when they were in sixth grade. They tested an additional group of third-grade children to assess cohort effects. The response patterns of the latter children were virtually identical to those found earlier by Singleton and Asher (1977). The pattern of results for the sixth-graders was very similar to the pattern when the same children were in third grade. The two small exceptions were that Black children showed a greater positive Black race bias in grade 6 than in grade 3, and all groups of children showed small declines in same-sex preferences between grades 3 and 6. Nevertheless, peer preferences based on sex were far stronger than those based on race.

Carter, DeTine, Spero, and Benson (1975) used a roster-and-rating method with seventh- and eighth-graders to assess how much they perceived classmates fulfilling their needs for academic acceptance (achievement recognition) and social acceptance. There were essentially no differences in the response patterns of adolescents in grades 7 and 8. Using analyses of variance, there were no race preferences by either Black males or Black females for academic acceptance. However, both groups preferred Black to White peers for social acceptance. Both White males and White females, on the other hand, preferred White peers for both types of acceptance. Using multiple regression analyses, a high grade point average (GPA) was the strongest predictor for all four race/sex groups for academic acceptance, with sex being the next strongest predictor for all but the Black males. Race had essentially no predictive value. For social acceptance, Black and White females most strongly preferred same-sex peers. A high GPA was an important, but secondary, factor for both. Black males most strongly preferred same-race peers, with a high GPA being the next important factor. White males most strongly preferred peers with a high GPA, and secondarily, same-sex peers. Thus, with the exception of Black males, and only in the realm of social acceptance, same-sex preferences were stronger than race preferences, a result consistent with the Singleton and Asher (1977, 1979) studies. The new findings in this study are the importance of GPA to students' academic and social preferences, and the relatively unique pattern for Black males.

Patchen (1982) reported a best-friends sociometric task in his study of public high school students. To the question concerning the number of other-race persons among students' five best friends, approximately 80 percent of both Black and White students reported "none." Approximately 11 percent reported "one." Thus, close interracial friendships were very infrequent. To the question concerning the racial composition of the informal group students "hung around with," approximately 72 percent of Black and White students said that their group was "all same race." Thus, strong racial preferences do not completely prevent secondary friendships from occurring.

The final two experiments to be discussed are those by Shrum and Cheek (1987) and Shrum, Cheek, and Hunter (1988). Recall that in both studies a best-friends sociometric procedure was used with the third- through twelfth-grade students in a single community school system. Shrum and Cheek found that the percentage of students who associated with peers in mixed-race groups was 83 percent in grade 3, 42 percent in grades 4 to 6, 0 percent in grades 7 and 8, and 0 percent in grades 9 to 12. The senior high school results are consistent with those reported by Patchen (1982) for his sociometric data. The discrepancy— 0 percent versus 28 percent—is only apparent, in that Shrum and Cheek based their findings on connected sets of best friends, whereas Patchen asked about the race of peers that students "hang around with." The latter are not necessarily restricted to best friends.

Shrum et al. (1988) report their results in two ways: the overall pattern of race preferences at each grade, and the pattern of same-race/same-sex preferences at each grade. Regarding the first, both Black and White groups showed increasing same-race preferences from grades 3 to 12, with White students, especially females, dramatically preferring same-race peers in grades 8 and 9. For same-race/same-sex preferences, in general all four sex/race groups evidenced a curvilinear relationship with grade level. These preferences were lowest at grade 3, highest in grades 6, 7, and 8, and lower at grades 11 and 12. Black students (male and female) were less self-segregated at the higher grade levels than White students; however, this is relative, in that same-race self-segregation was very marked from grade 7 on. Recall that Patchen (1982) found no differences between the two racial groups. Finally, Shrum et al. point out that from grade 7 on, self-segregation by race is a much stronger factor in intergroup relations than is sex segregation. In fact, the senior class in this school system had separate proms for Blacks and Whites.

In the above studies, a clear pattern of results was found with best-friends sociometric methods. In kindergarten, not controlling for sex, no same-race preferences were found. From grade 1 on, both Black and White children and adolescents showed strong same-race/same-sex preferences. These preferences peaked in grades 6 to 8, where self-segregation was particularly strong. In these and older grades, Blacks tended to be less race- or sex-segregated than Whites, and for both races, race was a more powerful factor in self-segregation than sex. The roster-and-rating results were quite different. In kindergarten and first grade, both Black and White children preferred Whites. In grades 3 through 8, there was a mild same-race preference, but a very strong same-sex preference. From grades 6 to 8, race became relatively more important for Blacks, particularly males. There are no data for senior high school students.

Two apparent contradictions emerge in the results from the two methods: (1) in best-friends techniques, race self-segregation markedly increases through grade 8, especially in comparison to sex segregation; whereas with roster-and-rating techniques, race is much less important than sex; (2) in best-friends methods, Whites in grades 6 to 8 are more racially self-segregated than Blacks, but with roster-and-rating methods, Black males have stronger race preferences than White males.

A plausible explanation of these contradictions is as follows. The best-friends method assesses students' actual practices, primarily in non-classroom settings. This includes unscheduled time, both in school and in off-campus activities. One's best friends, we learned from the non-classroom observational research, are of the same race and same sex. Roster-and-rating methods primarily emphasize in-school settings, usually in-class ones. These ratings thus have an academic emphasis, more so than do best-friends ratings. We learned from the classroom observational research that race is much less important than sex in peer preferences, especially for males. Thus, regarding the first apparent contradiction, same-sex preferences are strong with both methods, but the setting being assessed determines the relative importance of race. In classroom settings it is not very important, but outside of class, it is.

Regarding the second contradiction, it is not clear why Whites should have fewer Black best friends than the converse, unless one assumes that racial status differences in the culture continue to play a role well beyond preschool and kindergarten. The shift in a positive Black direction for Black males in roster-and-ratings probably reflects an attempt on their part to accommodate to a competitive disadvantage they have in the classroom setting. Recall the Carter et al. (1975) results indicating that with the multiple regression analyses, GPA was very important for both academic and social acceptance. It can be inferred from their analyses that Whites generally had higher GPAs than Blacks, and hence would tend to be preferred. But, as has been previously argued, males are more competitive than females, and hence would be less willing than females to concede a one-down status. Black males, by preferring other Black males for social and academic acceptance, would keep experienced status differences to a minimum.

We'll now relate these findings on discrimination to several of the hypotheses presented at the beginning of the chapter. Based on genetic/evolutionary considerations, it was speculated that males would discriminate along racial lines more than females would. In all studies but two, either there were no sex differences, or females discriminated more than males. Thus, this hypothesis is rejected. Given that there was no support for this hypothesis in the race prejudice literature, it is safe to conclude that this genetic/evolutionary consideration has no bearing in the domain of race for children and adolescents.

The hypothesis based upon cultural/historical considerations that, with increasing age, race discrimination would decrease more for Black than for White individuals is not supported. Most studies show no age-related differences, but some find Blacks more discriminatory than Whites, and others show the converse. There may be an age-related pattern for a particular methodology, but nothing consistent emerges across the various methods used. The lack of consistency fits with the race prejudice data. Hence, it is probably safe to conclude that this cultural/historical consideration also has no bearing in the domain of race for children and adolescents.

In findings similar to those for race prejudice, there is supportive evidence for developmental shifts in discrimination occurring at ages 4 and 7 years. Another shift occurs between 12 and 15 years, but that appears to be based on a marked increase in heterosexual interests, and not changes in group identity or cognitive development. That is, race discrimination peaks in the 12-to-15-year age range, and then declines somewhat afterwards. These findings are consistent with the absence of any shifts in race prejudice during this age range.

Concerning family influences on race discriminations, none of these studies report direct measures of parents' attitudes or behaviors in relation to adolescents' discrimination. Patchen (1982) reports correlations between adolescents' *perceptions* of parents' attitudes and the adolescents' own behaviors. The correlations were low to moderate for both Blacks and Whites, but we have no way of knowing how accurate these perceptions are. Two relatively objective measures that might be thought to have an impact—parents' education and extent of racial integration in adolescents' neighborhoods—were uncorrelated with discriminatory behavior. Thus, we leave open the question of family influences in this domain.

Development of Prejudice Towards People with Mental Retardation

Unlike research concerned with hearing-impaired persons, there is substantial literature dealing with prejudice of nonretarded children and adolescents towards their mentally retarded peers. As we noted in chapter 3, there are basically three levels of mental retardation: mild, moderate, and profound. Those with mild retardation (about 75 percent of all retarded persons) generally look like normally developing children but are somewhat different in behavior. Those with moderate retardation e.g., those with Down Syndrome, (about 20 percent of retarded persons) generally look different and act differently from nonretarded persons. Children with mild and moderate retardation are often mainstreamed in classes with nonretarded children for part of the school day. Those with profound retardation (about 5 percent of retarded persons) are markedly different from nonretarded persons and are usually segregated from them. As will be seen in the following discussion, the extent of similarity in appearance and behavior can have significant effects on children's attitudes.

The studies by Condon, York, Heal, and Fortschneider (1986), Gottlieb and Switsky (1982), Graffi and Minnes (1988), and Voeltz (1980, 1982) in part deal with the effects of nonretarded children's age and the amount of prejudice expressed. Unfortunately, the youngest age group studied was kindergarten age (only by Graffi and Minnes), and none of the research included adolescents. These experiments primarily included children in the second through sixth grades. Across the studies several different kinds of attitude measures were used. These include an adjective checklist, an acceptance scale of the mentally retarded, and various forms of a friendship scale that assess the types of activities that nonretarded children would be willing to carry out with mentally retarded peers.

With one exception, in all these experiments older nonretarded peers showed increasing positive attitudes and decreasing negative attitudes towards the mentally retarded. In the Graffi and Minnes study, third-graders had more positive attitudes than kindergarten children towards peers who were described as mentally retarded, in results consistent with the above. However, the kindergartners had more positive attitudes towards peers who were shown in photographs to have Down

Syndrome. These results are particularly puzzling because, in contrast to all the other research findings, the kindergarten children had more positive attitudes towards children with Down Syndrome than towards normal-appearing children.

In addition to the above studies, the experiments by Bak and Siperstein (1987a), Elam and Sigelman (1982), Hemphill and Siperstein (1990), Siperstein and Chatillon (1982), and Siperstein, Budoff, and Bak (1980) evaluated gender effects. In these studies, nonretarded children were presented with either audiotapes or videotapes of mentally retarded children reading alone or interacting with a nonretarded same-sex child. They were then administered attitude measures similar to those noted above.

In most of the research, girls were found to have either more positive attitudes or less negative attitudes towards mentally retarded peers than did boys. Graffi and Minnes (1988) reported no gender effects, and both Elam and Sigelman (1982) and Hemphill and Siperstein (1990) found girls to be more negative when the mentally retarded child was labeled as retarded, in addition to manifesting some behavioral deficiencies. The tendency for girls to have more positive attitudes than boys towards mentally retarded peers is consistent with the speculation based on genetic/evolutionary considerations. An alternative hypothesis is that in all cultures, girls are socialized to be more nurturant and responsible towards dependent individuals than are boys (Fishbein, 1984). Mentally retarded peers probably fall into this category, and hence would elicit more positive feelings from girls than from boys.

In contrast to the deaf, who comprise less than one half of 1 percent of all children, approximately 3 percent are classified as mentally retarded. Thus, it's likely that most nonretarded children have had some contact with retarded peers. Does the amount of contact influence attitudes? The studies by Condon et al. (1986), Siperstein and Chatillon (1982), and Voeltz (1980, 1982) compared children who had either no school contact with mentally retarded peers; low contact with them (classes for the retarded were located in the school, but there was no mainstreaming); or substantial contact with them (mainstreaming was practiced and/or special programs were held involving nonretarded and retarded peers). The results consistently show that the greater the current contact is that nonretarded children have with retarded peers, the more positive and/or less negative are their attitudes towards the retarded children. However, research that examined self-reports by nonretarded children of prior non-school contact with mentally retarded peers gives a somewhat different picture (Graffi & Minnes, 1988; Condon et al., 1986; Bourgondien, 1987). Bourgondien found that positive attitudes towards mentally retarded children correlated with amount of prior contact; but Graffi and Minnes and Condon et al. found no effects.

The results of school-based contact are consistent with the view that the more authorities, i.e., the school, approve of, or sanction, contact between retarded and nonretarded peers, the more positive will be the children's attitudes. Being in the same classroom reflects greater authority approval than only being in the same school. For the self-report data, we have no idea about the contexts and qualities of prior contact, and hence can make no clear statements about the inconsistent results.

As has been emphasized in our previous discussions, a central factor involved with the development of prejudice and discrimination is perceived behavioral differences between members of ingroups and those of outgroups. These differences were well defined in opposite-sex prejudice, discrimination towards the deaf (and its converse), and, to a lesser extent, racial prejudice. Several imaginative experiments have addressed this issue as it pertains to mentally retarded persons. In these studies, researchers investigated the effects of the social skills manifested by mentally retarded peers on the attitudes of nonretarded children.

Bourgondien (1987) showed videotapes to nonretarded girls of two normal-appearing girls interacting. In one tape, one of the girls acted inappropriately—e.g., she spoke too loudly, stared more, moved too close to the other girl; in the other tape, both girls acted appropriately. Half the participants were told that the inappropriately acting girl was in a special class for the retarded, and the other half were told only that she was in the same grade as they. In the Bak and Siperstein (1987a) study, nonretarded children were shown videotapes of normal-appearing peers, normal-appearing but mildly retarded peers, and peers with Down Syndrome. The children were shown first reading, and then discussing personal interests. The normal-appearing children read with ease, the mildly retarded ones made some errors, and those with Down Syndrome showed some difficulty reading a much lower-level text. In Siperstein et al. (1980), nonretarded children listened to an audiotape of two children participating in a spelling bee. One child (the control) was always a competent speller, whereas the other child (the target child) was either competent with difficult words, or incompetent with easy words. The subjects were shown photographs of the spellers. The control speller was always normal-appearing, whereas the target child was either normal-appearing or had Down Syndrome. In addition, the target child was labeled either as "mentally retarded" or as "a retard."

Finally, in Hemphill and Siperstein's (1990) study, a normal-appearing mentally retarded child was paired in conversation with a same-age nonretarded child. Through coaching of the mentally retarded child and skillful editing of the conversations, two videotapes were produced. In one, the mentally retarded child showed age-appropriate conversational abilities, and in the other, the child showed deficits characteristic of mentally retarded children, e.g., unexpected topic "leaps," repeating a small set of conversational topics, long pauses. As in the above studies, for half the participants, the target child was labeled as being in a special class for learning problems, and for the other half, the child was referred to as being in a "classroom like yours."

In all these experiments, irrespective of the label given the depicted children by the researchers, nonretarded children showed more positive attitudes towards the competent and/or socially appropriate peer than towards the incompetent and/or inappropriate peer. In the Bourgondien (1987) study, labeling of the target child as retarded had no effect on a measure of willingness by nonretarded children to interact with the child. In Bak and Siperstein's (1987a) study, nonretarded children showed similar attitudes towards a mildly retarded child and a child with Down Syndrome, both less positive than towards a normal-appearing child. In the Siperstein et al. (1980) study, labeling a normal-appearing child a "retard" had negative effects on children's attitudes, but labeling a child with Down Syndrome a "retard" had no differential effects, as compared to labeling him "mentally retarded."

In Hemphill and Siperstein's (1990) study, the conversationally deficient target was viewed less positively than the nondeficient target and as more likely to be rejected or isolated by peers. Labeling generally had no effects, with the exception mentioned above involving sex of rater. These studies indicate that nonretarded children's negative attitudes towards their mentally retarded peers are based primarily on the intellectually incompetent, socially inappropriate, or conversationally deficient behaviors of the retarded. Appearance differences from the "normal" seem secondary to behavior differences.

Development of Discrimination Towards People with Mental Retardation

Two types of studies are discussed in this section: those based on observations of interactions between mentally retarded and nonretarded peers, and those based on sociometric ratings. Regarding observations, which we'll discuss first, the majority of experiments that have been carried out deal with preschool-age children, and the remainder with junior and senior high school students. There are apparently no observational studies with children in grades K through 6.

Guralnick (1980) observed nonretarded and mildly, moderately, and severely retarded 4- to 6-year-old children during free-play periods in integrated preschool classrooms. Measurements were taken of play-mate preferences at the beginning and end of the academic year. The principal findings were that the nonretarded and mildly retarded children interacted more with one another than they did with the other two groups. Moreover, this discrimination increased from the beginning to the end of the year. The moderately and severely retarded children showed no interactional preferences among the four groups. It is important to note that the mildly retarded children were, on average, one year older than their nonretarded peers. Thus, it's possible that the principal factor determining playmate preferences for the nonretarded and mildly retarded groups was developmental level, e.g., mental age, and not relative developmental level, e.g., IQ.

The experiment by Guralnick and Groom (1987) answers the above question and provides important information about the social competencies of mildly retarded 4-year-olds. In their study, eight independent preschool play groups were constructed for a four-week period, each consisting of three nonretarded 4-year-olds, three nonretarded 3-year-olds, and two mildly retarded 4-year-olds who were matched in developmental level with the nonretarded 3-year-olds. However, the 3-year-olds had superior language ability relative to the retarded children.

Overall, nonretarded 4-year-olds most preferred playing with other nonretarded 4-year-olds and relatively avoided playing with children in the other two groups. The nonretarded 3-year-olds preferred playing with other nonretarded 3- and 4-year-olds and relatively avoided playing with their retarded peers. The retarded children most preferred playing with 4-year-old nonretarded peers, and relatively avoided playing with 3-year-old nonretarded peers. The retarded children engaged in more solitary play than children in the other two groups. In most of the other behaviors, e.g., leading peers in activities, modeling behaviors, following activities without instructions, the highest level of social competence was shown by 4-year-old nonretarded, then 3-year-old nonretarded, and finally 4-year-old retarded children. In contrast to their nonretarded peers, the retarded children were infrequently used as a resource by their peers, e.g., in seeking information or explanations from them. Finally, over the course of the four-week period, only children in the retarded group showed a decline in the ability to positively engage peers in social interactions. These findings suggest that young children most prefer playing with peers who are socially skilled. Mildly retarded children are deficient in this area. Does this deficiency also affect enduring social interactions, such as friendships?

The experiment by Guralnick and Groom (1988) addressed this question. They examined both unilateral and reciprocal friendships in the same group of children they had studied in 1987. A unilateral friendship was defined as one in which a child directed at least one third of positive peer-related interactions to a specific playmate. A reciprocal friendship involved two children, each directing at least one third of these interactions towards the other. Regarding unilateral friendships, there were essentially no differences between the three groups in frequency of occurrence. However, in a pattern consistent with the 1987 results, children in all three groups most preferred the 4-year-old nonretarded children for this type of friendship. The pattern for reciprocal friendships was quite different. The 4-year-old nonretarded children had the most reciprocal friendships, followed by the 3-year-old nonretarded children, and then the retarded children. Interestingly, the nonretarded children preferred same-age peers on this measure. Only two of the 16 retarded children had reciprocated friendships, so no pattern could be established for them. These results indicate that attempts at reciprocated friendships are far less successful when made by retarded than by nonretarded peers matched for either chronological or developmental age.

The next study, by Rynders, Johnson, Johnson, and Schmidt (1980), focused on the effects of competitive, individualistic, and cooperative structures on the interactions between adolescents with Down Syndrome and same-age (13 to 15 years) nonretarded peers. The two groups attended different schools, but were brought together one hour a week for eight weeks to bowl together. In the cooperative condition, the adolescents were instructed to help one another improve their bowling scores in order to maximize the group's score. In the competitive condition, they were instructed to try to get the best score in the group. In the individualistic condition, they were instructed to try to improve their scores by a certain amount each week. The authors coded numbers of positive peer interactions, e.g., praising, encouraging, under all three conditions. The results were striking. Both retarded and nonretarded adolescents in the cooperative condition directed about 10 times as many positive acts towards both categories of peers as did adolescents in the other two conditions. These results indicate that positive interactions can occur between retarded and nonretarded peers who are at very different developmental levels.

The study by Zetlin and Murtaugh (1988) used experimenter participant observation methods to investigate the nature of friendships among nonretarded and very mildly retarded (i.e., IQs averaging 73) adolescents attending the same senior high school. Retarded students were mainstreamed into several classes each day. The researchers attended classes with the students, hung out with them at lunch, between classes, and after school, and occasionally interviewed them. The study lasted an entire school year. Although the authors do not tell us the extent of friendship segregation among these students, it is clear from their discussion that very few friendships occurred between retarded and nonretarded peers.

Although friendship patterns within each group overlapped somewhat, there were substantial differences that would lead to friendship segregation between the two groups. Some of the most salient differences are as follows. Nonretarded students were much more likely than retarded ones to form large mixed-sex friendship groups. For about half of the retarded students, but few of the nonretarded ones, interactions with friends were mainly limited to the school setting and telephone conversations. Relative to those among nonretarded students, friendships among retarded students were generally less intimate; i.e., they disclosed fewer personal issues, were less empathic to the problems of a close friend, and often experienced frequent and intense conflicts. The latter characteristic led to less enduring friendships. The authors suggest that many of these differences are based on the relatively restricted experiences that retarded adolescents have had, and are probably unrelated to their retardation as such. The two main sources of restriction are classroom segregation and close parental supervision of their time out of school.

The above studies indicate that discrimination by nonretarded students towards their retarded peers is at least partially based on the lower level of social skills manifested by the latter group. For those children and adolescents with moderate and severe retardation, it is unlikely that these skills, even with training, could reach levels attained by nonretarded persons. For many mildly retarded persons, however, who comprise the majority of those with mental retardation, enhanced social skills are attainable. The Rynders et al. (1980) experiment indicates that interactions between moderately retarded and nonretarded peers can be positive, even if friendships do not occur.

Turning now to the sociometric studies, all but one used the roster-and-rating method (Stager & Young, 1981). Unfortunately, that experiment was the only one dealing with senior high school students. With the exception of the Guralnick and Groom (1987) and Strain (1985) experiments involving preschool children, all the remaining experiments were concerned with children between grades 2 and 7.

Recall that in the Guralnick and Groom (1987) experiment, independent groups consisting of 3- and 4-year-old nonretarded and 4-year-old mildly retarded children were observed. At the end of the four-week period, all the children were asked to rate each of their classmates on how much they like playing with them. The retarded children received lower average ratings and lower numbers of positive ratings than children in the other two groups, who received equivalent ratings. These results agree with the observational scores regarding the retarded children, but are somewhat discrepant regarding the two nonretarded groups. Recall that observations indicated that children in the 4-year-old nonretarded group were the most preferred. Strain (1985) measured various social and nonsocial behaviors of two groups of moderately retarded preschoolers. One group received relatively high sociometric ratings from their nonretarded peers, and the other group, relatively low ratings. Children in the higher-rated group were often observed to organize play, to share, to show affection, to help, and to act less negatively than children in the lower-rated group. Thus, social competence leads to relatively high sociometric ratings.

The experiments by Gottlieb, Semmel, and Veldman (1978), Roberts and Zubrick (1992), and Taylor, Asher, and Williams (1987) examined the relationship between nonretarded peers' evaluations of the behavior/personality of mainstreamed mildly retarded peers and liking of those peers. In all three studies, the children were in middle school, between grades 3 and 7. The specific measures employed by Gottlieb et al. and Roberts and Zubrick were similar and hence will be discussed first. In all these experiments, retarded children received lower friendship ratings than nonretarded children.

In the Gottlieb et al. (1978) study the social acceptance and social rejection of mildly retarded mainstreamed children were compared with peers' and teachers' perceptions of the retarded children's cognitive and disruptive behavior, and with the amount of time they were integrated into regular classes. Statistical analyses indicated that social acceptance was positively related to peer and teacher ratings of cognitive competence and unrelated to disruptive behavior. Social rejection was positively related to peer and teacher ratings of disruptive behavior and teachers' ratings of cognitive ability. The amount of time retarded children were integrated was unrelated to either social acceptance or rejection.

Roberts and Zubrick (1992) replicated and extended the Gottlieb et al. (1978) research by using very mildly retarded children (average IQs were 73). Statistical analyses indicated that social acceptance of *retarded* children was positively related to teachers' and peers' perceptions of their academic abilities and negatively related to peers' perceptions of their disruptive behavior. Social acceptance of *nonretarded* children was related only to teachers' and peers' perceptions of academic abilities. Different patterns emerged for social rejection. For *retarded* children, peers' perceptions of disruptive behavior constituted the only significant predictor. For *nonretarded* children, both peers' perceptions of academic abilities and disruptive behavior were significant predictors of social rejection.

The results of these two studies are not completely in agreement. However, they do point to two important conclusions. First, the bases of social acceptance and social rejection of retarded chidren by nonretarded peers are different. Being positively liked appears to depend on being academically competent, but being disliked depends on being disruptive. Second, nonretarded children seem to use different criteria in evaluating social acceptance and rejection when assessing retarded and nonretarded peers. This implies either that identifying peers as mentally retarded influences subsequent judgments about them, or that other behaviors that were not measured have an important role in determining social acceptance and rejection.

In the Taylor, Asher, and Williams (1987) experiment, mainstreamed mildly retarded and nonretarded children were compared on peer assessments of cooperation, disruptive behavior, shyness, fighting, and leadership, and teacher assessments of friendliness, avoidant behavior, bossiness, and aggressiveness. These two lists are similar, but not equivalent. Retarded children, relative to nonretarded ones, were seen by their peers as less cooperative, more shy, and less likely to be named as leaders. They were not seen to differ in disruptive or aggressive behavior. Teachers perceived retarded children as less friendly and more avoidant than nonretarded ones. No differences were found for bossiness or aggressiveness. Recall that the retarded children received lower friendship sociometric ratings than their nonretarded peers. These results indicate that perceived bossiness or aggressiveness do not underlie the relative dislike of retarded children by their nonretarded peers. Rather, in interactions with nonretarded peers, retarded children are shy or withdrawn and lacking in cooperative and leadership social skills. These characteristics were seen by Guralnick and Groom (1987) for mildly retarded preschool children, suggesting that they are deeply entrenched patterns when retarded children interact with nonretarded peers.

The above research indicates that various social and academic deficiencies underlie the low sociometric friendship ratings given by nonretarded children to their mildly retarded peers. The experiments by Bak and Siperstein (1987b) and Acton and Zarbatany (1988) address the issue of whether competence in a specific game situation can modify sociometric ratings. In the Bak and Siperstein experiment, groups of one mildly retarded and two nonretarded peers from the same classes (grades 4 to 6) were asked to play a beanbag-tossing game. The children were instructed to focus on the team's score, because they were in competition with other teams. The scoring was "rigged" such that the experimenter determined each player's performance outcome. For half the game, the retarded player "performed" the best, and for the other half, he or she "performed" as an average player. On days prior to and after the game playing, various sociometric measures were taken. The authors found that nonretarded children were much more likely to choose a highly successful retarded child as a partner in future games than to choose one who had only an average performance. However, game performance had no influence on nonretarded children's willingness to engage in other friendship-related activities with them. Thus, the specific positive competencies did not carry over into other interactional realms.

Acton and Zarbatany (1988) used the same rigged game with children in grades 2 to 6 that Bak and Siperstein (1987b) had used. The children played in pairs—one mildly retarded child, one nonretarded one—and the retarded child's scores were rigged to be average or poor. Additionally, half the pairs were instructed to encourage or coach each other because they were operating as a team (high interaction), whereas the other half were asked to sit quietly while their partner performed (low interaction). A variety of sociometric measures were taken on days before and after the game. Although the children attended the same school, they did not attend the same classes, unlike the children in Bak and Siperstein's study. The principal results, similar to those of Bak and Siperstein, were that game-playing competence had no effect on sociometric ratings. However, nonretarded children rated their game partners more positively than they rated other retarded children in their grades. Additionally, partners in the high-interaction condition were rated more positively by their nonretarded peers than were children in the low-interaction condition. These two findings are different from those of Bak and Siperstein, and lead to the following conclusion. For relatively unacquainted retarded and nonretarded children, a positive social experience will have generalized positive effects on how the retarded children are viewed by their nonretarded peers. But for children who are relatively well known to each other, one particular experience will have essentially no generalized effects.

In Stager and Young's (1981) experiment, mainstreamed mildly retarded senior high school students were sociometrically rated ("best friends") by their nonretarded classmates and by other retarded peers from their special education classes. Questions were also asked about the types of social contact that occurred with the mainstreamed students. The principal results were that retarded peers from special education classes were much more likely than nonretarded peers to be best friends with the mainstreamed students. Similarly, peers from special education classes had significantly more social contacts with their mainstreamed peers than did nonretarded peers. Indeed, there was virtually no social contact between retarded and nonretarded peers.

Measurements taken at the beginning and end of the semester were essentially the same. Thus, the picture already seen of social segregation in younger children strongly persists among older adolescents.

When the observational research is compared with the sociometric research, the major results are in complete accord: (1) nonretarded children and adolescents prefer interacting with and forming friendships with other nonretarded individuals; (2) these preferences are based on social and behavioral deficiencies of retarded peers; and (3) positive interactions and preferences by nonretarded children towards retarded peers can readily occur in highly specific situations such as game playing. Friendships can infrequently occur between nonretarded and retarded peers, especially if the latter have adequate social skills.

In comparing the prejudice and discrimination research, two inconsistencies emerge. First, none of the discrimination research points to reliable sex or age effects, whereas these do tend to occur in the prejudice literature. One plausible explanation is that social desirability issues concerning unknown peers influence prejudice but not discrimination judgments. Females and older children are more likely to respond positively to retarded peers than are males or younger children. It seems that with the former children generosity of spirit occurs relatively easily at a distance. The choosing of friends, however, has immediate and concrete effects. Second, in the prejudice research, increased contact leads to decreased prejudice, whereas in discrimination, length of contact appears to have no effect on friendship choices. Having kindly feelings towards mentally retarded individuals is obviously not enough to cause a nonretarded child to have them as friends. Both the prejudice and the discrimination literatures are in agreement that perceived social competence mediates positive choices and attitudes regarding the retarded by the nonretarded. Thus some socially competent retarded children will be valued positively and chosen as friends by their nonretarded peers. But the literature indicates that this is an uncommon occurrence.

Comparison Among the Groups

A poet once said that a rose was still a rose by any other name. That concept doesn't apply to the development of prejudice and discrimination. That is, prejudice and discrimination vary as a function of target group. For example, knowing how racial prejudice develops doesn't accurately inform us about the development of opposite-sex prejudice. Moreover, knowledge of the development of prejudice for any target group does not necessarily predict discrimination patterns towards that group. In other words, prejudice and discrimination generally follow somewhat different developmental paths. What have we learned in our survey about these effects? Let us first examine the prejudice literature.

Data on preschool children were available only for opposite-sex and race prejudice. For these groupings the emergence of prejudice (or its proxy, negative stereotyping) occurs by age 3 years, and is strongly evident in 4-year-olds. However, this statement must be qualified: Black preschool-age children often show prejudice towards Blacks. From age 4 on, different patterns are found for these two groupings as well as for prejudice towards mentally retarded peers. *Opposite-sex prejudice,* which is bidirectional, increases in strength until about age 8, and declines somewhat between ages 8 and 10 years. However, girls, but not boys, between the ages of 8 and 10 start to increasingly value opposite-sex characteristics. *Race prejudice* by Whites increases to age 7 or 8 years, declines or levels off between 8 and 12 years, and follows no consistent pattern at older ages. For Blacks, a positive White bias exists until about age 7, when it shifts to neutrality or White prejudice. Between 8 and 10 years, prejudice towards Whites declines slightly. No firm pattern emerges thereafter. *Prejudice towards the mentally retarded* is seen in nonretarded kindergarten children. It declines in strength thereafter, through age 12 years. Little is known for adolescents.

For all three groupings, males are found to be more prejudiced than or equally as prejudiced as females, a finding that is consistent with the genetic/evolutionary speculation based on the assumption of stronger group commitments by males than females. For all three groupings, behavioral differences were found to be correlated with prejudice; this is consistent with the genetic/evolutionary concept of "badging." This was especially pronounced for opposite-sex prejudice and prejudice towards the mentally retarded. In results consistent with the genetic/evolutionary prediction, development of opposite-sex and race prejudice were only weakly connected with parental values, and thus, by implication, were strongly tied to cultural values transmitted by other sources. There are no data on this issue regarding the mentally retarded.

Predictions based on cultural/historical considerations did not always have parallel results for opposite-sex and race prejudice. No relevant data are available for prejudice towards the mentally retarded. The predictions concerning the effects of subordinate status—that Blacks and females would acquire knowledge, behavior and values of male and White cultural norms prior to the converse—were supported. However, culturally/historically based predictions concerning self-esteem and age-related decreases in prejudice held for females in relation to males, but not for Blacks in relation to Whites.

Regarding the discrimination literature, observational data are available for preschool children for all four groupings. For *opposite-sex* and *race discrimination,* same-race/same-sex preferences are generally present in preschool children, and these preferences increase between ages 6 and 8 and either decline or level off until age 12. However, for race discrimination in classroom settings, females but not males continue to racially discriminate. Discrimination towards the *deaf* and *mentally retarded* by nonhandicapped children is present in preschool and remains high thereafter, with no apparent age-related trends. In preschool, mentally retarded children prefer interacting with nonretarded peers, whereas deaf children prefer interaction with teachers.

For the sociometric methods, with best-friends data, all four groupings show essentially the same patterns from grade 3 on: discrimination is quite marked at all ages. It is also stronger in this age range than it is for younger children. But ingroup/outgroup friendships do occur infrequently for all groupings.

In general, roster-and-ratings measures indicate far less discrimination than best-friends measures. This is especially the case for in-class or in-school academically oriented activities. Discrimination by sex appears much stronger than that by race. For nondisabled/disabled interactions, no comparable information is available.

For both observational and sociometric methods, ingroup/outgroup behavioral differences—badging—underlie the discrimination. This was most readily seen regarding the mentally retarded, for whom degree of social competence could be assessed. But it was also notable with the other groupings.

Regarding the genetic/evolutionary speculation concerning sex differences in discrimination, there was no support for it in the opposite-sex literature, and it was contradicted in the race literature. No reliable sex differences were identified for discrimination towards mentally retarded or deaf peers.

Not enough data are available to evaluate the genetic/evolutionary hypothesis about family effects. The cultural/historical predictions that discrimination of subordinates would decline relative to that of dominant groups were either unsupported (opposite-sex and racial discrimination) or not investigated (discrimination against deaf and mentally retarded persons).

Finally, there was strong support for age-related shifts in discrimination occurring in the first two periods, which were predicted by the group identity and cognitive development literature. Parallel findings occurred for the development of prejudice. Additionally, for opposite-sex prejudice, two later predicted age-related shifts were noted. These results suggest that the early development of prejudice and discrimination are linked with social cognitive development.

In summary, the early development of opposite-sex prejudice, race prejudice, and prejudice towards the mentally retarded is tied to group identity processes and social cognitive development. However, each of the three groupings has a unique pattern of development from preschool through junior high school. No consistent patterns emerge in senior high school. Badging mechanisms appear to underlie the various categories of prejudice. Discrimination follows different developmental paths than prejudice, and the various methods of assessing discrimination produce different patterns of results. One of the most consistent results is that within-school academically oriented discrimination is much lower than out-of-school or in-school socially oriented discrimination. In junior and senior high school, Blacks and Whites, males and females, deaf and hearing students, mentally retarded and nonretarded children all prefer ingroup to outgroup peers. Badging mechanisms likely play a role in these choices.

Summary

Psychological research, especially that carried out by Kenneth and Mamie Clark, had a significant impact on the U.S. Supreme Court decision that racial segregation of schools was unconstitutional. Using forced-choice methods with different-colored dolls, the Clarks found that both White and Black 4- to 7-year-olds reliably identified with the White dolls. Moreover, they attributed positive characteristics to White dolls, and negative ones to Black dolls. The Clarks concluded that Black, but not White, children were self-rejecting.

Research on the development of ethnic identity shows, counter to the Clarks' assertions, that young Black children may negatively evaluate their own ethnic group and still have high self-esteem. The explanation for this phenomenon is that personal identity and ethnic identity are somewhat independent developmental characteristics. Ethnic groups differ from one another along several major perceptual and behavioral dimensions, including language patterns. These differences can readily lead to ethnic conflicts. Children's development of an ethnic identity follows three stages: awareness of ethnic differences at ages 3 to 4 years; accurate ethnic awareness at 4 to 6 years; and accurate ethnic identity at ages 7 to 10 years. The last stage involves children's understanding of racial constancy.

Racial prejudice has different developmental paths for Black and White children. White children show White ethnic preferences by 4 years of age. The strength of these preferences increases until about age 8, and either levels off or declines between 8 and 12 years. No clear pattern emerges thereafter, but at all ages Whites prefer Whites. There is an indication that in adolescence and young adulthood, White females are less prejudiced than White males. Black children show White ethnic preferences between ages 4 and 6 years. Between 7 and 10 years they generally show Black preferences. Between 8 and 10 years, the positive Black preferences decline slightly and attitudes towards Whites become neutral. The data are inconsistent regarding age differences in adolescence or sex differences at any ages. Family influences on the development of prejudice by either Whites or Blacks are minimal. Age shifts predicted by the group identity and cognitive development literature are partially supported.

The three techniques to study race discrimination—observation, rating-and-roster sociometrics, and best-friends sociometrics—do not lead to equivalent conclusions. Observations show that Black preschool boys prefer playing with White boys, but White boys and girls and Black girls prefer same-race peers. From kindergarten through senior high school, in free-play or non-classroom settings, children prefer interacting with same-sex/same-race peers. In classroom settings in grades K through 8, females prefer same-race peers, but males show little or no racial preferences. With roster-and-ratings methods, kindergarten and first-grade children were found to prefer Whites to Blacks. In grades 3 through 8, a mild same-race preference, but a very strong same-sex preference occurs. There are no data for senior high school students. With best-friends methods, in kindergarten no race preferences were found. From grade 1 through senior high school, both Black and White children and adolescents preferred same-race, same-sex friends. These preferences were strongest in grades 6 to 8. Age shifts predicted by the group identity and cognitive development literature were partially supported.

Prejudice by nonretarded children towards their mentally retarded peers to some extent depends on the level of retardation. The youngest age group studied was in kindergarten. Between K and grade 6, older nonretarded children are less prejudiced than younger ones. Generally girls show less prejudice than boys, which is consistent with the speculation based on genetic/evolutionary considerations. As was the case with the other discussions of prejudice, behavioral differences were found to be the primary basis of nonretarded children's negative attitudes. Finally, increasing the amount of school contact between retarded and nonretarded children decreases the amount of prejudice of the latter group towards the former one.

Observational studies of discrimination by nonretarded children towards their mentally retarded peers is at least partially based on the lower level of social skills manifested by the latter group. Mildly retarded children and adolescents with competent skills do occasionally form friendships with nonretarded peers. All but one of the sociometric studies used the roster-and-rating method. Various social and academic deficiencies underlie the low sociometric ratings given mildly retarded children by their nonretarded peers. Specific positive competencies demonstrated by retarded children positively influence the interactions of nonretarded peers towards them. However, these effects do not carry over into areas other than that of the specific competency. In senior high school, nonretarded adolescents report virtually no social contacts with their mainstreamed mildly retarded peers.

In comparing the development of prejudice and discrimination among the four groupings discussed, there appear to be greater consistencies for prejudice than for discrimination. The results for opposite-sex prejudice and discrimination most closely fit the predictions based on genetic/evolutionary and cultural/historical conceptualizations. In all cases, behavioral differences between the groupings at least partially underlie both prejudice and discrimination. Finally, in all groupings, the first two age periods of change predicted by group identity conceptualizations emerge, indicating that social cognitive development partially underlies the early development of prejudice and discrimination.

Modifying Prejudice and Discrimination

Note: This chapter was written in collaboration with Catherine M. Johnson.

Introduction

There are five goals of this chapter. The first is to make predictions in terms of genetic/evolutionary and cultural/historical considerations about reducing prejudice and discrimination in children. The second is to describe the two theories that are most often associated with prejudice reduction: contact theory and Lewinian theory. The third goal is to briefly describe the types of measures used in studying the reduction of prejudice and discrimination. The fourth goal is to summarize the principal bodies of research that exist on the topic of the reduction of prejudice and discrimination. The fifth goal is to present an approach designed to reduce prejudice and discrimination in children and adolescents.

Two of the major legally mandated attempts aimed towards reducing cross-racial prejudice and discrimination have been school desegregation and mainstreaming of physically and mentally disabled persons. Substantial literature from the 1960s, 1970s, and 1980s exists for both of these. No similar legislation exists for reducing opposite-sex prejudice between children in schools.

Predictions

In regard to the first goal, one speculation and five predictions are made. The speculation, based on the genetic/evolutionary model, is that prejudice held by male children will be stronger than that held by female children. From this derives our first prediction: that it might be easier to change attitudes and behaviors of girls than those of boys. Based on the cultural/historical importance of dominance in establishing prejudice, modification of status will be an important factor in the reduction of prejudice and discrimination.

The second prediction is based on the fact that genetics and evolution, culture and history, and social development all play a role in the acquisition of prejudice and discrimination. Thus, interventions based on any one of these factors will probably have a limited effect in reducing prejudice and discrimination. Third, owing to the importance of authority acceptance in the acquisition of cultural knowledge, including prejudice and discrimination, one would expect that involvement by authorities in sanctioning acceptance of other groups would lead to a decrease in prejudice.

The fourth prediction is based on the importance of cooperation to group identity. One would expect children placed on a cooperative team to include their teammates, regardless of gender, race, ethnicity, or disability, in their ingroup. Behaviors and attitudes toward these teammates should become relatively positive. One would not expect, however, these attitudes and behaviors to extend to other people of that same race, ethnic group, sex, or disability, because these "other" people would not be part of their ingroup. Finally, one major prediction of the group identity and cognitive development literature is that there are shifts in the development of race prejudice at ages 4, 6 to 7, 10 to 12, 14 to 16, and 18 to 19 years. Consequently, one would expect differences in the effects of interventions to reduce prejudice and discrimination at these ages.

Contact Theory

One of the theories frequently cited to explain changes in prejudice is the contact theory (Allport, 1954). Allport cautioned that for contact to work in reducing prejudiced attitudes, these conditions must be present: the parties involved must share equal status, the community must sanction the change, the groups must be in the pursuit of common objectives (cooperation), and the association must be deep and genuine (intimate). The next few pages will be devoted to defining each of these factors in more detail and linking them to the genetic/evolutionary and cultural/historical models.

Differential power and status are important in the development of prejudice and discrimination. This suggests that equality of status is central to reducing those attitudes and behaviors. According to Allport (1954), equal status occurs for children when they have similar manners, modes of speech, moral attitudes, and mental ability, and when their parents have comparable amounts of property. Cohen's (1984) Status Equalization Project indicates that in school settings reading ability is also an important status factor for fifth- and sixth-grade Euro-American, African-American, Asian-American, and Hispanic-American students.

Norvell and Worchel (1981) discovered that the status children bring with them from other settings is often more important than their status in the current situation. Thus a student with high status, say as an athlete, would bring that status with her to classroom activities even if she did not excel scholastically. Robinson and Preston (1976) found that characteristics that indicate high status to Whites, e.g., reading ability, are occasionally different from those that indicate high status among Blacks. Thus there is agreement that status is an important factor in changing prejudice, but it is not so clear which factors influence status in a given situation.

Community sanction is linked to the concept of authority in the genetic/evolutionary model and cultural/historical model. By community sanction or institutional supports, Allport (1954) means law, custom, or local atmosphere that promotes changes in prejudice. Research supports Allport's hypothesis and indicates that the atmosphere regarding prejudice in the classroom, the school, and the surrounding community all impact a child's perception of community sanction (Lachat, 1972; Schofield, 1979).

As discussed above, cooperation is an important aspect of group identity. Allport (1954) defined cooperation as a pursuit of common objectives. This factor is of enough importance that a whole body of literature has been developed on the effects of cooperation on the reduction of prejudice and discrimination. Thus the concept of cooperation has been expanded and will be discussed in detail later in the chapter.

Like cooperation, intimacy is an aspect of group identity. Allport (1954) believed that casual contact reinforces stereotypes and prejudiced attitudes, while intimate contact serves to decrease prejudice. By intimacy he meant deeper and more genuine associations. Intimacy between individual members of groups, e.g., individual Euro-American and African-American children, develops when they work, study, and play together consistently over a period of time. The intimacy does not necessarily extend to all members of the outgroup. Thus, this factor should have a greater effect on discrimination than on prejudice.

There are data to support Allport's (1954) contact theory for prejudice reduction. Each of the forms of attitude change discussed in the remainder of the chapter will be considered in light of Allport.

Lewinian Theory

Lewinian theory is a form of field theory and postulates that a person's attitudes are at a quasistationary equilibrium (frozen) when driving forces are equal to restraining forces (Lewin, 1948). When the strength of a driving force (or restraining force) is altered, i.e., increased or decreased, the attitude will become unfrozen, change, and refreeze at a new level.

A simplified example might be helpful here. I (Cathy Johnson) have a specified amount of time each week that I allot to riding my horse. Factors that drive me toward riding more are these: I enjoy the activity; I enjoy being outdoors and in the woods; I wish to improve my skill level; it's more fun than cleaning the house; and my horse needs the exercise. There are factors that, if considered alone, would limit my riding (restraining forces): I have to earn money to pay for the horse; too much time in the sun is bad for my skin; most of my friends do not ride; and my horse also enjoys being out in pasture. Taken together, these driving and restraining forces help me balance my time. If either the driving or the restraining forces changed, I would spend a different amount of time riding. For example, my acquiring a second horse would increase the "horse exercise" driving force and I would spend more time riding. Additionally, my winning the lottery would reduce the "earning money" restraining force and increase my time riding.

Similarly, driving and restraining forces can apply to attitudes. First we will discuss restraining forces. Lewin (1948) indicated that group belongingness and interdependence of fate serve as restraining forces. Group belongingness is similar to group identity and therefore is tied to intergroup mechanisms and inclusive fitness. Allport's community sanction would be viewed by Lewin as a reduction of the "authority" restraining force. Interdependence of fate for Lewin is based on cultural/historical factors of collective memory of history, language, religion, and morality. Keep in mind that owing to cognitive/social development, the effects of this force on prejudice change with age, causing its influence to be stronger or weaker depending on the age group in question. Other scientists have used field theory to discuss additional restraining forces. Evans (1976) suggests that strain in social interactions, i.e. uneasiness, inhibition, and uncertainty, is one of the forces in the maintenance of prejudiced attitudes and thus a restraining force to the development of more positive attitudes. Donaldson (1980) hypothesizes that discomfort, a restraining force, is caused by the expectation of inappropriate social behavior by outgroups.

Factors like cognitive and social development serve as driving forces to attitude change. These factors are age-related, and thus the relative strength of driving forces will change with maturation. Additionally, Donaldson (1980) suggests that the empathy children feel toward others acts as a driving force to positive attitude change.

Measures Employed

Most of the measures utilized in prejudice reduction experiments assess either the cognitive or the behavioral predisposition component of attitudes. None measure the affective component. Measures of discrimination generally include friendship choice or playmate choice. The common measures are described below.

A social distance scale is one way to measure the behavioral predispositions component of prejudice. In a typical social distance scale, the subject is instructed to place a drawing of a child that represents the self into a number of different scenes. A scene might depict children working in the classroom, playing at recess, or playing at home. Scoring is done by actually measuring the distance between the "self" figure and other figures in the scene.

Activity preference scales also measure the behavioral intention aspect of prejudice. A typical one includes showing subjects a picture of a homogeneous group of students, e.g., same race/same sex, working together, and a similar picture containing a heterogeneous group. The subjects are then asked which group they would like to join or have as friends.

There are several ways to measure the cognitive aspect of prejudice, including attitude scales and stereotype rating scales. An example of an attitude scale is the PRAM II, which has subjects choose between Black and White figures in response to evaluative adjectives. A stereotype rating might list a series of unfavorable characteristics (e.g. sneaky, dirty, bad) and favorable characteristics (e.g. brave, strong, friendly). The subject is asked to identify whether all, most, some, few, or no children of a particular category have that characteristic. For younger children a picture story technique might be used to measure stereotypes.

The measures of discrimination generally include sociometrics or observation. Observation is used to measure playmate choice and is usually conducted during a short period of free time before and following any interventions. Sociometric scales can measure either playmate choice or friendship choice.

We have now identified the types of measures used in the prejudice and discrimination reduction literature. Throughout the following discussion, prejudice measures will be referred to as social distance scales, activity preference scales, stereotype ratings, and attitude scales. Discrimination measures are observation, sociometric playmate choice, and sociometric friendship choice.

Desegregation

On May 17, 1954, the United States Supreme Court handed down a decision in the case *Brown v. Board of Education* that brought an end to segregation in the public schools. The court's decision was based, in part, on the information in an *amicus curiae* brief signed by 35 psychologists, which stated that desegregation would decrease cross-racial prejudice, i.e., that of Black children toward Whites and of White children toward Blacks.

More than 40 years have passed since *Brown v. Board of Education,* giving researchers ample time to evaluate the results of school desegregation. One of the goals of this section is to give information on the results of those studies. In the discussion, attention will be paid, where possible, to differentiating results by age, sex, race, and geographic location. Consideration will be given to the effects of forced busing on prejudiced attitudes.

The second goal of this section is to interpret the data in terms of four of the predictions made above. First, girls' attitudes toward children of a different race will generally be more positive than those held by boys. Second, modification of status will be an important factor in the reduction of prejudice. Third, societal support of greater cross-racial acceptance will result in more positive cross-racial attitudes. Finally, one would expect differences in the results of desegregation based on age.

The third and final goal of this section is to discuss the results of desegregation in terms of contact theory and Lewinian theory.

The Studies

Table 6.1 contains information regarding 23 studies and was designed to give as clear a picture as possible of the factors that influenced the outcomes of desegregation. The column headings, or core characteristics, were chosen based on patterns that emerged from examining the literature. The response of the community to desegregation is identified as a core characteristic, although it is not mentioned in many studies. Allport (1954) identified it as an important factor, and a pattern is suggested when the available data are examined. The studies are listed in the table in this order: first, by amount of time elapsed since desegregation; second, by region of the country where the desegregation occurred; and third, by type of desegregation. This method was chosen to aid the reader in identifying important patterns.

The dependent measure, while important, was not listed as a core characteristic, because it did not seem to have a consistent impact on the outcome, and no patterns emerged. Three types of prejudice measures were used: stereotype ratings, attitude surveys, and social distance scales. In none of this research were sociometric data employed as the dependent measure.

The 23 experiments yielded 37 outcome results. Of these, 16 reveal an increase in prejudiced attitudes following desegregation; 10 show no change; and 11 indicate a decrease in prejudice. Approximately 40 percent of the studies show a decrease in prejudice for Blacks, while the corresponding decrease for Whites is only 25 percent.

Do the effects of desegregation change over time—for example, are effects different one year after a school has been desegregated from those seen five years after desegregation? The answer depends on the race of the child. Research falls into three time-related categories based on the length of time the school had been desegregated prior to the performance of the study. In short-term studies, initial data were collected prior to desegregation and the research was completed within one year following desegregation. No control groups were used in these studies. Medium-term data were compiled from schools that had been desegregated one to five years prior to the studies, with segregated schools used for control groups. Long-term studies compared schools desegregated for five years or more to segregated schools.

TABLE 6.1 Summary of Core Study Characteristics and Outcomes

Study	N	Grade	Time Since Deseg.	Region	Type of Deseg.	Community Response	Outcome Black	Outcome White
Barber (1968)	200	8	short	North	voluntary	negative	–	–
Carrigan (1969)	570	K–5	short	North	forced	?[a]	–	–
Dentler & Elkins (1967)	1230	3–6	short	North	natural	?	–	–
Evans (1969)	198	4–6	short	S–W[b]	forced	?	–	
Garth (1963)	94	9–12	short	South	voluntary	?	+	
McWhirt (1967)	152	10	short	South	voluntary	?	+	–
Campbell (1956)	746	8, 10, 12	short	South	forced	?		–
Lombardi (1963)	344	9–10	short	South	forced	neutral		0
Silverman & Shaw (1973)	?	7–12	short	South	forced	negative	0	0
Whitmore (1956)	?	8, 10, 12	short	South	forced	?		0
Green & Gerard (1974)	1769	K–6	short	West	voluntary	mixed	–	0
Webster (1961)	104	7	short	West	forced	?	+	–
Speelman & Hoffman (1980)	72	Pre, 1, 3	short	?	?	?		0

Study	N	Grade	Time Since Deseg.	Region	Type of Deseg.	Community Response	Outcome	
							Black	White
Armor (1972)	171	7–12	medium	North	voluntary	?	–	
Gardner, Wright, & Dee (1970)	260	6–8	medium	North	voluntary	?	+	+
Singer (1966)	136	5	medium	North	natural	?	+	+
Seidner (1971)	96	3	medium	South	voluntary	?	0	0
Friedman (1980)	?	K–3	long	North	natural	?		+
Koslin, Amarel, & Ames (1969)	129	1–2	long	North	natural	?	+	+
Lachat (1972)[c]	?	12	long	North	natural	neutral		–
Lachat (1972)	?	12	long	North	natural	positive		+
Herman (1967)	350	6	long	North	natural	?	0	–
Stephan (1977)	750	5–6	long	S-W	natural	?	–	–
Williams, Best, & Boswell (1975)	483	1–4	long	South	voluntary	?		0

[a]? indicates no information in the report.

[b]S-W indicates Southwest.

[c]Lachat is listed twice due to distinctly different community responses in the study.

When table 6.1 is examined for effects of time since desegregation, differences in prejudice on the part of Euro-American children show an interesting pattern. An increase in prejudice or no change following desegregation was seen for the White children when data were collected on a short-term basis. The children in medium-term conditions displayed a decrease in prejudice towards Blacks following desegregation in two of the studies, and no change in one. In the six long-term studies, seven results were reported for White students. Three revealed decreases in prejudice as a result of desegregation, three showed increases, and one showed no change in attitude.

The results for African-American children were mixed in all three time-related categories in table 6.1. Five short-term studies showed an increase in prejudiced attitudes, one revealed no change, and three indicated a decrease in prejudice towards Whites. Of the four medium-term results, two revealed a decrease in prejudice as a result of desegregation, one showed an increase, and one showed no change. One of the three long-term studies revealed a decrease in prejudice, one showed an increase, and one revealed no change.

One can conclude from these studies that for White children prejudice is at best unchanged immediately after desegregation, and that it decreases between one and five years following desegregation, but that after five years the results are mixed. The racial attitudes of Black students tend to be less affected by time: the results are mixed for all three time categories. Unfortunately, there are no published studies that have monitored the effects of desegregation in a single school system for more than one year. Hence, the longitudinal effects of desegregation are not known.

Regional differences, particularly discrepancies in results from Northern and Southern schools, are of interest. Examination of table 6.1 reveals eight studies that investigated prejudice of Northern Black children towards Whites. Of these, three found decreases in prejudice, four found increases, and one found no change. Ten outcomes for White students are also listed. Five of these show an increase in prejudice as a result of desegregation, and five reveal a decrease.

In the South, prejudice toward Blacks increased for White children in two of the studies and remained unchanged in the remaining four (see table 6.1). The picture for Black children in the South is different. Two studies demonstrated decreases in prejudice following desegregation and two showed no change. While conducting studies in the Southwest, Evans (1969) and Stephan (1977) discovered that Black children developed greater prejudice towards Whites following desegregation. Stephan's (1977) study revealed parallel findings for White children.

Some conclusions can be drawn from these data. Euro-American children in the North became either significantly more or significantly less prejudiced as a result of desegregation, while in the South their prejudice either increased or was unaffected. African-American students responded to desegregation in a way similar to that of Whites in the North, but in the South their prejudice was more likely to decrease or remain unchanged. Two studies are not enough to highlight the Southwest as a special case, but prejudice did increase for both White and Black populations.

Desegregation has typically occurred in three distinctly different ways, as indicated in table 6.1. *Forced* desegregation is generally the result of a school board order or court order and occurs within the entire school system of a given city. Students are bused from their own neighborhood to a school in another neighborhood. *Voluntary* desegregation can occur in an individual school or in an entire school system. Some of the students in these schools are also bused to other schools, generally through a process of open enrollment. An example of this would be a school in a predominately Black neighborhood offering advanced placement courses in order to attract White students from other neighborhoods. *Natural* desegregation occurs when the neighborhood is integrated and the school accurately reflects the neighborhood population.

It seems appropriate to mention a word about the difference between integration and desegregation. The two terms have similar meanings and are often used interchangeably to denote the ending of segregation and the coming together of people of various races and ethnic groups. Desegregation is the process of bringing the races together and integration is the condition that occurs following desegregation. Often the word "integration" is used to connote the condition that exists when the minority group is accepted on a completely equal basis (Pettigrew, 1971; St. John, 1975).

An examination of the results of the studies in table 6.1 based on the way desegregation occurred reveals some interesting patterns. First it should be noted that all of the forced-desegregation experiments were short-term in nature, while those that examined voluntary or natural desegregation spanned the entire time continuum. Research in which the attitudes of White children were examined following forced desegregation revealed an increase or no change in prejudice. The outcomes for White students following voluntary desegregation are mixed: three studies found no significant change, two found an increase, and one found a decrease. Of the eight outcomes for natural desegregation, half showed an increase in prejudice and the remaining half showed a decrease.

The outcomes for African-American children are mixed for all three types of desegregation. In situations in which the desegregation was forced, two studies found an increase in prejudice towards Whites, one found a decrease, and one found no change. For voluntary desegregation, prejudice increased in three studies, decreased in three studies, and remained unchanged in one. The results are similar in cases of natural integration. Two studies found increases in prejudice, two showed decreases, and one saw no change.

One can draw the following conclusions from these data. White children who experience forced desegregation tend to become more prejudiced. When desegregation is voluntary or natural, the results are mixed. No such patterns exist when the results for Black children are viewed by type of desegregation: the results are mixed for all three types.

Only three of the studies in table 6.1 differentiated results by sex. In general, White girls experienced more positive attitude changes as a result of desegregation than White boys, while Black girls' attitudes became more negative than those of Black boys (Dentler & Elkins, 1967; Silverman & Shaw, 1973; Singer, 1966). Singer studied fifth-grade children in naturally integrated schools. He found that both White girls and White boys displayed positive attitudes towards Blacks, but that girls showed the most positive attitudes and were more willing than members of any other group to associate with Blacks. However, Black girls held negative stereotypes of Whites, while the attitudes of Black boys were generally positive. Recall that it was speculated that girls would have more positive attitudes than boys toward other races, and that girls' attitudes would change more readily than boys'. This prediction is not supported for Blacks.

Does the age of the child at the onset of desegregation affect the outcome? The studies in table 6.1 are divided into three age-related categories for the following discussion. The first group of children experienced desegregation in preschool through second grade; i.e., they were less than 8 years old. For the second group the onset of desegregation was between the third and sixth grades (ages 8 to 12). The third group contained children in grades 7 through 12 (ages 12 to 18).

First let's look at the results for Black children. Five of the outcomes in table 6.1 include the youngest age category. Of these, three found an increase in prejudice as a result of desegregation, one showed a decrease, and one showed no change. The results for the middle age group are similar, with five showing an increase in prejudice; two, a decrease; and two, no change. For the oldest age group, two of these studies found an increase in prejudice, four showed a decrease, and one showed no change. Thus there is a tendency for the effects of desegregation to be more positive for the oldest group than for the two younger ones.

The picture for White children is different. Looking at outcomes for the youngest age group, two report an increase in prejudice; two, a decrease; and four, no change. For the middle age group the 11 outcomes are fairly evenly divided between an increase in prejudice, a decrease, and no change. In grades 7 through 12, White children's prejudice increased in five of the studies, decreased in two, and showed no change in three. Thus there is a tendency for the effects of desegregation to be more negative with the oldest group than with the two younger ones.

Recall that it was predicted that there would be differences in the results of prejudice intervention methods at certain ages, i.e., 4, 6 to 7, 10 to 12, 14 to 16, and 18 to 19 years. The results of table 6.1 do not support this prediction. There does seem to be a shift at age 12 to slightly more prejudice as a result of desegregation for White children, and a similarly age-related shift to less prejudice for Black students. It's not clear how to interpret these results.

Contact Theory

Why have we not seen a consistent decrease in prejudice for any groups of children as a result of desegregation? One possibility is that the conditions stipulated by Allport (1954) were not met. Recall that Allport's conditions included community sanction, equal status, cooperation, and intimate association.

The desegregation research supports Allport's (1954) suggestion that community sanction is an important factor in prejudice reduction. In the cases in which the community openly supported desegregation, prejudice decreased (see table 6.1). Five of the studies reported negative, neutral, or mixed community reactions. In all these cases either Black and White children became more prejudiced, or their attitudes did not change.

None of the schools attempted to modify or equalize status. Reading ability and economic factors play a role in determining status. In forced-busing situations the Black students often came from lower-economic-class neighborhoods and the White students came from suburban middle-class schools. Additionally, in many situations the level of education available in previously segregated Black schools was lower than that available in previously segregated White schools. When these students were brought together, reading ability differences existed. One can conclude that equal status was not attained for the children in the studies.

Allport (1954) also indicated that the pursuit of common objectives or cooperation is an important factor in reducing prejudice. None of the studies include cooperative contact. Hence this aspect of contact theory cannot be proved or disproved by the literature.

Allport (1954) believed that casual contact reinforces stereotypes and prejudiced attitudes, while intimate contact, or acquaintance, serves to decrease prejudice. Like that on cooperation, information on intimacy in the schools studied is lacking in table 6.1. Recall that short-term desegregation resulted in an increase or no change in prejudice for White students. This may, in part, be due to the fact that it takes time for intimacy to build, and one year is not enough.

Given the above considerations, it would be surprising if school desegregation had produced the expected decreases in prejudiced attitudes for children, since the contact theory conditions did not exist in any of the schools. We do know, however, that decreases in prejudice for both White and Black children are possible.

Lewinian Theory

From Lewinian theory one would expect desegregation to produce decreases in prejudice for both Black and White children. Let's look at some of the restraining and driving forces to see how they fit with the data presented in this section.

The expectation of socially inappropriate behavior and the discomfort caused by strain in social interactions are forces that restrain White and Black children from changing their attitudes. One would expect interactions in desegregated schools to lessen or eliminate these forces, since Black and White children play, interact socially, and perform in comparable ways. This display of socially acceptable behavior by both races of children did not have a consistent effect on reducing the prejudice of either group.

Also recall that respect for authority is a restraining force in Lewinian theory. The data in table 6.1 indicate that this force lessens when community support is in favor of desegregation. The result is a decrease in prejudice.

One of the driving forces to change prejudiced attitudes is empathy. One would expect that desegregation would increase empathy and therefore reduce prejudice. If this is happening, the effect is not consistent.

It does not appear that Lewinian theory is very helpful in explaining the results of desegregation. It is possible, however, that there was not enough interaction between the races in traditional schools for empathy to develop. Later in the chapter we will look at the importance of interaction in changing both attitudes and behavior.

Mainstreaming

Until 1975 the concept of equal protection under the law was not considered to include disabled children. The *Education for All Handicapped Children Act* changed that and initiated the concept of mainstreaming. Mainstreaming refers to the placement of children with disabilities into educational programs for and with nondisabled children (Karnes & Lee, 1979; Safford & Rosen, 1981; Tawney, 1981; Turnbull & Blacher-Dixon, 1981). Current terminology includes "inclusive education" and the "Regular Education Initiative."

The first goal of this section is to examine the mainstreaming research. When looking at the results of mainstreaming, many researchers primarily focus on changes in academic and social skills for disabled children. A few have examined changes in prejudice and discrimination on the part of nondisabled children toward the disabled as a result of mainstreaming. We will first look at the latter group of studies. Attention will be paid to differentiating results by type of disability, age, and sex. Next, the first body of literature will be discussed in light of the effect changes in academic and social skills may have on nondisabled children's prejudice and discrimination.

The second goal of this section is to interpret the data in terms of a speculation and a prediction made earlier in this chapter. First, it was speculated that girls' attitudes toward disabled children would generally be more positive than those held by boys. Second, it was predicted that age-related differences would be seen in the results of mainstreaming. The third and final goal of this section is to discuss the results of mainstreaming in terms of contact theory and Lewinian theory.

The Prejudice and Discrimination Studies

There is a moderate body of literature that examines the effects of mainstreaming on prejudice and discrimination by nondisabled children. Eleven studies are shown in table 6.2. Experiments dealing with cooperative learning in mainstreamed settings are not included, since these types of experiments are specifically dealt with in the next section. The first five studies compare a mainstreamed condition to a segregated condition, while the remaining six look at various aspects of mainstreaming. Six of the studies measure prejudice and the remaining five measure discrimination.

Does type of handicap affect prejudice or discrimination by nondisabled children? The answer is yes. Represented in the studies were children with mild, moderate, and severe mental retardation; orthopedic limitations; emotional disabilities; sensory impairments; and learning

TABLE 6.2 Summary of Mainstreaming Study Characteristics and Outcomes

Study	N	Grade	#/Type Disab.[a]	Independent Variable	Dependent Measure	Outcomes for Nondisabled
Archie & Sherrill (1989)	229	4–5	9/MR, PD, SI	Mainstreaming vs. Segregated Control	Attitude Scale	Mainstreamed found handicapped more fun and interesting vs. seg. control.
Gottlieb, Cohen, & Goldstein (1974)	499	3–6	30/MR	Mainstreaming vs. Segregated Control	Stereotype Scale	Mainstreamed less accepting of handicapped vs. seg. control.
Rapier, Adelson, Carey, & Croke (1972)	152	3–5	25/PD	Mainstreaming (before vs. after) Age Differences	Attitude Scale	Shift to less prejudice toward disabled after mainstreaming. Greater shift for 5th vs. 3rd grade
Sheare (1974)	400	9	30/MR	Mainstreaming vs. Segregated Control Sex Differences	Attitude Scale	Mainstreamed more accepting of disabled vs. seg. Girls more accepting vs. boys
York, Vandercook, Macdonald, Neff, & Caughey (1992)	181	7–9	24/MR, PD, SI	Mainstreaming (before vs. after) Academic and Behavioral Differences for Handicapped Kids	Sociometric Playmate	More accepting of disabled after mainstreaming. Perceived positive academic & social skills changes in disabled kids.

Study	N	Grade	#/Type Disab.[a]	Independent Variable	Dependent Measure	Outcomes for Nondisabled
Brewer & Smith (1989)	457	1–5	20/MR	Number of Years Mainstreamed (.7–5.7)	Sociometric Playmate	No differences based on years mainstreamed.
Goodman, Gottlieb, & Harrison (1972)	40	1–6	18/MR	Sex Differences	Sociometric Friendship	Girls more accepting of disabled vs. boys.
Miller, Richey, & Lammers (1983)	?	4–7	?/LD, SI, PD, MR	Type of Handicap	Social Distance Scale	Order of preference: LD, N, HI, PD, MR, VI.
Parish, Ohlsen, & Parish (1978)	131	5–7	?/LD, PD, ED	Type of Handicap	Attitude Scale	Order of preference: N, PD, LD, ED.
Roberts & Zubrick (1992)	194	3–7	97/MR	Academic and Behaviorial Differences for Handicapped Kids	Sociometric Friendship	Preferred MR kids with high-level social and academic skills.
Taylor, Asher, & Williams (1987)	64	3–6	34/MR	Behaviorial Differences for Handicapped Kids	Sociometric Playmate	MR displaying socially acceptable behavior preferred.

[a]#: Number of handicapped children in the study.

ED: Emotionally Disturbed   MR: Mentally Retarded   VI: Visually Impaired
HI: Hearing Impaired   SI: Sensory Impaired   Seg.: Segregated

disabilities. Some decrease in prejudice and discrimination by nondisabled children was found in relation to all these types of disabilities; however, most experiments did not differentiate results by type of disability.

Two studies specifically looked at the reactions of nondisabled children to different types of handicaps. Parish et al. (1978) used an attitude scale to assess the prejudice of nondisabled children towards children with three types of disabilities. The results indicated preferences ranked in the following order: physically challenged, learning disabled, and then emotionally disabled. In a similar study, Miller et al. (1983) used a social distance scale and determined that nondisabled children preferred learning-disabled children to nondisabled ones. Children with the remaining disabilities were preferred in this order: hearing-impaired, physically challenged, mildly mentally retarded, and visually impaired. Mainstreaming does generally create more positive attitudes and behaviors toward all types of disabilities. There does, however, seem to be a hierarchy of preference by type of handicap.

Examination of the studies in table 6.2 for differences based on the age of the nondisabled students reveals no general patterns; this result is inconsistent with predicted age effects. Rapier et al. (1972), however, did find some age differences. In their study, the attitudes of nondisabled third-, fourth-, and fifth-graders (ages 8 to 11) towards orthopedically disabled children were examined using an attitude scale. While the overall shift was from neutral to more positive attitudes, the shift was greatest for fifth-graders and smallest for children in the third grade. The failure to find predicted age effects is consistent with the desegregation studies. This implies that social cognitive factors play little part in these two types of nonspecific interventions. In the previous discussion of the prejudice and discrimination literature (chapters 4 and 5), the predicted age effects were found only for opposite-sex prejudice and discrimination. The other categories showed results consistent with the present findings: age had no systematic impact.

As predicted, there seem to be sex differences in prejudice and discrimination toward the disabled in this research (table 6.2). Sheare (1974) studied a group of nondisabled students, composed equally of boys and girls. Half of the students were placed with mildly mentally retarded children in their classes. The remaining students had no mentally retarded students in their classes. Sheare found that girls in both mainstreamed schools and segregated schools were less prejudiced than boys in both conditions. Similarly, Goodman et al. (1972) found that girls discriminated less than boys. These studies support the speculation that prejudice held by male children is stronger than that held by females.

The question remaining is this: Do higher social and academic skills of disabled children result in less prejudice and discrimination by their nondisabled peers? The answer is yes for discrimination, but there are no data for prejudice. Three of the studies in table 6.2 link reduced discrimination by nondisabled children with the socially acceptable behavior of disabled children.

York et al. (1992) studied nondisabled students in two schools that had been mainstreamed for one year when the final data were collected. The results indicated that the nondisabled students perceived positive social skills changes and academic changes in the disabled children, and also were more accepting of them than they had been prior to classroom integration.

The study done by Taylor et al. (1987) is also noteworthy. The researchers looked at the effects of mentally retarded children's social behavior on discrimination by nonretarded children. They found that retarded children who behaved in socially competent ways were more accepted by their nonretarded peers than those who displayed avoidant and withdrawn behavior or those who were aggressive and disruptive. In a similar study, Roberts and Zubrick (1992) found that both social and academic competency in retarded children was connected with the amount of discrimination by nonretarded children.

These data indicate that social and academic competencies in disabled children do result in less discrimination by their nondisabled peers. Additionally, it is probable that moderately and severely mentally retarded children will experience discrimination by their nondisabled peers, since they are less able to display social and academic competence. There is no evidence to suggest that changes in prejudice are related to social and academic skills.

The Social and Academic Skill Studies

Another outstanding question is whether the social and academic skills of disabled children improve as a result of mainstreaming. We know that social and academic competency for disabled children is associated with decreased discrimination by nondisabled children. We assume that mainstreaming will be effective in reducing discrimination by nondisabled children if improvements in social or academic skills for disabled children occur. Four studies were found that connect mainstreaming to the improvement of academic and social skills for primarily mildly mentally retarded preschool children (Cole, Mills, Dale, & Jenkins, 1991; Guralnick & Groom, 1988; Jenkins, Spelts, & Odom, 1985; Wylie, 1974).

Three of the four studies deal with the effects of mainstreaming on the social skills of disabled children (Guralnick & Groom, 1988; Jenkins et al., 1985; Wylie, 1974). The studies are similar with the exception of the subject population, and all of them show higher levels of social skills in the mainstreamed condition than in the segregated condition. Wylie studied mildly to moderately retarded preschoolers, Guralnick and Groom examined mildly mentally retarded preschoolers, and Jenkins et al. included mildly mentally retarded, orthopedically challenged, sensory-impaired, and nondisabled preschoolers. Wylie looked at social play interactions in mainstreamed and segregated settings. Interactions for all but two of the retarded children increased when the nonretarded children were introduced. The two children who did not display an increase in social play were nonverbal.

Two of the studies were designed to examine the academic skills of disabled children resulting from mainstreaming (Cole et al., 1991; Jenkins et al., 1985). The outcomes of these experiments are not consistent.

In Cole et al. (1991), mentally retarded preschoolers in mainstreamed classes were compared with similar students in segregated classes. All students were tested on general cognition, vocabulary, language, and early reading ability prior to beginning their first year of classes and at the end of the school year. The results showed that the higher-functioning students gained more academically from integrated classes, while those that were functioning at a lower level gained more from segregated classes. No significant differences were found between variously abled mainstreamed and similar segregated students in the study by Jenkins et al. (1985).

The data cited above indicate that the social and academic skills of high-functioning disabled preschool children improve as a result of mainstreaming. We saw earlier that this improvement is associated with a decrease in discriminatory behavior by nondisabled children. The results are different for lower-functioning moderately to severely mentally retarded children. The social and academic skills of these children do not improve in mainstreamed settings. Thus, discrimination by nonretarded children toward their low-functioning retarded peers probably remains unchanged.

Contact Theory

Can we explain the decreases in prejudice and discrimination on the part of nondisabled children toward disabled ones based on the contact theory? The answer seems to be no. As you will recall, the contact theory includes equal status, community sanction, cooperative contact, and intimate contact.

There is no evidence to suggest that equal status exists for disabled children, any more than it did for Black children following desegregation (Hertel, 1991). In many studies, where a decrease in prejudice or discrimination was seen among the nondisabled students, they were acting as role models for the disabled children (Snyder, Apolloni, & Cooke, 1977). Additionally, the nondisabled children interacted with the disabled children in a helping way, which seems to be an important factor in reducing discrimination (Cooper, Johnson, Johnson, & Wilderson, 1980; Johnson, Johnson, & Maruyama, 1983; Johnson, Rynders, Johnson, Schmidt, & Haider, 1979). This evidence indicates that equal status is not related to a decrease in prejudice or discrimination on the part of nondisabled children toward the disabled.

Community sanction is the second factor in the contact theory. As with desegregation, the community is not generally supportive. No studies examined community support of mainstreaming. There is, however, an ongoing debate about the effectiveness of mainstreaming, with strong opinions on both sides. The participants in this debate are parents, educators, and psychologists. There likely is not strong community support for a practice that is being argued so aggressively (Byrnes, 1990; Davis, 1989; Jenkins, Pious, & Jewell, 1990; Lieberman, 1990).

Cooperative and intimate contact are the final two components. None of these studies included cooperative interactions. Hence, this aspect of contact theory cannot be proved or disproved by the above literature. There is no evidence that intimate contact is required to change attitudes or behaviors of nondisabled students toward the disabled. This view is supported by research that found decreases in prejudice and discrimination toward disabled persons following lectures and video presentations (Donaldson, 1980; Lazar, Gensley, & Orpet, 1971; Sedlick & Penta, 1975).

Although the contact theory appeared to be helpful in explaining the results of desegregation, it does not seem to apply to mainstreaming. Most of the criteria were not present in mainstreamed schools where decreases in prejudice were found.

Lewinian Theory

Lewinian theory may better explain why mainstreaming causes a decrease in prejudice and discrimination. Let's examine some of the driving and restraining forces that are salient.

Recall that strain in social interactions is one of the forces in the maintenance of prejudiced attitudes, and thus a restraining force to the development of more positive attitudes. Seeing disabled children performing normal tasks in school alleviates this strain, and provides a reduction in the restraining forces.

The expectation of inappropriate social behavior by the disabled is another restraining force, and discovering that disabled children behave appropriately reduces the force. The study by Taylor et al. (1987) supports this conclusion. Recall their finding that mentally retarded children who behaved in socially acceptable ways were chosen as playmates by nonretarded children more often than those who were avoidant and withdrawn or aggressive and disruptive.

Finally, the empathy that nondisabled children feel toward disabled ones provides a driving force to positive change in attitudes. It is assumed that "helping behavior" of nondisabled children directed toward the disabled produces empathy, and hence, prejudice reduction (Donaldson, 1980).

Cooperative Interaction

The third substantial body of literature on prejudice and discrimination reduction is based on cooperative interaction. Let us begin by defining what is meant by cooperation and interaction. Cooperation implies that there must be positive goal interdependence, which can take the form of shared rewards, divided resources, or complementary roles (Johnson & Johnson, 1992). Interaction means that children work or talk together as opposed to simply occupying the same room.

The first goal of this section is to discuss the results of the cooperative interaction research. The second goal is to interpret the data in terms of two predictions made earlier. The first prediction is that one would expect cooperative interaction to reduce prejudice and discrimination toward outgroup members who become cooperative teammates. This reduction is not expected to generalize to all members of the same outgroup. The second prediction is that one would expect differences in the effects of prejudice and discrimination reduction interventions at ages 4, 6 to 7, 10 to 12, 14 to 16, and 18 to 19 years. The third and final goal of this section is to discuss the results of cooperative interaction in terms of contact theory and Lewinian theory.

The Studies

Table 6.3 contains 20 studies that examine the effects of cooperative interaction in academic settings on prejudice and discrimination toward different racial and ethnic groups, the opposite sex, and disabled persons. Three of the experiments measure prejudice and discrimination toward more than one comparison group (outgroup). Fourteen findings pertain to racial/ethnic prejudice or discrimination, three pertain to that towards opposite-sex individuals, and six, to that towards disabled children. The average sample size was 134 subjects, but the numbers ranged from 11 to 558. The children in these studies ranged in age from 7 to 18 (grades 2 to 12), but most were in the fifth through tenth grades.

The interventions took on average one hour each day for four weeks. The only brief intervention (15 minutes) was in the Katz and Zalk (1978) experiment. A variety of dependent measures were used. The first four studies listed in the table included some measure of attitude toward the outgroup in the general population. The second grouping of experiments, six in all, utilized observations to measure behavior toward classmates. The remaining 10 experiments collected sociometric data. Four of the experiments included follow-up data ranging from two weeks to nine months after the intervention.

Fourteen of the studies in table 6.3 had children working in cooperative teams as the single experimental condition. The majority of these experiments included some interaction between teams within a class. The control condition in 18 of the studies involved children working individually. Six of the experiments included two experimental conditions, one cooperative and one competitive. The results from the competitive conditions will be discussed together at the end of this section.

Opposite-Sex Prejudice and Discrimination

One of the studies in table 6.3 examines the effects of cooperative interaction on opposite-sex prejudice, and two examine its effects on discrimination. The first is by Johnson et al. (1978). White students were divided into cooperative and control conditions. In the cooperative condition the students worked in teams on math assignments, completing one answer sheet per team. They were instructed to share ideas and seek clarification from one another and were rewarded and praised as a group.

Two measures of opposite-sex prejudice were used following the intervention, an activity preference scale and an attitude scale. The results from both measures indicate that boys and girls in the experimental condition were less prejudiced toward members of the opposite sex than their counterparts in the control condition.

The cooperative condition for Cooper et al. (1980) and Warring et al. (1985) also included children working together on school assignments in teams. They found increases in opposite-sex friendship choices toward classmates following cooperative interaction, in contrast to children in the control group.

The three studies cited above indicate that cooperative interaction does reduce discrimination toward opposite-sex classmates and prejudice toward unknown members of the opposite sex. The latter results do not support the prediction that cooperative interaction will have effects only for the outgroup classmates worked with and not for unknown members of that outgroup.

TABLE 6.3 Summary of Cooperative Contact Study Characteristics and Outcomes

Study	N	Grade	Days/Hrs. per Day	Dependent Measure	Comparison Group	Outcomes/Follow-up Attitude	Outcomes/Follow-up Behavior
Attitude							
Weigel, Wiser, & Cook (1975)	324	7 & 10	100/1	Attitude Scale	Black	+0[a]	0
				Activity Preference	White	+0	0
				Sociometric Friend & Playmate	Hispanic	+0	+
					Euro[b]	+0	+
							+
Johnson, Johnson, & Scott (1978)	30	5–6	50/1	Activity Preference	Girls	+	+
				Attitude Scale	Boys	+	+
				Sociometric Friend			
Katz & Zalk (1978)	40	2 & 5	1/1/4	Attitude Scale	Black	0/0	0/0
				Social Distance	White	0/0	0/0
				Sociometric Friend			
				2-week follow-up			
Ziegler (1981)	146	5–6	10/1 1/2	Attitude Scale	Italian	+/0	+/+
				Sociometric Friend	Asian	+/0	+/+
				10-week follow-up	Greek	+/0	+/+
					West Indian	+/0	+/+
					Euro	+/0	+/+
Behavior: Observation							
Johnson, Rynders, Johnson, Schmidt, & Haider (1979)	30	7–9	6/1	Observation	Retarded		+
					Nonretarded		+

Study	N	Grade	Days/Hrs. per Day	Dependent Measure	Comparison Group	Outcomes/Follow-up Attitude	Behavior
Martino & Johnson (1979)	12	2–3	9/1	Observation	LD[c] Nondisabled		+ +
Rynders, Johnson, Johnson, & Schmidt (1980)	30	7–10	8/1	Observation	Retarded Nonretarded		+ +
Johnson & Johnson (1981)	51	4	16/1	Observation Sociometric Playmate	Black White		+ +
Rogers, Miller, & Hennigan (1981)	11	6	4/1/2	Observation	Black White		+ +
Johnson & Johnson (1982)	76	4	15/1	Observation Sociometric Friend 5-month follow-up	Black White		+/+ +/+
Behavior: Sociometric							
Ballard, Corman, Gottlieb, & Kaufman (1977)	200	3–5	40/1/2	Sociometric Playmate	Retarded Nonretarded		+ +
Blaney, Stephan, Rosenfield, Aronson, & Sikes (1977)	304	5	18/1	Sociometric Playmate	Black White Hispanic Euro		+ + + +
Slavin (1977)	65	7	20/1	Sociometric Friend	Black White		+ +

Table continues on p238.

TABLE 6.3 Summary of Cooperative Contact Study Characteristics and Outcomes—*Continued*

Study	N	Grade	Days/Hrs. per Day	Dependent Measure	Comparison Group	Outcomes/Follow-up Attitude	Behavior
DeVries, Edwards, & Slavin (1978)	558	7–12	18/4	Sociometric Friend	Black	+	
					White	+	
Slavin (1979)	294	7–8	50/1	Sociometric Friend 9-month follow-up	Black	+/+	
					White	+/+	
Armstrong, Johnson, & Balow (1981)	40	5–6	20/1 1/2	Sociometric Friend	LD	+	
					Nondisabled	+	
Cooper, Johnson, Johnson, & Wilderson (1980)	60	7	15/3	Sociometric Friend	Girls	+	
					Boys	+	
					Black	+	
					White	+	
					LD	+	
					Nondisabled	+	
Slavin & Oickle (1981)	230	6–8	50/1	Sociometric Friend	Black	+	
					White	+	
Johnson & Johnson (1985)	48	6	10/1	Sociometric Playmate	Black	+	
					White	+	
Warring, Johnson, Maruyama, & Johnson (1985)	125	4 & 6	11/1	Sociometric Friend	Girls	+	
					Boys	+	
					Black	+	
					White	+	

[a]+-0: Positive change toward classmates, no change in general attitude.
[b]Euro: Euro-American.
[c]LD: Learning disabled.

Racial and Ethnic Prejudice and Discrimination

Does cooperative interaction also affect attitudes and behaviors between different racial and ethnic groups? Fourteen studies in table 6.3 examined the effects of cooperative interaction on racial/ethnic prejudice and discrimination. Of the 17 outcomes reported, three measured prejudice and 14 measured discrimination.

Weigel et al. (1975) compared White and minority (African-American & Mexican-American) students in cooperative English classes with those in a control group. In the cooperative condition students worked in teams, and their grades were awarded individually, with bonus points given based on group performance.

A stereotype scale was used to assess prejudice toward classmates, while an attitude scale and an activity preference scale were used to measure prejudice toward unknown members of the other racial and ethnic groups. The results of the stereotype scale indicated a decrease in racial/ethnic prejudice towards classmates. The results of the other two measures showed no differences in racial/ethnic prejudice following either the cooperative intervention or the control situation.

Katz and Zalk (1978) had children put together jigsaw puzzles for fifteen minutes. The children in the experimental groups were White and Black. The control groups contained exclusively White children who also worked together on jigsaw puzzles. The dependent measures, an attitude scale and a social distance scale, were administered before the intervention, immediately following it, and two weeks later. The results showed no difference in cross-racial prejudice, either immediately following or two weeks after the intervention.

Ziegler (1981) did find changes in attitudes towards other ethnic groups following cooperative interaction. Conducted in Toronto, the study included Anglo-Canadians, West Indian–Canadians, Chinese-Canadians, Greek-Canadians, and Italian-Canadians. Children in the experimental condition learned material and then taught that material to their teammates. Quizzes were given biweekly and each child's grade was composed of an individual score and a home team score.

The dependent measure, an attitude scale, was administered before, immediately after, and 10 weeks after the intervention. At the end of the experiment the children in the cooperative condition showed a significantly greater increase in positive attitudes toward other ethnic groups than did those in the control condition. The effects had substantially decreased 10 weeks later and were no longer statistically significant.

The three studies taken together indicate that racial/ethnic attitudes toward the general population do not readily change as a result of cooperative interaction. When a change is noted, the effects disappear within 10 weeks. Although there are limited data, attitudes toward out-group classmates seem to improve following cooperative interaction.

No age effects were noted in any of these experiments. The studies included children in grades 2 through 10 (ages 7 to 16) and the results were the same regardless of the age group.

Of the 14 experiments in table 6.3 that measured racial/ethnic discrimination, three used observations as the dependent measure. The first of these, by Rogers et al. (1981), studied Black and White girls for two weeks during recess. Cooperative interactions consisted of playing cooperative games two days per week. The girls were observed prior to and following the experiment. Prosocial cross-racial interactions increased significantly on a pretest-posttest comparison.

In support of these data, Johnson and Johnson (1981, 1982) observed White and Black students in their two experiments. In the cooperative condition the students worked together in teams to finish their schoolwork. Each team completed one answer sheet and was rewarded as a group. In order for researchers to observe behaviors, 10 minutes of free time were given after each class. Significantly more cross-racial interaction was noted between students in the cooperative condition than between those in the control condition.

These three studies taken together indicate that cross-racial discrimination decreases as a result of cooperative interaction. The experiment by Johnson and Johnson (1982) indicates that the positive changes may be long-lasting (five months).

Thirteen studies in table 6.3 used sociometric data to measure racial/ethnic friendship and playmate choices as related to cooperative interaction. The first of these, by Weigel et al. (1975), Katz and Zalk (1978), and Ziegler (1981), were described earlier in this section. Both Weigel et al. and Katz and Zalk found no differences for Whites or Blacks between the cooperative condition and the control on measures of playmate or friendship choice. However, Weigel et al. and Ziegler did find positive changes regarding cross-ethnic (other than Black/White) preferences. Additionally, Ziegler's results held on follow-up 10 weeks later.

Slavin (1977, 1979), Slavin and Oickle (1981), and DeVries et al. (1978) measured cross-racial Black and White friendship choices before and after cooperative interactions. Slavin included Black and White students from two different English classes in both experiments. Slavin and Oickle and DeVries et al. included students studying a variety of subjects. The small teams of adolescents in the experimental condition listened to a presentation from the teacher and then worked together to learn the material. They were quizzed individually and each team was given a score based on the average performance of its members on the quizzes. The results of all four studies indicated a greater increase in cross-racial friendship choices following cooperative interaction than occurred in the control condition. Additionally, the Slavin (1979) experiment included a nine-month follow-up that indicated that the results were long-lasting.

Six similar experiments confirmed the above pattern of results (Blaney et al., 1977; Cooper et al., 1980; Johnson & Johnson, 1981, 1982, 1985; Warring et al., 1985). All found more racial/ethnic friendship or playmate choices following the cooperative condition than following the control condition. Johnson and Johnson (1982) showed that the effect was still present five months after the intervention.

These 13 studies taken together indicate that racial/ethnic discrimination generally decreases immediately following and up to nine months after cooperative interaction in classroom settings has occurred. Additionally, the results from the Blaney et al. (1977) experiment indicate that the decrease is greater toward cooperative teammates than toward other children in the class.

When examined together, the 14 studies on the effects of cooperative interaction on racial/ethnic prejudice and discrimination support the prediction that cooperative interaction would reduce prejudice and discrimination towards outgroup members who became cooperative teammates, but not toward unknown members of the outgroup. The Weigel et al. (1975) study showed less racial/ethnic prejudice towards teammates in the cooperative condition, but these results did not generalize to unknown members of another race or ethnic group. When racial/ethnic attitudes toward the general population did show some change, it was not long-lasting.

The results of these studies do not, however, support the second prediction made at the beginning of this section: that there would be age differences in the effects of cooperative interventions. In general, irrespective of age, attitudes toward unknown members of other racial/ethnic groups do not change as a result of cooperative interaction. Racial/ethnic attitudes and behaviors toward known classmates become more positive for children of all ages as a result of cooperative interventions.

Discrimination Towards Disabled Persons

The remaining group we need to evaluate results for is the disabled. None of the studies in table 6.3 measured attitude change towards the disabled as a result of cooperation. Six of the studies did, however, measure discrimination. Of these, three used observations and three used sociometric data.

Johnson et al. (1979) and Rynders et al. (1980) studied mildly mentally retarded and nonretarded students. In both studies, each child was placed into either a cooperative or a control condition. Those in the cooperative condition were instructed to improve their group bowling scores, while control condition students were instructed to improve their individual scores. Nonretarded children in the cooperative condition interacted positively with and cheered for the retarded children more than did those in the control condition.

In a similar study, Martino and Johnson (1979) used swimming instead of bowling and learning-disabled instead of retarded children. Observations were done in a 15-minute free-swim period after each class. In the cooperative condition, the number of friendly interactions between learning-disabled and non-learning-disabled children increased and the number of hostile interactions decreased over time, while those involving children in the individual condition stayed the same.

What happens when sociometric data are used in place of observations to measure discrimination? Ballard et al. (1977) studied mildly retarded and nonretarded children in a cooperative and a control condition. The cooperative experience was created by placing children in teams that worked together to produce a multimedia presentation (e.g., a slide show or skit). One of the teams in each classroom contained a retarded student and two or more did not. On completion of the presentations, new teams were formed for a second cycle of the process. Children in the control condition continued with their normal classwork throughout the eight-week experiment.

Sociometric playmate choice questionnaires were given before and after the experiment. Nonretarded children in the cooperative condition who had had a chance to work with a retarded student chose their retarded peers more often as playmates than did either those in the experimental condition who had not worked with a retarded child or those in the control condition. Additionally, since all nonretarded children in the experimental condition interacted positively with retarded children, their liking for their retarded peers increased compared to that of similar children in the control group.

Similar experiments were conducted by Armstrong et al. (1981) and Cooper et al. (1980). The Cooper et al. study was described earlier in this chapter. Differences between the two studies are noted in table 6.3 and include subject age and educational content. The results of both experiments indicated that non-learning-disabled students in the cooperative condition chose their learning-disabled peers more often as friends than did similar students in an individual setting.

Two predictions were made at the beginning of this section, one regarding outcomes toward cooperative teammates versus those toward unknown outgroup members, and one regarding age differences. Neither prediction made in this section is supported by the results of these six experiments. While it is evident from the above data that the behavior of nondisabled children toward their disabled classmates changes as a result of cooperative interaction, we do not know if this change generalizes to other handicapped persons, nor whether attitude changes as well. Additionally, there were no systematic differences in results based on age of the subject.

Competitive Studies

As mentioned at the beginning of this section, six of the experiments include a competitive condition. In four of these the competitive condition is confounded by mixing cooperation and competition, i.e., a cooperative team competes with another cooperative team for rewards (DeVries et al., 1978; Rynders et al., 1980; Johnson & Johnson, 1985; Warring et al., 1985). In the remaining two studies children in the competitive condition were instructed to outperform their teammates and rewards were given to the winners (Johnson & Johnson, 1982; Cooper et al., 1980). The results of these studies are mixed. Three of the experiments found less discrimination as a result of competitive interaction and three found no difference between the competitive condition and the control.

Contact Theory

Can the results of these cooperative interaction studies be understood in terms of contact theory? Let's look at each aspect of the theory.

Does equal status exist in cooperative interaction studies? In many of the studies the answer is yes, but in the studies on behavior toward disabled children particularly, the answer is no. In the majority of these studies, nonhandicapped children felt they helped their handicapped peers but did not feel that those peers helped them. Does cooperation exist? The answer to this question is definitely yes. How about community sanction? It would probably appear to the children that the teacher or facilitator is sanctioning working together; in many of these studies such behavior is actually rewarded by the authority figures present. So the answer is yes.

Finally, does intimacy exist? We have to answer yes to this question also. The contacts of children teaching, assisting, and encouraging one another in groups seem as intimate as most other types of contacts they may have. So it appears that with the exception that equal status does not exist between normally developing and disabled children, the contact theory does help us explain these results.

Lewinian Theory

Lewinian theory is also useful in explaining the results of this research. Let's examine some of the driving and restraining forces that are salient.

You will recall from the previous section on mainstreaming that strain in social interactions is a restraining force to the development of positive attitudes and behaviors. Working with children who were different from themselves (e.g., opposite-sex, differently abled, different-race children) over a period of time and finding out that they were not so very different would decrease this restraining force on given children.

A second restraining force that pertains to cooperative interaction is authority acceptance. This force is decreased when the authority figure (teacher) sanctions and rewards interacting together.

The final restraining force is the discomfort caused by the expectation of inappropriate social behavior. In many of these studies it was found that off-task or inappropriate behavior decreased in the cooperative setting. This would indicate that the children in these groups behaved appropriately and worked well together. Thus this restraining force would also seem to be decreased with cooperative interaction.

The development of empathy would be a driving force to change attitudes and behavior. The opportunity to work with and help their Black, disabled, or opposite-sex peers would aid in the development of empathy. The result of this would be to increase this driving force.

The Media

The effects of the media, particularly television and movies, on attitude change have been of high interest since the dawn of television. In their book on the influence of the media, Liebert and Sprafkin (1988) detail research showing that the media are effective in reinforcing existing attitudes and modifying rather than completely revising them. In a study done by Alper and Leidy (1970), they found that television was a useful medium for immediately changing attitudes, and that these changes were smaller but still present six months later. Given the evidence that the media affects attitudes, it is important to discuss how it affects prejudice in children.

There are two goals of this section. The first is to present the results of studies on the effects of the media on prejudice reduction in children. The second is to discuss the results in terms of contact theory and Lewinian theory.

The Studies

Four studies measuring the effects of television and film on prejudice in children are detailed in the next few pages (Gorn, Goldberg, & Kanungo, 1976; Houser, 1978; Kraus, 1972; and Westervelt & McKinney, 1980). The studies used a variety of methods to measure prejudice. The children in the studies ranged in age from 3 to 17 (preschool to eleventh grade).

The first study was by Kraus (1972) and included eleventh-grade (ages 16 to 17) White adolescents. An 11-minute film showing two teachers aiding an African-American student in applying and getting into a White private college was the experimental manipulation. Four versions of the film, varying the races of the teachers, were produced: both teachers were White; both teachers were Black; there were one White and one Black teacher; there were one Black and one White teacher (roles reversed). The study design included a pretest, a posttest, and a control group.

An attitude scale and a social distance scale were used to measure prejudice. The results indicated that both versions of the film that included both a Black and a White teacher were effective in reducing prejudice when compared to both the control group and the pretest data. The other two versions did not produce attitude change.

In the study by Gorn et al. (1976), White, English-Canadian preschoolers (ages 3 to 4) viewed *Sesame Street.* Professionally produced, two- to three-minute-long segments of children playing together in various settings were inserted into the program. Two versions of each segment were produced: an integrated version with White, Asian, and American Indian children, and a minority-only version, with Asian and American Indian children. Subjects in the experimental condition saw one of the two versions of the inserted segments, while those in the control condition watched *Sesame Street* with no inserts.

To measure prejudice, an activity preference scale was administered. The results indicated that children viewing either the integrated segment or the minority-only segment were significantly less prejudiced toward Asian and American Indian children than those in the control group.

The third study was by Houser (1978) and included White, Black, Asian, and Hispanic kindergarten through third-grade children (ages 5 to 9). For the experimental group, Houser created films showing children of different ethnic groups talking to each other. Much of the talk centered around the idea that appearance and skin color are not important when relating to others. Those in the control condition saw no films.

A stereotype rating scale was used to measure prejudice. The findings indicated that prejudice decreased following the experimental manipulations. The results held equally well regardless of age, sex, ethnicity of the subject, and ethnicity of the tester.

The final study was done by Westervelt and McKinney (1980). Fourth-grade (ages 9 to 10) boys and girls completed a pretest and a posttest. The experimental condition involved a 13-minute film showing physically disabled children in wheelchairs participating with nondisabled children in physical education and classroom activities. Children in the control group saw no films.

A social distance questionnaire and a stereotype rating scale were used to evaluate both a child in a wheelchair and another one with leg braces using crutches (as a test for generalization). Prejudice was assessed in three situations: in school, at home, and with a peer group. The measures were administered immediately following the film and again nine days later.

Both measures showed that prejudice toward children in wheelchairs decreased when compared both to the pretest and to the control group. However, attitudes toward children on crutches were unaffected. Nine days later the positive changes had disappeared.

The number of studies is limited, but the results show that television and film do reduce prejudice in children and adolescents. The films were effective regardless of the age, race, or sex of the subject. The effects were similar for prejudice toward Black, Asian, Hispanic, and wheelchair-bound children. It is interesting to note that in the Westervelt and McKinney (1980) study, prejudice reduction was found only toward the specific physical disability shown and the results did not generalize to children on crutches. Additional studies would be helpful in determining long-term effects.

Contact Theory

One might say that contact theory does not apply to these media studies because no actual contact exists. It is, however, interesting to note the aspects of the theory that are present. The films contain children that are working together (cooperation) in a way that denotes equal status and intimacy. We cannot know if the subject presumes that community sanction exists.

Lewinian Theory

Lewinian theory may be more helpful in explaining this research. Viewing children working and playing together would decrease the restraining forces that serve to maintain prejudice. The subjects could see that the different-race or disabled children in the film were similar to themselves in some ways and that they behaved appropriately. This would decrease the strain in social interactions and discomfort caused by expectations of inappropriate behavior. Additionally, empathy (driving force) would be increased as the subjects viewed and got to know the children on the screen.

Simulations

There is evidence that role-playing is an effective way to change attitudes. Research has shown that people will change their attitudes about an issue through simple role play (Janis & King, 1954; King & Janis, 1956; Mann & Janis, 1968; McGuire, 1985). A study done by Clore and Jeffrey (1972) revealed that college students became significantly less prejudiced toward those who are physically disabled after playing the role of a person in a wheelchair. Byrnes and Kiger (1990) found that White college students' attitudes towards Black people improved following a role play designed by Ms. Jane Elliott called "Blue Eyes–Brown Eyes" (Peters, 1985). Ms. Elliott designed this simulation following the death of Martin Luther King, Jr., to allow her third-grade students to feel the effects of discrimination.

The central question is this: Are role-playing simulations of any value in changing the attitudes of White children toward Black children, nondisabled children toward disabled ones, or boys toward girls? The first goal of this section is to examine the literature that investigates race prejudice and prejudice toward the disabled. No studies were found that examined the effectiveness of simulations in changing opposite-sex prejudice. The second goal is to discuss the results in terms of contact theory and Lewinian theory.

The Studies

Five simulation studies were found that dealt with changing prejudice in children through role play (Dahl, Horsman, & Arkell, 1978; Handlers & Austin, 1980; Margo, 1983; Marsh & Friedman, 1972; Weiner & Wright, 1973). The dependent variable in all of the experiments was prejudice. In none of the studies was discrimination measured.

Three of the studies included students role-playing disabilities involving motor skills (Dahl et al., 1978; Handlers & Austin, 1980; and Margo, 1983). All of these found a decrease in prejudice following the simulation. Dahl et al. used fifth-grade (ages 10 to 11) classes in their experiment. The classes were pre- and posttested using a social distance scale and an attitude scale. In the experimental condition, students spent 10 minutes experiencing each of three disabilities: a hearing, a visual, and a motor impairment. Decreases in prejudice toward deaf or blind people were not found. The only decrease in prejudice noted occurred toward the other physically impaired group, in connection to maneuvering a wheelchair.

The research done by Margo (1983) had similar results. In her study, each fifth- and sixth-grade (ages 10 to 12) student role-played four physical impairments by restraining fingers, using crutches and leg weights, and maneuvering a wheelchair. She found decreases in prejudice only towards people in wheelchairs when she compared the posttest to the pretest responses. There were no similar decreases in prejudice toward the other three impairments.

For both of these experiments the difference between simulations that decrease prejudice and those with no effects seems to lie in the "realness" of the simulation. Restraining a finger or using leg weights may produce an experience close to that of a disabled person, but everyone knows that disabled persons do not wear leg weights. The participants are also likely to realize the potential of their being in a wheelchair in their own lifetime, while the potential of waking up one morning to find two fingers fused together is nonexistent.

Blindness was simulated in three of the studies (Dahl et al., 1978; Handlers & Austin, 1980; Marsh & Friedman, 1972). Two of these experiments showed a decrease in prejudice toward the blind following the role play and one found no difference. Close inspection of the studies to determine the cause of these discrepant results revealed a difference in the settings of the experiments. The two studies that found a decrease in prejudice were part of a larger program that included discussions about stereotypes and the students' feelings about blindness and blind people, while the third study contained no such discussions. These data indicated that simulations that may have limited effect in isolation can have a greater effect if a well-facilitated, relevant discussion is held before and after the role play.

Only one of the experiments examined the effects of role-playing on race prejudice (Weiner & Wright, 1973). The simulation was based on Ms. Jane Elliot's "Blue Eyes–Brown Eyes," mentioned earlier. In their experiment Weiner and Wright divided a third-grade (ages 8 to 9) class into two groups distinguished by green and orange armbands. On the first day the class was told that the Orange students were smarter, cleaner, and better behaved than the Green students. Orange children were also granted special privileges and praised throughout the day, while the Green children were criticized. On day two the situation was reversed, allowing the Green children to be the superior group. The simulation became very real for the students, and tension between the groups developed.

The principal results using pretest-posttest comparisons were that the children held less racial prejudice and were more likely to commit to having future cross-racial interactions following the simulation. The effects were strong immediately following the role play and again two weeks later. The data fit nicely with the anecdotal evidence from Ms. Elliot's third-grade students, both when she performed the simulation and later, when the students had become adults (Peters, 1985).

These studies show that simulations can be effective in reducing prejudice in children. In order to be effective, they must be as real as possible. Discussions before and after the role play are important both to promote attitude change and to alleviate any stress felt by the participants during the experience.

Contact Theory

It is difficult to make the connection between the effectiveness of role-play simulations in reducing prejudice and contact theory. The factors in contact theory are equal status, community sanction, cooperative contact, intimate contact, and a real situation. Role plays do not promote equal status. As a matter of fact, simulations like the one done by Weiner and Wright (1973) seem to rely on the feelings of "superiority" and "inferiority" felt by the participants. Furthermore, community sanction, cooperative contact, and intimate contact are not present in these situations.

Lewinian Theory

Lewinian theory is useful in explaining the results of this research. The development of empathy for disabled persons or persons of other races during the simulation experience (Kiger, 1992) would be a driving force to developing more positive attitudes towards those persons. There are no obvious restraining forces produced by the simulations.

Individuation and Self-Acceptance

The final body of literature to be discussed is the research on individuation and self-acceptance. A definition of each will help get us started. Individuation is the process of differentiating people from one another. The process applies to separating oneself from others (self-individuation) or differentiating other individuals from the groups to which they belong. Self-acceptance is part of the self-individuation process (Aboud, 1988). It is defined by Rubin (1967a) to mean "a willingness to confront ego-alien as well as ego-syntonic aspects of the self and to accept rather than deny their existence" (p. 234). In other words, a person with high self-acceptance recognizes and accepts all aspects of the self, and a person with low self-acceptance sees and accepts only some aspects of the self, while denying that other aspects exist. The ego-alien or denied aspects of the self are generally those that society deems "unacceptable." It is important to note the difference between self-acceptance and self-esteem. Self-esteem, simply put, is pride in oneself. An individual can be low in self-acceptance and high in self-esteem—denying some aspects of the self while maintaining pride in who he believes himself to be.

Much of the literature on self-acceptance is based on the research detailed in *The Authoritarian Personality* (Adorno, Frenkel-Brunswick, Levinson, & Sanford, 1950). One of the conclusions of that research can be summarized as follows: Nonprejudiced people are aware of both their "acceptable" and their "unacceptable" characteristics, while prejudiced people tend not to see their "unacceptable" characteristics and fail to integrate them into their self-images.

A search through the literature locates nine studies that look at the relationship between individuation (self-acceptance) and prejudice. Of these, seven deal with people between the ages of 19 and 59 (Berger, 1952; Cook, 1972; Katz, McClintock, & Sarnoff, 1956, 1957; Rubin, 1967; Sheerer, 1949; and Stotland, Katz, & Patchen, 1972), and two deal with subjects between the ages of 9 and 18 (Phillips, 1951; Trent, 1957). A variety of measures have been used for both self-acceptance and prejudice. The next few pages contain more information on each experiment.

There are two goals of this section. The first is to present the literature on individuation, including the self-acceptance research. The second goal is to discuss the results in terms of contact theory and Lewinian theory.

Research on Children

Both of the studies that used children and adolescents as subjects were designed to determine if a correlation exists between self-acceptance and prejudice (Phillips, 1951; Trent, 1957). In both experiments two questionnaires were designed and validated, one to measure self-acceptance and one to measure racial/ethnic attitudes. Phillips administered his scales to White high school (ages 15 to 18) and college (ages 18 to 21) students. His attitude scale measured prejudice towards other racial and ethnic groups. Trent looked at self-acceptance and prejudice in 9- through 18-year-old (grades 4 to 12) Black children. His attitude questionnaire was organized according to the three dimensions of racial prejudice: cognitive, emotional, and behavioral intention. The results of both experiments showed a negative correlation between self-acceptance and racial/ethnic prejudice.

Research on Adults

Correlational studies have also been done with adults. Of the seven studies on adults, three examined the relationship between self-acceptance and prejudice. Sheerer (1949) studied counseling cases (White adults) for statements of self-acceptance and racial/ethnic prejudice. Berger (1952) measured self-acceptance and racial/ethnic prejudice for White college students (ages 18 to 21). In a study designed to assess the effects of contact with Blacks on White college students, Cook (1972) administered pre- and posttests measuring self-acceptance and racial attitudes. All three experiments showed a negative correlation between self-acceptance and racial/ethnic prejudice.

Sheerer (1949) also examined counseling cases for changes over time. She found an increase in self-acceptance during the course of therapy and a corresponding decrease in prejudiced attitudes. This was the first study to suggest that there was more than just a correlation between the two concepts.

Katz et al. (1956, 1957) and Stotland et al. (1972) also found a cause-effect relationship between self-acceptance and prejudice toward African-Americans. All three studies included White college students, and a series of pretests and posttests. Self-acceptance was assessed using a projective story completion test. Measures of prejudice were a stereotype scale and a social distance scale. In order to influence self-acceptance, each subject was asked to read a paper on denial and projection and a related case study. The case history described the life story of a college student and her struggles with denial and self-acceptance. It was designed to produce self-acceptance on the part of the subject. The results of all three experiments indicated that self-acceptance increased as a result of the manipulation. A corresponding decrease in prejudice was also noted.

In support of the above, Rubin (1967a, 1967b) found that prejudice towards Black people decreased following an intervention designed to increase self-acceptance. Rubin's study was detailed in two separate articles. His experiment studied White participants in a two-week sensitivity training workshop. The subjects ranged in age from 23 to 59 years, and the study design included a pretest, a posttest, and a control group. The participants served as their own control by being tested two weeks prior to the experiment and again at the onset of the study. A sentence completion test was used to measure self-acceptance and an attitude scale assessed prejudice towards African-Americans. Rubin found that as a result of the workshop the participants' self-acceptance increased and their prejudice decreased.

The nine studies described above showed that self-individuation leads to decreased prejudice. The first five experiments showed a correlation between self-acceptance (individuation) and prejudice. The remaining four studies indicated that interventions designed to increase self-acceptance also decreased racial/ethnic prejudice. There were no experiments measuring discrimination.

Individuation of Others

Only two experiments that connected individuation of others with prejudice were found (Katz, 1973; Langer, Bashner, & Chanowitz, 1985). The subjects in Katz's experiments were second- and sixth-grade (ages 7 to 8 and 11 to 12) White and Black students from integrated schools. An attitude scale, a social distance scale, and a stereotype scale were administered before and after the experimental manipulation. The White children in the experimental condition were taught to differentiate between pictures of Black people with various skin tones, hair, and facial expressions. The African-American children performed the same task with pictures of Euro-American people. All the children in the control condition were simply shown pictures of White and Black people. The results indicated that the children in the experimental group were less prejudiced both than they themselves had been on the pretest and than the control group.

The Langer et al. (1985) experiment looked at how individuation of others for nondisabled sixth-graders (ages 11 to 12) affects prejudice towards people who are wheelchair-bound, are blind, are deaf, or have only one arm. During the five-day intervention, the children in the experimental condition were taught to make distinctions between different types of disabled people and to distinguish between beliefs about the disabled and reality. For example, the children were shown a picture of a person in a wheelchair working as a newscaster and were given written information about that person. The children wrote down what was occurring in the photograph, four reasons why the pictured individual would be good at her job, and an explanation of how the depicted person could do her job. In the control condition pictures were shown with no differentiation manipulation. A social distance scale and an activity preference scale assessed prejudice towards the disabled. The results indicated that following the experimental condition, nondisabled children were less prejudiced towards the disabled than those in the control condition, and than they had been in their own pretest results.

The number of studies are limited (two) but they do suggest that individuation of others can lead to decreased prejudice both toward people of other races and toward the disabled. Neither of the experiments measured discrimination.

Contact Theory

Contact theory cannot be used to explain why individuation leads to decreased prejudice. Recall that cooperation, intimacy, community sanction, and equal status are factors in contact theory. No contact exists in the self-individuation studies. The experiments on individuation of others do include viewing pictures of and learning about disabled people or people of another race. This may be indirectly related to intimacy. There is, however, no cooperation, and no information on either status or community sanction is available.

Lewinian Theory

Lewinian theory is more helpful in explaining the data. Let's examine some of the driving and restraining forces. Learning about people from outgroups in order to differentiate between outgroup individuals serves to develop empathy (driving force) and decrease strain in social interactions (restraining force). Also recall that cognitive development and individuation serve as driving forces to attitude change.

A Multiple-Factor Approach

Based on the fact that prejudice and discrimination are determined by multiple factors (genetics and evolution, culture and history, and social development), and moreover, that these factors have different effects on different targets, interventions based on any one of these factors should have a limited impact. We saw that desegregation had little effect on reducing racial prejudice and discrimination. Mainstreaming had a moderate impact on decreasing prejudice and discrimination towards the disabled. Cooperative interaction was highly effective in reducing discrimination towards other racial/ethnic groups, the disabled, and the opposite sex, as well as decreasing opposite-sex prejudice. It had no impact on changing attitudes towards other racial/ethnic groups or towards the disabled.

Research on media effects was limited; however, it showed that reductions in prejudice towards both other racial/ethnic groups and the disabled did occur. Similarly, the limited data on simulations showed decreases in prejudice towards both the disabled and other racial groups. Likewise, increasing individuation of self and others reduces prejudice towards both other racial/ethnic groups and the disabled. No data are available concerning the impact of films, simulations, and individuation on discrimination.

Based on these findings, we suggest that multiple approaches be used in the schools to combat prejudice and discrimination. Due to its consistent access to large numbers of children, the school system is the ideal situation for interventions designed to reduce prejudice and discrimination. We saw that desegregation by itself has limited effect in changing attitudes and behaviors. However, cooperative learning has been shown to have strong widespread effects on reducing discrimination. We believe that this form of teaching should become an integral part of the education system, especially in racially integrated and mainstreamed settings. An added benefit of this approach is that it gives students the impression that those in the community, especially its authority figures, support the importance of changing attitudes and behaviors toward members of other groups. Mainstreaming has been shown to be a moderately effective approach in reducing prejudice and discrimination toward the disabled. Recall that the effects are limited when the disabled student is moderately to severely mentally retarded. Therefore, cooperative learning in these cases should be done cautiously.

In that individuation of self and others is effective in reducing prejudice, we believe that teaching methods promoting self-acceptance and valuing differences among people should become an integral part of the normal education process. This fits well with local and national efforts to promote the valuing of diversity. Aboud (1988) suggests the use of psychological tests that reveal personal profiles to help individuals discover unique aspects of self. These profiles can then be compared with those of others to look for similarities and differences. Finally, films and role-playing are effective tools in reducing prejudice, and therefore should be used intermittently throughout the academic year. Other than cooperative interaction, there are no known methods of reducing opposite-sex prejudice.

These proposed changes are quite dramatic. Many might question whether they are feasible. However, there are school systems in the United States that have successfully instituted cooperative learning programs. Additionally, many schools throughout the country are including individuation and valuing diversity programs in their curricula. It is clear that the social, educational, and emotional problems created by prejudice and discrimination will not be resolved if we continue with the status quo. We need strong viable interventions to resolve the issues. The proposed changes may go a long way towards alleviating these problems.

Summary

There are two theories frequently cited to explain changes in prejudice and discrimination: contact theory and Lewinian theory. The important conditions in contact theory are equal status, community sanction, cooperation, and intimacy. Contact theory helps us understand the results of the research on desegregation, cooperative interaction, and the media. It is less helpful in explaining the literature on mainstreaming, simulations, and individuation.

Lewinian theory is a form of field theory that emphasizes the influence of driving and restraining forces. The forces that restrain children from changing their prejudiced attitudes include authority acceptance, intergroup mechanisms, ingroup favoritism, strain in social interactions, and the expectation of inappropriate social behavior by outgroup members. Driving forces include cognitive development, individuation, and empathy. Lewinian theory is useful in discussing the results of the research on mainstreaming, cooperative interaction, the media, simulations, and individuation. It does not aid us in understanding the results of the desegregation experiments.

Data from 23 studies on the effects of desegregation on prejudice and discrimination yield some interesting conclusions. Desegregation is largely ineffective in decreasing either prejudice or discrimination. The results, however, tend to be more positive for Black children than for Whites. In general, there were no systematic differences in outcomes between boys and girls, and no age effects were noted in the experiments. The absence of equal status between students and lack of community support appear to be important factors in these studies.

Fourteen studies were discussed on the effects of mainstreaming on prejudice and discrimination on the part of nondisabled children toward the disabled. Mainstreaming does create more positive attitudes toward all types of handicaps, but is less effective on prejudice toward the moderately to severely mentally retarded. There are differences based on the ages of the nondisabled children, with older children (ages 10 and up) developing more positive attitudes than younger ones (ages 8 and below). Mainstreamed girls tend to be less prejudiced than their male peers.

Cooperative interaction implies positive goal interdependence and children working or talking together. Twenty studies have been done on the effects of cooperative interaction (predominantly cooperative learning) on prejudice and discrimination toward different racial and ethnic groups, the opposite sex, and the disabled. There are lasting effects on discrimination (nine months), but not on attitudes. Cooperative interaction does affect both opposite-sex prejudice and discrimination. Attitudes toward other racial/ethnic groups are not impacted by cooperative interaction, but racial/ethnic discrimination does decrease. The discriminatory behavior of nondisabled children toward their disabled classmates decreases as a result of cooperative interaction.

Four studies that measured the effects of media, particularly television and movies, on attitude change were detailed. Television and film do affect prejudice in children and adolescents. The films were effective regardless of the age of the subject, and seemed to impact all three aspects of prejudice. The effects are present for prejudice toward the disabled and other racial/ethnic groups. No studies were found that examined the effectiveness of films in changing opposite-sex prejudice or in changing discrimination toward any group.

There is evidence that role-playing is an effective way to change attitudes; there is no information on discrimination. Examination of the literature reveals five studies that investigated race prejudice and prejudice towards the handicapped. No studies were found that examined the effectiveness of simulations for changing opposite-sex prejudice or for reducing discrimination towards any group. In order to be effective, simulations must be as real as possible. Discussions before and after a role play are important both to promote attitude change and to alleviate any stress felt by the participants during the experience.

Individuation is the process of differentiating people from one another, and can apply to the self (self-acceptance) and to others. Nine studies were discussed on the relationship between self-acceptance and prejudice, but no experiments on discrimination were found. A negative correlation exists between prejudice and self-acceptance; nonprejudiced people are high in self-acceptance, while prejudiced individuals have low self-acceptance. Manipulations designed to increase self-acceptance result in decreased racial/ethnic prejudice and prejudice toward the disabled. Two experiments dealing with the connection between individuation of others and prejudice were presented, but no data were available on discrimination. Teaching children to differentiate among disabled people and among individuals from other racial/ethnic groups causes a decrease in prejudice towards the differentiated group.

A multiple-factor approach is needed to produce decreases in prejudice and discrimination towards the opposite sex, those who are disabled, and other racial/ethnic groups. Cooperative learning and processes that promote self-acceptance and valuing of differences among people must become an integral part of our academic programs. Finally, films and role-playing are useful tools to decrease prejudice and should be used intermittently throughout the academic year.

CHAPTER

Recapitulation

Dominant and Subordinate Groups

As I reflect about the intellectual journey I have been on while writing this book, my mind keeps being drawn to the worldwide horrors currently being produced by prejudice and discrimination. In 1994 the Northern Irish Protestants and Catholics are still violent opponents, the Bosnian Serbs and Muslims have yet to sit together and discuss peace, and the Rwandan Hutus and Tutsis are still massacring each other—the numbers stagger the mind. Ethnic differences at least partly underlie the violence in these cultures. I think, too, about the abolition of apartheid in South Africa and the election of a Black president in that tortured yet hopeful country. The agonizing history of African-Americans makes one fear that peace and equality will not come quickly to South Africa, but progress will occur.

The account I've given in this book describes prejudice and discrimination between the dominant and subordinate groups as being an integral part of the social knowledge of American culture—they are expected and normative reactions by group members. Thus, the absence, not the presence, of prejudice and discrimination in individuals might be a surprise. Prejudice and discrimination are sustained because members of the dominant groups benefit from them. These members, such as White males, ensure the continued well-being of their families and friends by maintaining and reinforcing their value systems in all the major institutions of our society: family, schools, media, religion, politics, business, justice system, and armed forces. Children in the dominant groups are socialized to incorporate these values and beliefs into their social knowledge and to act in ways consistent with that knowledge. Given the consistent reinforcement children receive for holding the values of the dominant group, they become adolescents and then adults committed to these values.

People are seekers of consistency. When experiences occur that don't comfortably fit with what we believe and "know" to be true, we find ways to explain the discrepancies. We often create categories called "exceptions" or "special cases" to do so. The social knowledge that includes prejudice and discrimination towards outgroups is constantly being challenged by reality. "The Chairman of the Joint Chiefs of Staff is Black? He looks almost White." "The president of a Fortune 500 company is a woman? She's probably very masculine." "A young man with Down Syndrome is a television star? There's not another like him." "A deaf person is now a college president? He used to be hearing." Sometimes the number of exceptions mounts up and they can no longer be easily seen as exceptions. Then members of the dominant group find different ways to disqualify others; for example, "Affirmative action unfairly got them where they are."

The stigmas attached to subordinate groups are deep in our subconsciousness. In some cultures, for example, the contamination of women during menstruation prohibits their contact with men until the flow has stopped. But the potential for contamination is always present. The subordinate groups in North American cultures are seen as having the ability to contaminate others. Children seem to learn this at an early age, but the costs of acquaintanceship or friendship with outgroup members are not very high, and thus can occur.

Members of the subordinate groups in North American cultures have also been socialized by the value system of the dominant groups. This usually leads to a devaluation of their own groups. Thus, Blacks, females, the deaf, and the mentally retarded grow up believing that their group is inferior to the dominant groups. Moreover, members of subordinate groups often act in ways that perpetuate the belief in their inferiority, as was seen in the discussion of patriarchy and female socialization.

I painfully witnessed this self-deprecation by Blacks a number of years ago when I was practicing family therapy. The wife of a middle-class Black couple related an incident that occurred when she and her husband went to a movie theater in a White neighborhood. She described the strange looks and extra distance given her and her husband by the other patrons while waiting in line. But the part that stays with me was her statement that prior to leaving home for the movie, she had bathed and put on perfume to ensure that she was clean and smelled good. She said she didn't want to offend any of the White people she would encounter.

Since societies are open systems, the values of the dominant groups are not static but are susceptible to a variety of influences from both within and outside the culture. Immigration of different ethnic/racial groups has had profound effects in challenging the alleged superiority of Euro-Americans. An inordinate number of academically and artistically talented individuals are of Asian descent. Gifted Hispanic political leaders have emerged in the past decade. And of course, there is no shortage of women and African-Americans who have succeeded academically, artistically, politically, and economically.

Equal opportunity is becoming more of an American reality than in previous decades, and this has often led to dominant and subordinate groups performing equally in a wide variety of tasks and settings. Because of this, sexism, racism, and handicappism are being chipped away with each passing decade; but values long held by the dominant groups in the culture are still strongly believed.

Cultural Change

The positive changes in the treatment of females, African-Americans, the deaf, and the mentally retarded were clearly seen in the "Brief Cultural Histories" chapter. The changes described were quite marked, though there were setbacks along the way. In the Colonization period (1607–1770), for example, women's place was in and around the home, tending their gardens and rearing children. Since families were economically self-reliant, women had major economic functions. However, schools were usually closed to girls, women could not legally own land or businesses independently of their husbands, vote, sit on juries, hold public office, or be officials of the church. In the last period, Postwar Growth and Change (1945–the present) women have very definitely been out of the home and into the schools, churches, the judiciary, the political and economic marketplace, and even the military. Some of the greatest gains were made in times of war, when new demands and opportunities opened for them. However, women themselves created many of these opportunities through political skills they had acquired over many years of fighting social inequities.

Despite the gains, prejudice and discrimination towards these groups still exist. Members of the most dominant group, i.e., White males, view other groups as being inferior, frequently basing this assessment on "scientific" evidence. The dominant group has attempted to control sexuality, education, and job opportunities for all four subordinate target groups. As the laws have changed to support equity and equality, members of the dominant culture have had to find more covert means for maintaining discrimination. The "old boys" network is still intact and powerful.

The positive changes in discrimination and prejudice did not occur solely because of "enlightened" self-interest or through the acquisition of a newer and higher moral sense by White males, although a little of both probably played a part. Abraham Lincoln wished to abolish slavery because it was wrong, but his initial political stance was to limit its spread. Moreover, it's clear from his writings that he was not particularly interested in social integration of the races.

Although I assume that prejudice towards the four target groups has declined across historical time, the extent of this trend is not clear. However, it is obvious that overt discrimination has dramatically decreased. From these histories, it appears that three factors together led to the positive change. First, members of the target groups, or their families, had to strongly advocate for themselves. They had to publicly declare that their treatment by the dominant culture was prejudicial. They had to organize and collaborate with group members to combat this unfairness. Some of our most powerful and eloquent speeches and literature were produced by these people. Every time I hear Martin Luther King, Jr.'s "I have a dream" speech I get chills. The self-advocates appealed to the human sense of justice and fairness, but also to the fears all persons— both dominant and subordinate—have about social unrest.

Self-advocacy by subordinate groups is insufficient by itself to produce substantial positive social change, unless it leads to revolution. It often induces increasing numbers of the dominant group to take up their cause. It is likely that dominant group members already believed that treatment of a particular subordinate group was unfair. Lincoln, after all, did not invent abolition. Some members of the dominant group were awakened by the self-advocates of the subordinate groups, and some were reawakened; their submerged feelings of justice and fairness reemerged. With the constant pressure provided by the subordinate groups, dominant group members stimulated one another to advocate for change. In many cases these dominant group advocates enacted changes themselves. They could open up job or educational opportunities. They could help integrate neighborhoods, churches, and private clubs. They could extend their hand in friendship to members of subordinate groups. These are all important acts. But they usually don't go much beyond the local level.

Widespread changes in discrimination occurred when powerful members of the dominant group made changes in the law. These changes occurred because of the continued self-advocacy by subordinate groups and advocacy from members of the dominant group. Changes in the law offer opportunities for enforcement. Initially this must be carried out by the dominant group (who may drag their feet) but eventually subordinate group members gain positions of power to enforce the laws themselves; they sit on juries, are judges, lawyers, and police. When the laws change, some of the official power held by the dominant group is transferred to subordinate groups. This is a remarkable process. Several years ago I heard a talk about this by a Black state treasurer. He said that when the White community trusts you with their money, you know you've made real progress.

Genetic/Evolutionary Predispositions

Underlying the culturally persistent acts of prejudice and discrimination is a strong genetic/evolutionary predisposition to make significant distinctions between one's own and other groups. Our analysis shows that we are fundamentally tribal beings. In human evolutionary history the tribe—a genetically and culturally related community of subsistence groups—emerged as the central mode of social organization. This is different from that of gorillas, chimpanzees, and bonobos, for which the single subsistence group is the primary social organ. Different subsistence groups for them are actual or potential enemies. For humans, enemies are different tribes. For the apes an outsider is an individual that is not known. For human hunter-gatherers, an outsider is not only unknown, but also a person who is not a member of the tribe.

People are identified as tribal members by the various perceptual "badges" they display: language, dialect, dress, specific behavioral habits and customs. Because of the importance of badges, we have developed exquisite sensitivities to recognize them. Failure to identify outsiders can lead to physical harm or death. Spying by foreign agents is a modern version of the attempt to conceal one's true tribal (national) identity in order to harm the enemy.

The two major genetically predisposed effects of distinguishing "own group" from "other group" are that we favor members of our own tribe relative to outsiders, and that we are wary of and often hostile to members of other tribes. The former effect is part of the nature of Darwinian selection processes. The latter is a feature of intergroup relations, seen in gorillas, chimpanzees, bonobos, and human hunter-gatherers. We infer that intergroup hostility is an ancient evolved characteristic dating back to at least the common ancestor of the four species. These two predispositions lead to very simple and very safe ways of interacting with others: be friendly to tribal members; be wary of those from other tribes. It is important to point out that these are behavioral *predispositions,* not *reflexes.* Individual learning plays a part in determining how these predispositions develop into behavioral interaction tendencies. We learn that some tribal members are to be avoided and that some outsiders can be trusted.

A third genetic/evolutionary predisposition directly relates to the complexity of human hunter-gatherer societies relative to the apes, and indirectly to the development of prejudice and discrimination: authority acceptance. In order to be a contributing member of these societies one has to acquire an inordinate amount of diverse information in a relatively short period of time. Learning by conditioning, trial and error, and imitation are inadequate to complete the task. Authority acceptance directs us to accept as true the messages transmitted by the authorities in our culture. In its most positive manifestation, cultural authorities share their wisdom and knowledge, which includes personal histories as well as the history of the culture. In hunter-gatherer societies, which are egalitarian, this knowledge is relatively benign, regarding status differences among members. Some of the knowledge directs tribal members to attend to badges that distinguish them from outsiders. In industrial societies, however, the authorities' knowledge and wisdom include "known" characteristics of dominant and subordinate groups and thus serve to maintain the power and status of the dominant ones. This is part of the basis of prejudice and discrimination.

From a developmental perspective, authority acceptance is operative by about age 2 years. Own-group preferences and intergroup hostility, however, start to come into play when children are older and have acquired a group identity. Some of the most salient groups in our society are based on sex, ethnicity, and presence or absence of disabilities. Because of physical and behavioral differences (badges) between these groups, distinctions among them readily occur. Moreover, societal authorities indicate that distinguishing these groups is important. Thus, authority acceptance and group processes reinforce each other and enhance status differences among groups.

Psychological research indicates that group identification starts to emerge at about age 3 and is relatively stable by age 4. By age 7, children's understanding of group processes has grown substantially. These findings suggest that the nature of prejudice and discrimination will change in systematic ways between ages 4 and 7.

Finally, behavior genetics research dealing with individual differences in prejudice indicates that the psychological influences coming from parents have a small effect on the development of prejudice, whereas the genetic influences are substantial. This conclusion fits well with other research concerned with individual differences in intelligence, psychopathology, and personality. Since parents are the first major authority figures in children's lives, how is it that degree of parental prejudice has little consistent impact on children's prejudice? There are at least three possible answers to this question. First, parents convey a large amount of information to their children, nearly all of which is consistent with generalized societal norms. Thus, inadvertently, parents mediate culturally held beliefs and values about the various groups in the culture. Second, a variety of authorities in the culture tend to convey the same kinds of messages to everyone. Perhaps children assimilate this information with some type of averaging process. Parents' views may be important, but not the only important ones. Third, the research may not reflect the effects of extremist views on prejudice and discrimination. Perhaps parents who are members of the American Nazi party or the Ku Klux Klan have a stronger effect on their children than parents with more moderate beliefs and values.

Development of Prejudice and Discrimination

As defined, prejudice and discrimination are different, but typically related, psychological phenomena. Numerous studies with adults show that there is often a discrepancy between the two—between attitudes and overt behavior. One of the principal distinctions between measures of prejudice and measures of discrimination in children is that the former primarily assesses reactions to unknown others, whereas the latter assesses reactions to known peers. Thus, it should not be surprising that individuals may be prejudiced towards a particular group in the abstract, but have friendly relations with familiar peers of that group. The converse may also hold. Prejudice seems to be closely tied to the acceptance of cultural values, whereas discrimination seems more closely tied to one's experiences in a particular context. The above considerations suggest that prejudice and discrimination may have different developmental paths.

In addition to the above, prejudice and discrimination may develop differently depending upon the involved target groups. It's possible that our genetic/evolutionary heritage differentially predisposed us to respond to the badges displayed by different groups. This question has not been explored. However, we know that in each culture the various dominant and subordinate groups are differentially valued. Moreover, individuals are often members of dominant and subordinate groups at the same time; for example, White females are members of the dominant White group, but the subordinate female group. We don't know the calculus people use for combining and evaluating these combinations.

The research surveyed in this book supports the above ideas. Prejudice and discrimination have different developmental trajectories, which additionally vary with the target groups being examined. In all cases prejudice does emerge by age 4 years. Thereafter, opposite-sex prejudice, race prejudice, and prejudice towards the mentally retarded show different age-related patterns. For all three groupings many predictions based on genetic/evolutionary considerations were supported. For example, males were generally more prejudiced than females, and ingroup-outgroup behavioral differences (badges) were correlated with degree of prejudice. Opposite-sex and race prejudice were only weakly associated with parental values.

Predictions based on cultural/historical considerations were differentially supported for opposite-sex and race prejudice. For opposite-sex prejudice, females were more likely than males to acquire opposite-sex knowledge, behavior, and values. The age-related decline in opposite-sex prejudice was greater for females than for males. Also, female self-esteem was strongly associated with male values but male self-esteem was not associated with female values. For race prejudice, Blacks were more likely to acquire knowledge, behavior, and values of White cultural norms than the converse. However, the predictions concerning self-esteem and age-related decreases in prejudice were not supported.

The discrepancies between opposite-sex and race prejudice concerning the cultural/historical predictions are quite interesting. The dominant culture apparently gives a consistent and lifelong message about the relative value of males and females and Whites and Blacks. There are few opposing groups that successfully contradict those values dealing with gender. In a sense, there can't be, because the salient cultural norms are those of White males, not just those of males. Thus, females can oppose males, but how do they oppose Whites, especially since the majority are themselves White? Additionally, most females form families with males, and thus become part of a system that supports male values. For the Blacks, there is a strong opposing group that often successfully contradicts the White values. Blacks can form highly supportive and nurturant relations with other Blacks. To some extent they have a separate culture from Whites, and that culture often provides a solid grounding for positive self-esteem and racial pride. To get along in a predominantly White culture, however, they have to be knowledgeable about White values, behaviors, and norms.

The discrimination literature is much more complicated than that for prejudice, because the various measures of discrimination often lead to different conclusions. Using observational methods, race and opposite-sex discrimination are clearly seen in 4-year-olds, increase to about age 8, and decline or level off until adolescence. In classroom, as opposed to free-play settings, females but not males evidence race discrimination. Discrimination towards the deaf and mentally retarded are also strongly present in 4-year-olds and remain high thereafter, with no particular age trends seen.

With best-friends sociometric data, all four groupings show very marked discrimination at all ages, especially after age 8. Ingroup-outgroup friendships *infrequently* occur in all groupings, for example, those between nonretarded and mentally retarded peers. Roster-and-ratings measures indicate far less discrimination than best-friends measures. Children and adolescents are much more likely to discriminate in social than in academic settings. Thus children from different groups who willingly help each other with schoolwork will usually not eat lunch together, and certainly not hang out with the same set of friends. These findings reinforce the idea that for discrimination, context is very important.

For all four groupings there is firm support for the view that behavioral differences underlie some of the observed discrimination. Males and females, Blacks and Whites, mentally retarded and nonretarded, deaf and hearing persons often act and interact differently from each other. Certainly language use varies across these groups (the extreme, of course, occurs in deaf versus hearing individuals), but the types of social skills employed in interactions are often discrepant. Given that badging mechanisms are deeply ingrained in our genetic makeup, it's not surprising that ingroups and outgroups should be sensitive to behavioral nuances. Of course, since culture categorizes people into these groups, we tend to exaggerate even slight differences among them. We probably also "perceive" differences that are more imagined than real.

There was consistent support for the two age-related shifts in discrimination predicted by the group identity literature (the shifts were also seen in the prejudice literature). These findings indicate that social cognitive developmental processes play a role in the early development of prejudice and discrimination. That is, as the nature of children's social understanding changes, the ways in which they enact prejudice and discrimination also change.

Finally, essentially none of the other genetic/evolutionary predictions or those based on cultural/historical considerations were supported in the discrimination literature (in many cases no data were available). Although the discrepancy here with the prejudice literature supports the idea that the underlying processes between the two are very different, it is nevertheless puzzling. In my 1976 book I stated that "evolutionary processes are fundamentally involved with the acquisition of information or knowledge about the environmental niche of the species." *Knowledge* was related to effective *action* in the environment. Presumably, cultural knowledge has similar positive effects on action. But the research shows many genetic/evolutionary and several cultural/historical links with knowledge (prejudice) and few with action (discrimination). One possible explanation for this dilemma is that discrimination is based on a number of general and specific knowledge considerations, including prejudice, and these must be weighed before action is taken. Prejudice is more or less pure knowledge, which only implies action, but doesn't require it.

Modifying Prejudice and Discrimination

Prejudice and discrimination will be eliminated when perceived and believed differences *between* groups are reconstrued as differences *within* groups. That is, when Americans view all Americans as belonging to the same group as opposed to different and opposing ones, then the core problem will disappear. Everyone knows that people differ from one another. These differences are usually accepted by ingroup members; but when they appear in members of outgroups, they are often identified as being unacceptable. The goal of transforming "between" to "within" is occasionally achieved. For example, a sense of "we" as opposed to "us versus them" occurs during crises, the prime example being wartime. But crises are neither normative nor desirable.

An alternative goal is to attempt to change people such that they accept and equally value members of other groups—that is, to encourage people to maintain the belief that ingroups and outgroups are different, and yet not favor their own group or disfavor others. I think that this goal flies in the face of our genetic/evolutionary heritage, and hence is likely to fail.

We saw that merely putting children together as in school desegregation and mixed-gender classes had essentially no impact on modifying prejudice and discrimination. However, cooperative learning was very effective in reducing discrimination (although it had limited effect on reducing prejudice). Mainstreaming of disabled children and adolescents had a moderate effect on decreasing prejudice and discrimination towards them by the nondisabled. Research on media effects, simulations, and individuation all indicated some effectiveness in decreasing prejudice. No data were available for discrimination.

These approaches were successful for a variety of reasons, but what they seemed to share was implied or explicit community sanction. That is, the authority structure of the school or other community institutions "stated" that members of the various groups should be treated with fairness and respected as individuals. This, of course, capitalizes on the genetic/evolutionary factor of authority acceptance. Another shared aspect in these successful approaches is that directly or indirectly they helped individuals see that members of different groups were similar in many ways to their own groups. As perceived differences become diminished, it is a short step to view others as members of one's own group.

No single one of the above approaches was successful in reducing prejudice and discrimination across all ingroups and outgroups. This is understandable because the processes underlying them are multiple, and as we previously noted, prejudice and discrimination vary with developmental status and target group. We recommend, however, that cooperative learning in integrated and mainstreamed schools be the linchpin for change. It embodies an essential ingredient for maintaining group cohesion: cooperation. It has been shown to be effective in reducing discrimination, and it is at least as effective as other approaches in promoting academic achievement. Integral also in our recommendation is the incorporation of teaching methods or content that promote self-acceptance and acceptance of individuals who differ from ourselves. This approach has been shown to effectively reduce prejudice. Films and role-playing should periodically be employed because they too have been effective in reducing prejudice.

The strongly implied message of the proposed dramatic changes is that the authority structure of all our communities endorse, even mandate, these changes. We cannot readily change the genetic structure of our species as a means of eliminating prejudice and discrimination. But we can positively use the characteristics with which we are endowed. The paradox in our proposal is as follows. Prejudice and discrimination serve to maintain the power and status of the dominant groups. These are typically the same groups whose members are the authority figures in our culture. We are proposing that the authority figures initiate changes that will ultimately reduce their power and status through the merger of ingroups and outgroups. Of course, if those in the authority structure can be persuaded to see these changes as promoting their self-interest, then it is no paradox at all.

A Final Note

I've been discussing the ideas in this book with friends and colleagues for several years. Two related questions keep recurring. Doesn't the genetic/evolutionary view mean that prejudice and discrimination will always be with us? How does the genetic/evolutionary view help us attempt to modify prejudice and discrimination? I tell them, in response to the first question, that the underlying pressures for prejudice and discrimination will always be with us. This implies that we have to be vigilant and make strong efforts to combat these tendencies. In response to the second, I tell them that we have to make use of the underlying processes towards different ends. It's not in our genes to be prejudiced and discriminatory against groups within our society; but it is in our genes to favor ingroup members, disfavor outgroup members, and accept what authorities tell us. The latter is the key to successful change. It often takes courage for the authorities to take new positions on these matters. Fortunately they occasionally do so, as President Truman did in racially integrating the armed forces and as the Congress and President Johnson did in passing civil rights legislation.

No one can legislate changes in our hearts and souls. Prejudiced attitudes, by their nature, are relatively unresponsive to new and contradictory information. Certainly new messages from authorities will speed the process of change, but since these attitudes infuse a large number of our beliefs and actions towards outgroup members, additional experiences will be required. My belief is that challenging discrimination is more likely to succeed in modifying prejudice than challenging prejudice directly. Mandated cooperative interactions between ingroups and outgroups is likely to be the most successful set of new experiences for accomplishing this goal.

Finally, I believe that our success in modifying prejudice and discrimination in children will be severely limited unless prejudice and discrimination are modified in adults. Adults not only have to create the circumstances that will promote change in our children, but we must also give a consistent message based on our own behavior. To do otherwise is to belie the earnestness of our intentions.

REFERENCES

Aboud, F. (1988). *Children and prejudice.*
Oxford: Basil Blackwell.

Aboud, F. E., & Mitchell, F. G. (1977). Ethnic
role-taking: The effects of preference and
self-identification. *International Journal
of Psychology, 12,* 1–17.

Abramenkova, V. V. (1983). Joint activity in the
development of a humane attitude toward
preschool peers. *Soviet Psychology, 22,*
38–55.

Acton, H. M., & Zarbatany, L. (1988).
Interaction and performance within
cooperative groups: Effects on
nonhandicapped students' attitudes toward
their mildly mentally retarded peers.
*American Journal of Mental Retardation,
93,* 16–23.

Adorno, T. W., Frenkel-Brunswick, E.,
Levinson, D. J., & Sanford, R. N. (1950).
The authoritarian personality. New York:
Harper.

Albert, A. A., & Porter, J. R. (1988). Children's
gender role stereotypes: A sociological
investigation of psychological models.
Sociological Forum, 3, 184–210.

Allport, G. W. (1954). *The nature of prejudice.*
Cambridge: Addison-Wesley.

Alper, S. W., & Leidy, T. R. (1970). The impact
of information transmission through the
television. *Public Opinion Quarterly, 33,*
556–562.

Andrews, P. (1985). Improved timing of
homonoid evolution with a DNA clock.
Nature, 314, 498–499.

Antia, S. D. (1982). Social interactions of
partially mainstreamed hearing-impaired
children. *American Annals of the Deaf,
127,* 18–25.

Aptheker, H. (1971). *Afro-American history:
The modern era.* Secaucus, NJ: The
Citadel Press.

Archie, V. W., and Sherrill, C. (1989). Attitudes
toward handicapped peers of
mainstreamed children in physical
education. *Perceptual and Motor Skills,
69,* 319–322.

Armor, D. J. (1972). The evidence on busing.
Public Interest, 28, 90–126.

Armstrong, B., Johnson, D. W., & Balow, B.
(1981). Effects of cooperative vs.
individual learning experiences on
interpersonal attraction between learning-
disabled and normal-progress elementary
school students. *Contemporary
Educational Psychology, 6,* 102–109.

Arnold, D., & Tremblay, A. (1979). Interaction
of deaf and hearing preschool children.
Journal of Communication Disorders, 12,
245–251.

Bagley, C., & Young, L. (1988). Evaluation of
color and ethnicity in young children in
Jamaica, Ghana, England, and Canada.
*International Journal of Intercultural
Relations, 12,* 45–60.

Bak, J. J., & Siperstein, G. N. (1987a).
Similarity as a factor effecting change in
children's attitudes toward mentally
retarded peers. *American Journal of
Mental Deficiency, 91,* 524–531.

Bak, J. J., & Siperstein, G. N. (1987b). Effects of
mentally retarded children's behavioral
competence on nonretarded peers'
behaviors and attitudes: Toward
establishing ecological validity in attitude
research. *American Journal of Mental
Deficiency, 92,* 31–39.

Baker, J., & Fishbein, H. D. (1993). The
development of homosexual prejudice and
race prejudice in children and adolescents.
Paper presented at the Annual Convention
of the American Psychological
Association, Toronto, Canada.

Ballard, M., Corman, L., Gottlieb, J., & Kaufman, M. J. (1977). Improving the social status of mainstreamed retarded children. *Journal of Educational Psychology, 69* (5), 605–611.

Barber, R. W. (1968). *The effects of open enrollment on anti-Negro and anti-white prejudices among junior high students in Rochester, New York.* Unpublished doctoral dissertation, University of Rochester.

Baruch, G. K., & Barnett, R. C. (1986). Father's participation in family work and children's sex-role attitudes. *Child Development, 57,* 1210–1223.

Bassey, K., & Bandura, A. (1992). Self-regulatory mechanisms governing gender development. *Child Development, 63,* 1236–1250.

Benderly, B. L. (1980). *Dancing without music.* Washington, DC: Gallaudet University Press.

Berger, E. M. (1952). The relationship between expressed self-acceptance and expressed acceptance of others. *Journal of Abnormal and Social Psychology, 47,* 778–782.

Berry, M. F., & Blassingame, J. W. (1982). *Long memory: The black experience in America.* New York: Oxford University Press.

Bethlehem, D. W. (1985). *A social psychology of prejudice.* New York: St. Martin's Press.

Bettelheim, B. (1943). Individual and mass behavior in extreme situations. *Journal of Abnormal and Social Psychology, 38,* 417–452.

Beuf, A. H. (1977). *Red children in white America.* Philadelphia: University of Pennsylvania Press.

Bigler, R. S., & Liben, L. S. (1993). A cognitive-developmental approach to racial stereotyping and reconstructive memory in Euro-American children. *Child Development, 64,* 1507–1518.

Blaney, N. T., Stephan, C., Rosenfield, D., Aronson, E., & Sikes, J. (1977). Interdependence in the classroom: A field study. *Journal of Educational Psychology, 69* (2), 121–128.

Bourgondien, M. E. Van. (1987). Children's responses to retarded peers as a function of social behaviors, labeling, and age. *Exceptional Children, 53,* 432–439.

Brackett, D., & Henniges, M. (1976). Communicative interaction of preschool hearing impaired children in an integrated setting. *The Volta Review, 78,* 276–285.

Braine, L. G., Pomerantz, E., Lorber, D., & Krantz, D. (1991). Conflicts with authority: Children's feelings, actions, and justifications. *Developmental Psychology, 27,* 829–840.

Branch, C., & Newcombe, N. (1980). Racial attitudes of black preschoolers as related to parental civil rights activism. *Merrill-Palmer Quarterly, 26,* 425–428.

Branch, C., & Newcombe, N. (1986). Racial attitude development among young black children as a function of parental attitudes: A longitudinal and cross-sectional study. *Child Development, 57,* 712–721.

Brand, E. S., Ruiz, R. A., & Padilla, A. M. (1974). Ethnic identification and preference: A review. *Psychological Bulletin, 81,* 860–890.

Brewer, N., & Smith, J. M. (1989). Social acceptance of mentally retarded children in regular schools in relation to years mainstreamed. *Psychological Reports, 64,* 375–380.

Brody, G. H., & Stoneman, Z. (1981). Selective imitation of same-age, younger, and older peer models. *Child Development, 52,* 717–720.

Brody, G. H., & Stoneman, Z. (1985). Peer imitation: An examination of status and competence hypotheses. *Journal of Genetic Psychology, 146,* 161–170.

Brown v. Board of Education. 347 U.S. 483 (1954). 349 U.S. 294 (1955).

Brown, P. M., & Foster, S. B. (1991). Integrating hearing and deaf students on a college campus. *American Annals of the Deaf, 136,* 21–27.

Brown, R. (1965). *Social psychology.* New York: Free Press.

Brown, R. (1986). *Social psychology* (2nd ed.). New York: Free Press.

Btaugh, C., & Liss, M. B. (1992). Home, school and playroom: Training grounds for adult gender roles. *Sex Roles, 26,* 129–147.

Bukowski, W. M., Gauze, C., Hoza, B., & Newcomb, A. F. (1993). Differences and consistency between same-sex and other-sex peer relationships during early adolescence. *Developmental Psychology, 29,* 255–263.

Buss, D. M. (1994). The strategies of human mating. *American Scientist, 82,* 238–249.

Bussey, K., & Bandura, A. (1992). Self-regulatory mechanisms governing gender development. *Child Development, 63,* 1236–1250.

Byrnes, D. A., and Kiger, G. (1990). The effect of a prejudice-reduction simulation on attitude change. *Journal of Applied Social Psychology, 20* (4), 341–356.

Byrnes, M. (1990). The regular education initiative debate: A view from the field. *Exceptional Children, 56* (4), 345–351.

Caldera, Y. M., Huston, A. C., & O'Brien, M. (1989). Social interactions and play patterns of parents and toddlers with feminine, masculine, and neutral toys. *Child Development, 60,* 70–76.

Campbell, E. Q. (1956). *The attitude effects of educational desegregation in a Southern community.* Unpublished doctoral dissertation, Vanderbilt University.

Cantwell, D. P. (1990). Depression across the early life span. In M. Lewis and S. M. Miller (Eds.). *Handbook of developmental psychopathology.* New York: Plenum Press.

Carrigan, P. M. (1969). *School desegregation via compulsory pupil transfer: Early effects on elementary school children.* Ann Arbor, MI: Public Schools.

Carter, D. E., DeTine, S. L., Spero, J., & Benson, F. W. (1975). Peer acceptance and school-related variables in an integrated junior high school. *Journal of Educational Psychology, 67,* 267–273.

Chance, M. R. A. (1975). Social cohesion and the structure of attention. In R. Fox (Ed.), *Biosocial anthropology.* London: Malaby Press.

Cherry, F., & Byrne, D. (1977). Authoritarianism. In T. Blass (Ed.), *Personality variables in social behavior.* Hillsdale, NJ: Erlbaum.

Clark, K. B. (1963). *Prejudice and your child.* (2nd ed., enlarged). Boston: Beacon Press.

Clore, G. L., & Jeffery, K. M. (1972). Emotional role-playing, attitude change, and attraction toward a disabled person. *Journal of Personality and Social Psychology, 23* (1), 105–111.

Cohen, E. (1984). The desegregated school: Problems in status, power and interethnic climate. In N. Miller and M. B. Brewer (Eds.), *Groups in contact: The psychology of desegregation.* New York: Academic Press.

Colby, A., Kohlberg, L., Gibbs, J., & Lieberman, M. (1983). A longitudinal study of moral development. *Monographs of the Society for Research in Child Development, 48* (Nos. 1–2).

Cole, K. N., Mills, P. E., Dale, P. S., & Jenkins, J. R. (1991). Effects of preschool integration for children with disabilities. *Exceptional Children, 58* (1), 36–45.

Condon, M. E., York, R., Heal, L. W., & Fortschneider, J. (1986). Acceptance of severely handicapped students by nonhandicapped peers. *Journal of the Association for Persons with Severe Handicaps, 11,* 216–219.

Cook, S. W. (1972). Motives in conceptual analysis and findings of social psychology. In J. Brigham & T. Weissbach (Eds.), *Racial attitudes in America: Analysis and findings of social psychology.* New York: Harper & Row.

Cooper, L., Johnson, D. W., Johnson, R., & Wilderson, F. (1980). The effects of cooperative, competitive and individualistic experiences on interpersonal attraction among heterogeneous peers. *Journal of Social Psychology, 111,* 243–253.

Cross, W. E. (1987). A two-factor theory of racial identity. In J. S. Phinney and M. J. Rotheram (Eds.). *Children's ethnic socialization.* Beverly Hills: Sage.

Dahl, H. G., Horsman, K. R., and Arkell, R. N. (1978). Simulation of exceptionalities for elementary school students. *Psychological Reports, 42,* 573–574.

Damico, S. B., & Sparks, C. (1986). Cross-group contact opportunities: Impact on interpersonal relationships in desegregated middle schools. *Sociology of Education, 59,* 113–123.

Damon, W., & Hart, D. (1988). *Self-understanding in childhood and adolescence.* New York: Cambridge University Press.

Davis, W. E. (1989). The regular education initiative debate: Its promises and problems. *Exceptional Children, 55* (5), 440–446.

Dentler, R. A., & Elkins, C. (1967). Intergroup attitudes, academic performance, and racial composition. In R. A. Dentler, B. Mackler, & M. E. Warshauer (Eds.), *The urban R's.* New York: Praeger.

DeVos, G., & Wagatsuma, H. (Eds.). (1966). *Japan's invisible race.* Berkeley: University of California Press.

DeVries, D. L., Edwards, K. J., and Slavin, R. E. (1978). Biracial learning teams and race relations in the classroom: Four field experiments using teams-games-tournament. *Journal of Educational Psychology, 70* (3), 356–362.

Donaldson, J. (1980). Changing attitudes toward handicapped persons: A review and analysis of research. *Exceptional Children, 46* (7), 504–514.

Duckitt, J. (1992). Psychology and prejudice: A historical analysis and integrative framework. *American Psychologist, 47,* 1182–1193.

Ehrlich, H. J. (1973). *The social psychology of prejudice.* New York: Wiley.

Eisenberg, N., Wolchik, S. A., Hernandez, R., & Pasternack, J. F. (1985). Parental socialization of young children's play: A short-term longitudinal study. *Child Development, 56,* 1506–1513.

Elam, J. J., & Sigelman, C. K. (1983). Developmental differences in reactions to children labeled mentally retarded. *Journal of Applied Developmental Psychology, 4,* 303–315.

Elser, R. (1959). The social position of hearing handicapped children in the regular grades. *Exceptional Children, 25,* 305–309.

Emerton, R. G., & Rothman, G. (1978). Attitudes towards deafness: Hearing students at a hearing and deaf college. *American Annals of the Deaf, 123,* 588–593.

Erikson, E. H. (1963). *Childhood and society* (Rev. ed.). New York: Norton.

Etaugh, C., & Liss, M. B. (1992). Home, school and playroom: Training grounds for adult gender roles. *Sex Roles, 26,* 129–147.

Evans, C. L. (1969). *The immediate effects of classroom integration on the academic progress, self-concept and racial attitudes of Negro elementary children.* Unpublished doctoral dissertation, North Texas State University.

Evans, J. H. (1976). Changing attitudes toward disabled persons: An experimental study. *Rehabilitation Counseling Bulletin, 19,* 572–579.

Evans, S. M. (1989). *Born for liberty.* New York: The Free Press.

Eysenck, H. J. (1992). Roots of prejudice: Genetic or environmental? In J. Lynch, C. Modgil, & S. Modgil (Eds). *Prejudice, polemic or progress?* London: The Falmer Press.

Fagot, B. I. (1985). Beyond the reinforcement principle: Another step toward understanding sex role development. *Developmental Psychology, 21,* 1097–1104.

Fagot, B. I., & Hagan, R. (1985). Aggression in toddlers: Responses to the assertive acts of boys and girls. *Sex Roles, 12,* 341–351.

Fagot, B. I., Hagan, R., Leinbach, M. D., & Kronsberg, S. (1985). Differential reactions to assertive and communicative acts of toddler boys and girls. *Child Development, 56,* 1499–1505.

Fagot, B. I., & Leinbach, M. D. (1989). The young child's gender schema: Environmental input, internal organization. *Child Development, 60,* 663–672.

Finkelstein, N. W., & Haskins, R. (1983). Kindergarten children prefer same-color peers. *Child Development, 54,* 502–508.

Fischer, K. W., & Bullock, D. (1984). Cognitive development in school-age children: Conclusions and new directions. In W. A. Collins (Ed.), *Development during middle childhood: The years from six to twelve.* Washington, DC: National Academy of Sciences Press.

Fishbein, H. D. (1976). *Evolution, development, and children's learning.* Pacific Palisades, CA: Goodyear.

Fishbein, H. D. (1984). *The psychology of infancy and childhood.* Hillsdale, NJ: Erlbaum.

Fishbein, H. D., & Imai, S. (1993). Preschoolers select playmates on the basis of gender and race. *Journal of Applied Developmental Psychology, 14,* 303–316.

Fishbein, H. D., Stegelin, D., & Davis, N. (1993). Playmate preferences among urban multicultural preschool children. Paper presented at the Annual Conference of the National Association for the Education of Young Children, Anaheim, California.

Forbes, H. D. (1985). *Nationalism, ethnocentrism, and personality.* Chicago: University of Chicago Press.

Foster, S., & Brown, P. (1989). Factors influencing the academic and social integration of hearing impaired college students. *Journal of Postsecondary Education and Disability, 7,* 78–96.

Franklin, V. P. (1984). *Black self-determination: A cultural history of the faith of the fathers.* Westport, CT: Hill.

Frederickson, G. M., & Knobel, D. T. (1980). A history of discrimination. In T. F. Pettigrew, G. M. Frederickson, D. T. Knobel, N. Glazer, & R. Ueda (Eds.), *Prejudice.* Cambridge: Harvard University Press.

Freidl, E. (1975). *Women and men: An anthropologist's view.* New York: Holt, Rinehart & Winston.

Friedman, P. (1980). Racial preferences and identifications of white elementary school children. *Contemporary Educational Psychology, 5,* 256–265.

Gannon, J. R. (1981). *Deaf heritage: A narrative history of deaf America.* Silver Spring, MD: National Association of the Deaf.

Gardner, E. B., Wright, B. D., & Dee, R. (1970). *The effects of busing black ghetto children to white suburban schools.* Unpublished manuscript. (ERIC Document Reproduction Service No. ED 048 389)

Garth, C. E. (1963). *Self-concept of Negro students who transferred and did not transfer to formerly all-white high schools.* Unpublished doctoral dissertation, University of Kentucky.

Gilbert, D. T. (1991). How mental systems believe. *American Psychologist, 46,* 107–119.

Goffman, E. (1963). *Stigma.* Englewood Cliffs, NJ: Prentice-Hall.

Goodall, J., Bandora, A., Bergmann, E., Busse, C., Metama, H., Mpongo, E., Pierce, A., & Riss, D. (1979). Intercommunity interactions of the chimpanzee population of the Gombe National Park. In D. A. Hamburg & E. R. McCown (Eds.), *The great apes.* Menlo Park, CA: Benjamin/Cummings.

Goodman, H., Gottlieb, J., & Harrison, R. (1972). Social acceptance of EMRs integrated into non-graded elementary school. *American Journal of Mental Deficiency, 76,* 412–417.

Goodman, M. E. (1952). *Racial awareness in young children.* Cambridge, MA: Addison-Wesley.

Gorn, G. J., Goldberg, M. E., & Kanungo, R. N. (1976). The role of educational television in changing the intergroup attitudes of children. *Child Development, 47,* 277–280.

Gottlieb, G. (1991). Experimental canalization of behavioral development: Theory. *Developmental Psychology, 27,* 4–13.

Gottlieb, J., Cohen, L., & Goldstein, L. (1974). Social contact and personal adjustment to attitudes toward educable mentally retarded children. *Training Bulletin, 71,* 9–16.

Gottlieb, J., Semmel, M. I., & Veldman, D. J. (1978). Correlates of social status among mainstreamed mentally retarded children. *Journal of Educational Psychology, 70,* 396–406.

Gottlieb, J., & Switsky, H. N. (1982). Development of school-age children's stereotypic attitudes toward mentally retarded children. *American Journal of Mental Deficiency, 86,* 596–600.

Graffi, S., & Minnes, P. M. (1988). Attitudes of primary school children toward the physical appearance and labels associated with Down syndrome. *American Journal of Mental Retardation, 93,* 28–35.

Graham, D. L. R., & Rawlings, E. I. (1991). Bonding with abusive dating partners: Dynamics of Stockholm Syndrome. In B. Levy (Ed.), *Dating violence: Young women in danger.* Seattle: Seal Press.

Green, J., & Gerard, H. (1974). School desegregation and ethnic attitudes. In H. Fromkin & J. Sherwood (Eds.), *Integrating the organization, a psychological analysis.* New York: Free Press.

Greenfield, P. M., & Childs, C. P. (1991). Developmental continuity in biocultural context. In R. Cohen & A. W. Siegel (Eds), *Context and development.* Hillsdale, NJ: Erlbaum.

Groce, N. E. (1985). *Everyone here spoke sign language: Hereditary deafness on Martha's Vineyard.* Cambridge, MA: Harvard University Press.

Grusec, J. E. (1971). Power and the internalization of self-denial. *Child Development, 42,* 92–105.

Guralnick, M. J. (1980). Social interactions among preschool children. *Exceptional Children, 46,* 248–253.

Guralnick, M. J., & Groom, J. M. (1987). The peer relations of mildly delayed and nonhandicapped preschool children in mainstreamed playgroups. *Child Development, 58,* 1556–1572.

Guralnick, M. J., & Groom, J. M. (1988a). Friendships of preschool children in mainstreamed groups. *Developmental Psychology, 24,* 595–604.

Guralnick, M. J., and Groom, J. M. (1988b). Peer interactions in mainstreamed and specialized classrooms: A comparative analysis. *Exceptional Children, 45* (5), 415–425.

Haller, J. S., Jr., & Haller, R. M. (1974). *The physician and sexuality in Victorian America.* Urbana: University of Illinois Press.

Hallinan, M. T. (1981) Recent advances in sociometry. In S. R. Asher and J. M.

Gottman (Eds.), *The development of children's friendships*. New York: Cambridge University Press.

Hamilton, D. L., & Trolier, T. K. (1986). Stereotypes and stereotyping: An overview of the cognitive approach. In J. F. Dovidio and S. L. Gaertner (Eds.), *Prejudice, discrimination, and racism.* New York: Academic Press.

Hamilton, W. D. (1964). The genetical evolution of social behavior. *Journal of Theoretical Biology 7,* 1–52.

Hamilton, W. D. (1975). Innate social aptitudes in man: An approach from evolutionary genetics. In R. Fox (Ed.), *Biosocial anthropology.* London: Malaby Press.

Handlers, A., & Austin, K. (1980). Improving attitudes of high school students toward their handicapped peers. *Exceptional Children, 47* (3), 228–229.

Harding, V. (1981). *There is a river: The black struggle for freedom in America.* New York: Harcourt Brace Jovanovich.

Harter, S. (1993). Causes and consequences of low self-esteem in children and adolescents. In R. F. Baumeister (Ed.), *Self-esteem: The puzzle of low self-regard.* New York: Plenum Press.

Harter, S., & Pike, R. (1984). The pictorial scale of perceived competence and social acceptance for young children. *Child Development, 55,* 1969–1982.

Hartup, W. W. (1983). Peer relations. In P. Mussen (Ed.), *Handbook of Child Psychology.* (4th ed., Vol. 4). New York: Wiley.

Hayden-Thomson, L., Rubin, K. H., & Hymel, S. (1987). Sex preferences in sociometric choices. *Developmental Psychology, 23,* 558–562.

Heller, M. (1987). The role of language in the formation of ethnic identity. In J. S. Phinney and M. J. Rotheram (Eds.), *Children's ethnic socialization.* Beverly Hills: Sage.

Hemphill, L., & Siperstein, G. N. (1990). Conversational competence and peer response to mildly retarded children. *Journal of Educational Psychology, 82,* 128–134.

Herman, B. E. (1967). *The effect of neighborhood upon the attitudes of Negro and white sixth grade children toward different racial groups.* Unpublished doctoral dissertation, University of Connecticut.

Hertel, R. (1991). Changing negative attitudes of able-bodied children toward their handicapped peers: The novel stimulus and equal status hypothesis. *Dissertation Abstracts International, 51,* 5029–5132. (University Microfilms No. 9107074)

Hetherington, E. M. (1965). A developmental study of the effects of sex of the dominant parent on sex-role preference, identification, and imitation in children. *Journal of Personality and Social Psychology, 2,* 188–194.

Higgins, P. C. (1980). *Outsiders in a hearing world.* Beverly Hills, CA: Sage.

Hinde, R. A. (Ed). (1983). *Primate social relationships.* London: Blackwell Scientific Publications.

Houser, B. B. (1978). An examination of the use of audiovisual media in reducing prejudice. *Psychology in Schools, 15,* 116–121.

Hrdy, S. B. (1977). *The langurs of Abu.* Cambridge: Harvard University Press.

Hus, Y. (1979). The socialization process of hearing-impaired children in a summer day camp. *The Volta Review, 81,* 146–156.

Huston, A. C. (1983). Sex-typing. In P.H. Mussen (Ed.), *Handbook of child psychology* (4th ed., Vol. 4). New York: Wiley.

Huston, A. C. (1985). The development of sex-typing: Themes from recent research. *Developmental Review, 5,* 1–17.

Irwin, C. J. (1987). A study in the evolution of ethnocentrism. In V. Reynolds, V. Falger, & I. Vine (Eds.), *The sociobiology of ethnocentrism.* Athens: University of Georgia Press.

Isaacs, H. R. (1965). *India's ex-touchables.* New York: John Day.

Janis, I. L., & King, B. T. (1954). The influence of role-playing on opinion change. *Journal of Abnormal and Social Psychology, 49,* 211–218.

Jarrett, O. S., & Quay, L. C. (1984). Crossracial acceptance and best friend choice. *Urban Education, 19,* 215–225.

Jenkins, J. R., Pious, C. G., & Jewell, M. (1990). Special education and the regular education initiative: Basic assumptions. *Exceptional Children, 56* (6), 479–491.

Jenkins, J. R., Speltz, M. L., & Odom, S. L. (1985). Integrating normal and handicapped preschoolers: Effects on child development and social interaction. *Exceptional Children, 52* (1), 7–17.

Johnson, D. W., and Johnson, R. T. (1981). Effects of cooperative and individualistic learning experiences on interethnic interaction. *Journal of Educational Psychology, 73,* 444–449.

Johnson, D. W., & Johnson, R. T. (1982). Effects of cooperative, competitive, and individualistic learning experiences on cross-ethnic interaction and friendships. *The Journal of Social Psychology, 118,* 47–58.

Johnson, D. W., & Johnson, R. T. (1985). Relationships between Black and White students in intergroup cooperation and competition. *The Journal of Social Psychology, 125* (4), 421–428.

Johnson, D. W., & Johnson, R. T. (1992). Implementing cooperative learning. *Contemporary Education, 63,* 173–180.

Johnson, D. W., Johnson, R., & Maruyama, G. (1983). Interdependence and interpersonal attraction among heterogeneous and homogeneous individuals: A theoretical formulation and a meta-analysis of the research. *Review of Educational Research, 53,* 5–54.

Johnson, D. W., Johnson, R. T., & Scott, L. (1978). The effects of cooperative and individualized instruction on student attitudes and achievement. *The Journal of Social Psychology, 104,* 207–216.

Johnson, R., Rynders, R., Johnson, D. W., Schmidt, B., & Haider, S. (1979). Interaction between handicapped and nonhandicapped teenagers as a function of situational goal structuring: Implications for mainstreaming. *American Educational Research Journal, 16,* 161–167.

Jolly, A. (1972). *The evolution of primate behavior.* New York: Macmillan.

Jones, E. E. (1985). Interpersonal distancing behavior of hearing-impaired versus normal-hearing children. *The Volta Review, 87,* 223–230.

Kanner, L. (1964). *A history of the care and study of the mentally retarded.* Springfield, IL: Charles C. Thomas.

Karlins, M., Coffman, T. L., & Walters, G. (1969). On the fading of social stereotypes: Studies in three generations of college students. *Journal of Personality and Social Psychology, 13,* 1–16.

Karnes, M. D., & Lee, R. C. (1979). Mainstreaming in the preschool. In L. Katz (Ed.), *Current Topics in Early Childhood Education* (Vol. 2). Norwood, NJ: ABLEX.

Katz, D., Sarnoff, I., & McClintock, C. M. (1956). Ego defense and attitude change. *Human Relations, 9,* 27–45.

Katz, D., Sarnoff, I., & McClintock, C. M. (1957). The measurement of ego defense as related to attitude change. *Journal of Personality, 25,* 465–474.

Katz, I. (1979). Some thoughts about the stigma notion. *Personality and Social Psychology Bulletin, 5,* 447–460.

Katz, I. (1981). *Stigma: A social psychological analysis.* Hillsdale, NJ: Erlbaum.

Katz, P. A. (1973). Stimulus predifferentiation and modification of children's racial attitudes. *Child Development, 44,* 232–237.

Katz, P. A. (1983). Developmental foundations of gender and racial attitudes. In R. L. Leahy (Ed.), *The child's construction of social inequality.* New York: Academic Press.

Katz, P. A., & Boswell, S. (1986). Flexibility and traditionality in children's gender roles. *Genetic, Social, and General Psychology Monographs, 112,* 105–147.

Katz, P. A., Sohn, M., & Zalk, S. R. (1975). Perceptual concomitments of racial attitudes in urban grade school children. *Developmental Psychology, 11,* 135–144.

Katz, P. A., & Zalk, S. R. (1978). Modification of children's racial attitudes. *Developmental Psychology, 14,* 447–461.

Kennedy, P., & Bruininks, R. H. (1974). Social status of hearing impaired children in regular classrooms. *Exceptional Children, 40,* 336–342.

Kennedy, P., Northcott, W., McCauley, R., & Williams, S. M. (1976). Longitudinal sociometric and cross-sectional data on mainstreaming hearing impaired children: Implications for preschool programming. *The Volta Review, 78,* 71–81.

Kerig, P. K., Cowan, P. A., & Cowan, C. P. (1993). Marital quality and gender differences in parent-child interaction. *Developmental Psychology, 29,* 931–939.

Kiger, G. (1992). Disability simulations: Logical, methodological and ethical issues. *Disability, Handicap and Society, 7* (1), 71–78.

King, B. T., & Janis, I. L. (1956). Comparison of the effectiveness of improvised versus non-improvised role-playing in producing opinion change. *Human Relations, 9,* 177–186.

Kochman, T. (1987). The ethnic component in Black language and culture. In J. S.

Phinney & M. J. Rotheram (Eds.),
Children's ethnic socialization. Beverly
Hills: Sage.

Kohlberg, L., & Ullian, D. Z. (1974). Stages in
the development of psychosexual concepts
and attitudes. In R. C. Friedman, R. M.
Richart, R. L. Vande Wiele (Eds.), *Sex
differences in behavior.* New York: Wiley.

Koslin, S., Amarel, M., & Ames, N. (1969). A
distance measure of racial attitudes in
primary grade children: an exploratory
study. *Psychology in Schools, 6,* 382–385.

Krantz, M. (1987). Physical attractiveness and
popularity: A predictive study.
Psychological Reports, 60, 723–726.

Kraus, S. (1972). Modifying prejudice: Attitude
change as a function of the race of the
communicator. In A. Brown (Ed.),
Prejudice in children. Springfield, IL:
Charles C. Thomas.

Kuhn, D., Nash, S. C., & Brucken, L. (1978).
Sex role concepts of two and three year
olds. *Child Development, 49,* 445–451.

Lachat, M. (1972). *A description and
comparison of the attitudes of white high
school seniors toward black Americans in
three suburban high schools: An all white,
a desegregated, and an integrated school.*
Unpublished doctoral dissertation,
Teachers College, Columbia University.

Ladd, G., Munson, H., & Miller, J. (1984).
Social integration of deaf adolescents in
secondary-level mainstreamed programs.
Exceptional Children, 50, 420–428.

LaFreniere, P., Strayer, F. F., & Gauthier, R.
(1984). The emergence of same-sex
preferences among preschool peers: A
developmental ethological perspective.
Child Development, 55, 1958–1965.

Lamb, M. E., Easterbrooks, M. A., & Holden,
G. W. (1980). Reinforcement and
punishment among preschoolers:
Characteristics, effects, and correlates.
Child Development, 51, 1230–1236.

Lamb, M. E., & Roopnarine, J. L. (1979). Peer
influences on sex-role development in
preschoolers. *Child Development, 50,*
1219–1222.

Lane, H. (1984). *When the mind hears: A history
of the deaf.* New York: Random House.

Lange, L. (1983). Woman is not a rational
animal: On Aristotle's biology of
reproduction. In S. Harding & M. B.
Hintikka (Eds.), *Discovering reality.*
Dondrecht, Holland: D. Reidel.

Langer, E. J., Bashner, R. S., & Chanowitz, B.
(1985). Decreasing prejudice by
increasing discrimination. *Journal of*

Personality and Social Psychology, 49,
113–120.

La Piere, R. T. (1934). Attitudes versus actions.
Social Forces, 13, 230–237.

Lazar, A. L., Gensley, J. T., & Orpet, R. E.
(1971). Changing attitudes of young
mentally gifted children toward
handicapped persons. *Exceptional
Children, 37,* 600–602.

Lederberg, A. R. (1991). Social interaction
among deaf preschoolers. *American
Annals of the Deaf, 136,* 21–27.

Lederberg, A. R., Ryan, H. B., & Robbins, B. L.
(1986). Peer interaction in young deaf
children: The effect of partner hearing
status and familiarity. *Developmental
Psychology, 22,* 691–700.

Lerner, G. (1986). *The creation of patriarchy.*
New York: Oxford University Press.

Lever, J. (1978). Sex differences in the
complexity of children's play and games.
American Sociological Review, 43,
471–483.

Levy, G. D., & Fivush, R. (1993). Scripts and
gender: A new approach for examining
gender-role development. *Developmental
Review, 13,* 126–146.

Levy-Shiff, R., & Hoffman, M. A. (1985).
Social behavior of hearing-impaired and
normally-hearing preschoolers. *British
Journal of Educational Psychology, 55,*
111–118.

Lewin, K. (1948). *Resolving social conflicts.*
New York: Harper & Row.

Lewin, K. (1951). *Field theory in social science.*
New York: Harper & Brother.

Lieberman, L. (1990). REI: Revisited...again.
Exceptional Children, 56, 561–562.

Liebert, R. M., & Sprafkin, J. (1988). *The early
window: Effects of television on children
and youth.* Elmsford, NY: Pergamon
Press.

Lobel, T. E., Bempechat, J., Gewirtz, J. C.,
Shoken-Tozpaz, T., & Bashe, E. (1993).
The role of gender-related information and
self-endorsement of traits in
preadolescents' inferences and
judgements. *Child Development, 64,*
1285–1294.

Locksley, A., Ortiz, V., & Hepburn, C. (1980).
Social categorization and discriminatory
behavior: Extinguishing the minimal
intergroup discrimination effect. *Journal
of Personality and Social Psychology, 39,*
773–783.

Lombardi, D. N. (1963). Factors affecting
changes in attitudes toward Negroes

among high school students. *Journal of Negro Education, 32,* 129–136.

Lorenz, K. (1969). Innate bases of learning. In K. Pribram (Ed.), *On the biology of learning.* New York: Harcourt, Brace, and World.

Lou, M. W. (1988). The history of language use in the education of the deaf in the United States. In M. Strong (Ed.), *Language learning and deafness.* New York: Cambridge University Press.

Lumsden, C. J., & Wilson, E. O. (1981). *Genes, mind and culture.* Cambridge: Harvard University Press.

Lytton, H., & Romney, D. M. (1991). Parents' differential socialization of boys and girls: A meta-analysis. *Psychological Bulletin, 109,* 267–296.

Maccoby, E. E. (1980). *Social development.* New York: Harcourt Brace Jovanovich.

Maccoby, E. E. (1988). Gender as a social category. *Developmental Psychology, 24,* 755–765.

Maccoby, E. E. (1990). Gender and relationships: A developmental account. *American Psychologist, 45,* 513–520.

Maccoby, E. E., & Jacklin, C. N. (1987). Gender segregation in childhood. In E.H. Reese (Ed.), *Advances in Child Development and Behavior* (Vol. 20). New York: Academic Press.

Mann, L., and Janis, I. L. (1968). A follow-up study on the long-term effects of emotional role-playing. *Journal of Applied Psychology, 8,* 339–342.

Marger, M. N. (1991). *Race and ethnic relations* (2nd ed.). Belmont, CA: Wadsworth.

Margo, B. C. (1983). Modifying attitudes toward physically handicapped children. *Perceptual and Motor Skills, 56,* 1002.

Marsh, V., and Friedman, R. (1972). Changing public attitudes toward blindness. *Exceptional Children, 38,* 426–428.

Martin, C. L. (1989). Children's use of gender-related information in making social judgments. *Developmental Psychology, 25,* 80–88.

Martino, L., & Johnson, D. W. (1979). Cooperative and individualistic experiences among disabled and normal children. *The Journal of Social Psychology, 107,* 177–183.

Massad, C. M. (1981). Sex role identity and adjustment during adolescence. *Child Development, 52,* 1290–1298.

McCauley, C., & Stitt, C. L. (1978). An individual and quantitative measure of stereotypes. *Journal of Personality and Social Psychology 36,* 929–940.

McCauley, R. W., Bruininks, R. H., & Kennedy, P. (1976). Behavioral interactions of hearing impaired children in regular classrooms. *The Journal of Special Education, 10,* 277–284.

McConnell, S. R., & Odom, S. L. (1986) Sociometrics: Peer-referenced measures and the assessment of social competence. In P. S. Strain, M. J. Guralnick, and H. M. Walker (Eds.), *Children's social behavior.* New York: Academic Press.

McGuire, W. J. (1985) Attitudes and attitude change. In G. Lindzey and E. Aronson (Eds.), *Handbook of social psychology* (3rd ed. Vol. 2). New York: Random House.

McHale, S. M., Bartko, W. T., Crouter, A. C., & Perry-Jenkins, M. (1990). Children's housework and psychosocial functioning: The mediating effects of parents' sex-role behaviors and attitudes. *Child Development, 61,* 1413–1426.

McKirdy, L. S., & Blank, M. (1982). Dialogue in deaf and hearing preschoolers. *Journal of Speech and Hearing Disorders, 25,* 487–499.

McWhirt, W. J. (1967). *The effects of desegregation on prejudice, academic aspiration, and the self-concept of tenth grade students.* Unpublished doctoral dissertation, University of South Carolina.

Meier, A., & Rudwick, E. (1976). *From plantation to ghetto* (3rd ed.). New York: Hill and Wang.

Miller, M., Richey, D. D., & Lammers, C. A. (1983). Analysis of gifted students' attitudes toward the handicapped. *Journal for Special Educators, 19,* 14–21.

Milner, D. (1983). *Children and race.* London: Sage Publications.

Moore, J. W., Hauck, W. E., & Denne, T. C. (1984). Racial prejudice, interracial contact, and personality variables. *Journal of Experimental Education, 52,* 168–173.

Moores, D. F. (1982). *Educating the deaf* (2nd ed.). Boston: Houghton Mifflin.

Musselman, C. R., Lindsay, P. H., & Wilson, A. K. (1988). An evaluation of recent trends in preschool programming for hearing-impaired children. *Journal of Speech and Hearing Disorders, 53,* 71–88.

Nash, G. B., Jeffrey, J. J., Howe, J. R., Frederick, P. J., Davis, A. F., & Winkler, A. M. (Eds.). *The American people* (2nd ed.). New York: Harper & Row.

Norvell, N., & Worchel, S. (1981). A reexamination of the relation between equal status contact and intergroup attraction. *Journal of Personality and Social Psychology, 41* (5), 902–908.

O'Brien, M. (1992). Gender identity and sex roles. In V. B. Van Hasselt & M. Hersen (Eds.), *Handbook of social development.* New York: Plenum Press.

Padden, C., & Humphries, T. (1988). *Deaf in America: Voices from a culture.* Cambridge: Harvard University Press.

Parish, T., Ohlsen, R., & Parish, J. (1978). A look at mainstreaming in light of children's attitudes toward the handicapped. *Perceptual and Motor Skills, 46,* 1019–1021.

Pasanella, A. L., & Volkmor, C. B. (1981). *Teaching handicapped students in the mainstream* (2nd ed.). Columbus, OH: Charles E. Merrill.

Passin, H. (1955). Untouchability in the far east. *Monumenta Nipponica, 2,* 27–47.

Patchen, M. (1982). *Black-White contact in schools.* West Lafayette, IN: Purdue University Press.

Patterson, C. J. (1992). Children of lesbian and gay parents. *Child Development, 63,* 1025–1042.

Patton, J. R., Payne, J. S., & Beirne-Smith, M. (1990). *Mental retardation.* (3rd ed.). Columbus, OH: Charles E. Merrill.

Peters, W. (Producer and Director) (1985). *A class divided* [Film]. Washington, DC: Public Broadcast Station Video.

Petersen, A. C., Compas, B. E., Brooks-Gunn, J., Stemmler, M., Ey, S., & Grant, K. E. (1993). Depression in adolescence. *American Psychologist, 48,* 155–168.

Pettigrew, T. F. (1971). *Racially separate or together?* New York: McGraw-Hill.

Phillips, E. L. (1951). Attitudes toward self and others: A brief questionnaire report. *Journal of Consulting Psychology, 15,* 79–81.

Phinney, J. S. (1990). Ethnic identity in adolescents and adults: Review of research. *Psychological Bulletin, 108,* 499–514.

Piaget, J. (1948. Originally published in 1932). *The moral judgment of the child.* New York: Free Press.

Piaget, J. (1971). *Biology and knowledge.* Chicago: University of Chicago Press.

Plomin, R., & Daniels, D. (1987). Why are children in the same family so different from one another? *Behavioral and Brain Sciences, 10,* 1–60.

Pomerleau, A., Bolduc, D., Maleint, G., & Cossette, L. (1990). Pink or blue: Environmental gender stereotypes in the first two years of life. *Sex Roles, 22,* 359–367.

Porter, J. D. R. (1971). *Black child, white child.* Cambridge, MA: Harvard University Press.

President's Committee on Mental Retardation (1976). *Changing patterns in residential services for the mentally retarded.* Washington, DC: U.S. Government Printing Office.

President's Committee on Mental Retardation (1977). *Mental retardation past and present.* Washington, DC: U.S. Government Printing Office.

Qualls, R. C., Cox, M. B., & Schehr, T. L. (1992). Racial attitudes on campus: Are there gender differences? *Journal of College Student Development, 33,* 524–529.

Quigley, S. P., & Paul, P. V. (1986). A perspective on academic achievement. In D. M. Luterman (Ed.), *Deafness in perspective.* San Diego: College-Hill Press.

Rapier, J., Adelson, R., Carey, R., & Croke, K. (1972). Changes in children's attitude toward physically handicapped. *Exceptional Children, 39,* 219–223.

Reynolds, V. (1987). Sociobiology and race relations. In V. Reynolds, V. Falger, & I. Vine (Eds.), *The sociobiology of ethnocentrism.* Athens: University of Georgia Press.

Roberts, C., & Zubrick, S. (1992). Factors influencing the social status of children with mild academic disabilities in regular classrooms. *Exceptional Children, 59* (3), 192–202.

Robinson, J. W., & Preston, J. D. (1976). Equal-status contact and modification of racial prejudice: A reexamination of the contact hypothesis. *Social Forces, 54* (4), 911–924.

Rogers, M., Miller, N., & Hennigan, K. (1981). Cooperative games as an intervention to promote cross-racial acceptance. *American Educational Research Journal, 18* (4), 513–516.

Rossi, A. S. (1977). A biosocial perspective on parenting. In A. S. Rossi, J. Kagan, & T. K. Hareven (Eds.), *The family.* New York: W.W. Norton.

Rotatori, A. F., Schwenn, J. D., & Fox, R. A. (1955). *Assessing severely and profoundly handicapped individuals.* Springfield, IL: Charles C. Thomas.

Rotheram, M. J., & Phinney, J. S. (1987). Introduction. In J. S. Phinney & M. J. Rotheram (Eds.), *Children's ethnic socialization.* Beverly Hills: Sage.

Rotheram-Borus, M. J., & Phinney, J. S. (1990). Patterns of social expectations among Black and Mexican-American children. *Child Development, 61,* 542–556.

Ryan, M. P. (1975). *Womanhood in America.* New York: New Viewpoints.

Rynders, J. E., Johnson, R. T., Johnson, D. W., & Schmidt, B. (1980). Producing positive interaction among Down Syndrome and nonhandicapped teenagers through cooperative goal structuring. *American Journal of Mental Deficiency, 85,* 268–273.

Rubin, I. M. (1967a). Increased self-acceptance: A means of reducing prejudice. *Journal of Personality and Social Psychology, 5,* 233–238.

Rubin, I. M. (1967b). The reduction of prejudice through laboratory training. *Journal of Applied Behaviorial Science, 3* (1), 29–50.

Sacks, O. (1989). *Seeing voices: A journey into the world of the deaf.* Berkeley: University of California Press.

Safford, P. L., & Rosen, L. A. (1981). Mainstreaming: Application of philosophical perspectives in integrated kindergarten programs. *Topics in Early Childhood Education, 1,* 1–10.

St. John, N. H. (1975). *School desegregation outcomes for children.* New York: John Wiley.

Scarr, S. (1992). Developmental theories for the 1990s: Development and individual differences. *Child Development, 63,* 1–19.

Schlesinger, H. (1986). Total communication in perspective. In D.M. Luterman (Ed.), *Deafness in perspective.* San Diego: College-Hill Press.

Schofield, J. W. (1979). The impact of positively structured contact on intergroup behavior: Does it last under adverse conditions? *Social Psychology Quarterly, 42,* 280–284.

Schofield, J. W., & Francis, W. D. (1982). An observational study of peer interaction in racially mixed "accelerated" classrooms. *Journal of Educational Psychology, 74,* 722–732.

Schofield, J. W., & Sagar, H. A. (1977). Peer interaction patterns in an integrated middle school. *Sociometry, 40,* 130–138.

Sedlick, M., & Penta, J. B. (1975). Changing nurse attitudes toward quadriplegics through use of television. *Rehabilitation Literature, 36,* 274–278.

Seidner, J. (1971). *Effects of integrated school experience on interaction in small biracial groups.* Unpublished doctoral dissertation, University of Southern California.

Selman, R. L. (1980). *The growth of interpersonal understanding.* New York: Academic Press.

Semaj, L. (1980). The development of racial evaluation and preference: A cognitive approach. *The Journal of Black Psychology, 6,* 59–79.

Serbin, L. A., & Sprafkin, C. (1986). The salience of gender and the process of sex typing in three- to-seven-year-old children. *Child Development, 57,* 1188–1199.

Seyfarth, R. M. (1983). Grooming and social competition in primates. In R. A. Hinde (Ed.), *Primate social relationships.* London: Blackwell Scientific Publications.

Shapiro, H. (1988). *White violence and black response.* Amherst: The University of Massachusetts Press.

Sheare, J. B. (1974). Social acceptance of EMR adolescents in integrated programs. *American Journal of Mental Deficiency, 78,* 678–682.

Sheerer, E. T. (1949). An analysis of the relationships between acceptance of and respect for self and acceptance of and respect for others in 10 counseling cases. *Journal of Consulting Psychology, 13,* 169–175.

Sherif, M., Harvey, O. J., White, B. J., Hood, W. R., & Sherif, C. W. (1961). *Intergroup conflict and cooperation: The robbers-cave experiment.* Norman, OK: University of Oklahoma Book Exchange.

Sherif, M., & Sherif, C. W. (1953). *Groups in harmony and tension.* New York: Harper.

Shrum, W., & Cheek, N. H., Jr. (1987). Social structure during the school years: Onset of the degrouping process. *American Sociological Review, 52,* 218–223.

Shrum, W., Cheek, N. H., Jr., & Hunter, S. M. (1988). Friendship in School: Gender and racial homophily. *Sociology of Education, 61*, 227–239.

Siegal, M. (1987). Are sons and daughters treated more differently by fathers than by mothers? *Developmental Review, 7*, 183–209.

Siperstein, G. N., Budoff, M., & Bak, J. J. (1980). Effects of the labels "Mentally Retarded" and "Retard" on the social acceptability of mentally retarded children. *American Journal of Mental Deficiency, 84*, 596–601.

Siperstein, G. N., & Chatillon, A. C. (1982). Importance of perceived similarity in improving children's attitudes toward mentally retarded peers. *American Journal of Mental Deficiency, 86*, 453–458.

Signorielli, N., & Lears, M. (1992). Children, television, and conceptions about chores: Attitudes and behaviors. *Sex Roles, 27*, 157–170.

Silverman, I., & Shaw, M. (1973). Effects of sudden mass school desegregation on interracial interactions and attitudes in one Southern city. *Journal of Social Issues, 29* (4), 142–144.

Singer, D. (1966). *Interracial attitudes of Negro and white fifth grade children in segregated and unsegregated schools.* Unpublished doctoral dissertation, Teachers College, Columbia University.

Singleton, L. C., & Asher, S. R. (1977). Peer preferences and social interaction among third-grade children in an integrated school district. *Journal of Educational Psychology, 69*, 330–336.

Singleton, L. C., & Asher, S. R. (1979). Race integration and children's peer preferences: An investigation of developmental and cohort differences. *Child Development, 50*, 936–941.

Slavin, R. E. (1977). How student learning teams can integrate the desegregated classroom. *Integrated Education, 15* (6), 56–58.

Slavin, R. E. (1979). Effects of biracial learning teams on cross-racial friendships. *Journal of Educational Psychology, 71* (3), 381–387.

Slavin, R. E., & Oickle, E. (1981). Effects of cooperative learning teams on student achievement and race relations: Treatment by race interactions. *Sociology of Education, 54*, 174–180.

Sluckin, A. M., & Smith, P. K. (1977). Two approaches to the concept of dominance in preschool children. *Child Development, 48*, 917–923.

Smetana, J. G. (1986). Preschool children's conceptions of sex-role transgressions. *Child Development, 57*, 862–871.

Smith, G. J. (1985). Facial and full-length ratings of attractiveness related to the social interactions of young children. *Sex Roles, 12*, 287–293.

Snyder, L., Apolloni, T., & Cooke, T. P. (1977). Integrated settings at the early childhood level: The role of nonretarded peers. *Exceptional Children, 43*, 262–266.

Soder, M. (1990) Prejudice or ambivalence? Attitudes toward persons with disabilities. *Disability, Handicap & Society, 5*, 227–241.

Speelman, D., & Hoffman, C. D. (1980). Personal space assessment of the development of racial attitudes in integrated and segregated schools. *Journal of Genetic Psychology, 136*, 307–308.

Spence, J. T., & Helmreich, R. L. (1978). *Masculinity and femininity: Their psychological dimensions, correlates, and antecedents.* Austin: University of Texas Press.

Spencer, M. B. (1983). Children's cultural values and parental rearing strategies. *Developmental Review, 3*, 351–370.

Spencer, M. B., & Markstrom-Adams, C. (1990). Identity processes among racial and ethnic minority children in America. *Child Development, 61*, 290–310.

Stager, S. F., & Young, R. D. (1981). Intergroup contact and social outcomes for mainstream EMR adolescents. *American Journal of Mental Deficiency, 85*, 497–503.

Stephan, W. G. (1977). Cognitive differentiation and intergroup perception. *Sociometry, 40*, 50–58.

Stephan, W. G. (1985). Intergroup relations. In G. Lindzey and E. Aronson (Eds.), *Handbook of social psychology (3rd ed., Vol. 2).* New York: Random House.

Stevenson, H. W., & Stevenson, N. G. (1960). Social interaction in an interracial nursery school. *Genetic Psychology Monographs, 61*, 37–75.

Stevenson, M. R., & Black, K. N. (1988). Paternal absence and sex-role development: A meta-analysis. *Child Development, 59*, 793–814.

Stokoe, W. C., Jr. (1960). *Sign language structure* (Reissued). Silver Spring, MD: Linstok Press.

Stotland, E., Katz, D., & Patchen, M. (1972). The reduction of prejudice through the arousal of self insight. In J. Brigham and T. Weissbach (Eds.), *Racial attitudes in America: Analysis and findings of social psychology.* New York: Harper & Row.

Strain, P. S. (1985). Social and nonsocial determinants of acceptability in handicapped preschool children. *Topics in Early Childhood Special Education, 4,* 47–58.

Strain, P. S., & Kerr, M. M. (1981). *Mainstreaming of children in schools.* New York: Academic Press.

Strayer, F. F., & Trudel, M. (1984). Developmental changes in the nature and function of social dominance among young children. *Ethology and Sociobiology, 5,* 279–295.

Strum, S. C. (1987). *Almost human.* New York: W. W. Norton.

Tajfel, H. (1981). *Human groups and social categories.* Cambridge: Cambridge University Press.

Tajfel, H., & Turner, J. C. (1986). The social identity theory of intergroup behavior. In S. Worchel & W. G. Austin (Eds.), *Psychology of intergroup relations* (2nd ed.). Chicago: Nelson-Hall.

Tawney, J. W. (1981). A cautious view of mainstreaming in early education. *Topics in Early Childhood Education, 1,* 25–36.

Taylor, A. R., Asher, S. R., & Williams, G. A. (1987). The social adaptation of mainstreamed mildly retarded children. *Child Development, 58,* 1321–1334.

Terry, R. & Coie, J. D. (1991) A comparison of methods for defining sociometric status among children. *Developmental Psychology, 27,* 867–880.

Tindale, N. B. (1974). *Aboriginal tribes of Australia.* Berkeley: University of California Press.

Tonnesmann, W. (1987). Group identification and political socialization. In V. Reynolds, V. Falger, & I. Vine (Eds.), *The sociobiology of ethnocentrism.* Athens: University of Georgia Press.

Tooby, J., & DeVore, I. (1987). The reconstruction of hominid behavioral evolution through strategic modeling. In W. G. Kinzey (Ed.), *The evolution of human behavior: Primate models.* Albany: State University of New York Press.

Trent, R. (1957). The relation between expressed self-acceptance and expressed attitudes towards Negroes and whites among negro children. *Journal of Genetic Psychology, 91 ,* 25–31.

Turiel, E. (1983). *The development of social knowledge.* New York: Cambridge University Press.

Turnbull, A. P., & Blacher-Dixon, J. (1981). Preschool mainstreaming: An empirical and conceptual review. In P. Strain and M. Kern (Eds.), *Mainstreaming children in schools.* New York: Academic Press.

Vandell, D. L., Anderson, L. D., Ehrhardt, G., & Wilson, K. S. (1982). Integrated hearing and deaf preschoolers: An attempt to enhance hearing children's interactions with deaf peers. *Child Development, 53,* 1354–1363.

Vandell, D. L. & George, L. B. (1981). Social interaction in hearing and deaf preschoolers: Successes and failures in initiations. *Child Development, 52,* 627–635.

Van den Berghe, P. L. (1981). *The ethnic phenomenon.* New York: Elsevier.

Vaughn, B. E., & Langlois, J. H. (1983). Physical attractiveness as a correlate of peer status and social competence in preschool children. *Developmental Psychology, 19,* 561–567.

Vaughn, G. M. (1987). A social psychological model of ethnic identity development. In J. S. Phinney & M. J. Rotheram (Eds.), *Children's ethnic socialization.* Beverly Hills: Sage.

Voeltz, L. M. (1980). Children's attitudes toward handicapped peers. *American Journal of Mental Deficiency, 84,* 455–464.

Voeltz, L. M. (1982). Effects of structured interactions with severely handicapped peers on children's attitudes. *American Journal of Mental Deficiency, 86,* 380–390.

Waddington, C. H. (1957). *The strategy of genes.* London: Allen & Unwin.

Waddington, C. H. (1960). *The ethical animal.* London: Allen & Unwin.

Walkerdine, V. (1981). Sex, power, and pedagogy. *Screen Education, 38,* 14–24.

Walkerdine, V. (1990). *Schoolgirl fictions.* London: Verso.

Wallen, J. E. W. (1955). *Education of mentally handicapped children.* New York: Harper.

Warring, D., Johnson, D. W., Maruyama, G., & Johnson, R. (1985). Impact of different types of cooperative learning on cross-ethnic relationships. *Journal of Educational Psychology, 77,* 53–59.

Watson, M. W., & Fischer, K. W. (1980). Development of social roles in elicited and spontaneous behavior during the preschool years. *Developmental Psychology, 16,* 483–494.

Webster, S. W. (1961). The influence of interracial contact on social acceptance in a newly integrated school. *Journal of Educational Psychology, 52* , 292–296.

Weigel, R. H., Wiser, P. L., & Cook, S. W. (1975). The impact of cooperative learning experiences on cross-ethnic relations and attitudes. *Journal of Social Issues, 31* (1), 219–244.

Weiner, M. J., & Wright, F. E. (1973). Effects of undergoing arbitrary discrimination upon subsequent attitudes toward a minority group. *Journal of Applied Social Psychology, 3* (1), 94–102.

Weisner, T. S., & Wilson-Mitchell, J. E. (1990). Nonconventional family life-styles and sex typing in six-year-olds. *Child Development, 61,* 1915–1933.

Westervelt, V. D., & McKinney, J. D. (1980). Effects of a film on nonhandicapped children's attitudes toward handicapped children. *Exceptional Children, 46* (4), 294–296.

Whitmore, P. G. (1956). *A study of school desegregation: Attitude change and scale validation.* Unpublished doctoral dissertation, University of Tennessee.

Wicker, A. W. (1969). Attitudes versus actions: The relation of verbal and overt behavioral responses to attitude objects. *Journal of Social Issues, 25,* 41–78.

Williams, J. E., Best, D. L., & Boswell, D. A. (1975). The measurement of children's racial attitudes in the early school years. *Child Development, 46,* 494–500.

Wilson, E. O. (1975). *Sociobiology: The new synthesis.* Cambridge: Harvard University Press.

Wilson, E. O. (1980). *Sociobiology: The abridged edition.* Cambridge: Harvard University Press.

Wilson, R. S. (1978). Synchronies in mental development: An epigenetic perspective. *Science, 202,* 939–948.

Wolfensburber, W. (1976). The origin and nature of our institutional models. In President's Committee on Mental Retardation, *Changing patterns in residential services for the mentally retarded.* Washington, DC: U.S. Government Printing Office.

Wrangham, R. W. (1987). African apes: The significance of African apes for reconstructing human social evolution. In W. G. Kinzey (Ed.), *The evolution of human behavior: Primate models.* Albany: State University of New York Press.

Wylie, R. E. (1974). Integrating handicapped and nonhandicapped preschool children: Effects on social play. *Childhood Education, 51,* 360–364.

Yee, M. D., & Brown, R. (1992). Self-evaluations and intergroup attitudes in children aged three to nine. *Child Development, 63,* 619–629.

York, J., Vandercook, T., Macdonald, C., Heise-Neff, C., & Caughey, E. (1992). Feedback about integrating middle-school students with severe disabilities in general education classes. *Exceptional Children, 58,* 244–258.

Zalk, S. R., & Katz, P. A. (1978). Gender attitudes in children. *Sex Roles, 4,* 349–357.

Zetlin, A. G., & Murtaugh, M. (1988). Friendship patterns of mildly learning handicapped and nonhandicapped high school students. *American Journal on Mental Retardation, 92,* 447–554.

Ziegler, S. (1981). The effect of cooperative learning teams for increasing cross-ethnic friendship: Additional evidence. *Human Organizations, 40* (3), 264–268.

Zigler, E., & Hodapp, R. M. (1986). *Understanding mental retardation.* New York: Cambridge University Press.

INDEX

AAMD. *See* American Association on Mental Deficiency

Abolitionism, 97–99

Abortion rights, 93

Aboud, F., 5, 129, 182, 184–186, 254

Abramenkova, V. V., 68, 70

Acton, H. M., 205–206

African-Americans, 2, 130, 172–180, 208, 210
  cultural history of, 20–22, 36–37, 77, 94–105, 122–124, 259
  discrimination against. *See* Racial discrimination
  racism toward, 39, 96. *See also* Racial prejudice
  as research focus, 16–17, 84, 85
  and White cultural norms, 172, 177, 181, 208, 264–265

Albert, A. A., 151

Allport, Gordon, 3, 5–7, 22–24, 33–36, 215–217, 219, 225–226

Altruism, 57–58, 129

Ambivalence, 16–17, 27, 36, 130

American Anti-Slavery Society, 98

American Association on Mental Deficiency (AAMD), 118–119

American Association on Mental Retardation, 115

American Sign Language (ASL), 108–113, 125

Antia, S. D., 162

Anti-Semitism, 25–27, 37

Appeal (Walker), 99

Aristotle, 29–30

Armed forces, 83–84, 98, 103, 123, 124, 268

Asher, S. R., 188, 189, 193, 194, 204, 205

ASL. *See* American Sign Language

Attitudes, 4, 6–8, 10, 38, 216–217, 244, 247, 263
  as sex-typing factor, 136–137(table), 138

Attucks, Crispus, 96

Authoritarian Personality, The, 25–28, 37, 250

Authority, 24, 26, 28, 34, 244, 255
  acceptance of, 42, 56, 58–62, 68, 79, 80, 133, 262, 268
  and prejudice reduction, 214, 226, 262, 267, 268

Badging, 66, 80, 133–135, 146, 178–179, 208–210, 261, 262

Bak, J. J., 198–200, 205, 206

Ballard, M., 242

Bandura, A., 152

Bayes' Rule, 12–13

Behavior, 8, 35, 41–44, 46–50, 60–61, 77–79, 158
  and discrimination, 263, 265
  and group identity, 178–179, 199, 208–210, 212
  and prejudice, 8–9, 36, 128, 217, 264
  in sex-typing, 136–137(table), 138, 148
  social, 42–43, 49, 52, 56–58, 63–65, 69–81
  and stereotypes, 12–13

Behavior genetics, 48–50, 79, 263

Beliefs, 59, 61–62, 128, 136–137(table), 138

discrimination toward, 39, 84, 122, 159–167, 169, 209, 265
Delaney, Martin, 99
Depression, 149–150
Descartes, Rene, 61–62
Desegregation, 40, 103–104, 124, 214, 218–219, 222–226, 253–255, 266
DeVos, G., 17, 18, 20
DeVries, D. L., 240
Disabled persons, 16–17, 77, 129–130
    mainstreaming of, 227, 230–234, 253, 254
    prejudice against, 227, 230–234, 241, 243, 246–248, 252–256
    See also Deaf persons; Mentally retarded persons
Discrimination, 14, 35, 73, 93, 128, 134, 147
    and authority, 62, 80
    causes of, 22–24, 33, 37, 83, 124
    in culture, 83–85, 123–126, 257–258, 266
    against deaf persons, 84, 122, 159–167, 169, 209
    decrease in, 84, 259–261
    development of, 38–40, 209, 210, 212, 263–266
    against disabled persons, 227, 230–232, 241–243, 255–256
    by gender. See Opposite-sex discrimination
    genetic/evolutionary aspects of, 34–35, 38, 41–42, 51, 55–56, 58, 266, 268
    and group identity, 42, 68, 80, 172, 261–263, 265
    hostility in, 76–77, 81
    against mentally retarded persons, 84, 122, 172, 200–207, 209, 211–212, 231–232, 265
    and prejudice, 7–9, 36, 207, 263–264, 266
    by race. See Racial discrimination
    reduction of, 214, 216, 218, 234–235, 239–244, 254–256, 266–268

study of, 128, 130–133, 167–168
Dominance hierarchies, 53, 59, 71, 80
Dominant groups, 84, 121–123, 125, 126, 134–135, 258–262
Du Bois, W. E. B., 101, 103

Economy, 19, 23, 84, 99, 122
Education for All Handicapped Children Act (1975), 120, 227
Ehrlich, Howard, 3–5, 7, 9
Eisenberg, N., 140
Elser, R., 164
Emerton, R. G., 165
Empathy, 244, 255
Employment, 87–93, 99, 101–102, 106, 121, 125
Environment, 33, 34, 41, 43–44, 46, 48–50, 79
Epigenesis, 43–44, 46, 50, 55
Equality, 86, 88–94, 96, 103, 122, 124, 259
Equal Rights Amendment, 30
Eta people, 18, 19
Ethnic groups, 10–12, 14–15, 176–177, 179, 210
Ethnic identity, 35, 39, 66–67, 175–181, 183, 210
Ethnocentrism, 25–27, 37, 58
Eugenics, 117, 118
Evolution, 41–44, 51–53, 56, 62, 64–65, 68
    and culture, 44, 45(fig.), 46–48, 50, 58–59, 79
    and prejudice, 33–34, 37, 38, 65
Eysenck, H. J., 49, 50

Fagot, B. I., 140, 144–146
Family, 54, 60–61, 142–144
    and discrimination development, 196–197, 209
    and prejudice development, 172, 184–186, 208, 211, 263, 264
    sex-typing influence of, 134, 135, 138–141, 144, 147, 168, 172

Fard, W. D., 103
Fascism, 26, 28–29
Feminism, 30, 88, 89, 91, 93
Finkelstein, N. W., 187, 188
Fischer, K. W., 71, 72, 134
Fishbein, H. D., 48, 141, 187–188, 190
Foster, S. B., 166, 167
Francis, W. D., 189, 191

Gallaudet, Thomas H., 108, 109
Gallaudet College, 109, 112
Garrison, William Lloyd, 98
Garvey, Marcus, 102
Gauthier, R., 155
Gender, 65, 79, 128, 135, 140, 147–150, 168
  and discrimination, 187–196, 209, 211, 265
  and opposite-sex prejudice, 84, 147–150, 155, 157–158, 172, 208, 264
  and prejudice degree, 65, 172, 183–184, 186, 198, 207, 208, 211, 218, 264
  and prejudice development, 80, 134, 147
  and prejudice reduction, 214, 224, 227, 230, 255
Genetics, 41–44, 45(fig.), 46–53, 56–57, 79, 114
Genotypes, 33–34
George, L. B., 160
Gilbert, D. T., 61–62
Goffman, Irving, 14–15
Goldstein, Max, 110
Gorn, G. J., 245
Gottlieb, G., 43, 44, 48
Gottlieb, J., 204
Graffi, S., 197–199
Greenfield, P. M., 47–48
Groce, Nora Ellen, 106
Groom, J. M., 201–203, 205
Group identity, 65–68, 78, 80, 214–217, 261–262
  and behavior, 69–76, 178–179, 199, 208–210, 212
  and discrimination, 68, 169, 265

emergence of, 42, 68–73, 81, 178–179, 262
multi-group, 66–68
and prejudice, 66–68, 80, 133–134, 154, 158–159, 172, 210, 212, 265
Grusec, J. E., 61
Guralnick, M. J., 200–203, 205

Hagan, R., 145
Hamilton, D. L., 9, 13–14
Hamilton, William D., 56–58
Haskins, R., 187, 188
Hayden-Thomson, L., 156
Heller, M., 179
Helmreich, R. L., 149
Hemphill, L., 198–200
Henniges, M., 160
Hepburn, C., 76
Hetherington, E. M., 60
Hodapp, R. M., 114
Holmes, Oliver Wendell, 118
Homosexuality, 93, 143–144
Hostility, 3, 42, 76–77, 80, 81, 134, 172, 262
Houser, B. B., 245–246
Hunter, S. M., 155, 156–157, 194
Hunter-gatherers, 42, 50–51, 54–55, 62–65, 67–68, 78–80, 262
Huston, A. C., 135, 138–141, 148
Hymel, S., 156

Imai, S., 187–188, 190
Inclusive fitness, 42, 56–58, 66–68, 80, 217
India, 17–20, 36
Individual difference, 22–24, 37, 79, 263
Individuation, 249, 250, 252–256, 267
Industrial societies, 42, 55, 78–79, 81, 262
Inferiority, 121–122, 125, 258
Ingroup favoritism, 42, 68, 75–76, 80, 134, 255, 261, 268
Integration, 83–84, 103–104, 120–121, 123, 268
  and desegregation, 171, 173, 210, 223

Intelligence, 28, 117–118
Intimacy, 216, 226, 243, 255
Irwin, C. J., 57, 66
Isaacs, H. R., 17, 18, 20

Jacklin, C. N., 155
Japan, 17–20, 36
Jarrett, O. S., 192, 193
Jews, 10, 11(table), 14, 17, 29
Johnson, Andrew, 99
Johnson, D. W., 235, 240–242
Johnson, Lyndon B., 103, 268
Johnson, R., 242
Johnson, R. T., 240, 241
Joseph P. Kennedy, Jr. Foundation,
    119

Katz, I., 15–17, 36, 129–130
Katz, P. A., 129, 151, 235, 239, 240,
    252
Kennedy, John F., 103, 119
Kennedy, P., 163, 164
King, Martin Luther, Jr., 100, 103,
    104
Kochman, T., 179
Kraus, S., 245
Kuhn, D., 150
Ku Klux Klan, 101

Ladd, G., 165, 167
LaFreniere, P., 155, 156
Lamb, M. E., 146
Langer, E. J., 252
Language, 67, 107, 111, 160, 179,
    210
La Piere, R. T., 8
Lederberg, A. R., 161
Legislation, 90, 117–119, 126, 261
    civil rights, 92, 99, 103, 123–124,
        268
    for desegregation, 171, 173, 210,
        214, 218
    Jim Crow, 100–101, 124
Leinbach, M. D., 140
Lerner, G., 31
Lewin, K., 217
Lewinian theory, 40, 214, 216–217,
    226, 253, 255
    and prejudice reduction, 233–
        234, 244, 246–247, 249

Lieben, L. S., 14
Lincoln, Abraham, 99
Lippmann, Walter, 9
Lobel, T. E., 153–154
Locksley, A., 76
Lumsden, C. J., 44, 46, 47
Lytton, H., 139

McCauley, C., 11–12
McCauley, R. W., 162
Maccoby, E. E., 155, 157, 169, 179
McKinney, J. D., 246
Mainstreaming, 40, 112, 120, 197,
    206, 214, 230–234
    effects of, 253–255, 266–267
    research on, 227, 228–
        229(table), 230
Marger, M. N., 7, 23–24, 33–35
Margo, B. C., 248
Marriage, 56–57
Martin, C. L., 153, 154
Martino, L., 242
Massad, C. M., 149
Media, 244–247, 253, 255, 256, 267
Mentally retarded persons, 77,
    113–121, 123, 125, 214, 242,
    259
    discrimination toward, 84, 122,
        172, 200–208, 211–212, 231–
        232, 265
    mainstreaming of, 120–121, 197,
        206, 227, 230–232
    prejudice toward, 39, 84–85,
        118, 121, 172, 197–200, 210–
        212, 264
Mental retardation, 113–115, 118,
    197, 201, 211
Miller, J., 165
Milner, D., 5, 8, 9, 36
Minnes, P. M., 197–199
Munson, H., 165
Murtaugh, M., 202

NAACP. *See* National Association
    for the Advancement of
    Colored People
Nash, S. C., 150
National Association for Retarded
    Children, 118

Turner, Nat, 97

Untouchability, 17–20, 36, 77

Values, 59, 128, 258–259
Vandell, D. L., 160–161
Van den Berghe, P. L., 66–67
Vaughn, G. M., 181
Veldman, D. J., 204
Voting rights, 88, 90, 99, 100, 103–104

Waddington, C. H., 34, 48, 58, 59
Wagatsuma, H., 17, 18, 20
Walker, David, 99
Walkerdine, Valerie, 32–33, 93
Watson, M. W., 71, 72
WCTU. *See* Women's Christian Temperance Union
Weigel, R. H., 239–241
Weiner, M. J., 248, 249
Weisner, T. S., 142
Westervelt, V. D., 246
Williams, G. A., 204, 205
Wilson, Edward, 33, 44, 46, 47
Wilson-Mitchell, J. E., 142
Wolfensberger, W., 115, 116
Women, 29–31, 77, 84–94, 122–124, 126, 135, 259

in children's socialization, 31–33, 37, 139–141
prejudice toward. *See* Opposite-sex prejudice
Women's Christian Temperance Union (WCTU), 89
Women's rights, 85–93, 124
Wrangham, Richard, 62–64
Wright, F. E., 248, 249

X, Malcolm, 104

Yee, M. D., 69, 70, 76
York, J., 231
Young, R. D., 206
Young Women's Christian Association (YWCA), 89
YWCA. *See* Young Women's Christian Association

Zalk, S. R., 151, 235, 239, 240
Zarbatany, L., 205–206
Zetlin, A. G., 202
Ziegler, S., 239, 240
Zigler, E., 114
Zinacantecos, 47–48, 50
Zubrick, S., 204, 231

ABOUT THE BOOK AND AUTHOR

The development of prejudice and discrimination has its roots in our genetic/evolutionary heritage. Although the specific targets of prejudice are primarily determined by the culture and history of the society in which people reside, the particular socialization experiences children and adolescents have can alter these influences. As Harold Fishbein explains, research shows that prejudice and discrimination have different developmental courses, and moreover, that development within each domain—ethnicity, gender, deafness, mental retardation—is somewhat unique.

Fishbein contends that prejudice and discrimination can be reduced. Desegregation and mainstreaming have had little positive effect by themselves, but cooperative learning in classroom settings among different ethnic groups, different genders, or handicapped and non-handicapped individuals has been consistently found to have positive effects. One factor that appears to have a powerful influence in both the transmission of prejudice and its reduction is the sanction of members of the most dominant groups in a culture. Thus, prejudice and discrimination from a societal point of view are top-down phenomena.

This book is a valuable text for advanced courses in developmental and social psychology as well as useful supplemental reading for courses in biological or evolutionary psychology. It is also appropriate for advanced education courses in multiculturalism and diversity. The book will especially appeal to those with strong multidisciplinary interests.

Harold D. Fishbein is professor of psychology at the University of Cincinnati. He is the author of *Evolution, Development, and Children's Learning* and *The Psychology of Infancy and Childhood*.